Along the Shore

REDISCOVERING TORONTO'S WATERFRONT HERITAGE

M. JANE FAIRBURN

ECW Press

Published by ECW Press
2120 Queen Street East, Suite 200, Toronto, Ontario, Canada M4E 1E2
416-694-3348 / info@ecwpress.com

LIBRARY AND ARCHIVES CANADA CATALOGUING IN PUBLICATION

Fairburn, M. Jane
Along the shore : rediscovering Toronto's waterfront
heritage / M. Jane Fairburn.

Includes bibliographical references.
ISBN 978-1-77041-099-2 (PBK); 978-1-77090-360-9 (PDF); 978-1-77090-361-6 (EPUB)

1. Waterfronts—Ontario—Toronto—History. 2. Toronto (Ont.)—
History. I. Title.

FC3097.4.F35 2013   971.3'541   C2012-907527-2

Editor for the press:	Jen Knoch
Front cover design:	Barbara Breuner
Text design:	Tania Craan
Cover images:	Bluffer's Park Beach, 2008, Jane Fairburn. Overlay: People in a Rowboat, Ashbridge's Bay, 1910, City of Toronto Archives, F1244_it181A.
Author photo:	Cynthia Vail
Typesetting:	Kendra Martin
Printing:	Friesens 5 4 3 2 1

The publication of *Along the Shore* has been generously supported by the Canada Council for the Arts which last year invested $20.1 million in writing and publishing throughout Canada, and by the Ontario Arts Council, an agency of the Government of Ontario. We also acknowledge the financial support of the Government of Canada through the Canada Book Fund for our publishing activities, and the contribution of the Government of Ontario through the Ontario Book Publishing Tax Credit. The marketing of this book was made possible with the support of the Ontario Media Development Corporation. *Along the Shore* was produced with the support of the City of Toronto through the Toronto Arts Council.

PRINTED AND BOUND IN CANADA

A NOTE ON THE CREDITS

For the sake of brevity, some abbreviations were used in the image credits: AO (Archives of Ontario), CTA (City of Toronto Archives), CT/MS (City of Toronto, Museum Services), LAC (Library and Archives Canada), PC (Private Collection), SA (Scarborough Archives), TPA (Toronto Port Authority Archives), TPL (Toronto Public Library), YUL/CTSC (York University Libraries, Clara Thomas Archives & Special Collections).

Permission for use of Gwendolyn MacEwen's poems "Dark Pines Under Water" and "Animal Syllables" was provided by the author's family.

To my husband, Mark Rodger,
and to our children, Callum, Kathleen, and Lachlan

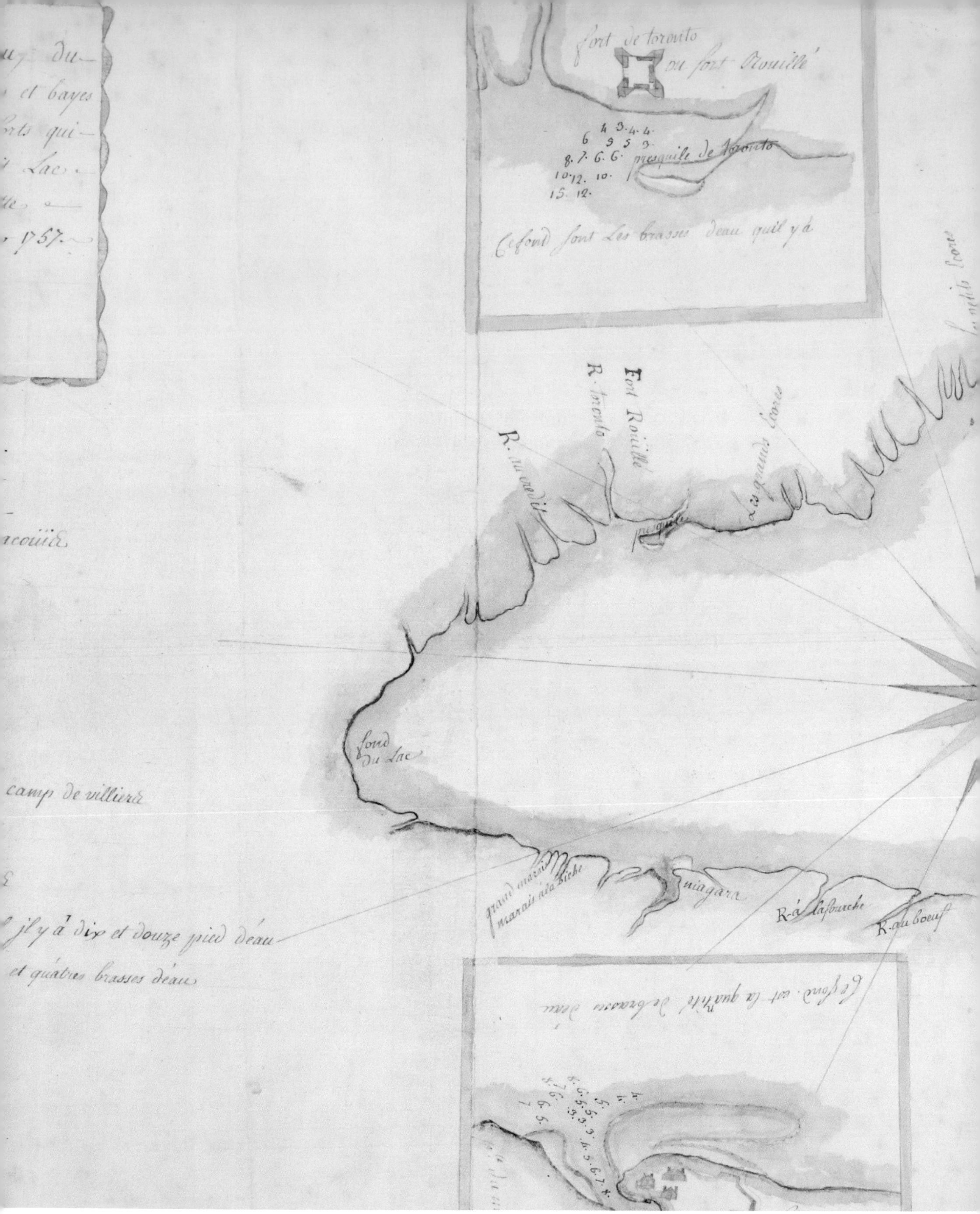

fort de toronto
ou fort Rouillé

4. 3. 4. 4.
6   3. 5.
8. 7. 6. 6. presqu'ile de toronto
10. 12. 10.
15. 12.

Cefond sont Les brasses d'eau qu'il y à

du
et bayes
rts qui
Lac
1757.

rcouïlé

R. du cœur it

R. toronto

Fort Rouillé

presqu'ile

a la grandes croix

la petite croix

fond
du Lac

camp de villiers

il y à dix et douze pied d'eau

et quatres brasses d'eau

grand marais
marais à la biche

niagara

R. à lafourche

R. au bœuf

Cefond est de qualité de bonne glaise

4.
4.
6. 5. 5.
7. 6. 5. 5. 3.
7. 6. 5. 5. 3.
5. 5.   4. 3. 6. 7. 8.
7.

Carte au plan nouveau du lac Ontario, 1757

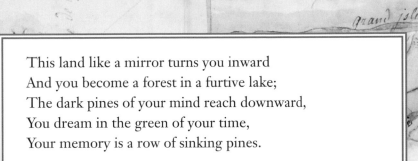

This land like a mirror turns you inward
And you become a forest in a furtive lake;
The dark pines of your mind reach downward,
You dream in the green of your time,
Your memory is a row of sinking pines.

Explorer, you tell yourself, this is not what you came for
Although it is good here, and green;
You had meant to move with a kind of largeness,
You had planned a heavy grace, an anguished dream.

But the dark pines of your mind dip deeper
And you are sinking, sinking, sleeper
In an elementary world;
There is something down there and you want it told.

Gwendolyn MacEwen,
"Dark Pines Under Water," *The Shadow-Maker*

TABLE OF CONTENTS

Introduction

CANADIAN CLASSICAL PIANIST Glenn Gould once said that Toronto was one of the few cities in the world in which he could live because it imposed no "cityness" upon him. This statement may seem somewhat curious, given that at the time of its utterance Toronto was a rapidly growing conurbation of over two million people, with suburbs that radiated out in all directions from a busy central core. Yet perhaps not. Perhaps Gould's view was, in part, influenced by where he was raised, Toronto's Beach, where within a short five or ten minute stroll down a hill, or through a leafy ravine, he could reach the limit of the city and stand along the shore of one of North America's massive inland seas, Lake Ontario.

Though Gould's favourite place in the Beach was the water's edge, he also roamed Toronto Bay, tracking the freighters from far-off exotic locales that cruised up the St. Lawrence from the Atlantic Ocean into Lake Ontario, finally arriving at Canada's great interior maritime city, Toronto. Lieutenant Governor John Graves Simcoe, who visited Toronto Bay in May of 1793, was also attracted to the site but for different reasons: the sandy peninsula in front of the mainland made for a natural sheltering harbour in the event of an anticipated American attack. Toronto also stood at the junction of two ancient aboriginal transportation corridors: the relatively flat Lakeshore Trail and the Toronto Carrying Place, whose two branches, near the mouths of the Rouge and Humber Rivers, served as access points to the Upper Great Lakes and the interior regions of Canada. Attracted by its strategic position, Lieutenant Governor Simcoe named the site York in 1793, though it was later re-named Toronto.

Glenn Gould out in Lake Ontario, the Beach, 1956

Jock Carroll, LAC, e011067053

The length of the shoreline of modern Toronto has greatly increased since its inception in 1793, and it now stretches from the Rouge River in the east to Etobicoke Creek in the west. Likewise, as the city has grown, the northern boundary of Toronto has moved farther and farther away from the water's edge, so much so that for many city residents today, the lake may seem somewhere on the periphery and not part of their active awareness. Everywhere and always, beyond the crumbling Gardiner Expressway and the rooflines of the Royal York Hotel, the peaks and crevices of the Scarborough Bluffs, the near shore waters of the Island, and the mouth of the Humber River, stretch the waters of Lake Ontario, within our reach yet perceived by many of us as being almost impossibly remote.

Yet in the early days of settlement, the lake was the source of Toronto's existence. It provided a vital hub for industry, trade, transportation, and the movement of goods, which made pioneer settlements possible, many of which began at or near the shore. Early on in Toronto's development, the lake was also a key destination for leisure, sport, and entertainment, with a series of pleasure grounds, hotels, and amusement parks established at or near the lakefront by the late nineteenth century.

Even the many people who enjoy the waterfront today may take the lake itself for granted, yet the sheer magnitude and breadth of Lake Ontario often astounds the newcomer. We often forget that Lake Ontario is part of a series of lakes that live up to their attribution as great. Unparalleled anywhere in the world, the Great Lakes contain more than eighty per cent of North America's fresh water, or about one-fifth of the world's supply. Only the polar ice caps contain more fresh water than these enormous basins. Lake Ontario — though the smallest of the Great Lakes, with a surface water area of some 7,340 square miles, and more than 700 miles upriver from the Atlantic — remains our gateway to the ocean and all that lies beyond.

I have now lived a significant portion of my life along Toronto's eastern shore. My experience with the lake is personal and remains one of connection, and for many years I have had at least one toe in the water. Yet it took an unanticipated close encounter with the lake about fifteen years ago to cement this relationship and set me on a journey of discovery — a journey that continues to this day.

While running high above the lake on a frigid midwinter afternoon, I slipped on black ice on the first step down to the Scarborough Bluffs, an extremely steep incline known locally as Killer Hill. Below the hill, the Scarborough Bluffs plunge to the water some 250 feet below. As I lay there stranded, my cries were blown away by the gusts of wind that swirled around me. With my right ankle hanging from my leg at an unnatural angle,

Scarborough Bluffs, 2012

Keith Ellis

I could do nothing but wait to be discovered. Far below me the ice fog swirled along the surface of the lake, weaving its intricate patterns over the grim grey water. Despite being on the outskirts of Canada's most densely populated city, it seemed as though I had tumbled into a wilderness that remained raw and uncivilized. It was a lake I had never known.

To be sure, I was at last seen and eventually rescued, and then I was promptly delivered into the hands of a marvellous surgeon. But long after my body had fully recovered, the time I had spent on the slope stayed with me. Where had I been? What was that all about? I found quite early in my journey that the questions I was asking related, first and last, to the spirit, the innermost nature of a particular place.

That place is the water's edge, where the city rubs shoulders with the natural world. *Along the Shore* turns our gaze back to the lake and four distinct communities and districts that remain connected to the waterfront and hug its shores, from the Rouge River in the east to Etobicoke Creek in the west: the Scarborough shore, the Beach, the Island, and

3

the Lakeshore (composed of the communities of Humber Bay, Mimico, New Toronto, and Long Branch). Moving from east to west, I'll examine the unique landscape and geography, history, and people that make up each of these special places. Though each retains a separate identity, collectively they are a place rich in memory and imagination.

Along the Shore does *not* cover what we today still think of as the downtown core, nor does it address the communities near the water's edge that at one time were more directly connected to the lake, particularly those communities to the west of downtown that lie east of the Humber River, Parkdale and Swansea, and Leslieville, which is situated east of the Don River. Although the core has its own fascinating history, some 160 years have passed since downtown Toronto could be thought of as simply a waterfront community. With the advent of the railway age in the mid 1850s came a rapid period of industrialization and commercialization that saw the downtown develop into a centre of finance, commerce, government, and public entertainment.

During this period of innovation and change, ambitious landfill projects pushed many sections of the shore farther and farther to the south to make way for industry, shipping, and the railway. The iron horse, while facilitating the industrial age, was also a barrier to the lake. As rail and road transportation advanced into the twentieth century, the Port of Toronto declined in importance, and the Gardiner Expressway, itself a monument to the automobile age, further physically and psychologically separated many Torontonians from the water.

Recently there has been a shift in perspective. Neighbourhoods that were once cut off from the lake are finding their way back to the water. Degraded sections of the shore and near-shore areas are being revitalized and former industrialized sites adjacent to Lake Ontario are being converted into new, exciting multi-use waterfront communities. Only now, with intense pressure everywhere on living space, with the cost and inconvenience of commuting from the more distant suburbs, and with a proliferation of condominium buildings, is the downtown of Toronto beginning to look like a reconfigured waterfront community — but that is a subject for another book.

The experience that set me on the path to writing this book bore no relation to my experience of modern Toronto. On the contrary, I was suddenly faced with the fact that the Toronto shore was once a wilderness governed by nature. So I set about looking for places along the waterfront that, on some level, were still connected with the lake and had kept some memory, some vestige of the past. I found that these waterfront communities and districts I have identified, places that often began as outlying settlements within the former County of York, have retained something of their village character,

despite a daily, intimate involvement with Toronto. Such places never were nor are even now mere offshoots of the centre. And so it was in them that I found something of what, unconsciously, I had been seeking.

Lake Ontario Ice, *New Toronto, c. 1948* George Paginton, Courtesy Tony Paginton

———◆———

THE FORMATION OF Toronto's shoreline began about 12,500 years ago, as the last period of glaciation came to an end and a layer of ice, half a mile thick, began to melt northwards, releasing its tenacious hold on the region. As the ice retreated, the boulders and debris beneath it carved out the lake basin and an intricate network of rivers, valleys, and ravines. Toronto's present shoreline took shape relatively recently, about 3,000 years ago, though extensive infilling projects in the nineteenth and twentieth centuries have pushed the water's edge far to the south of the original shoreline in many sections of the city.

A wild place it must have been, punctuated by verdant ravines, deep river valleys and creeks, sandy beaches, soaring high cliffs, and fecund marshlands, in some sections

Introduction

fronted by a narrow peninsula of sand. Beyond the shore was a freshwater ocean of seemingly endless proportions. The fusion of water and landscape makes this city unique, as did the carving of the land by the retreating glacier, to which we owe the complex system of valleys and ravines that run from the north down through the city and out to the shore of the Lake. Each of the major valleys contains a substantial watercourse — the Don, the Humber, the Rouge — that empties into the lake at or near one of the waterfront communities and districts that still exist today, most prominent among them the Scarborough shore, the Beach, the Island, and the Lakeshore.

Despite the differences in their land formations, each of these waterfront areas is part of a continuum. Together they retain a memory of the pastoral — a little of the natural world within the urban landscape. There is still a spirit alive in this land, one that wanders through the interconnected network of ravines and woodlands and waterways that lead down to and along the shore.

AS I STARTED MY exploration of Toronto's waterfront communities and districts, I quickly realized "Where am I?" cannot be answered without reference to the dimension of time and the history of these special places. Rather than an end in itself, history became my compass and guide for answering my initial question. Although I approached each region as an entity unto itself, an unexpected pattern emerged as I moved along the shore from east to west. Each region, to some extent, took on certain characteristics that are common to them all.

The successive groups of Aboriginal peoples who moved through the lower Humber River Valley in turn were to be found on the Island and at the mouths of the Rouge River and Etobicoke Creek. As Mohawk traditionalist William Woodworth Raweno:kwas reminds us, there are footprints on this land and on this shore that tell a story of human habitation that begins shortly after the retreat of the last glacier. Ever since, different groups of first peoples have periodically hunted, camped, and fished at the river mouths along the lakefront.

European presence along the present-day Toronto shore occurred sometime in the seventeenth century, with the French in the eighteenth century establishing two successive trading posts near the mouth of the Humber River and Fort Rouillé, near the west end of the present Canadian National Exhibition grounds. With the arrival of Lieutenant Governor John Graves Simcoe in 1793, a garrison, later known as Fort York, was erected and land was cleared at the east end of Toronto Bay for a town, signalling a change from an economy based on hunting, trapping, and the fur trade to one of settled agriculture and industry.

As archaeologist Ronald F. Williamson notes, the first permanent European settlements along the waterfront in the vicinity of Toronto followed the earlier pattern of habitation at the river mouths established by the successive groups of first peoples, the forerunners of the communities and districts on or near the Rouge, Don, and Humber Rivers and Mimico and Etobicoke Creeks. Rather than relying exclusively on York for survival, newcomers who settled in these isolated areas picked up, to varying degrees, the patterns of resource harvesting, agriculture, and water transportation that were in many cases long established. The same rivers that gave the Aboriginal people their hunting and fishing and agriculture made commerce and, in due course, industry possible for the early European settlers, so that an overlapping use of land emerged over time.

Many of these early settlers — the fishermen, the market gunners, the boat builders and captains, the tradesmen, and even some of the pioneer families — moved fluidly along the waterfront during the nineteenth century. The pioneers cleared the land, laid

Introduction

Yachts, ferries, and Toronto as seen from the busy lagoon near the Queen City Yacht Club on Algonquin Island

Jane Fairburn

the roads, often along pre-existing aboriginal pathways, and established the sawmills, gristmills, and woollen mills at the river mouths along what was then a waterfront of dispersed districts, villages, and farmland. A system of trade and development took shape, with dairy, produce, grain, and many other farm goods from the hinterlands; milled lumber from the Humber, Don, and Rouge Rivers; vegetables and flowers from Kew Gardens at the Beach; fish from the Island and Mimico Creek; and potash and grain from Scarborough. Gradually, the shoreline became one interconnected whole as the city filled in around the markets and Toronto Harbour.

After the pioneer era, these outlying areas contained within them a series of seasonal resorts, parks, and entertainment areas, which were first accessed by the steamers and schooners that plied the Toronto shore and many other locales farther afield in the nineteenth and early twentieth centuries. Later, many of these places were accessed by an interconnected system of streetcars and radials, which at one time ran along the main arterial east-west routes of the city and outlying areas, from West Hill in the east to Long Branch and beyond in the west. By the early decades of the twentieth century,

each area contained within its boundaries a fully established, year-round residential community or communities. If we were to get into a boat and survey the Toronto shore today, we would see most of them there still, interspersed among the other notable waterfront landmarks along the shore.

Spanning almost eleven miles from the Rouge to the Beach, the gentle river marshes and craggy precipices of the Scarborough Bluffs are home to the largest waterfront district in the Toronto area, the Scarborough shore. At the west end of the Bluffs stands the R.C. Harris Water Treatment Plant (also known as the Waterworks), itself a cultural monument to our connection with the lake and the unofficial dividing line between the Bluffs and the Beach.

Just to the west of the Waterworks, the cliffs give way to a wide strip of sand some two miles long. Here the Beach community stretches from the Kingston Road to the sands of Lake Ontario, with the Boardwalk, a wooden promenade along the lakefront, acting as the community's unofficial main street. Immediately to the west of the Beach's Ashbridge's Bay Marina is the Leslie Street Spit, a man-made peninsula that has evolved

Mouth of the Humber River, 2012

Keith Ellis

into a waterfront park and nature sanctuary, which is now an adjunct of the wider community.

As we continue to move westward we reach the Eastern Gap or, as it is officially known, the East Gap. On the west side of the gap is the Island, which, geographically speaking, is really a series of sandbars, waterways, and ponds off the mainland of downtown Toronto. A full-time residential community thrives there, with about 650 residents on Wards and Algonquin Islands, although the population is greatly diminished from its zenith in the first half of the twentieth century. As we sail around the Island, our course angles inward toward the Canadian National Exhibition grounds and Ontario Place, a waterfront park and entertainment centre now undergoing a period of transition. Just west of here, past the Argonaut Rowing Club, is the tony Boulevard Club, which began as the Parkdale Canoe Club in 1905. Next are the Palais Royale and the Sunnyside Bathing Pavilion, the only remnants of the once wildly popular Sunnyside Beach Amusement Park. Still moving west, we can see the bold arch of the Humber River Pedestrian and Cycling Bridge casting a shadow over the water at the entrance to the Toronto Carrying Place Trail, which was travelled by Aboriginal people for millennia. To the west of the bridge, past the giant condominiums in Humber Bay, the other Lakeshore communities, Mimico, New Toronto, and Long Branch, still hug the line of the water.

These special communities and districts — the Scarborough shore, the Beach, the Island, and the Lakeshore — fan out over the southern limits of the city at Lake Ontario and form a complex and diverse network of landscapes and people. Though historically connected, each of these places maintains a distinct sensibility and separate identity. Each has its own stories, many known only to the old-time residents of these communities. For us as Torontonians, these stories are the collective yarns of an almost forgotten waterfront culture that is uniquely ours, waiting to be rediscovered.

The Scarborough Shore

PART I

Cathedral Bluffs, Scarborough Bluffs Park, 2011

Keith Ellis

CHAPTER ONE

The Nature of the Place

On the evening of July 29, 1793, the *Mississauga*, a British government vessel, set sail from Niagara for Toronto Bay. Arriving at Toronto before dawn the next morning, the vessel was piloted into the bay after daybreak by Jean-Baptiste Rousseaux, an Indian Department interpreter and trader who lived nearby. Mrs. Simcoe, the wife of the lieutenant governor of Upper Canada, John Graves Simcoe, awoke on board the ship later that morning and was met with a sublime view of the pristine basin.

The bay, as later described by Colonel Joseph Bouchette in *The British Dominions in North America; etc.*, revealed a plush carpet of Carolinian forest, which cast its image on the lake, blurring the line of demarcation between the water and beach. Just to the west of the inlet was the Rousseaux home, which was at the mouth of an ancient river now known as the Humber. For countless centuries the riverbank had served as a passageway to the hinterlands and the inland regions of Canada. To the south of the mainland was a peninsula that formed the outer periphery of the bay, beginning in the west, at the mouth of the inlet, and stretching easterly as a finger of white sand as far as the eye could see.

Toronto Harbour in 1793

(engraving) Anonymous, with permission
of the Royal Ontario Museum © ROM, 958.13.7

Within days of her arrival at Toronto, Mrs. Simcoe rode on horseback easterly across this peninsula, now known as the Island. Continuing east, along a sandy beach on the north shore of the lake, she found herself in the vicinity of what we now know as the Beach and from there, despite the restrictions of a proper eighteenth-century lady's dress, climbed into a small boat and had herself rowed farther still, until she saw a line of immense and imposing cliffs stretching far into the distance. Of the experience she wrote in her diary: "After rowing a mile we came within sight of what is named, in the map, the highlands of Toronto. The shore is extremely bold, and has the appearance of chalk cliffs, but I believe they are only white sand. They appeared so well that we talked of building a summer residence there and calling it Scarborough." Although the Highlands had been known to early European explorers since the seventeenth century, and for countless centuries before that to the Aboriginal people who frequented the lakefront, it was Mrs. Simcoe who first recorded the sense of mystery and imagination that they continue to evoke to this day.

It was one thing for Mrs. Simcoe to write about the Highlands. It was another thing

Along the Shore

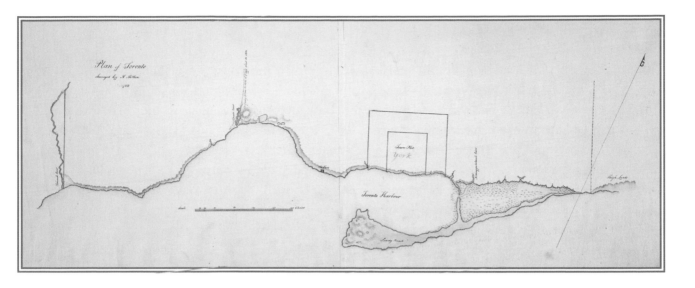

entirely, during those times, to consider living on top of them, replete as they were with insects — notably black flies — and beasts of all description and lacking road access to York, which lay,

Alexander Aitken's Plan of Toronto *(1788) clearly shows the peninsula Mrs. Simcoe rode across on her way to the Highlands (noted on the far right of the map)*

AO, F 47-5-1-0-1, Simcoe family maps of Upper Canada

at a minimum, five and a half miles distant to the west. To say the least, this was a thoroughly unconventional idea for an English gentlewoman of her times. But Elizabeth Simcoe was by no means conventional. She appreciated and rejoiced in the unspoiled beauty of the landscape, enough so to envision herself right from the beginning on the top of the cliffs, in the middle of nature, gazing out at an unending sea of blue.

In time these cliffs came to be known as the Scarborough Highlands and, later in the twentieth century, as the Scarborough Bluffs. In 1850 the whole region — bordered on the west by what is now Victoria Park Avenue, on the north by what was then the

The Bluffs as Viewed by Elizabeth Simcoe, c. 1793

Risto Turunen, Courtesy Mural Routes Heritage Trail

17

The Scarborough Shore

Township of Markham, on the east by what was then the Township of Pickering, and on the south by Lake Ontario — was incorporated as Scarborough Township within the County of York. The shoreline area of the township originally included the cliffs and, directly to the east, the Highland Creek River Valley, which lies just to the west of the present-day West Rouge area. (The Scarborough waterfront displays a northeast alignment from approximately Victoria Park Avenue, though for our purposes, directions along the Kingston Road, which has generally run parallel with the shore since the nineteenth century, are expressed as east-west, with the shore situated to the south of the highway.)

Since the nineteenth century, industrial and commercial building on and in the vicinity of the Toronto shore has destroyed much of the natural beauty first seen by Mrs. Simcoe. The steady march toward the future has too often reduced our shoreline to a by-product of Toronto's progress, so much so that many sections of today's waterfront would be virtually unrecognizable to the Simcoes. Yet some places remain where one can stand in silence and respond to the natural world, not with picks and shovels but with dreams and love. The Scarborough shore is one such place.

———◆———

ALTHOUGH MRS. SIMCOE was the first to record the grandeur of the Bluffs, others have been making the journey to the Scarborough shore ever since. There was Jack Heron and Ruth Heron (née McCowan), who lived almost 100 years ago in the Beach at what was then the easternmost edge of Toronto. As it turns out, the couple was distantly related through a common ancestor, Sarah Ashbridge, whose family were the first settlers in the greater Beach area and were also pioneers of the Scarborough shore.

I was told by one of their children, Ruth Sutherland (née Heron), that in the long and lovely days of summer her parents sometimes gathered their children and picnic baskets and set out for a day in the open country. They made

Radial car travelling westbound down Trout's Hill, c. 1915

Courtesy SA

Along the Shore

their way along the Kingston Road to a spot near Victoria Park Avenue where the radial car route — the electric tram that spanned the breadth of the Township of Scarborough, from Birch Cliff in the west all the way east to West Hill — began. There they joined a group of locals waiting for the trolley that took them just a few more miles to the east and into a different and seemingly distant land. They were going to have a day in the Bluffs, still known in those days as the Scarborough Highlands.

As they glided along the Kingston Road, sometimes in the car with a cupola of coloured glass, they passed Sir Donald Mann's Fallingbrook, a stately mansion with extensive grounds that overlooked the lake. Moving east, they next passed the Toronto Hunt, an exclusive country club whose presence on the Scarborough shore dated from 1895. Beyond this elegant property the rapidly expanding Birch Cliff community continued, which had begun decades earlier as a seasonal cottage area.

As the train climbed Trout's Hill to the east of these places, they passed another impressive residence whose three-storey turret surveyed the lake lying to the south, beyond the tableland known locally as the Flats. In later years, this property would be known as the White Castle Inn. Rising over the crest of the hill, they had their first

sight of Scarborough's gentle meadows, spread out like a patchwork quilt before them and framed on the south by Lake Ontario, an ever-present expanse of blue glimpsed fleetingly through the trees.

Within minutes they passed the Halfway House, which still welcomed weary wayfarers off the Kingston Road, as it had from earliest times, when it was a popular stagecoach inn. To the southeast, beyond the cows that dozed in the shade of oak and elm, stood the twin citadels of the Roman Catholic Church's St. Augustine's Seminary and St. Joseph's-on-the-Lake, a convent and novitiate. These structures stood in stark contrast to the

St. Augustine's Seminary (pictured in the background of this postcard) also operated as a working farm in the first half of the twentieth century Courtesy Archives of the Roman Catholic Archdiocese of Toronto (ARCAT)

The Scarborough Shore

unassuming barns and homesteads of the original pioneers, among them those of the McCowans and the Cornells, whose lands still sprawled south from the Kingston Road down to the lake.

Just past St. Joseph's-on-the-Lake was Scarborough Heights Park, a pleasure ground that had been a popular destination for day trippers since the early 1900s. The family opted to avoid the raucous crowds at the park, however, and continued a little farther, where they finally arrived at Markham's Road, as it was then called. There, near the dilapidated smithy of Scarborough Village, which by then was almost deserted, they got off the radial.

The children ran ahead while their parents meandered along the time-worn path strewn with buttercups and wild strawberry. Only the freshness of the air hinted at the

An early twentieth century postcard of the moonlight over the Scarborough Bluffs

TPL, PC 3035

height of land as they moved steadily uphill toward the sumac that lined the top of the meadow. Finally, at the top of the field, they parted the brush and the brambles and sat down, drinking in the deep aquamarine and indigo tones of the still and silent lake that stretched out to the south.

Years later, the Herons solidified these summer sojourns by building a romantic stone house near the edge of this very cliff. One of the main features of this lovely home was a simple square window, which at night perfectly framed the moon hanging low on the southern horizon, casting a pathway of silver light across the waters of the lake. The memory of that simple "blue window" is cherished to this day.

———•———

THE SCARBOROUGH SHORE, remarkable for its beauty, is also notable for its size and scale. Presently stretching from the R.C. Harris Water Treatment Plant, which borders the Beach community, in the west to the mouth of the Rouge River in the east, it is almost eleven miles in length, more than twice the length of

Along the Shore

the next longest shoreline featured in this book, the Lakeshore.

Volume 1 of Adam and Mulvany's *History of Toronto and County of York, Ontario; etc.* refers to Scarborough as being "abundantly watered." Four of the seven watersheds within the city of Toronto flow through Scarborough, and two of the three significant remaining marshlands in the city are just east of the Bluffs, at the mouths of Highland Creek and the Rouge River. Many sections of the Scarborough shore are designated as ecologically and/or scientifically significant. Together with Highland Creek and the Rouge Park lands, which are soon to be designated an urban national park, the Scarborough shore is an ecosystem of unparalleled diversity within the city of Toronto.

The Scarborough shore is perhaps most impressive when viewed from the perspective that Mrs. Simcoe first saw it, at the water's edge. From Lake Ontario, the cliffs appear as multi-layered cakes of white, grey, and rust punctuated by richly foliated ravines. In some sections, underwater streams and rivulets dribble down the cliff face, and in other sections the cliffs bear distinctive ridge-like patterns, worn from the waves of an ancient glacial lake that preceded Lake Ontario.

Farther to the east, near the highest point of the cliffs, stands the formation known as the Cathedral Bluffs or the Needles. Here the Bluffs take on a more malevolent appearance, where the jagged-toothed, perpendicular cliff faces, complete with spires, pinnacles, and buttresses, rise almost 300 feet out of the water.

The geological termination of the Scarborough Bluffs is at East Point Park, a quarter mile west of the mouth of Highland Creek. Early mariners called this area Centre Point, as it was halfway between the active ports of Toronto and Whitby. While the geological formation of the Bluffs actually ends here, the Scarborough shore continues east and includes the mouths of Highland Creek and, today, beyond the historic area of Port Union, the Rouge River at the city limits.

———— ◆ ————

LONG BEFORE THE ARRIVAL of the Simcoes, the Bluffs were known to the French explorers, traders, and coureurs de bois as Les grands Ecores. One interpretation of *"écore"* found in an 1873 dictionary of French etymology defines it as a steep place on the shore, although the term is no longer in common use, and in Toronto did not survive the arrival of the British in 1793. Mrs. Simcoe thought of naming a summer residence on the Bluffs "Scarborough" because the cliffs reminded her of those at Scarborough, England, a resort town on the North Sea Coast. Unlike so many other transplanted British place names, this one was apt, not only for the resemblance seen by Mrs. Simcoe but also for

The Scarborough Shore

Doris McCarthy's Fool's Paradise, 2005, now an Ontario Heritage Trust property Jane Fairburn

etymological reasons of which she likely knew little or nothing.

The secondary meaning of the word "scar," according to the *Oxford Reference Dictionary*, is "a precipitous craggy part of a mountain-side or cliff." Archaeologist and historian David Boyle, editor of *The Township of Scarboro 1796–1896*, points out that the word "scar" is also curiously related to the Saxon word "sciran," meaning to divide, which is apt because the shore divides the land from the water. The second half of the word, "borough," also resonates in its plain meaning of a village or town, for there has been an intermittent human presence near the edge of the shore since as far back as 11,000 years ago.

Boyle also points out that the word "borough" is historically connected with the Anglo-Saxon word "beorgan," translations of which include "to cover, to hide, or to protect." It is in this sense that the present-day communities along the Scarborough shore are best defined — as hidden places that exist in relative isolation from the rest of Toronto. Unlike the Beach and the Island, which are still at some level village-like, the Scarborough shore, including the Bluffs and the Highland Creek and Rouge River Valleys, are more properly a series of enclaves, each one somewhat different in character

Along the Shore

but all "sub" urban, in the original non-pejorative sense of the word, existing within a complex system of parks, ravines, gullies, and water.

In stark contrast to the natural world of the lake, the Kingston Road lies on the height of land at the north end of the community. This multi-lane highway, dotted with seedy motels and strip malls erected during the height of the automobile age, effectively cuts the Bluffs off from the rest of the city, both visually and psychologically.

North of the highway lies another Scarborough. While the knee-jerk characterization of this Scarborough as an urban ghetto is grossly unfair — a Statistics Canada report released in 2009 shows many sections of Scarborough, including the vast majority of the Scarborough Bluffs district, to be *at or below* the average rate of violent crime in Toronto — it is nevertheless more difficult to recognize a connection to the lake in the concrete housing developments and cookie-cutter bungalows that appeared almost overnight on the abandoned farmlands north of the Kingston Road after the Second World War. It is only as you travel south from the highway and approach the water that you leave all this behind. Here the orientation shifts outward, toward the expanse of Lake Ontario, where you experience, in the words of Canadian painter and long-time resident Phil Richards, "a psychological freedom not normally associated with city living."

The development of these permanent residential areas was significantly different in Scarborough compared with the other waterfront areas, which transitioned into a series of full-time residential communities and districts in the early decades of the twentieth century. The Scarborough shore, with the exception of its westerly edge at Birch Cliff, remained largely rural in character and kept up many of the traditions and practices of an agrarian society right up to the early 1940s. There are still residents of the Scarborough shore who remember the southernmost edge of the township as farmland and who know the place not by its assigned street names and paved-over concession lines but by the topography of the land and shore.

There is a spirit in these last remaining wild spaces, in the untended apple and cherry orchards of Scarborough's lakeside parks and the wide suburban lots built near the shore-cliff of an ancient glacial lake, a spirit that recalls another time and place in the history of the former township. It is at the decrepit Ashbridge farmhouse, the abandoned Cornell barn, and the Osterhout log cabin standing in Guildwood Park that we feel most keenly a yearning for our collective rural past, a past that was all but obliterated in the successive waves of industrialization that hit the present-day Toronto shore in the nineteenth and twentieth centuries. Despite the inevitable intrusions of progress, the cliffs and major watercourses remain, anchoring us to the past and grounding us in the present.

CHAPTER TWO

Beginnings

The story of the Scarborough shore reaches back some 75,000 years, to a time when the Wisconsin Glacial Episode, the last glacial period occurring within the ice age, began. The present-day Scarborough shore stood at an outlet of an enormous river that, during warm periods, flowed through the Laurentian Channel from Georgian Bay into a much larger ancestral Lake Ontario. Deposits from the delta of this river, including fossil pollen and lake organisms, collected at the mouth of the basin and were thickest in the Scarborough area, where they formed a peninsula that jutted far out into the lake.

After the beginning of the last glacial period, material continued to be deposited at the base of this great delta. When the Laurentide Ice Sheet began its final retreat from the Toronto region about 12,500 years ago, a massive body of water, much larger than today's Lake Ontario, was left in its wake. Known as Lake Iroquois, this body of water quickly drained away about 12,200 years ago, as temperatures continued to rise and the previously blocked St. Lawrence River Valley was freed of ice. (To maintain consistency with the majority of the published archaeological and geological literature, the dates

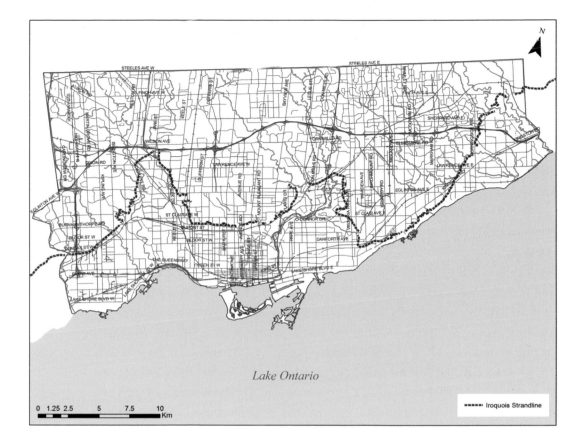

This map of Toronto shows the Lake Iroquois shorecliff, marked in red
Courtesy Archaeological Services Inc.

presented here are uncalibrated radiocarbon years before present [1950]. The difference between uncalibrated radiocarbon years and calibrated or calendar years is generally inconsequential for most purposes, although the gap typically increases as one progresses back in time. For example, the estimated retreat of the Laurentide Ice Sheet circa 12,500 years ago would be calibrated to about 14,475 years ago.)

Though Lake Iroquois has long since disappeared, the shorecliff of this ancient glacial lake remains a prominent feature of the Toronto landscape. It is the hill on which Casa Loma stands, which bisects midtown Toronto at about St. Clair Avenue and eventually intersects with the Scarborough shore near the midpoint of the Scarborough Bluffs, in Cathedral Bluffs Park (the park holds the dual distinction of being the highest point on the Scarborough Bluffs and on Lake Ontario). There it runs parallel with the present shore until turning northeastward, roughly at Markham Road in Scarborough.

After Lake Iroquois drained, a much smaller body of water than the present Lake

Ontario remained, known as Lake Admiralty. According to geologist Nicholas Eyles in "Ravines, Lagoons, Cliffs and Spits: The Ups and Downs of Lake Ontario," the original shoreline of this smaller basin was at least three miles to the south of the present Lake Ontario. It was during the Lake Admiralty phase that the rivers feeding into the freshwater basin began to cut deep ravines and stream gullies into the land adjacent to the Toronto shore. These ravine systems are prominent in the Bluffs and also evident in the Highland Creek and Rouge River Valleys.

With the retreat of the Laurentide Ice Sheet, pressure on the land was released, and it began to slowly rise, a process known as post-glacial crustal rebound. Since that time, the outlet of what we now know as Lake Ontario has been gradually rising faster than the lake itself, as the earth's crust readjusts after the retreat of the massive ice sheet. The rising outlet has been slowly refilling the Ontario basin and has created, in time, Lake Ontario. Rising lake levels have also backed up the tributary rivers and streams along the Toronto shore, and, as environmental archaeologist Robert MacDonald writes, "reduced the slope" of the waterways, "creating extensive coastal wetlands at their drowned mouths and forcing them to meander and broaden their valleys." According to *Waterfront Toronto: Archaeological Conservation and Management Strategy*, it was only relatively recently, about 3,000 years ago, that the present-day Toronto shoreline assumed a profile similar to what the British found at the time of settlement.

Because the water was considerably lower during the Lake Admiralty phase, much of the deposits that collected during the glacial period were exposed in the Scarborough area, contributing to a giant promontory that extended far out into the lake. This enormous shorecliff was the precursor of the Scarborough Bluffs. As lake levels continued to rise over the millennia, silts and sands from the shorecliff slowly eroded and moved westward, creating the present-day Toronto shoreline. A narrow sandy spit that ran westward also took shape, just offshore, all the way from today's Beach community to what we now know as Toronto Island. The sandbar was loosely connected to the mainland near present-day Woodbine Avenue in the Beach and farther west near the outlet to the Don River.

———— • ————

THE FIRST EXTENSIVE scientific examination of the Bluffs was made in the 1870s by English geologist George Jennings Hinde. As he stated in his lecture to the Canadian Institute in 1877, "On its northern shores . . . the banks of the lake [Ontario] are generally low and without features of importance, [but] this general deficiency is more than compensated by the display, perhaps unequaled anywhere around the lake, of glacial strata at the Scarboro' Cliff."

Internationally acclaimed Canadian geologist Arthur Philemon Coleman continued the study of the Bluffs in the twentieth century and produced one of the first maps of the glacial deposits of the Toronto region that included the Scarborough Bluffs and the related strata at the Don Valley Brickyard. The Bluffs continue to be studied for the secrets they reveal about the last glacial age and climate change — an issue that is especially relevant today.

The sedimentary deposits of the Scarborough Bluffs, stacked one upon the other, are the layers of time. From the top of the cliff, the Bluffs' successive strata of clay and sand reach down toward the shore, each one revealing a more distant time period but not yet fully understood. As geolo-

gists classified the strata, in some cases they used the names of the small communities that still remain at the top of the cliff. At the sub-glacial layer of the Bluffs lies the Meadowcliffe diamict, named for the community that has been my family's home for over a decade. Farther back in time, down the face of the cliff, sits the Seminary diamict, referencing St. Augustine's Seminary, which has stood near the highest point of the Bluffs since 1913. Still more distant in time, near the base of the Bluffs, are the yellow sands of the Scarborough Formation from the commencement of the Wisconsin Glacial Episode.

Geologist Arthur Philemon Coleman was also an accomplished artist and painted this image of the Scarborough Bluffs during one of his many trips to the Highlands in the early twentieth century

Arthur Philemon Coleman, with permission of the Royal Ontario Museum © ROM, 932.39.315

The Scarborough Shore

Afternoon on Scarborough Bluff
Flats, *September 1925* James Jervis
Blomfield, TPL, 982-9-7

Nicholas Eyles indicates in *Toronto Rocks* that "virtually an entire section of the Toronto Pleistocene" may be seen at Cathedral Bluffs Park, the highest point of the Scarborough Bluffs. Here an immense convex cliff of clay and sand, displaying the Scarborough and Thorncliffe Formations and the Sunnybrook, Seminary, and Meadowcliffe diamicts, rises from the narrow beach.

Marine historian C.H.J. Snider in his "Schooner Days" column in the *Evening Telegram* of September 23, 1944, noted that "the Bluffs were gouged and scored by the rains of centuries into gullies and gables, revetments and ravines . . . their height close-in is only a first step toward great elevation. As high again above it, but sometimes miles further inland, rises the second step, tree-plumed, cleared in steep fields which zig zag down to the plateau where rise century-old elms and farm houses with their orchards as ancient."

The variations in land elevation at the top of the cliffs, as described by Snider, are still evident today. In many sections, from the vicinity south of Kennedy Road in the west to Guildwood Village in the east, the land immediately adjacent to the cliff is best described as a flat plain that is separated from the higher ground farther inland by an imposing hill that in many places intersects with the old Lake Iroquois shorecliff. This plain, known to pioneers and many of Scarborough's oldest residents as the Flats, is in fact the bottom of the ancestral Lake Iroquois. Some of Scarborough's earliest homesteads were built on this land nearest the cliff, which lies between the steep embankment leading up to the present-day Kingston Road and the edge of the Bluffs.

While some of Scarborough's earliest homesteads were located on the Flats, the deep ravines and stream gullies flowing down to the lake provided encampment sites and areas rich in game for first people, who migrated into the region shortly after the retreat of the last ice sheet. Today these woodlands, ravines, and gullies support a diverse range of plant life and form important corridors for the surprising amount of wildlife that continues to inhabit the shore area, the river marshes, and the flat tableland on the cliff face.

Several areas of the Scarborough shore, including the Bluffs, East Point Park, the Highland Creek Swamp, and the lower Rouge Valley, have received the provincial designation of a Life Science Area of Natural Scientific Interest (ANSI). A report prepared for the former Metropolitan Toronto and Region Conservation Authority in 1996 indicates that the lower Rouge alone contains thirty-two regionally rare vascular plants and identifies the Rouge River area, along with the Scarborough Bluffs, as sites of rare or significant populations of breeding birds, reptiles, and mammals. The report also notes the presence of important migratory bird habitats in the Scarborough Bluffs, East Point, and Rouge River areas and significant rare species in East Point.

Added to these designations are many individual sites singled out by the Toronto and Region Conservation Authority as Environmentally Significant Areas (ESAs). There are nine such sites at or connected to the Scarborough shore, with many of them forming key animal and plant refuge areas. The Scarborough shore also contains many woodland sites, including the Fallingbrook Woods and Guild Woods ESAs, which are characterized as remnant Carolinian forests. This lush deciduous forest type, widespread in the eastern United States, extends only into southern Ontario and once sprawled across most of the Toronto region and down to the lakefront.

The Highland Creek Wetland Complex has recently been affirmed as provincially significant, as have the coastal marshes at the mouth of the Rouge River. The latter marshes are contained within the biologically and ecologically diverse Rouge Park,

The Scarborough Shore

which extends north from the lake, adjacent to the community of the West Rouge, to well beyond the city limits. Twelve times the size of New York's Central Park, it is soon to be designated Canada's first national park in an urban area.

———•———

OVER THE MILLENNIA, the natural process of erosion that created the present-day Toronto shore and the Island caused the Scarborough cliffs to move continuously northward and inland. Erosion is most prevalent at the base of the cliff, where the water laps the shore, but groundwater, seeping through the layers of clay and sand at the top of the cliff, has also played a part.

Erosion was helped along in the nineteenth century by stonehooking. In the nineteenth and early twentieth centuries, hundreds of tons of stone and gravel were removed from the shorelines and near-shore waters of the greater Toronto area and hauled onto ships. This material, used in foundations and road construction, fuelled the growth of Toronto. Some stonehooking ships sailed out of Port Union, although a larger fleet worked out of Port Credit, west of Etobicoke Creek.

With the settlement of Scarborough in the nineteenth century came deforestation, a factor that served to further accelerate the rate of erosion at the cliffs. Jean Little, in "The Neilsons of Scarborough," recalls a story about her family's homestead on the edge of the cliffs, west of the mouth of Highland Creek: "The electrical storms over the lake were usually severe, but some were worse than others. One wild night that Grandmother recalled very clearly was when the waves undercut the bluff and a huge section collapsed and slid into the lake, taking the old log barn on a neighbouring farm along with it. The barn had not been used for some time because of its dangerous position and it now had followed the abandoned log house, which had dropped over the lake bank many years before."

Twentieth century homes have not been immune to the same fate. As early as the 1920s, articles in the *Toronto Daily Star* report significant erosion in the Scarborough Bluffs. In an attempt to counter the perpetual wave action, some residents began throwing refuse over the side of the cliff. In the twentieth century, municipal authorities filled some of the rapidly eroding ravines that led down to the shore with garbage, a practice that continued for several decades. Indeed, before the development of Bluffer's Park in the 1970s, the southerly end of Brimley Road near the lake operated as a municipal garbage dump; a massive landslide occurred in the ravine in 1991, blocking access to Bluffer's Park for some time.

An article in the *Toronto Daily Star* of February 21, 1951, indicates that nineteen

houses on the Bluffs were in jeopardy of falling over the cliff. Mr. Robinson, who farmed
the Cherry Orchard, now Sylvan Park, lost his
house to the cliffs in the 1940s, as did other

*House on the edge — here's what remains
of comedian Billy Van's house on the
Scarborough Bluffs, 2011* Jane Fairburn

property owners near St. Joseph's-on-the-Lake, in today's Cathedral Bluffs neighbourhood. At the time of writing, the former cottage of comedian Billy Van clings to the
crumbling edge of the Bluffs on our street, while millions of dollars are poured into
the Toronto and Region Conservation Authority's Meadowcliffe Drive Erosion Control
Project, initiated to halt further disasters from occurring along the edge of the Bluffs.

It was the visionary Spencer Clark, co-founder of the Guild of All Arts and former
owner of the Guild Inn, who first installed a barge filled with concrete at the water's edge
to stem erosion at the foot of the Bluffs underneath his property. In the 1960s, hundreds
of thousands of truckloads of fill were trucked down to the shore, through a roadway
built in the gully lying to the east of the Guild of All Arts.

Eventually the former Metropolitan Toronto and Region Conservation Authority
followed suit, installing a series of groynes and armoured revetment walls at the shore.
More recent developments have seen the piecemeal installation of a waterfront trail at
the foot of the cliff in many sections of the Bluffs. While these measures have curbed
erosion, most of the narrow, natural beaches at the shore have been lost. The angle of

The Scarborough Shore

the cliff faces, now starved of continual wave action, is being reduced. The slopes are becoming more stable and vegetation is taking hold. This process has already eliminated, to a significant degree, the unique geological feature of the Bluffs in many areas, as well as the possibility of discovering other archaeological sites near the shore.

———•———

THE FIRST HUMANS in the Toronto region were the Paleo-Indians, who moved through the present shoreline area as early as eleven thousand years ago. Very little evidence of this initial group has been discovered across the Toronto lakefront, since earlier habitation sites are presumably now submerged under the lake. Much of the evidence we do have of very early human presence in Scarborough has been found near the old Lake Iroquois shorecliff, which may have served as a useful lookout point during hunting periods.

As early as 1896, David Boyle, the father of Canadian archaeology, noted a grave that contained the remains of five Aboriginal people of a relatively recent date near the Bluffs. Scarborough's pioneers and farmers participated in the discovery of many artifacts that provide clues to the presence of the earlier people who occupied the area near the present-day Toronto shore. Some of them they saved; others they simply chucked out over the back of the wagon during the course of baling hay or gathering the harvest.

The largest collection of Archaic period artifacts ever documented in Scarborough were gathered over many years by the Helliwell family, who held lands in the vicinity of the historic village of Highland Creek. This area, west of the Rouge River, takes its name from the waterway that flows down to Lake Ontario. The Helliwells farmed lands in the Highland Creek Valley, as well as the surrounding tablelands, so it's important to recognize that this collection was gathered from a vast area, and not just from the area adjacent to the creekbed. This group of artifacts, examined by archaeologist Peter Pratt in the 1950s, contained many projectile points (spearheads and arrowheads) from the Laurentian Archaic culture, from about BC 3,500 to 2,500, as well as many Late Archaic artifacts, including projectile points, from about BC 2,500 to 1,400. Based on Pratt's description, thirty-one late pre-contact Huron-Wendat projectile points were noted that date somewhere in the AD 1400s to 1500s. According to archaeologist Dana Poulton, "Basically, what you have in the Helliwell collection is a slice though about 5,000 years of First Nations history in Scarborough."

In the early twentieth century, the McCowan brothers found relics of the Late Paleo-Indian and Early Archaic periods at two sites farther to the west, one close to today's Cathedral Bluffs and the other close to today's intersection of Kingston and McCowan

Roads. This private collection, examined by archaeologist Bruce Schroeder in 1989, points to evidence of human occupation in the Bluffs as early as 10,000 years ago, making these finds among the oldest artifacts in all of Toronto.

As recently as 2005, an archaeological dig conducted by Catherine Crinnion of the Toronto and Region Conservation Authority near the mouth of Highland Creek revealed an Early Woodland or Late Archaic camp that was likely a tool manufacturing and rejuvenation site. These investigations, and others conducted in the vicinity of the river and creek mouths near the shore, have produced many artifacts from different time periods and indicate ongoing use of the present shoreline area across thousands of years, both for temporary encampments and semi-permanent villages.

Historian Carl Benn points out that the transition to Iroquoian horticultural societies in the lower Great Lakes occurred about 1,100 years ago. By about 800 years ago, the Iroquoian societies on the north shore of Lake Ontario, including those in the Toronto region, known as the ancestral Huron-Wendat, had become clearly defined sedentary communities. By this time, the Huron-Wendat, along with other Iroquoian groups, lived in longhouses and practised farming and the growing of the "three sisters"— corn, squash, and beans — as well as sunflowers and tobacco.

Archaeologists Ronald F. Williamson and Robert MacDonald write that by the fourteenth century there were a number of communities along the major waterways in the Toronto region, including the Rouge, Don, Humber, and Highland Creek drainage systems. They point out that these sites were usually around two hectares in size (about five acres). Many sites grew to approximately ten to twelve acres by the early sixteenth century. These farming societies had immense resource needs, and they typically exhausted their habitation sites in fewer than twenty years.

While humans have long been present at or near Toronto's lakefront, this presence has *not* been continuous. The

Ancient point from the R.A. McCowan collection, found in the vicinity of the Cathedral Bluffs

James McCowan Memorial Social History Society

mid-fifteenth century saw a movement toward the consolidation of Iroquoian groups in the Great Lakes region, including the ancestral Huron-Wendat located on the north shore of Lake Ontario. By the end of the sixteenth century, the Iroquoian people of the north shore of Lake Ontario, including those of the Toronto region, deserted the lakefront and moved northward to join the Huron-Wendat Confederacy, located in the areas of Lake Simcoe and the southeastern region of Georgian Bay. While the reasons for this migration are complex, the merger with other groups north of the lake undoubtedly left them in a stronger position to defend against attacks from their enemies, the Iroquois Confederacy from the south. While the Huron-Wendat were of the same linguistic family as the Iroquois Confederacy, they were of a different cultural affinity.

Reasons for hostilities between these distinct cultural groups are not fully understood. Yet they are undoubtedly connected to some degree to the presence of the Europeans, who had reached the Toronto region by the seventeenth century. Carl Benn reminds us that the Europeans brought with them a previously unknown host of diseases that decimated local Aboriginal populations and heightened tension among the various first peoples as they competed for trade with the French, Dutch, and English.

In the 1640s and 1650s, the Iroquois Confederacy launched a campaign against its enemies on the north shore of the lake. Many Huron-Wendats perished, while others were absorbed by the Iroquois Confederacy. Still others were dispersed and some fled eastward, establishing themselves in what is now the province of Quebec. The Huron-Wendat people, whose historic homeland lies in the region of Georgian Bay and Lake Simcoe, currently reside in an enclave of Québec City called Wendake (formerly called Jeune-Lorette).

In the mid-1660s, one of the members of the Iroquois Confederacy, known as the Seneca, moved from their homeland in present-day New York State northward to the Toronto region for a short period. The Seneca established two villages near the north shore of the lake at Toronto, part of a larger movement that saw other Iroquois villages established to the east and west of Toronto along the shore.

It was during this time that Ganatsekwyagon, Scarborough's earliest known village, was founded. Ganatsekwyagon was located about a mile and a half up from the mouth of the Rouge River. Its sister village, Teiaiagon, was situated about the same distance up the Humber River, some sixteen miles to the west.

An archaeological report prepared by Mayer, Pihl, Poulton and Associates in 1988 estimates that 500 to 800 people lived at Ganatsekwyagon, which is roughly translated as "place among the birches." About the same number of people are estimated to have lived

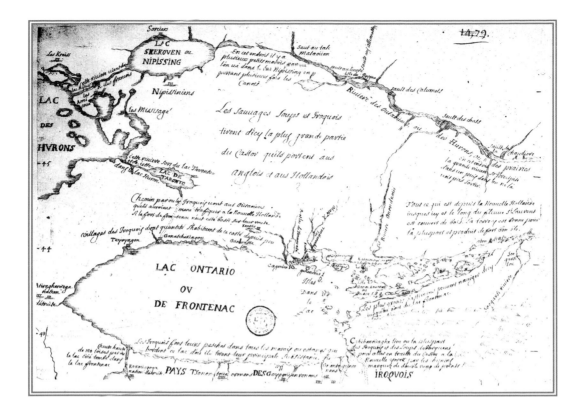

This map was likely drawn by Claude Bernou from information provided by explorer Louis Joliet. It shows the two Seneca villages at what is now Toronto and the eastern branch of the Carrying Place Trail leading north from Ganatsekwyagon. South of Teiaiagon, the Island is barely visible. Lake Simcoe is shown as Lac de Taronto.

Map and Data Library, University of Toronto, Toronto, original held at Service historique de la marine, Paris

at Teiaiagon. The placement of both villages was highly strategic, enabling residents to farm and access the rich hunting and fishing grounds in the marshland areas and at the mouth of the lake. Also, the rivers were only navigable up to the villages, allowing residents to control access to the sites.

Ganatsekwyagon and Teiaiagon were strategically placed at the foot of the eastern and western branches of the Toronto Carrying Place Trail, a lengthy route through the highlands north of Lake Ontario to the Holland River, eventually connecting with Lake Simcoe and Georgian Bay. The trail was a passageway to the hunting territory north of Lake Ontario and acted as a shortcut to the Upper Great Lakes region and all that lay beyond. The Seneca villages at the bottom of the trail were likely erected to establish control over the new territory as well as command control of the complex fur trade network that had developed after the appearance of the Europeans in the region in the seventeenth century.

Ganatsekwyagon was also connected to Teiaiagon in the west by an overland lakeside trail that ran along the edge of the lake, though the primary route to the village may have deviated substantially to the north in Scarborough, according to archaeologist Dana Poulton.

Percy J. Robinson, in *Toronto During the French Régime*, holds that the first recorded European visitors to Ganatsekwyagon were probably the French explorers and traders Jean Péré and Louis Joliet in 1669. Later that same year, a mission was established by the Sulpician fathers, under the direction of François d'Urfé. Robinson states that d'Urfé, along with Abbé Fénelon, passed a punishing winter at Ganatsekwyagon in 1669, their presence establishing the "first recorded residence of white men in the neighbourhood of Toronto" and, for our purposes, the first Europeans to inhabit the vicinity of the Toronto shore. A close reading of Dollier de Casson's *History of Montreal 1640–1672* suggests that the Abbé Fénelon in fact passed that winter alone at Ganatsekwyagon, without d'Urfé. Robinson further suggests that the French encampment is memorialized in the place name Frenchman's Bay, which according to present knowledge lies just to the east of Ganatsekwyagon, though recent scholarly thinking suggests otherwise. The French name for Toronto's most easterly waterway does, however, live on in the "*Rouge*" River.

Bead Hill, near the mouth of the Rouge, has been tentatively identified as Ganatsekwyagon. According to an archaeological report prepared by archaeologists Mayer, Pihl, Poulton and Associates in 1998, it includes a burial ground and a village site along with the presence of a much earlier indeterminate aboriginal campsite. Evidence suggests that the primary focus of the village was on the fur trade, though Poulton notes that it "was well situated for the exploitation of natural food and other resources . . . being in close proximity to the rich biomass of the Rouge Marsh."

The earliest reference to Bead Hill appears to be in 1849. In *America: A Four Years' Residence in the United States and Canada*, published that year, William Brown describes a burial ground that his workmen found near a sawmill he was renting nearby:

> My men, who had one day strayed to the top of a neighbouring hill . . . discovered that the place had a long time ago been a favorite burying ground of the Indians. . . . There were pieces of broken pottery, broken guns, and flint heads of some very handsome tobacco pipes which the men brought away. They intended to go in again. . . . But I persuaded them to let the dead to rest in peace, going, however, to view the place myself; and I found that about forty acres had been

Iroquoian villages in the Toronto area would have looked much the same as this recreated site at the Longwoods Conservation Area near London, Ontario Courtesy Ronald F. Williamson, Archaeological Services Inc.

appropriated as a place of sepulture, and that no grave had been deeper than about two feet from the surface. The whole steep bank of the river had been used, and the graves being one above the other in the hillside, they looked like steps from the top to the bottom.

Bead Hill, though largely unknown, was designated a site of national historical significance in 1991. According to one assessment of the site noted in Barbara Myrvold's *The People of Scarborough: A History*, it is "of international importance by virtue of the fact that it includes burials and that it is the only one of the seven Iroquois villages on the north shore known to have escaped destruction by urban development." The site has yielded some 3,500 artifacts, including 278 glass trade beads, which were highly valued by first peoples involved in the early days of the fur trade.

The Scarborough Shore

Ganatsekwyagon may have lasted for a period of just over twenty years before the Iroquois abandoned the north shore of the lake, perhaps as a result of a treaty or ongoing hostilities with the French. Other historians point to the oral tradition of the Anishinabe. Their history holds that a number of decisive battles won by the Anishinabe in south and central Ontario in a conflict known as the Beaver Wars forced the Iroquois back to their original territory.

Unfortunately few images exist that tell the story of the Aboriginal presence at Toronto. Here is an etching by Mrs. Simcoe of Canise, or "Great Sail," a Mississauga who frequented the greater Toronto shore area, c. 1794 TPL, x18-27b

After the Iroquois had left the north shore of the lake, a treaty was signed in 1701 between New France and many Aboriginal nations and groups in the northeast of North America, including the Iroquois Confederacy. Under this treaty, called the Great Peace of Montreal, the confederacy agreed to remain on the south shore of Lake Ontario. By this time an Anishinabeg group called by the Europeans the Mississaugas had moved into southern Ontario. The territory of the Mississaugas of the Toronto region now stretched eastward from Long Point on Lake Erie to the Niagara River, down the river to Lake Ontario, and along the north shore of the lake, ending at the Rouge River, and extending back inland to the height of land.

As hunter-gatherers, the Mississaugas likely occupied the area around Ganatsekwyagon on a seasonal basis, moving through the entire present-day Toronto shore area, hunting and fishing at the river mouths and practising some garden farming during the summer months. The Mississaugas were also present at the Humber River near Teiaiagon and may have occupied a separate village there on the west side of the waterway. They gathered at the mouth of the Credit River in the spring and fall.

The Mississaugas also named many of the major watercourses that drained into Lake Ontario along the present-day Toronto shore. According to surveyor Augustus Jones's 1796 list of "Names of the Rivers, and Creeks, as they are called by the Mississaugas," the Mississaugas gave Highland Creek the name "Yat-qui-i-be-no-nick" (creek comes out under high [lands]), while the Rouge was listed as "Che-Sippi," meaning "large creek."

The transition to a rural, agrarian society began with the arrival of the Simcoes in 1793, and as settlement took hold, the Mississaugas' traditional hunting and fishing grounds gradually became depleted, though they clung to their traditional ways as long as possible. Sadly, disease and alcoholism also played its part in the demise of many band members. Perhaps author John Spilsbury describes the plight of the Mississaugas best in *Fact and Folklore*, a local history of the eastern area of Scarborough: "Their historic farming and hunting lands had been taken over by the white man. They had nowhere to go. It is a matter of record that they were a gentle people."

By the late summer of 1826, the majority of the remaining Toronto-region Mississaugas had converted to Christianity and moved to the banks of the Credit River, near Lake Ontario, in the present-day city of Mississauga, led by their heroic and proud Chief Kahkewaquonaby, also known by his English name, the Reverend Peter Jones. We will also meet Jones in the Island and Lakeshore sections of the book.

It is interesting to note that though the consolidation of the Mississaugas on the Credit River cleared the way for further uninhibited settlement, the lands along the Scarborough shore may have never been properly ceded to the British. The Mississaugas were signatories to Treaty 13 of 1805, which confirmed the Toronto Purchase of 1787, an earlier land deal for much of what is modern-day Toronto. The Scarborough lands, however, were not included in that purchase. A later agreement, contained within the Williams Treaties of 1923, attempted to rectify this situation, but the Mississaugas did not sign this document; neither do they accept the wording, which attempts to fix the earlier omission of the Scarborough lands. The Mississaugas were, however, compensated in 2010, in the Toronto Purchase Settlement, for the lands contained in Treaty 13.

A little more than 210 years before the Toronto Purchase Settlement, the first European settlers arrived in Scarborough. During this time, the Mississaugas were still roaming freely through this vast district, and their ability to survive and thrive in the harsh Canadian climate must have been a wonder to many newly arrived Europeans, who set about hacking themselves out of the bush, one log at a time.

CHAPTER THREE

Settlement

As the population of Ontario, and in fact Canada, has become increasingly urban, we have all but forgotten the hardships associated with pioneer life: the loneliness of the log cabin with the wind whistling under the door and the wolves howling outside, the torturous swarms of mosquitoes and blackflies, and the back-breaking clearing of trees. Scarborough was not York, where the Queen's Rangers, upon arriving in Toronto Bay, began to hew the logs and set out the roads and infrastructure of a town. Scarborough was a distant and different place, more akin to descriptions in Susanna Moodie's *Roughing It in the Bush* of recently arrived immigrants doing battle with a malevolent wilderness. The nature and character of these early immigrant families and the hardships they faced would shape the texture of the community for years to come.

The earliest settlements in Scarborough took place in two distinct areas. One group of pioneers chose to settle near the edge of the cliffs, known in those days as the Front. Another group, including Scarborough's first settlers, David and Mary Thomson, chose the heavily forested territory inland, along the rivers and creeks leading down to the

The Settler's Lullaby, *1893*

Ernest Thompson Seton, CT/MS, 1996.5.1

shore that in previous centuries had been frequented by successive groups of Aboriginal peoples.

In "The Backwoodsman" Susanna Moodie wrote,

Son of the isles! rave not to me
Of the old world's pride and luxury;
Why did you cross the western deep,
Thus like a love-lorn maid to weep
O'er comforts gone and pleasures fled,
'Mid forests wild to earn your bread ?
. . . .
Beneath his axe, the forest yields
Its thorny maze to fertile fields;
This goodly breadth of well-till'd land,
Well-purchased by his own right hand,
With conscience clear, he can bequeath
His children, when he sleeps in death.

The Scarborough Shore

Brothers David and Andrew Thomson, along with their wives and children, left Dumfriesshire, Scotland, in 1796 and arrived in Newark (Niagara) in June of that year. These men, both skilled stonemasons, were joining their brother, Archibald, a carpenter and businessman who was already well established in the New World. Archibald Thomson, a United Empire Loyalist, had previously arrived in Johnstown, in what is now New York State, in 1773 and had served in the Loyalist militia during the American War of Independence.

In 1797, the three Thomson brothers and their families moved to York, where they were active in the construction trade. David and Andrew worked on the brick walls of the first Parliament Building at York, and all three brothers were involved in construction projects at the Garrison in 1815. York in those days was concentrated near the north-easterly shore of Toronto Bay. Mary Thomson, like so many others, feared the diseases that were thought to be associated with living so close to the low-lying marshes of the

Don River. In the spring of 1799 she and her husband, David, left Toronto Bay at York and walked into the Scarborough forest, along an old aboriginal trail that led northeast, likely the same trail that once led toward the Iroquois village of Ganatsekwyagon. They moved inland, setting up camp along Highland Creek, roughly two and a half miles from the cliffs. There they established their homestead, becoming Scarborough's first permanent European settlers. This area was named Bendale in the late nineteenth century.

In 1801 the Archibald Thomson family moved to Scarborough, settling close to David and Mary on Highland Creek. The Andrew Thomson family followed one year later, along

St. Andrew's Cemetery sits on part of David Thomson's original holdings and houses some of Scarborough's oldest pioneer families. A memorial erected to the memory of David and Mary Thomson reads in part: "To their honor who redeemed the Township from the wilderness." Jane Fairburn

with a few others originally from Dumfriesshire. In 1819 these Scots built St. Andrew's Church on a corner of David and Mary Thomson's property. Often referred to as the Auld Kirk, it became a centre of religious and community life for Scots in Scarborough, both in Bendale and for another Scottish community that developed a few decades later at the Front. A later church, built in 1849, still stands today and houses the oldest religious congregation in Scarborough.

Life in the bush was anything but easy, and *The Township of Scarboro 1796–1896* recounts some of the Thomson family's trials. Left alone in the woods with her children while David worked in York, Mary is said to have stopped a bear from running off with her livestock by attacking it with an axe. David, as sturdy as his wife, reportedly had his leg amputated — without anaesthetic.

By the time Scarborough was formally incorporated as a township within the County of York in 1850, the three original Thomson families had substantially expanded. The Thomson family now numbers in the thousands and includes some notable Canadians, among them media magnate David Thomson, Third Baron Thomson of Fleet, and author Farley Mowat, who carries a fascination with the wilderness, perhaps due to his own Thomson blood.

———— • ————

AFTER THE ARRIVAL of the Simcoes in 1793, many of the initial land patents near or along the lakefront at Toronto were given to prominent residents of York and Upper Canada, including government and military officials and a few United Empire Loyalists, former residents of Britain's American colonies who remained loyal to the Crown after the American Revolutionary War. As in other areas of the city, the vast majority of the patents in Scarborough were never taken up but were held for purposes of land speculation and, in time, were sold to other settlers. (The Toronto real estate market was competitive even then.) This practice slowed early growth in some regions of the Front in Scarborough. For example, the jurisdiction of the West Rouge (originally within the Township of Pickering and transferred to the Borough of Scarborough in 1974) was not settled by Henry Cowan until 1843. Up to that date the land had been held by the original patentee, William Holmes, Esquire.

The first land patent in Scarborough was granted in May of 1796 to Captain William Mayne, who received property in the eastern area of the present-day Birch Cliff area. In August 1796, John White also received a patent for extensive lands in the township, including property in what we now know as the community of Birch Cliff. White was the first attorney general of York, who was shot dead in a duel with John Small, the clerk of the executive council, in 1800.

The 1811 *Patent Plan, Scarborough Township*, indicates that Sarah Ashbridge and her son Jonathan, formerly from Pennsylvania, were also original patent holders at the Front, with Jonathan and Sarah holding lands that extended down to the Bluffs, near today's Cliffside neighbourhood. Family members also held patents in the vicinity of Toronto's present-day Beach community. Unlike so many early patent holders, the Ashbridges eventually did take up settlement near the cliffs, after originally settling on Ashbridge's Bay in 1794.

Apart from the American Ashbridges, other early Americans from the former thirteen colonies, often confused with Loyalists, settled at the Front shortly after the turn of the nineteenth century. By 1801, the *York, Upper Canada Minutes of Town Meetings and Lists of Inhabitants 1793–1823* lists one "Wm Cornwell" and three others from the same residence in the Township of "Scarboro." Boyle's *The Township of Scarboro 1796–1896* indicates that the first of this group to settle at the Front in Scarborough was William Cornell, who reportedly crossed the lake with his family just prior to 1800, taking up Lots 17 and 18 near today's Cliffcrest, in the vicinity of Kingston and Markham Roads. A word of caution: *The Township of Scarboro 1796–1896* presents a fascinating and invaluable portrait of life in early Scarborough, though Boyle, in large measure, relied on the oral tradition of local residents in preparing the book, and he notes, "It is quite certain that numerous omissions, and perhaps some errors, will be noticeable."

According to *The Township of Scarboro 1796–1896*, Cornell and his family spent the first winter out on the lake in their schooner, seemingly at the base of the Scarborough Bluffs. Boyle also reports that Cornell established the first gristmill in the township, and in 1804 the first sawmill on Highland Creek, reportedly hauling the millstones for the gristmill all the way from Kingston on his sled. Boyle also reports that Cornell planted the first orchard in the township, said to be in the vicinity of what is now Sylvan Park, two years after landing at the cliffs. Recent research suggests that Cornell may have initially come to the vicinity of Port Hope, Ontario, before he set foot in the Township of Scarborough. Furthermore, common sense dictates that Cornell may have passed his first years in the township farther east, near his mill in the Highland Creek Valley, though these details may never be definitively established.

William Cornell was also reportedly very active in the lake trade that primarily took place at the mouths of Highland Creek and the Rouge River. The "Schooner Days" column of July 13, 1935, reports that Cornell built a small schooner at the mouth of the Rouge River sometime between 1800 and 1812. It is also hypothesized that he may have begun boat-building operations there, with the promontory located to east of the outlet possibly named for him. (In previous years the promontory was known as Billy's Point.)

William Cornell passed his entrepreneurial spirit down through the generations, including to his descendant James Cornell, who was the reeve of the Township of Scarborough and farmed the original homestead in the earlier part of the twentieth century. He, along with farmer and future premier of Ontario George Henry, established a co-operative dairy in 1909 with about 500 milk producers. The Farmers' Dairy Company, with headquarters at 367 Queen Street West and, later, at what is now Walmer Road and McPherson Avenue, ran until 1929, when it was bought out. Sealtest Foods took over operations in the 1960s.

Another early American settler of local renown was Thomas Adams, referred to as Uncle Tommy Adams or the American Dutchman. Adams, who may have come to Canada as early as 1808, built a log house on the ridge overlooking the lake near the future village of Port Union, in the area we now know as the West Rouge. It is highly probable that Adams Creek, the remnants of which still flow out to Lake Ontario in the West Rouge, was named for this early settler.

Though the details vary, one story holds that Adams was the captain of an American sailing ship during the War of 1812 and was forced to take refuge in Highland Creek. Fearing that his load of wares might be seized, he threw them overboard. Other stories tell of a British pay ship being chased into Highland Creek, then a navigable waterway for at least a mile, where it discharged its load of silver coins overboard. Successive generations of treasure hunters have searched the bottom of the creek for the treasure, including, in 1936, one long-time Scarborough resident, Ivan Annis. C.H.J. Snider interviewed Annis in his "Schooner Days" column "One Try for the Treasure" in 1942. The story goes that Annis, along with some friends, dug a hole some thirty-four feet deep in the Highland Creek marsh, probably in the vicinity of Stephenson's swamp, before the walls collapsed. Annis, emerging from the incident unharmed, maintained, "If I ever get 1,000 or 1,500 dollars that I can spare, I'll have another try for that gold — and I'll be happy if I only get part of the money back."

Shortly after the conclusion of the American Revolution, an ancestor of Ivan Annis, Charles Annis, is said to have crossed the Niagara River with his wife and children, eventually camping on unsurveyed land overlooking the Bluffs east of Markham Road. First settling to the east in what is now Whitby, Annis returned to the Scarborough Front and took up possession of these lands, stretching from the lakefront to north of today's Olde Stone Cottage Pub and Patio, which was later built by one of his descendants.

The Scarborough Shore

Jeremiah Annis stone house, c. 1910, now The Olde Stone Cottage Pub and Patio

Courtesy SA, image restoration Jeremy Hopkin

According to *A History of Scarborough*, edited by Robert Bonis, when first asked by an officer of Lieutenant Governor Simcoe if he had fought against the British during the Revolution, Charles Annis replied, "I will always fight for my home and where my property is." He may not have been a Loyalist, but his frank answer apparently impressed Simcoe.

Many early American pioneers in fact became very loyal citizens of Scarborough and Upper Canada. It is said that Levi Annis's house was used as quarters for British soldiers on their way between Kingston and Niagara during the turbulent years before and after the War of 1812. Legend has it that some of these soldiers, warned of an imminent American invasion, buried their valuables and money in Gates Gully. Many generations of children, including my own, have spent countless hours searching for lost treasure in that gully.

WHILE BRITISH SOLDIERS marched through the wilderness along the newly opened Kingston Road during the War of 1812, most were unaware that they were treading a time-worn path followed by others for countless centuries, if not millennia. David Boyle reminds us that "It is not unusual to find that the first roads opened in lakeshore (or first opened) townships followed tortuous Indian trails, as these always led along routes presenting fewest difficulties and most advantages . . . it is probable that the Kingston, Danforth and other old roads in this township were laid out on the lines pursued by ancient paths."

In 1799, Asa Danforth was contracted to build a road to connect York to the Bay of Quinte, along the backwoods aboriginal trail that led the Thomsons into Scarborough. This trail may also once have been the primary link between the Seneca villages of Ganatsekwyagon and Teiaiagon, which lay to the west. Danforth's route through Scarborough, however, was problematic. The trail went too far to the north, especially for the settlers who were rapidly populating the Front.

Settlers in the south end of the township needed a road that offered access to the lake through the Highland Creek and Rouge River Valleys and one that would also provide overland access to the markets of York, Kingston, and beyond. To this end, in 1801 William Cornell and Levi Annis, son of Charles Annis, cut the Kingston Road (also referred to locally as the Front Road) out of the bush, following another pre-existing aboriginal path along the lake. In a very short period of time, the Kingston Road, near the lakeshore, overtook the Danforth in popularity and became the arterial route into York from the east.

In 1817 Samuel Purdy began operating what may have been the first stagecoach line over the Kingston Road in winter, departing from Brown's Inn in Kingston on Monday and arriving in York on Thursday. The state of the road was so deplorable that Purdy suspended his stagecoach service entirely during the summer months, resuming it only in the winter. Captain Basil Hall's account of his journey along the Kingston Road from York in *Travels in North America in 1827 and 1828* stands in for the experience of many the early traveller. He writes, "When we least expected a jolt, down we went smack! dash! crash! . . . at other times, . . . grinning like grim death . . . expecting a concussion which, in the next instant, was to dislocate half the joints in our bodies." Needless to say, travel by boat in the early days was preferable by far to taking the deeply potholed, corduroy

Road Between Kingston and York, Upper Canada

47

The Osterhout log cabin at Guildwood Park is a tangible reminder of the Scarborough shore's pioneer past

Jeremy Hopkin, 2005

arterial road that connected York to Kingston.

The trajectory of the Kingston Road in the Township of Scarborough was quite different from the road we know today. In the early years, the road dipped down to the Flats overlooking the lake to accommodate some of the original settlers who had built their log cabins near the cliffs. Shortly after the War of 1812, the Kingston Road was straightened out, with the entire course heading somewhat generally to the north to take advantage of better grades. This new section provided a safe and convenient "front road" but no longer offered views of the lake. (The alignment of the Kingston Road was again changed in 1833).

————◆————

STILL STANDING ON what was formerly Lot 14, Concession C, in what is now Guildwood Park, is an intact one-and-a-half-storey, two-door log cabin of the pioneer period, one of only a few such remaining structures left in the Toronto area. Several theories have been put forward as to the origin of this unique structure. Some have argued that the original patent holder for these lands, United Empire Loyalist William Osterhout, may have erected the cabin. However, a historical and archaeological research paper edited by Grace Ryan establishes that Osterhout never settled in Scarborough and that the land upon which the cabin still stands was transferred quite early to Alexander McDonell, a member of York's early establishment who was elected Speaker of the House of Assembly in 1805. Though there is no evidence that McDonell built the cabin or improved the land upon which it stands, his familial relationships were nonetheless interesting: he was the brother-in-law of Colonel Samuel Smith, a prominent figure in the Lakeshore section of the book, and the uncle of the future attorney general John MacDonell. The latter's story is told in the Island section.

Local lore also suggests that the cabin may have been built and used by Augustus Jones, a surveyor in Upper Canada in the late eighteenth and nineteenth centuries and the father of the Reverend Peter Jones, also known as Kahkewaquonaby. Augustus Jones was commissioned by Lieutenant Governor Simcoe to survey the lakeshore of the townships east from York to the Trent River, including Scarborough, an area that at that time was known as Glasgow Township. The theory goes that Jones and his survey crew built the cabin and used it as a shelter while they were surveying the Scarborough lakeshore. Research led by archaeologist Martha Latta refutes this theory, citing a lack of "artifactual evidence for any occupation before the middle of the nineteenth century." By 1845, James Humphrys of County Tyrone, Ireland, acquired this land in present-day Guildwood Park, along with other adjacent property, and it is likely that the structure was erected during the period of his ownership. Regardless of the cabin's origin, it remains a fascinating and tangible connection to the pioneer history of the Scarborough shore and the township.

Another early log cabin, long since disappeared, was situated at Springbank Farm near the edge of the Bluffs in the Meadowcliffe area. Though the date is not definitely established, it was erected as early as 1833 by the James McCowan family, who were part of a later Scottish immigration that brought over 200 people to the Front from the vicinity of Lanarkshire, beginning in about 1825.

Shortly after arriving in Canada in 1833, several members of the James McCowan family perished, apparently from typhus fever and cholera. In the summer of 1834, days before his own death, McCowan penned the following lines to friends from Springbank Farm: "We have in the course of God's Providence lost one of our famlie . . . our Dear daughter Mary Ann Hunter McC is no more . . . this letter I have penned sittin at my son Willm's bedhead just waiting on him . . . the cholera is again very sore . . . I am so confused and wuried that I hardly know what I do, not having got much rest for three days and two nights. I am, Dear Sir, your Sincair old friend with I hope a new face."

The Scarborough Shore

Although suffering the inevitable hardships and heartbreaking losses associated with pioneer life, the McCowans, like many of their neighbours, went on to establish prosperous farms along the Front and are today counted among the district's oldest continuing residents.

The Scots were a clannish bunch who valued their own traditions and way of life. Their fierce independence and toughness also made them successful farmers in the wilds of the Front. One early story features the Auld Kirk's Presbyterian minister, the Reverend William Jenkins, and the Reverend John Strachan. Strachan was himself a Scot and raised a Presbyterian. After immigrating in 1799, he joined the Church of England, becoming a prominent member of York society and eventually the first Anglican bishop of Toronto. In a reported exchange between the two men, Strachan commented to the backwoods Jenkins that his coat was looking a little threadbare, to which Jenkins replied, "Aye, Jock, but I hae nae turned it."

By the early part of the nineteenth century, Scarborough had begun to develop a distinct culture and flavour from the British presence at York, hinging on the traditions and practices of many of its early settlers, including the Scots. Unique to the Scots was the game of curling, which in the early years was played on the frozen watercourses leading down to the lake. Historian Edwin C. Guillet notes that "among the townships, Scarborough was pre-eminent for its curlers." According to David Boyle, friendly matches were being arranged as early as

Letter from James McCowan to William Begg,
Springbank Scarborough, August 20, 1834
James McCowan Memorial Social History Society

Along the Shore

1832 and 1833, with "players passing along the Kingston Road with their besoms." (A besom was the broom used in curling, though the term is no longer in common usage.)

The Scots valued education, and one of Scarborough's early teachers was John Muir, an immigrant from Lanarkshire, Scotland, who settled north of the Front near Bendale in 1833. John Muir's son, Alexander Muir, who composed the lyrics of "The Maple Leaf Forever," was also, for a short period, a teacher in Scarborough. After leaving the township, he became the principal of a number of schools in the greater Toronto area, including the Leslieville School in present-day Leslieville.

Early Scarborough had a strong literary tradition that extends far beyond Muir's patriotic lyrics. The township counted poet Alexander (Sandy) Glendinning as an early settler. As noted by T.B. Higginson, in "Alexander Glendinning — 'The Scarborough Settler,'" some of Glendinning's work was published in 1871 in a rare little book entitled *Rhymes*, which expressed the early hardships of pioneer life in Ontario and the longing for home. Perhaps his best-known work is the "Scarborough Settler's Lament," which was later set to music by legendary folk singer Stan Rogers. (Rogers's version replaces the word "Scarboro" in the first two lines of the poem with the word "Canada.")

AWA WI' SCARBORO'S MUDDY CREEKS

Awa wi' Scarboro's muddy creeks,
And Scarboro's fields of pine;
Your land o' wheat's a goodly land
But yet it isna mine.

The heathy hill, the grassie dale,
The daisie-spangled lea,
The trottin' burn and craggie lin,
Auld Scotland's glens gie me

. . . .

But fancy oft at midnight hour,
Will steal across the sea;
Yestreen, amid a pleasing dream,
I saw the auld countrie.

Each well-known scene that met my view
Brought childhood's joys to min';
The blackbird sang in Fushie lin
The song he sang langsyne.

But like a dream, time flees away;
Again the morning came,
And I awoke in Canada,
Four thousand miles frae hame.

———•———

SCARBOROUGH, IN ITS earliest days of settlement, was to a degree a separate place, not directly tied to York through its transportation systems, commerce, or trade. As has been noted, the most effective means of transportation during these early years was the lake, accessed through the many waterways that led down to the shore, including the Highland Creek and Rouge River systems. These waterways were far deeper than today: historical geographer Wayne Reeves notes that in the 1830s, a ninety-five-ton schooner was able to navigate one mile up Highland Creek, which today slows to just a trickle in certain sections during July and August. Likewise, pioneers in the Markham area reportedly came down to the lake via the Rouge River.

Currency belonging to Jordan Post the Younger, Upper Canada, 1815 TPL, 1815, Currency

Encouraged by an abundant supply of virgin forest, both from the valleys and the surrounding lands that were transitioning to farms, the Rouge River and Highland Creek waterways supported a growing industrial base in the early nineteenth century that was independent of York. As we have seen, William Cornell reportedly built the first sawmill on Highland Creek. This mill was closely followed by a profusion of others on Highland Creek, the "little" Rouge River (a tributary of the Rouge), and the Rouge River itself. Boyle indicates that by 1850, there were twenty-three sawmills operating in Scarborough.

Jordan Post, a wealthy clockmaker and land owner in York, whose name is memorialized, along with that of his wife Melinda, on two streets in downtown Toronto, moved to Scarborough sometime between 1829 and 1834.

Drawing of a stonehooker, c. 1850s, first published in John Spilsbury's Fact and Folklore Courtesy Nell LaMarsh

Acquiring 500 acres in the Highland Creek area, he established a sawmill and floated his lumber downstream to a point known as Cornell's Landing, where it was shipped to various ports on Lake Ontario.

The influence of Post and many other early Scarborough settlers on lake navigation and trade should not be forgotten. Some of the township's earliest pioneers built schooners of their own and carried out a tidy business marketing goods and by-products from the forest and developing homesteads. Stonehookers (shallow-draft, flatter-bottomed schooners) were built at the mouths of Highland Creek and the Rouge River, as well as at other rivers and creeks along the present-day Toronto shore, and gathered gravel, stone, and Dundas shale from the near shore waters of the lake.

C.H.J. Snider indicates in "The Last of the Stonehookers" that the earliest recorded of these vessels was the *Wood Duck*, built at the Rouge River in 1822.

Early pioneer traders shipped goods as far away as the Bay of Quinte and Kingston as well as Oswego in New York State. Goods traded from Scarborough farms included ashes, potash, shingles, grain, and other farm produce in return for flour, salt, lime, and other settlers' effects. Cordwood, though transported overland to Toronto, was also part of this early trade. According to Boyle, the previously mentioned Uncle Tommy Adams, who settled in the area of the present-day West Rouge, was "a pioneer flax grower." Making bags, mattresses, and ropes, he plied his trade between Port Union and Oswego, on the south shore of the lake. In 1834 he built a small sailing ship, or schooner, the *Mary Ann*, at the bottom of his property, near the mouth of Highland Creek. Along with partner John Allen, he carried out a similar trade to ports of call along the lake.

The Highland Rangers were locally built schooners that served the farmers of the Front and the backwoods of Scarborough. These schooners had the advantage of coming up on shore to meet the farm wagons transported through the gullies and at the mouths of Highland Creek and the Rouge River. Early reports indicate that William Cornell carried out such a local business, though his ship is said to have been confiscated by the Americans during the War of 1812. Another Ranger of note was the *Highland Chief*, which, according to C.H.J. Snider, frequented Port Credit, the Humber, Frenchman's Bay, and Presqu'île Point. The *Duke of York* was another Ranger built at the Rouge during this early period, about 1820, and was said to be the fastest on the lake, cutting two to five hours off the return trip between Oswego and York.

During the first half of the nineteenth century, the Crown imposed a tariff on goods coming to York and surrounding districts, including a stiff tax on all the necessities for the pioneer homesteader — leather, tea, tobacco, and other sundries — and on salt, over which the government had a monopoly until a brisk smuggling trade developed with the United States. The free traders, as they were called on both sides of the border, landed their schooners just off the Bluffs and traded in tariff-free goods in the region's gullies and ravines. Scarborough's relative isolation made these areas ideal hiding places for such merchandise, which was later carried up the crevices in the cliffs and transported along the Kingston Road to points east and west, including York.

The steamship *Canada* was also built at the mouth of the Rouge, in the winter of 1825–26, and was perhaps the most noteworthy vessel constructed along the Scarborough shore. Built by Joseph Dennis and others and towed to Toronto, where her engines were installed, she was the first steamship made in the Toronto region and, in fact, one

of the earliest steamers on the lake. The *Loyalist* of 1826, as quoted in *Robertson's Landmarks of Toronto*, highlights the *Canada's* "combined excellence of the model and machinery" and notes "the trip to Niagara was performed in four hours and some minutes."

Another ship that has attracted a considerable amount of lore is the *Charlotte of Pickering*, built at Rosebank, at the mouth of the Rouge, sometime before the winter of 1837. One unconfirmed story relates that shortly after the Rebellion of 1837 at York, a group of rebels engaged the ship's captain, William Quick, to take them across to America, where they would be free from charges of treason. Quick took them out into the lake, only to turn and bring them back into the harbour at York, delivering them into the hands of the authorities.

———◆———

WHILE TORONTO'S WATER ACCESS made transportation easier, Lake Ontario could be perilous. As told by John Spilsbury in *Fact and Folklore*, Port Union entrepreneur William Helliwell recounted the following incident involving business partner Will Hetherington in his diary in 1848: "Mr. Hetherington, his son and a sailor were working on their small schooner. Mrs. Hetherington called them to dinner. They got into a small punt with only a pole and the off-shore gale blew them out into the angry lake. They were driven onto the U.S. shore about midnight and walked to [the] Niagara River where they caught the Transit Steamer to Toronto and arrived at Port Union at 9:00 p.m. the following day, to the surprise of their grieving relatives."

Plying the waters near the Highlands was especially treacherous. In bad weather, schooners and steamers could easily drift onto the underwater shelf of deltaic deposit that extends out from the Bluffs, leaving the boats vulnerable to breaking up, which could be as dangerous for sailors as sinking in deep water.

On a black, stormy night in about 1855, a number of bedraggled men struggled up the steep, muddy slope of what was then known as Nigger Gully, located near the foot of today's Guild Inn. These men were survivors of the *Jessie Woods*, a ship carrying supplies including tea, sugar, shoes, cutlery, marble, and dry goods. The captain had struggled to keep the boat on course, but, weighed down by the marble in the hull, it had drifted into the shallow offshore waters, floundered on the bank, and broken up.

According to C.H.J. Snider, in his column of November 29, 1941, the men followed the flicker of a single candle that they saw through the dense wood of the gully, emanating from the log cabin of William Humphrey [*sic*] (perhaps the Osterhout log cabin). The men engaged the help of the Cornell family, who lived northwest of where the ship lay in distress. The Cornells were no strangers to the shipping trade, old William himself being both a sailor and a ship owner. The Humphrey and Cornell boys went back to the gully that night and guarded the hold of the *Jessie Woods* from potential pilferers. When dawn broke, the men and the crew began the arduous journey of hauling the goods up the ravine to the Kingston Road. A handsome Waterbury clock that stood in the Cornell farmhouse thereafter is said to have been a reward from the ship's captain for a job well done.

As late as the 1930s, evidence of many earlier wrecks and disasters was piled up at the foot of the Bluffs, along the narrow beach. On August 3, 1915, the paddle wheeler *Alexandria* was caught in a horrific storm that threatened to pummel the ship against the side of the cliffs. Newspaper articles of the time indicate that the ship, a wooden steamer under fifty-horsepower strong, was carrying a light load (about 300 tons), including various food stuffs, canned goods, cast-iron sinks, kegs of brass hooks, and even high-quality rubber boots. After leaving Port Hope, Ontario, she ran into bad weather and high seas, described by *The Scanner* as a "dirty southeasterly blow." As she moved into range of the Highlands, the captain maintained her engines at full steam, purged much of her cargo, and yet could not stop the slow drift toward the cliffs. In

Wreck of the Alexandria, *1915*
CTA, F1244_it02383a

the late afternoon, she ran up against the shallow bottom of the lake 150 to 200 yards offshore.

Early distress calls from the ship brought farmers, vacationers, and radial employees to the edge of the cliff shortly after the ship ran aground. Some of these folk scaled the treacherous slope, while others ran down Gates Gully to get to the panicked men, who were clinging to the side of the ship, unwilling or unable to jump into the swells and swim to shore. As the waves continued to pummel the vessel and the ship began to break up, the crew launched a lifeboat, which quickly capsized in the pounding surf. Then the brawny Ed Middleton, at one time the caretaker of St. Joseph's-on-the-Lake and himself a former engineer on the lake boats (or Lakers as they were called), waded into the surf. He tied a rope around his waist, had it secured to the shore, and succeeded in getting the line to the lifeboat, bringing the capsized men safely to the shore.

The *Toronto Daily Star* reported one crew member as saying, "Suddenly we heard a shout that sounded quite close to us . . . and we saw a man fighting for his footing just a

57

few feet from us. It was magnificent! . . . How he managed to get as far as he did without being swept off his feet by the rushing waves or snatched under the surface by the deadly undertow is amazing. But he made it." Those standing at the shore eventually formed a human chain and dragged the sailors out of the perilous surf. Miraculously, the entire crew of the *Alexandria* was rescued and finally made it to the top of the cliff, where the local farming community attended to them.

When calm seas returned to the Bluffs the next morning, the pilferers moved in. Residents who lived near the shore, from the Bluffs all the way over to the Island, were said to have no shortage of sugar or tomatoes for a few seasons to come. Long-time Scarborough resident Robert (Bob) McCowan relates that the *Alexandria* quickly disappeared, piece by piece, salvaged for other uses by residents of the Front, scrap metal being scarce during the First World War. Many of the farming families who lived near the cliffs managed to get their own little memento of the ship, including the McCowans, who for years afterward put one of the main ship's cables to use on their farm. Even my street may have its own memento: an enormous anchor set out on the front lawn of one of our neighbours that was reportedly recovered from the *Alexandria*.

The wreck itself lasted for decades, with local children spending many a long summer's day swimming out to dive off the walking beam of the old ship. Today what is left of her rests within twenty or thirty feet of shore. Her boiler is out there still and may be seen at periods of low water every summer, sticking up out of the blue, just beyond the Queen Anne's Lace that lines the shore.

———— ❖ ————

TO THE EAST of the Bluffs was a robust commercial fishing industry at Port Union that began about 1840 and lasted through to the 1920s. Francis Portwine, or "Old Portwine," was a fisherman who lived with his wife in a cottage just to the east of Port Union Road in the late nineteenth century. Along with other local residents and farmers, Portwine used the Fishery Road, a trail along Highland Creek from the lake to the Kingston Road that is now subsumed in the Colonel Danforth Trail. The Lang family, fishermen from Woodbine Beach in today's Beach community, was fishing out of Port Union after about 1910.

The catch at Port Union was plentiful and supplied the ready markets at Toronto, where, up to 1920, according to Spilsbury, "catches of 2,000 pounds of white fish and trout were not uncommon." One early report indicates that the Scottish pound net was used at the mouth of the Rouge and Highland Creek by 1850, while Spilsbury describes the technique used offshore at Port Union as that of deep-sea fishing, with

the use of nets, sinkers, and floats.

Fishing was not confined to the commercial trade, however. Many early settlers on the Front, including Nelson Gates, who operated a farm

This sketch of Portwine's cottage was first published in John Spilsbury's Fact and Folklore *in 1973*

Courtesy Nell LaMarsh

and inn on the Kingston Road, took advantage of the rich source of fish in the many streams, creeks, and waterways. William Brown's *America: A Four Years' Residence in the United States and Canada* describes the fish supply in the Rouge in the 1840s:

> Being within about two miles from the mouth of the river, we were visited every month with a fresh shoal of fish, which came up periodically. In the month of May we had the black bass; in June we had the red and yellow bass. In July we had other sorts and in August we had the Salmon. Country farmers came in large parties at these particular seasons with nets to catch, for curing, some of whom would procure five or six barrels. We never interfered with them, except in the salmon season, and then we made the most we could of the fish.

According to popular legend, the fish were not only plentiful but on occasion large. One early story, related in Boyle's history, holds that Andrew Thomson, fishing in

An active, though modest, fishing industry continued at Port Union and other nearby ports of call, including Frenchman's Bay (shown here c. 1924), east of the Rouge River. Note the presence of the fishing nets and the schooner in the harbour CTA, F1548_s393_it19335

Highland Creek with a companion, caught, "hooked and landed a fish so large that when suspended from a pole run through its gills and resting on the shoulders of the two men, its tail touched the ground." The men were reportedly five foot nine, and the man-sized fish is thought to have been a sturgeon.

Scarborough's lakefront connection to trade and transportation reached its zenith when the Scarborough and Pickering Wharf Company was established in 1847 near the mouth of the Rouge by local farmer and entrepreneur William Helliwell along with his partners, Daniel Knowles and Will Hetherington.

Robertson's Landmarks of Toronto tells us that Helliwell's father, Thomas, after emigrating from Yorkshire, England, began a brewery and distillery on the banks of the Don River in 1820. This area became known as Todmorden Mills, and the brewery operations continued until the building was destroyed by fire in 1847. Helliwell then moved to

Old Port Union Village • EST. 1865 (Post Office) → C. 1856-1895

1. Thomas Laskey's Hotel c. 1860
2. Laskey Hotel Driveshed
3. G.T.R. Steam Engine
4.
5. G.T.R. Freight Shed
6. G.T.R. Water Tower
7.
8. G.T.R. Depot (Station) & Post Office — 1865-
9.
10. G.T.R. Foreman's House
11.
12. Granary for Wharf
13. Scarborough, Markham & Pickering Wharf Co. est. 1847
14. Apple Storehouse for Wharf
15. Schooner
16. The Grand Trunk Railway est. 1856
17. Andrew Annis' farmhouse - 1852 -

Lake Ontario

© Jeremy F. Hopkin, Feb 1999

[WHARF WAS APPROXIMATELY 50 FEET WIDE, 350 FEET LONG]

✹ NOTE: THIS IS JUST A CONCEPT BASED ON INFORMATION / PLEASE KNOW MAY BE INACCURATE. ALSO: AT ONE TIME THERE WERE MORE STRUCTURES IN THE VILLAGE.

This conceptual drawing by Jeremy Hopkin gives us a very good idea of what the village of Port Union looked like in the 1860s, though by this time, the activities of the port itself were greatly diminished

Courtesy Jeremy Hopkin

the Highland Creek Valley, where in 1849 and 1850 he, along with his partners, capitalized on the active trade already taking place and built a wharf (originally located on the Scarborough and Pickering town line at the bottom of present-day Lawrence Avenue and Port Union Road) and storehouses at the shore that moved goods from the three townships directly onto ships.

Many of the original pioneer families from the Scarborough Front held interests in the Scarborough and Pickering Wharf Company. The little village of Port Union grew up around the wharf and storehouses near the edge of the lake. At the shore end of the pier, sometimes lined up all the way up to the Kingston Road, farmers stood with their teams, waiting their turn to load their goods, among them grain, potash, and apples, into the storehouses, a stopover on their journey to markets beyond. By the early 1850s, Port Union was booming. Will Hetherington opened the Union Hotel, which

61

The Halfway House, 1912 TPL, E 5-12b

catered to the influx of farmers waiting to offload their goods near the wharf. During these years, Hetherington and Helliwell also joined forces to build the *Caledonia*, probably built on the beach at nearby Port Union. It and the *Northerner* (1856) were among the last of the schooners built at the Scarborough shore.

Port Union's importance as a shipping centre should not be overstated however. By and large it never *received* any substantial quantities of cargo. Rather, its function was to transport goods from the developing farm community to markets along the lake. The Scarborough and Pickering Wharf Company was financially viable for only a short period of time. The coming of the Grand Trunk Railway in 1856 and improvements to the Kingston Road greatly diminished the need to move goods by water. Trade with other lake ports dwindled, while overland trade with Toronto became increasingly consolidated. The new railway traversed the outlets of both Highland Creek and the Rouge and blocked access to small natural harbours at the mouth of both of these waterways. In "Scarborough 1861," census enumerator for Ward 2 Frank Helliwell remarked that by this time, gristmills and numerous sawmills located on the waterways had also declined, with few significant stands of timber remaining in the township.

Regardless of the decline of the milling industries and the pioneer shipping trade, Port Union carried on, one of its main functions now to service the Grand Trunk Railway. As John Spilsbury notes, the village was also a "water, wood, freight and passenger stop."

Along the Shore

Thomas Laskey optimistically opened another hotel in 1860, though by 1861 the port was only shipping small amounts of cordwood. The wharf was washed away in a fierce storm in 1895, leaving only its piles behind.

Industry came to Port Union again with the opening of the Johns-Manville Plant in 1948. When the plant closed, near the end of the twentieth century, the lands were redeveloped as a residential area. This area of the lakefront has a pretty waterfront trail running right over the place where the wharf stood for so many years.

———— •◆• ————

THE SECOND HALF of the nineteenth century was a prosperous time for agriculture in Scarborough, with many productive farms stretching out over the undulating landscape, right down to the Flats, which overlooked the lake. With Toronto close by, large towns never developed in Scarborough, although many significant hamlets and villages sprung up, including Highland Creek, named for the waterway that coursed through the community, located in the township's easterly corner, near the Front. Highland Creek boasted all the services and trades necessary for a pioneer homestead and included, according to Scarborough historian Richard Schofield in *Scarborough: Then and Now (1796–1996)*, "millers, grist millers, cobblers, merchants, . . . blacksmiths [and] ship-builders" as well as the township's first smithy. From about 1856, Irish immigrants working on the Grand Trunk Railway came to live along today's Morningside Avenue. This area became distinguished from Highland Creek and was known as Cork Town, later named West Hill. Scarborough Village, located near the junction of Eglinton and Markham Roads, included a large area of farmland that stretched southward to Lake Ontario, east to the Highland Creek River, and west to McCowan Road. It was home to Scarborough's first post office and sported an array of early businesses, including Nelson Gates's Scarboro Inn, Chester's General Store, and a blacksmith and wagon shop.

Before the railways, the Kingston Road was the main overland transportation route to York. The Front Road was populated with rest stops that catered to the traveller, many offering refreshments, overnight accommodation, and a place to stable and water horses. Some of the more popular establishments, which stretched from present-day Victoria Park to Highland Creek, were the Six Mile Inn, located near present-day Birchmount Road, Gates's Scarboro' Inn, the William Wallace Inn, near present-day Scarborough Golf Club Road, and William Helliwell's Scarboro' Valley Inn, at Highland Creek.

One of the longest-lasting inns was the Halfway House, built in 1850 and located on the northwest corner of today's intersection of Midland Avenue and Kingston Road.

The Halfway House was so named because it was equidistant on the stagecoach route between Toronto and Dunbarton, a village east of today's Pickering. Improvements in transportation rendered some of these inns obsolete by the turn of the twentieth century, but the Halfway House carried on, becoming a centre of activity for the local community and for an increasing number of visitors to the township.

During the second half of the nineteenth century, life in the Township of Scarborough remained for the most part uncomplicated and wholly rural. After the pioneers had done their work, clearing the fields and establishing the infrastructure to support a rural agrarian community, the population of the township actually began to decrease, as was the case in many rural areas across the province. Many young men were lured west as the Prairies opened up or just a few miles to the big city, seeking employment opportunities in what was now the fastest-growing urban centre west of Montreal.

In the coming decades, the Scarborough shore would provide respite from intense industrialization and the crush of humanity in Toronto at the close of the nineteenth century. The sleepy south end of the Township of Scarborough, with its natural beauty, its Bluffs, its river, and its creeks, was poised to be discovered.

CHAPTER FOUR

Resort Era

The Toronto of the late nineteenth century bears little resemblance to the twenty-first century post-modern metropolis we know today. For one thing it was smaller, and most people lived in cramped quarters downtown. The rapidly growing economy was driven by unbridled industry, which produced jobs but lacked even the most basic environmental controls. The hot summers were particularly difficult for the working and emerging middle classes. Before the exodus to cottage country, Torontonians sought refuge along their own lakefront, from the Rouge River in the east to Etobicoke Creek in the west.

A series of privately owned parks populated the lakefront during this time. Many Torontonians packed up their picnic baskets, gathered their families, and spent the day at one of these parks, though accommodations were often available for more lengthy stays. Transportation to the earliest parks was by steam or sail, departing from the downtown harbour at regular intervals during the summer. Victoria Park, established in 1878 in the southwest corner of the Township of Scarborough, was one of the first parks.

Dear mother —
hope your are having a good
time everything is all right —
one of our nice places
and it is not in Portland
either
George

*On the beach at Victoria Park, c. 1900
— a postcard from George to his mother*
TPL, PC 966.2.23

It is described in Adam and Mulvany's history as "one of the most pleasant and popular of the summer resorts of Toronto" and a refuge to "large numbers of pleasure seekers and wearied citizens in search of a brief respite from the toil and worry of urban life." They go on to describe the park itself: "There is a broad, sandy, shelving beach, running back to a high clay bluff. The front portion consists of a smooth, grassy expanse, fringed with trees, overlooking the lake. A summer hotel and pavilion have been provided for the accommodation of the public. To the rear is the park proper, sloping gradually upwards, retaining most of the natural characteristics of the forest, excepting that the underbrush has been cleared away in places, and winding paths have been made in every direction."

Other later amusements at Victoria Park included a steam merry-go-round, a zoological garden, and a shooting gallery. The wharf at Victoria Park straddled the boundary between the Township of Scarborough and the developing Beach community. A further discussion of the park may be found in the Beach section of this book.

Rosebank, another recreational area, began drawing Torontonians as early as 1880. Presently within the city of Pickering, Rosebank began as a farm in 1860, when William Cowan, son of the previously mentioned Henry Cowan, purchased lands on the east side of the Rouge River. Later in the nineteenth century, Torontonians arrived there by boat and train and camped by the shores of the lake. Old Portwine, the fisherman we met earlier, is said to have supplemented his income at Port Union by ferrying patrons across the Rouge to the resort, while Ron Brown notes in *Toronto's Lost Villages* that the Grand Trunk Railway built a special station near Rosebank and "added picnic specials to their trains" to accommodate passengers. The original farmhouse, known as Rosebank House, was renovated in 1897–98 and then again in 1907–08, allowing for increased patronage. In 1898 a new pavilion accommodated a growing number of day trippers and cottagers. In its heyday, the resort included a dance hall, a picnic area, and a campground and had an overall capacity of more than a hundred people. By 1910, a full-blown cottage community had developed there, with twenty-five families housed in cottages and tents.

In addition to Victoria Park and Rosebank, the Toronto Hunt, a private country club, came in 1895 to what is presently the Birch Cliff area. The Toronto Hunt is widely accepted as having been established in 1843 by Colonel William Elliot of the Royal Canadian Rifles. While the emphasis was on hunting, complete with horses and dogs, in the early years at Scarborough, William Gray's *A History of the Toronto Hunt 1843–1993* indicates that other sports, including polo, golf, tennis, and cricket, were already established by the first decade of the twentieth century. By the 1920s, as the Birch Cliff area expanded, the hounds were moved from Scarborough. In the 1930s, the Hunt sold the part of its property that lay north of the Kingston Road, but it still maintains a strong presence along the waterfront, just east of the Beach.

Canadian landscape painter Doris McCarthy, herself raised in the Beach, remembered the luxuriant Christmas parties held at the Hunt in the early part of the twentieth century. In *A Fool in Paradise: An Artist's Early Life*, McCarthy recalls: "There was a baronial dining room, a table to seat thirty, silver shining, glassware sparkling, a huge fire blazing on a hearth at one end of the room. For me, the most exciting features were the row of waiters in uniform standing behind us, and ginger ale as common as milk."

The year 1914 saw the official opening of the Scarboro Golf Clubhouse and course, financed by a group of Toronto investors, including stockbroker A.E. Ames, whose country estate, Glen Stewart, stood south of the Kingston Road in the Beach during this period. According to Denis Matte, general manager of the club, the story goes that Ames was originally a member of the Toronto Golf Club, which in its early days was located north of the Old Woodbine Racetrack, near the vicinity of the present-day Beach community. In the early twentieth century, the Toronto Golf Club moved west to the banks of Etobicoke Creek. Rather than following the club, Ames pursued the building of a "local" club and looked to the pastoral lands of the Scarboro Heights.

The Scarborough Shore

Still located north of the juncture of Scarborough Golf Club and Kingston Roads, the site of some 144 acres features the original elegant Victorian clubhouse and wraparound veranda. In 1924 renowned golf architect A.W. Tillinghast redesigned the course to take advantage of the naturally undulating, picturesque landscape and Highland Creek, which winds its way through the property. The Scarboro Golf and Country Club is noted as one of the top-forty golf clubs in Ontario and has hosted the Canadian Open four times, in 1940, 1947, 1953, and 1963.

Hunting, both for sport and for economic gain, took place along most of Toronto's lakefront in the nineteenth century. In the early days of York's and Toronto's development, hunting was centred on the peninsula, which stretched from the present-day Island to Ashbridge's Bay in the east, close to what is today Woodbine Avenue. The waterfront was alive with wildlife in the nineteenth and early twentieth centuries. Many families of eagles nested on the Scarborough Bluffs, but they were hunted to the point of extinction. A story told by Ernest Thompson Seton in George Fairfield's anthology *Ashbridge's Bay* recounts the experience of hunter Bill Loane:

> He noticed that at Scarborough Heights, just east of Ashbridge's Bay, there was a solitary pine at the water's edge, where a long ravine came in from the north. This was a favourite perch with the eagles. So Loane made a hide at the foot of it and left this hide for a month or so till the birds got accustomed to it. Then before daylight one day, when there was a northwest gale, he hid inside with his gun and waited. Presently an eagle alighted. Loane poked out his gun and dropped the bird, but continued in hiding. Before the day was over, he had killed seven eagles. All were white-heads but one, which was a Golden.

Another hunter during the same era was not so lucky. According to Seton he shot an eagle in the wing, causing the eagle to fall down the slope of the Bluffs. As the man closed in on the wounded animal, "The eagle seized his thigh with both the talons of his powerful feet, and held on despite the man's most desperate struggles. In the morning his anxious friends found him dead, the eagle still holding on, and his claws driven deep into the femoral artery; while, all around, the blood and marks showed how the gunner had struggled for his life."

David Boyle's history reports that the last black bear in the Scarborough Bluffs was rousted from a cave, presumably on the beach, in 1885. The last lynx was caught well off the lakefront in 1891 or 1892. Today we must content ourselves with the many deers, foxes, and coyotes, not to mention the hawks and peregrine falcons, that still make the Bluffs, the creek and river valleys, and the backyards of lakeside houses, their home.

Sir Donald Mann's Fallingbrook

THE POTENTIAL FOR THE development of the Scarborough Bluffs as a residential community was first acknowledged by William Canniff in his description of Scarborough in "An Historical Sketch of the County of York": "The Heights of Scarboro are noted for their romantic beauty. The shore from Toronto along the front of the township is fast becoming the permanent or summer residence of gentlemen who belong to the city. Private enterprise has . . . exhibited itself in the erection of pleasant villas with delightful grounds overlooking the lake."

The most prominent area of such early development was just east of present-day Victoria Park Avenue near the lake, where the gentry of Toronto went to escape the rigours of city life on a permanent or semi-permanent basis. In 1905 Donald Mann (later knighted in 1911) acquired lakefront property adjacent to the Toronto Hunt from Edgar Jarvis. A much earlier owner, the Reverend Charles Winstanley, had purchased the property in 1844 and built a house there, calling it Falling Brook, perhaps after the streams and springs that were prevalent along the Bluffs in those early days.

In 1907 railway magnate Donald Mann erected a stunning English Tudor estate overlooking the Bluffs and furnished it with rare antiques, oil paintings, and a substantial library. Tragically, Sir Donald Mann's personal and financial fortunes declined rapidly when he lost control of his Canadian Northern Railway in the late 1910s, which he built with Sir William Mackenzie, culminating in the loss his home, Fallingbrook, to fire in 1930. Though the house was destroyed, the gatehouse survives and has been incorporated into the residential community that developed there after the fire.

Impressive estates still standing in the general vicinity of the former Fallingbrook include the home at the foot of Fallingbrook Road, built by Henry P. Eckardt, and the Château des Quatre Vents, another seasonal mansion, located on Rockaway Crescent. The Château has commonly been mistaken for Sir Henry Pellat's seasonal property that was also built in the area, known as Cliffside. Pellat, a prominent businessman and close associate of Sir Donald Mann and Sir William Mackenzie, also built Casa Loma, the imposing castle that still stands on Spadina Avenue. Sadly, Pellat's personal fortune declined in the Great Depression. Cliffside fell to the wrecking ball in the mid-1930s, and in his last remaining years Pellat retreated to the Lakeshore district, where he lived in a more modest home overlooking what was then Lake Shore Road, near the mouth of Mimico Creek, until his death at the age of eighty-one.

Up on the Kingston Road, to the east and west of Fallingbrook and the Toronto Hunt, was the developing cottage community of Birch Cliff, which began in the 1890s. It was here, among the birch trees that lined the top of the cliffs, that Torontonians built their more modest seasonal homes and summer cottages. We do not know definitively when the Birch Cliff community began, but John Stark is said to have erected a cottage on what is now Springbank Avenue in 1892, calling it Birch Cliff. A picture of the original Stark cottage reveals a wooden Victorian structure of modest proportions with a generous wraparound porch. According to Richard Schofield, it is possible that this building may still stand on Springbank Avenue, though it would now be renovated beyond recognition.

Stark cottage, Birch Cliff Courtesy SA

The dignified country estates of southwest Scarborough were by no means exclusive to this little corner of the township. In fact, during the late nineteenth and early twentieth

The White Castle Inn looked out over the lake in the early 1950s, though its first occupants, the Gowanlock Trouts, were long gone TPL, S 1-1094

centuries, many country estates were built in the vicinity of the Scarborough shore. During the nineteenth century, Jennie Kidd Trout (née Gowanlock), who was the first Canadian woman licensed to practise medicine, and her husband, Edward, often retreated to an impressive residence on the height of land overlooking the Bluffs, in the vicinity of Trout's Hill, just east of Glen Everest Drive and the Kingston Road. An imposing white stucco home with a turret, in later years it became known as the White Castle. It was eventually operated as a hotel until it succumbed to fire midway through the twentieth century.

Farther to the east stood Ranelagh Park, constructed in 1914 by Colonel Harold Child Bickford, a decorated military man, in the English arts and crafts tradition. Now known as the Guild Inn, Ranelagh Park was once the seasonal residence of the Bickford family. It included a horse stable, Bickford being an avid polo player. Bickford sold

Miller Lash House, 2011. The exterior of the house is clad in stone from Highland Creek.

Keith Ellis

the property in 1921. It then became the St. Frances Xavier China Mission Seminary, which housed the Scarboro Foreign Mission, founded by Monsignor John M. Fraser in 1918. The Scarboro Foreign Mission Society, as it is now known, later moved to its present location, adjacent to St. Augustine's Seminary on the Kingston Road. In 1932 Rosa Breithaupt Hewetson bought the building and grounds and, with her husband, Spencer Clark, established the Guild of All Arts, conceived as a co-operative arts and crafts community.

Standing in the Highland Creek Valley on the University of Toronto Scarborough campus is an elegant arts and crafts bungalow, constructed in 1913 by Miller Lash, a Bay Street lawyer and entrepreneur. As a young girl growing up in West Hill, I remember peering up at the slightly tired seventeen-room estate, some 150 feet long, which was tucked away in the ravine, close to the creek. As strange as it may seem, it appeared to have always been a part of the natural landscape, nestled so perfectly on the side of the ridge and clad in local river stone. Thanks to a committed group of volunteers, the home was restored in the 1990s and remains one of the best examples of the arts and crafts tradition in the Toronto region. A contemporary of Frank Lloyd Wright, E.B. Greene of the firm Greene and Wicks in Auburn, New York, was probably the architect.

In 1913 lawyer, author, and parliamentarian William Henry Moore built another large stone house in the same arts and crafts tradition on the east side of the Rouge River, just beyond Rosebank House. The property included lands that were formerly held by the original patentee on both sides of the Rouge at the river mouth, William Holmes. The house, along with its extensive gardens, artesian well, and grand swimming pool — more than 175 acres in all — was known as Moorlands. Sadly, the original home, known locally as "the castle," burned down in 1935, though generations of Moores continued to reside on the property until it was taken over by the Metropolitan Toronto and Region Conservation Authority in the 1960s. It was officially opened as the Petticoat Creek Conservation Area in 1975. Moorlands was my mother's home and the repository of my first waterfront memories.

THE HOLIDAY PLACES and high-end residences along Scarborough's shore might have remained somewhat isolated exceptions to the otherwise rural landscape of the township for decades had it not been for the appearance of the Toronto & Scarboro Electric Railway, incorporated in 1892 with the aforementioned Henry Pellat as one of its directors. These relatively roomy cars, known as interurbans, ran on a single track and covered a much greater distance than their urban cousin, the streetcar. With more frequent stops than the conventional railway, the lines offered a relatively inexpensive, practical alternative to travelling through the countryside near Toronto, including the Scarborough shore, the Lakeshore, and even places as far away as Sutton on Lake Simcoe. Needing only one or two attendants per car, the radial travelled over vast regions and was the harbinger of suburban development in both the Scarborough and Lakeshore districts of the waterfront.

The first foray into mass public transportation in Scarborough was the Toronto Street Railway Company's horse-drawn Kingston Road Tramway. Begun in 1874, it operated from the Don River to the westerly fringe of the township at Blantyre Avenue from 1878 to 1887. Six years later, the Toronto & Scarboro Electric Railway Light and Power Company began operations along the Kingston Road, with service from Queen Street east to Blantyre Avenue. As Robert Stamp notes in *Riding the Radials*, in the early and mid-1890s, the Toronto & Scarboro line and the western route, the Toronto & Mimico line, were taken over by the Toronto Railway Company (TRC), owned by the entrepreneurial giant William Mackenzie. Service was extended east to the Toronto Hunt in 1898 and in 1901 to the Halfway House at Midland Avenue.

In 1904 the Toronto and York Radial Railway Company (TYRRC) was born as a subsidiary of the TRC, with William Henry Moore of Moorlands as the general manager. In 1906 the line was extended one final time to West Hill, near the Pickering–Scarborough border. The Hydro Electric Power Commission of Ontario took over the TYRRC in 1922, controlling the intra-urban and streetcar routes along the lakeshore until the 1930s, when the tracks were removed from all sections of the Scarborough route.

Long-time Lakeshore resident Ross Gamble fondly recalled such visits to the Bluffs — of hopping on the radial at New Toronto to visit his Aunt Dolly, whose cottage on the Scarboro Heights overlooked the Lake. Using the radial and connecting streetcars, he could get back home in the west end in time for dinner.

As in the Beach and Lakeshore districts, Mackenzie's Scarborough line benefitted from the patronage of day trippers. Even after the radial was extended to West Hill, many folks still ended their journey at the Halfway House and meandered down to the edge of the cliffs through the leafy pathways. A dance floor and bar were eventually added to the second floor of the Halfway House, while on the south side of the Kingston Road, a cool drink could be had at the refreshment stand before pushing on back into the city.

Several years after the establishment of the Scarborough line, Mackenzie opened Scarborough Heights Park on sixty acres of land south of the Kingston Road, near present-day McCowan Drive, stretching down to the Bluffs. Other such "electric" parks, operated under the umbrella of the TRC, figured prominently in the Beach

William Henry Moore, general manager of the Toronto Railway Company, heads up Yonge Street

Courtesy Anthony Moore, cartoon by Frise

Along the Shore

and the Lakeshore districts. The radial brought patrons right into Scarborough Heights Park on a stump line. The park included a pavilion and bandstand, featuring regular dances and frequent appearances by local performers. Unlike the classic amusement parks of Scarboro Beach in the Beach, Hanlan's Point on the Island, and Sunnyside to the east of the Lakeshore district, Scarborough Heights Park remained first and foremost a pleasure ground, offering people the opportunity to meet and socialize in a natural environment.

Although getting to the Bluffs was made easier with the radial line, getting to the beach was still difficult and often perilous. As early as 1901, the Township of Scarborough responded to mounting public pressure and constructed a series of steps down the ravine to the lakefront at Fallingbrook Road, known as the Hundred Steps. The Township later followed suit at Lakeside Avenue in Birch Cliff and then close to present-day Glen Everest Drive in 1921. According to Jack Cavanagh, in "Parks in Scarborough Remembered," the township established lifeguard facilities at these locations in 1929 in response to "the hundreds of children and adults who reportedly spent many hours a week enjoying the beaches."

The radial and streetcars no doubt had a role to play in transporting employees of the T. Eaton Company to two privately run facilities that overlooked the Scarborough lakefront. In 1917, Eaton's Boys Camp was established, for the well-being of employees, on part of the former grounds of Victoria Park. Shortly after, land was purchased at the foot of present-day Brooklawn Avenue in the Scarborough Bluffs, where the Young Men's Country Club was established. According to Donica Belisle in "A Labour Force for the Consumer Century," "The boys and men who attended these places slept in tents, played sports, held 'concerts and shows,' and entertained female guests during 'Friday evening socials and dances.'"

About the same time as Donald Mann built his impressive Fallingbrook in 1907, a boathouse, refreshment stand, and dance hall were erected below the Mann estate, at the foot of the Hundred Steps, on the beach. Known as the Fallingbrook Pavilion, this establishment developed a bit of a nefarious reputation over the years and carried the nickname of the "Bucket of Blood" due to the various donnybrooks that erupted there, both inside the premises and on the beach. The Fallingbrook Pavilion burned down in the 1930s. It was only one of a number of dance halls and pavilions that were prevalent in the city and along the greater Toronto waterfront up to the early 1960s.

By the 1930s a number of private parks had been established along Scarborough's waterways that led down to the shore, including the Willows Park, located on Highland

The Scarborough Shore

The Fallingbrook Pavilion

Courtesy SA

Creek near Lawrence Avenue and Galloway Road. Many of these parks, including Ferguson's Beach, established in the 1940s at the mouth of the Rouge, catered to overnight guests and offered outdoor amusements. Summer cottages were also built on the premises and were later converted into full-time residences, most notably during the Great Depression and the housing shortage that ensued after the Second World War. As we will see in other areas of the waterfront, this era was marked by a degree of anti-Semitism: author Don Allen notes that the Willows, along with other similar facilities, restricted admission to non-Jewish patrons.

Another dance pavilion, located at the foot of Scarborough Crescent, directly south of the Ashbridge property that overlooked the Bluffs, was the much-loved Paradise Pavilion, built and operated by three local brothers, Pat, Tom, and Vic Burd, in 1924. In the daytime, the establishment operated as a park, and a steep pathway at the southeast corner of the pavilion ran down the side of the cliff to the Beach below.

Paul Burd, son of Tom, remembers as a small boy seeing the couples dance around the floor of the pavilion in the afternoon to the big band tunes of the day on the Wurlitzer. The well-known Niosi Brothers played there, as well as the east-end band George Wade and His Corn Huskers. Former patron George Gordon recalls in *Let's Dance:*

A Celebration of Ontario's Dance Halls and Summer Pavilions that Wade's Corn Huskers produced a live coast-to-coast radio broadcast from the pavilion on Saturday nights. The pavilion was located near the highest point of the Bluffs, known as the Cathedral Bluffs or the Needles. Erosion was, and continues to be, a significant issue in this area, and the Paradise Pavilion came within twenty-five feet of the abyss before it was finally torn down near the end of the Second World War.

Stretching down from the Kingston Road to the Flats, and adjacent to the Paradise Pavilion at its southern edge, was the Cliffside Golf Club. As long-time Bluffs resident Paul Burd says, "We saw more golf balls go over those cliffs than anyone would ever believe." Shortly after the Paradise Pavilion was torn down, the golf course was closed in 1950, washed away by a tidal wave of change that swept across Scarborough and her southern shore. The era of post-war suburbanization had begun.

Over the past three or four decades, many city dwellers have come to think some-what disdainfully of the inner suburbs, districts that once lay outside the city but have since been absorbed into a "greater" Toronto. These suburbs are thought to be somehow of less worth than the city centre, simply by virtue of their geographical location. For many, the very word "suburb" conjures up an image of row upon row of hastily erected, faceless houses that sit awkwardly on a denuded rural landscape. Even though a majority of Torontonians — comprising many different ethnic backgrounds — now live in these suburbs, the image persists that they represent a banal, homogeneous society, bereft of culture and with no ethnic diversity. For some people the picture is even bleaker, with the narrative of suburban life now rife with images of gang wars, disconnection, and spiritual decay.

Yet there was a time in the not too distant past when the terms "suburb" and "suburbia" conjured up quite a different image. In the late nineteenth and early twentieth centuries, in reaction to the overpopulated and cramped conditions of urban life,

Taylor's Drug Store was conveniently located next to the radial line in Birch Cliff CTA/TTC. F16_s71_ it5366

with its slums and pollution brought on by rapid and unregulated industrialization, many people romanticized rural life as a simpler and more innocent time. Accordingly, city residents, both the wealthy and those of modest means, set out to escape to the outlying areas on the fringe of the countryside, especially to those near the water's edge.

However, after the Second World War, people's concept of and attitude toward these outlying areas changed, as mass suburban development took hold, not just in Toronto but throughout North America and in many other parts of the world. As noted Canadian sociologist S.D. Clark relates in *The Suburban Society*, the combined effects of the baby boom, chronic housing shortages, and economic prosperity shifted the principal focus to finding land and accommodation, regardless of the location. During this period, housing "filled in" beyond the outer fringes of the old city of Toronto, including at the Scarborough shore in the east and the Lakeshore district in the west. The "filling in" that occurred in both these areas did not take place, however, on wholly uninhabited lands, but rather around earlier-established residential patterns that were rooted in a different philosophy of suburban development.

The Scarborough Shore

Along the Scarborough shore and with the exception of the southwestern corner, the process of suburbanization evolved very slowly in the first decades of the twentieth century and continued in a piecemeal fashion until the end of the Second World War. When full suburbanization took hold in the 1950s, it ushered in a period of great social transformation. The result was the same in Scarborough in the 1950s as it was in the Lakeshore district and in many other areas on the outskirts of the city: the death of an established rural society.

Regardless of the loss occasioned by this great societal shift to suburbia, the Scarborough shore remains, by and large, an example of a healthy, stable suburban neighbourhood that is linked to the lake and the natural world. It also offers us unique insights into the roots of the original nature and formation of suburban culture, an ethos that was all but lost after mass suburbanization took hold across Toronto.

The self-styled "pioneer" of the Kingston Road and Scarborough lakeside development was Cecil (also known to some as "Cec") White, who controlled White & Co. Real Estate. A death notice posted in the *Globe and Mail* noted that White was a native of Hillsdale, Michigan, who came to Toronto in 1910. Also active on the Humber River and in the Lakeshore, he was credited with the "opening up of the Scarboro Bluffs district" and was primarily responsible for the establishment of the early infrastructure — roads, waterways, and electrical systems — that enabled suburban development to begin in the Scarborough Bluffs and farther east, at the mouth of the Rouge River, in the first half of the twentieth century.

In the years prior to the First World War, White began several developments, both north and south of the Kingston Road, for various income levels. An advertisement in the *Toronto Daily Star* on October 23, 1913, promotes six- and seven-room bungalows with electric light, furnaces, and three-piece baths. While White did sell packaged, standardized bungalows for the working and middle classes, as far as suburban development was concerned, the early twentieth century was first and foremost the era of the self-built home. During this period, White's primary focus remained on the development of lots and services, while the purchasers built their own houses, according to their own specifications and financial resources.

Stylized Cecil White logo, c. 1910

Courtesy Jeremy Hopkin

Most of the early-twentieth-century development that took place along the Scarborough shore proffered the natural beauty of the area as a means to attract prospective buyers. A sixteen-page brochure produced by the Toronto & Canadian Building Company, for the development of Sandown Park sometime after 1912, geared its marketing strategy to prospective immigrants from England. In a section entitled "In the Midst of One of Nature's Beauty Spots," the similarity of the features of the Scarborough Bluffs to Scarborough, England, "the Queen of the North," were noted: "On the opposite side of Kingston Road are the Scarboro' Heights and Scarboro' Bluffs, admittedly the most delightful of nature's beauty spots within the Toronto district. Those who know Scarborough, England, will readily recognize the similarity of the coast line and the beauty of the cliffs."

Likewise, White and others promoted the radial — which by 1906 ran through the southwest region of Scarborough, along the Kingston Road to West Hill — to draw buyers into the area. Accordingly, it was here, in the radial-serviced Birch Cliff area, that Cecil White started his early Scarborough colonization, aimed squarely at the workingman *and* the developing middle class. Beyond the opportunities for leisure, the radial opened up, for the first time, the possibility of living in the township and working in the city. This, combined with the availability of inexpensive land, resulted in an intense housing boom in the southwest corner of the township in the early years of the twentieth century.

One of White's early developments was Kalmar Heights, located north of the Kingston Road and running to just beyond present-day Danforth Avenue. With small lots and prices set at twelve to fifteen dollars a foot, the development was advertised in the *Toronto Daily Star* in October 1912 as "A close-in subdivision at suburban prices." Another subdivision, Edgely Park, was featured in the same paper as "RIGHT ON THE CAR LINE; IT GIVES A BEAUTIFUL VIEW OF THE LAKE; COOL IN SUMMER . . . If you want a home at a moderate price, build in EDGELY PARK . . . Prices are $18.00 per foot upwards."

By the late 1920s, many people had settled closer to the lake, in refurbished cottages or in subdivisions such as R.B. Rice and Sons' Kingsbury Park, located just east of the Toronto Hunt. Birch Cliff's transition to a streetcar suburb was complete in 1928, when the radial lines were pulled up and streetcar tracks laid in the middle of the road from Victoria Park to Birchmount. By this time, Birch Cliff residents could readily access a variety of services that had sprung up along the Kingston Road, including Mitchell's store, established in 1908, which for some years also served as the post office. The community's expansion was so significant that the Township of Scarborough began conducting its business there in 1922 and continued to do so for the next twenty-five years.

The Scarborough Shore

Stylized image of Mitchell's store, c. 1930s

Courtesy SA, image colourized by Jeremy Hopkin

A more affluent community developed farther to the west, on the east side of Victoria Park Avenue, after Sir Donald Mann's estate, Fallingbrook, was destroyed by fire in 1930. In the years that followed, an upper-middle-class suburb developed in this area and came to be associated with the Beach community lying immediately to the west. Richard Harris, in *Unplanned Suburbs*, points out that many of the fine homes in this area were originally financed by Dominion Housing Act loans. These loans, while purportedly assisting the middle class, financed the construction of large homes in other similar upper-class neighbourhoods, including Forest Hill and Lawrence Park.

Apart from the southwest corner of Scarborough, where the relative proximity of the Beach and the radial brought about a period of rapid growth in the early twentieth century, the rest of Scarborough remained quite rural. It would be a mistake, however, to think that residential development and settlement along the rest of the Scarborough shore was simply a product of the rapid suburbanization that took place after the Second

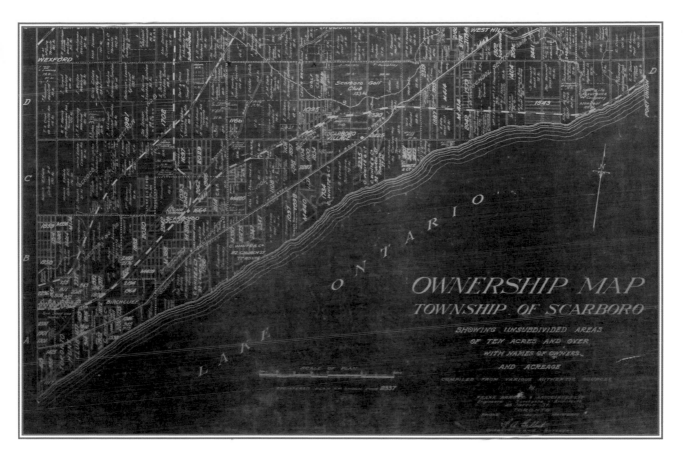

World War. In fact, the Ownership Map, Township of Scarboro, located in the Scarborough Archives and dating from about 1924, indicates that a large number of the original farm lots south of the Kingston Road

Ownership map of the Township of Scarboro, c. 1924 Courtesy SA

had already been subdivided by the mid-1920s, although few of these subdivisions had yet been developed. Clark writes in *The Suburban Society* of a necessary "proving up" that occurred in suburban communities before full-scale suburbanization began, and this was certainly true of the Scarborough shore. D.B. McCowan in "A Lakefront Estate Residential Development" recounts that farmer-developers had registered subdivision plans in at least one area of the Bluffs by the late nineteenth century, with local entrepreneurs following suit in the early twentieth century. It was time for Scarborough's new wave of pioneers to move east and begin the transition.

Not guided by any master plan, pockets of habitation took root along the cliffs, facilitated by but not dependent upon the radials. Each of these communities had a different origin and character, yet each was focused on an appreciation of the lake. It

St. Augustine's Seminary of Toronto,
as it appeared at sunset, 2008 Jane Fairburn

was precisely the piecemeal nature of this development opment that enabled the exurban enclaves of artists and religious communities to take hold along the water's edge, where residents experienced something closer to a rural way of life yet with access to the city.

Each of these early Bluffs communities, whether consciously or unconsciously, came to embrace the suburban ideal in its earliest form, in which, according to Hrag Vartanian, the "individual is freed from the city and brought closer to nature." In the Bluffs, the emphasis was, and still is, on the private life while remaining in an essentially urban setting that is masked or veiled by the great expanse of the cliffs and the lake.

One such early community was St. Augustine's Seminary, opened in 1913. St. Augustine's was financed largely through the efforts of Toronto brewer Eugene O'Keefe and was known in the community as "the house that beer built." According to author Karen Booth, it originally stood on about 140 acres of land that stretched down to the water. It was the first major seminary constructed in English-speaking Canada for the training of Roman Catholic priests. A fine example of the Beaux-Arts tradition, St.

Augustine's still stands in one of the last open fields that remain south of the Kingston Road and is the principal seminary for the Archdiocese of Toronto. Outdoor activity figured prominently in the lives of the young seminarians in the earlier part of the twentieth century. Canadian painter Phil Richards, who was raised a short distance from the seminary, recalls participating in the hockey games on the rink on the grounds. Some of the braver seminarians participated in the annual "cliff climb" that took place on the almost vertical cliff face at the south end of the property.

A short distance to the east, the Sisters of St. Joseph established St. Joseph's-on-the-Lake Convent and Novitiate in 1918. The imperious three-storey neo-Gothic structure stood near the highest point of the Bluffs, until it was torn down to make room for development in the early 1960s. The only remnant of St. Joseph's today is Cathedral Bluffs Drive, which runs south from the Kingston Road and was formerly the long driveway that led south to the convent above the cliffs.

Having arrived in Toronto in 1851, the sisters already had a long tradition of service in the city. Some years previously they had sold their farm in the Beach and had established another property in Scarborough, located at present-day St. Clair and Warden Avenues, to grow food for their House of Providence Charity Centre in downtown Toronto. This tradition of service continued in the Bluffs, with the sisters offering Catholic education to boys and girls. The convent also operated as a working farm, infirmary, and home for retired sisters.

Lifelong Bluffs resident Bob McCowan recalls that one of the main sources of water at the novitiate came from the lake, pumped halfway up the side of the cliff and held in a large cistern. He remarks that this was a clever departure from the practices of the local farmers, who, in dry summers, resorted to digging successive wells on their

This otherworldly image shows one brave seminarian descending to the shore below Courtesy Archives of the Roman Catholic Archdiocese of Toronto (ARCAT)

The Scarborough Shore

properties. He recalls that the nuns went out routinely to the Bluffs for picnics: "They had a path, and took their exercise down there. . . . To this day I remember what they looked like playing badminton in those dog-gone long dresses."

The Annals of the Sisters of St. Joseph of 1919 describe the setting at St. Joseph's-on-the-Lake as "beautifully quiet, intensely spiritual . . . the nature and surroundings are so inspiring," and add, "May its fruits be lasting." Mrs. Barbara (née Beech) Kennedy had fond memories of attending St. Joseph's School in the 1940s. As she lay in her bed during the long nights of winter, her mind would drift to the stern but fair Sister Frances Xavier, whom she imagined standing on the balcony in the luminous moonlight, overlooking the lake.

———•———

DESPITE THE EARLY SIGNS of development along the Scarborough shore, rural life in the community carried on. The First World War came, and Jack Heron, whom we met at the beginning of this section, though recently married, went off to the conflict overseas, along with many other Scarborough men. In one letter Jack wrote to his wife, Ruth, he remarked, "We are all in dugouts now. We had a deep hole dug in the side of a chalk hill and built our little home right in the hold and buried it. I was just telling George, that when we get home, we're not going to bother hunting up houses or flats any more, we'll just go down to the lake bank and dig one."

The contributions of these brave men and women, who fought in both World Wars and the Korean War, including those from the Scarborough lakefront, are memorialized in the cenotaph that stands at the junction of the Kingston Road and Danforth Avenue, north of the Bluffs. On the south side of this cenotaph, a stone from the residents of Scarborough, England, also commemorates their sacrifice.

The outbreak of the First World War ended Cecil White's plans for the rapid suburban development of the Scarborough shore, but there were other reasons as well. The most essential group of city residents, the rising middle class, had simply failed to show sufficient interest. Although the radial did bridge the gap between country and city, the commute was far too long and there were too few stops to attract large numbers of city workers. There were also too few local industries and, therefore, few opportunities for employment available in the rural community.

Nonetheless, settlement did continue, though at a snail's pace. In addition to the trickle of middle-class residents who did decide to commute from the suburbs, there came two groups in particular — the well off and the poor — who made what S.D. Clark describes as their own "backlands utopias" in these otherwise rural areas. It was there, in the forests and flats overlooking the lake, that "the rich could live out a private, unencumbered, genteel life, while the very poor had their first chance at home ownership."

It was on a road near the cliffs and adjacent to a gully, on part of an original garden suburb plan laid out by Cecil White in 1911, that sculptor and model-maker Fred Coates and his wife, Louise, an accomplished painter and craftswoman, began construction of their lifelong home, Sherwood, in 1919. When the couple died, the University of Toronto presented an exhibition of their life's work in the late 1990s. For the occasion, Paul Makovsky edited a catalogue, entitled *The Stuff Dreams Are Made Of: The Art and Design of Frederick and Louise Coates.*

Fred Coates was raised in England, and their home, described as "one of the most romantic houses in Canada," mirrored the old English cottage and English arts and crafts tradition, as revived and popularized by artist and architect William Morris. Fred Coates was long associated with the University of Toronto and for many years taught model-making at the School of Architecture, as well as holding the position of art director of the Hart House Theatre. Louise Coates is reported to have said, "I taught art before we were married, but afterward stayed in the house. Everything we had went into it." Designed by the Coateses themselves, the house includes a secret passageway, light wells, and many handmade sculptural elements. The Coateses are said to have been informally associated with the Group of Seven, holding many elaborate parties at Sherwood over the years.

Writer Hrag Vartanian describes the early-twentieth-century Chine Drive community as "the Utopian arts and crafts suburban colony." While it is unlikely that any formal artistic community ever existed, there is some evidence that links the Coateses and their neighbours, the

Pencil and pastel drawing of Louise Coates (known to her friends as "Brownie"), c. 1920, Anonymous

PC

The Scarborough Shore

Gieseckes, to the Beech Grove crafts group. Whether by design or chance, it was clear that the Chine Drive community had and still retains at its core a disproportionate number of artists, with painters, sculptors, and writers coming together in one place — inspiring others in the general area to refer to it as "At Oddity's End." It is perhaps an appropriate name, given the former presence of eccentrics of local renown, such as George Giesecke, known to the neighbourhood children simply as "the Colonel." A landscape architect by profession, he was also accomplished at the sport of fencing, and he often helped children learn how to swim down at the foot of the Bluffs.

———— • ————

THE 1929 STOCK MARKET CRASH and ensuing economic ruin was the final nail in the coffin that ended Cecil White's dream of a widespread middle-class migration to the Scarborough shore and of a broad pattern of planned settlement into developments like Sandown Park. While the radial lines were removed along the Kingston Road during the

Great Depression, first from Scarborough Village to West Hill in 1930 and then from Scarborough Village to Birchmount Road in 1936, isolated patches of self-built housing sprung up on the partially laid out streets and the empty lots of subdivisions like Sandown Park, often with no direct access to water mains (and indoor plumbing). More isolated makeshift dwellings, some of them mere tarpaper shacks, were to be found near the waters of the lake, for example, in the vicinity where Guildwood Village is today. Likewise, other communities developed along the Highland Creek and Rouge River Valleys, where many former slapdash summer cottages were now occupied year round. In one such community, the Willows, located

John Alexander skates in Cecil White's Sandown Park development, which amounted to a ragtag collection of homes in an open field in the 1930s
Courtesy John Alexander

Along the Shore

on the banks of Highland Creek, at least seventeen cottages literally collapsed into the water in October of 1954, courtesy of Hurricane Hazel.

In 1935 Sydney Alexander, who emigrated from England in 1929, moved with his family to Sandown Park, north of the Kingston Road at Midland Avenue. Like some of his neighbours, Sydney was unable to find steady work and was on relief. Yet although times were tough and people struggled, conditions were not desperate. His son, John Alexander, recalls a tight community that was to a degree self-reliant, keeping large gardens and even hens, goats, and rabbits. Sometime around 1941, the Alexanders acquired a large lot at Sandown Park from the groundskeeper of the Rouge Hills Golf Course, Bill Frankum, who also lived at the park. On this lot was a wooden building that had begun life as a chicken coop but had never been used for this purpose. From these humble beginnings, the family erected a self-made home and improved it over time with materials from the locomotive grave-yard at Midland and St. Clair Avenues. In stages they added bedrooms, indoor plumb-ing, and electricity, as well as a large garden and orchard of about one acre. According to John, "It had everything you needed; it was very comfortable." A large grove of willow trees in the undeveloped subdivision became a play area for the children, though even in this happy childhood the reminders of the misfortune of others were never far off. John remembers, "There was a lot of old tin cans laying around in one of the groves where the ponds were and at one point I think it had been a hobo jungle, during the Depression." Another of Cecil White's projects that did not see completion during the intervening years of the Depression was the ambitious

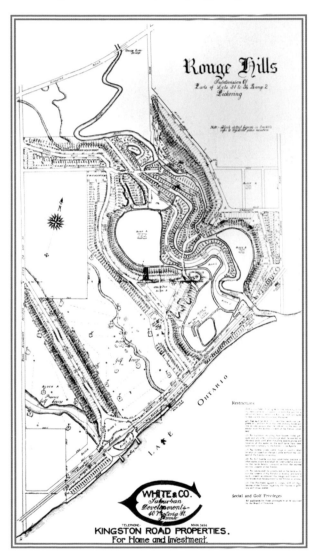

Map of Rouge Hills subdivision, c. 1920s

West Rouge Community Centre

The Scarborough Shore

Rouge Hills development, located on both banks of the Rouge River. As early as 1922, White had acquired lands from the original settlers in the area, the Cowan family, to complete his grand vision. His self-styled Venice of North America in the Rouge River flats was promoted in the *Toronto Daily Star* of June 30, 1926 as a high-end "summer residential recreational community" with a golf course as its centrepiece. The promotional article further stated:

> COME AND SEE
> Rouge Hills
> You will be fascinated by this beautiful spot — you will love it — you will re-visit
> it — you will want to live there . . . trees, hills, lake, river, Venetian waterways,
> golf, tennis, swimming, canoeing, boating, dancing, dining — life at its very best.

Another article on the same page indicated that "Rouge Hills is not a 'free for all' place. It is reserved for select people who will make congenial neighbours. The kind of people who are desired are those who . . . appreciate the niceties of life and who enjoy clean sport and the great out-of-doors." Later in the article mention was also made of a group of "responsible business people" from across North America who had already invested in the development.

In the 1920s, a nine-hole golf course and a clubhouse were opened, and canals were dredged into the mouth of the Rouge River, with at least two bridges built to islands in the Rouge delta. Wayne Reeves reports that a roadway and some homes were also built before the Depression intervened in the 1930s and White's grand plan was stalled. Despite these setbacks, including the death of White himself in 1946, his estranged wife, Gladys, continued on. Gladys's niece Sue Johanson, the author, nurse, and sex educator, fondly remembers the Sunday walks they would take through the West Rouge before full-scale development took hold. (Gladys White successfully developed other lands adjacent to the Rouge, including the Chesterton Shores subdivision.) The Rouge Hills Golf and County Club continued until 1971, and, although the lands were later developed, the lovely clubhouse still remains as the local community centre. Hurricane Hazel wiped out all evidence of White's grand vision for the waterway, though the canals, or lagoons, are still present at the river mouth if you look closely, though now in an altered, naturalized form.

The Dirty Thirties, up to and including the years of the Second World War, marked the final days of rural Scarborough. The Kennedy family, suffering a business downturn during the Depression, moved from the tony neighbourhood of Forest Hill to Park Hill, a Cecil White development geared to the upper-middle class and still located today south of the Kingston Road, between Bellamy and Markham Roads. An advertisement

for Park Hill appearing in the *Toronto Daily Star* on September 22, 1911, some twenty years earlier, promoted "Lakeside Homes for Particular People" on lots from one-half acre to three acres, with winding streets, much like the garden suburb design found at Chine Drive. The advert encouraged, "If you are going outside of the city centre to live — stick to the Lake. The air is purer. The temperature is more even — warmer in the winter and cooler in the summer because of the well-known equalizing virtue of a big body of water. The outlook is better — for no bit of scenery or landscape is ever complete without its fair proportions of land, water, hill, and dale."

It was in this area, in the 1930s, after the hell of the First World War was long over, that Jack and Ruth Heron built their elegant retirement retreat: a stone house on a three-acre lot overlooking the water. Many of these homes were influenced by the arts and crafts movement, including a gracious home built by J.C. Cornell, a descendant of the previously mentioned William Cornell. This structure, featured in the *Evening*

Telegram on July 20, 1920, was faced in stones from the beach at the bottom of the Bluffs.

Though some with ties to the local community did eventually come to live in Park Hill, most of the people who built in the area were, according to Barbara Kennedy, "successful business people, writers, and professionals who were seeking a simpler life. It was a place where they could buy a lot and be self sufficient with the beauty of nature all around you."

Kennedy remembers lying at the top of the bank at Park Hill as a child with her friends, quietly observing a curious "lady painter" hammering nails into the roof of her house on the Flats below. This land was the location of the original nineteenth century McCowan homestead. In the twentieth century, it became home to Canadian landscape painter Doris McCarthy, who acquired twelve acres on the easterly portion of the Flats from Cecil White in 1939. In the 1940s farmers and newcomers alike marvelled at the spectacle of the *unmarried* McCarthy in her jeep, flying up the roadway that White had carved out of the hill.

With the acquisition of the little cottage overlooking the lake on the Flats, McCarthy became another early self-builder in Scarborough. As McCarthy noted in *A Fool in Paradise*, she initially camped in a tent on the property and did not acquire electricity until after the end of the Second World War. Her mother referred to the property as that "Fool's paradise of yours," a moniker McCarthy ultimately adopted as the name of her property. Yet it was to this partially built "little white box of a house with a blue roof . . . looking as if the first strong wind would blow it away" that McCarthy would return, first on weekends and then to live in year-round for seven decades.

McCarthy was no stranger to Lake Ontario and the greater Toronto shore area. She had been raised in the Beach. As a young child she spent her summers by Lake Ontario, both at the foot of Balsam and MacLean Avenues and in her earliest years at a cottage in Long Branch, in the Lakeshore district. Her father, George McCarthy, was a civil engineer under R.C. Harris (whom we will meet in the Beach section), and had helped build the Bloor Street Viaduct, which bridges the distance between Bloor Street and Danforth Road over the Don Valley. According to Doris McCarthy, he also designed the romantic Venetian Bridge at Centre Island.

———•———

SOME TWELVE YEARS AGO, I walked down the street from our family home and visited Doris McCarthy at Fool's Paradise. She told me the story of a warm June day in 1921, when her father invited her to canoe with him east from the Beach into the wild reaches

Post Romano, Fool's Paradise, *1948* Doris McCarthy, © The Estate of Doris McCarthy, PC

of the Scarborough Bluffs. Excited at the prospect of sharing some time with her normally busy and aloof father, and equally curious to explore an unseen landscape, she eagerly accepted his invitation.

Near the remains of the *Alexandria* they came ashore to light a fire and picnic on the sandy beach. Those very Bluffs would provide Doris McCarthy with a lifetime of inspiration, and, in a strange convergence of circumstances, McCarthy made her lifelong home in the open pasture above the beach where she and her father had picnicked some seventeen years earlier. The land and the simple house she built there became, in her own words, her "solace and retreat," and her "favourite work of art." When I asked her to describe the connection she felt to the landscape at Fool's Paradise, she said, "Well, I never married. My home is my root, it's my husband. . . . You own down here because you want land and therefore you love it."

McCarthy, a student of the Group of Seven's Arthur Lismer, went on to a painting career that spanned eight decades and offered a deeply personal interpretation of place within the diverse regions of Canada and beyond. She became, in the words of another member of the Group of Seven, A.J. Casson, "a woman with a vision who stuck to it"; who, after forty years of teaching painting at Toronto's Central Technical School, received the Order of Canada, the Order of Ontario, several honorary doctorates, and, in 1999, the McMichael Canadian Collection's first Artist of Honour award.

Others aside from McCarthy felt a similar draw to the Meadowcliffe area, formerly known as the Bellamy Bluff. In 1939 Harvey Robert Pollock, founder of the former Pollock Shoe Company, built his gracious country mansion, Lakewood, on the grounds of the original Rae estate, which overlooked the Flats and the lake. The home, now slated for demolition but which at the time of writing still stands, was built in the Georgian revival style and originally sat on about thirty-seven acres, commanding excellent views out over Lake Ontario. Harvey Pollock's son, Robert, remembers wonderful times spent riding with friends along the edge of the Bluffs, where, on occasion, they would dismount and hurtle down the cliff face for a swim below. Robert told me, "It was like being on a Coney Island parachute, almost. We'd hit the sand, but it would give way, and you'd have the feeling you were floating. We never recognized the danger at the time — of course, when you're a kid, you're invincible anyway."

Robert told me that his father's trek back into Toronto was sizable, but that it was a lifetime dream of Pollock Sr.'s to own and maintain horses. Lakewood fulfilled this dream, in an idyllic setting overlooking Lake Ontario, in the declining years of rural Scarborough in the 1940s. Among the visitors to the estate was Lieutenant Governor Louis Breithaupt, whose daughter, Rosa Breithaupt Clark, had some years previously purchased Cliff Acres, formerly known as Ranelagh Park, located approximately two miles to the east.

Cliff Acres, which in previous years had also served as the St. Francis Xavier Mission Seminary, included the remnants of an old-growth Carolinian forest. Shortly after acquiring Cliff Acres, Rosa married Spencer Clark. The Clarks were political idealists whose beliefs were rooted in the arts and crafts movement. Their ideals, also prevalent in the Chine Drive community (which was a little farther west), were deeply entwined with nostalgia for the rural life and a desire to recreate the communities that were disappearing as a result of industrialization.

It was in this spirit that the Clarks established the Guild of All Arts, conceived as an arts and crafts colony and co-operative. The Clarks' vision was to build a community where artists could reside and focus on creative pursuits in a natural, rural setting. During

The Guild Inn, c. 1940s
Courtesy Jeremy Hopkin

the 1930s, in the midst of the Great Depression, the Clarks organized studios and workshops that focused on a variety of arts and crafts, including weaving, woodworking, sculpture, batik, and metalworking. Some of the artists' work was sold at the onsite craft shop.

They took on artists and apprentices, and the Clarks' vision was met with some initial success, though Carole Lidgold, in *The History of the Guild Inn*, indicates that "the co-operative was a constant financial struggle." To finance its activities, the Clarks began to receive visitors and serve dinners, and by the early 1940s the Guild had added guest-room facilities.

During the war years, the government leased the Guild from the Clarks to serve as a training base for the Women's Royal Naval Service (WRENS) and was known as the HMCS Bytown II, and at the end of the war, it served as a military hospital. Otherwise known as Scarborough Hall, it specialized in the treatment of nervous disorders brought about by the war, and many local residents volunteered there. The hospital closed its doors in 1947.

After the war, the Clarks converted the main residence into a first-class inn that would also serve as a key centre for arts and culture in the decades to come. In the post-war years, the Clarks also began a sculpture garden, which today contains more than sixty architectural remnants salvaged from old Toronto buildings that were demolished during the early and middle years of the last century.

The Scarborough shore had another significant, but little-known, role to play during the Second World War, with the installation of Research Enterprises Limited's radar training facility, established at the foot of Eastville Avenue near the edge of the cliffs. According to W.E. Knowles Middleton's *Radar Development in Canada*, the federal government established Research Enterprises Limited (REL) in 1940 and completed a factory in Leaside in 1941. Radar was a developing technology during the Second World War, and REL was the focal point for all of the design and production of radar equipment used by the Canadian Armed Forces. William W. McLachlan indicates that forty-one radar units were established in Canada in all, with radar-operating personnel trained at REL in Scarborough, at the bottom of Eastville Avenue.

Greek Theatre archway Jane Fairburn

Many Bluffs residents considered themselves lucky to obtain local employment during the war at what was referred to as the REL plant, including Sydney Alexander. Patrolled by soldiers, the operations of the plant were top secret. Paul Burd, whose father and uncles ran the Paradise Pavilion, recalls the huge radar antennas that were installed near the edge of the cliff. He says he and his friends sat for hours at the water's edge, watching the free show, which included the intermittent appearance of corvettes and, on one occasion, submarines. Spitfires routinely sped over the surface of the lake, trying to avoid detection by the radar beam and then, in the nick of time, veered skyward, in what seemed an impossible attempt to avoid a head-on collision with the face of the cliff.

It was just after the end of the war that Paul Burd, about fourteen by then, spent his final summer with his friends along the lakefront, ranging through what remained of the open lands at the top of the cliffs and down at the lakefront, before suburban development took hold in earnest.

This fascinating photo from the William James collection shows two men standing on
a precarious point of the Scarborough Bluffs known as "No Man's Land," c. 1909 CTA, F1244_it12-26

In the spring of 2011, he shared with me a tragedy that marked his life:

> We were down on the beach one day and one of my chums decided he was going
> to scale a cliff just slightly west of what is now called Bluffers Park. That was the
> area we called No Man's Land. It was almost a sheer cliff face, and had a needle
> that went straight up. On the top of the needle, lying out from the Flats, was a big
> piece of property that we walked out to on a hard, narrow path. On either side of
> the path, the cliff face plummeted down to the Beach, almost 300 feet below.
>
> My friend tried to climb up the face of the needle from the lakeside. He got
> halfway up and a large slab of clay slid away and knocked him over with him
> under it and it crushed him. Yeah, that's the last day I ever went down to the
> Bluffs. I never went back. My dog wouldn't leave him. I tried to get my dog to
> come home, but he wouldn't leave until they actually took the body away.

This boy's tragic fall came at a pivotal moment in the life of the township. The
Second World War had ended, and full-scale suburbanization of the Scarborough shore
was about to take hold — and with it, a measure of destruction and loss.

CHAPTER SIX

Destruction and Loss

I n the years immediately following the war, returning servicemen, along with many new immigrants and refugees, crowded into the city of Toronto in search of accommodation and work. People settled down, got married, and had, by today's standards, many children. By the early 1950s, these trends — together with an increase in economic prosperity, the corresponding affordability of the car, and the relatively low cost of land in the outlying areas of the city — created the ideal conditions for a mass migration into the suburbs.

Government policy during these years certainly helped and encouraged this movement. The Veteran's Land Act (VLA) attempted to resettle returning servicemen, granting veterans small tracts of land on the edge of major urban areas. By 1950, veterans were eligible for loans to build their own homes. Grants were also awarded, pursuant to the Veteran's Charter, based on service. The Gordonvale subdivision, on the old Neilson farm north of the Kingston Road and St. Joseph's-on-the-Lake, was one such government-supported subdivision. According to long-time resident Bob McCowan, the government acquired about thirty or forty acres of this farm. Veterans built their own homes on half-acre lots, with many of the returning servicemen growing their own food in large garden plots.

Another government institution that facilitated the migration to the suburbs was the Central Mortgage and Housing Corporation (CMHC), which administered the National Housing Act and Home Improvement Loans Guarantee Act and oversaw the financing, administration, and construction of Canadian homes. Examples of these original CMHC, or "wartime," homes may still be seen along the Scarborough shore today. One style commonly found in the Bluffs is the one-and-a-half-storey-frame "berry box," which is quite similar in style to Plan No. 47-1 in the CMHC's catalogue of *67 Homes for Canadians*, published in 1947. Now often renovated and complete with all the modern conveniences, these modest homes provided affordable housing both to war veterans and first-time buyers.

The acute shortage of housing, coupled with available financing for potential buyers, brought the developers on board, and large-scale residential development began in the early 1950s. Homes in the $12,000 to $20,000 range presented the opportunity for many Torontonians to own a home. Young families, predominantly WASPs (white, Anglo-Saxon, and Protestant), who had no particular ties to the city and were living in their parents' basements or in cramped one-bedroom apartments, simply packed up their possessions and their children, got into their cars, and drove out to the suburbs. Their need for their own home, as S.D. Clark points out in *The Suburban Society*, trumped every other concern.

PLAN No. 47-1

Suitable for construction anywhere in Canada. Area—730 sq. ft. Cubic contents—16,790 cu. ft. Required lot frontage, without driveway—42'-0" with driveway—44'-0"

6½ rooms, including Living Room, Kitchen–Dining Room, 4 Bedrooms and Bathroom. Full Basement.

THIS plan combines an efficient layout with a very pleasing exterior appearance.

The front entrance gives access to a vestibule which has a coat closet of ample size and with natural light. The living room is of good size and proportion and contains flush wood or coal burning fireplace and side bookcases. There is a splendid window arrangement.

The kitchen opens off the living room and is spacious with dining nook and storage closet. Stair to basement leads from the kitchen. There is also a direct outside trade or service entrance.

The post-war "berry box" may still be seen in many areas of older suburban Toronto, including the Scarborough shore

Canada Mortgage and Housing Corporation (CMHC)

The Scarborough Shore

In the Way of Progress, *1996–97, Mural Routes Heritage Trail* Jennifer, Jamie, and Phil Richards, Courtesy Mural Routes Heritage Trail

Between one harvest and the next, farmer's fields with undulating rows of potatoes were traded for dormitory suburbs that each housed 500 people or more and were complete with paved roadways and electric lighting. In 1951 Scarborough had a population of 56,292. Over the course of one decade that number increased almost fourfold, to 217,286.

In 1954, in the middle of this transition, Jack Heron died very suddenly. The lovely stone house on the Bluffs was sold in 1956, and Ruth and one of her daughters took an apartment back in the city. In 1960 the sisters of St. Joseph's-on-the-Lake vacated their retreat on the Scarborough shore. Soon after, the grand building that had overlooked the water for decades succumbed to the wrecking ball. A strip mall was planted shortly thereafter in the sisters' front field adjacent to the Kingston Road. The long driveway down to the lake remained, but it was now "in-filled" with housing on either side. In the mid-1960s, the Halfway House, an icon of Scarborough rural life, was unceremoniously uprooted and carted off to Black Creek Pioneer Village, where it was restored and still stands.

The Kingston Road, the former pathway carved out of the woods by William Cornell and Levi Annis, had by this time been developed into a multi-lane highway. The little ma-and-pa shops that had sprung up along the roadside at the radial stops in the earlier part of the century now gave way to the accoutrements of the car culture — gas stations, used car lots, and strip malls — which facilitated and encouraged suburbia's reliance on the automobile. Few acknowledged what was lost in this transition. It was easier just to forget.

A wall mural entitled *In the Way of Progress*, painted by the artist Phil Richards and other members of his family, stands on the south side of the Kingston Road, just east of St. Augustine's Seminary, and reminds us of the loss and of Scarborough's forgotten agricultural past. The mural depicts a cow lazing in the roadway, blocking the movement of a truck and radial car, themselves both symbols of the new age, as a little girl looks on wistfully behind.

Much of my childhood was spent in a suburb in southeast Scarborough, in the 1960s and early 1970s, and despite the negative connotations that are so often now associated with suburban life, I count those days as some of the happiest of my life thus far. Rather than experiencing the alienation so often attributed to suburban life, we gloried in wide-open spaces as well as the deep ravines and gullies of Highland Creek. We revelled in the sense that we were somehow living in a borderland, on the edge of the urban world yet within the embrace of a rural past. Tobogganing down abandoned gravel pits or sitting in a makeshift fort under long-abandoned apple trees was a way of life.

———— •✦• ————

IN 1953 SPENCER AND ROSA CLARK began Scarborough's first planned community when they sold some 400 acres of land around the Guild Inn to make way for Guildwood Village. An artist's sketch of the village plan, published in the *Toronto Daily Star* on April 9, 1955, reveals a mixed-income community. Though the rendering includes apartments and some homes ranging from $13,000 to $20,000, it also proposes many other areas above this price category, and therefore outside the range of the average first-time home buyer of that era. A small article published in the same paper on October 17, 1955, stated that the original development was anticipated to house about 7,000 residents and included one and a quarter miles of frontage along Lake Ontario.

Like the earlier suburban development at Don Mills, the Clarks' concept was to build a community with all of the services — a ready-made town or village of sorts that included shopping, community centres, restaurants, and other commercial features, rather than a series of homes with no perceptible centre or social focus. Dr.

The Scarborough Shore

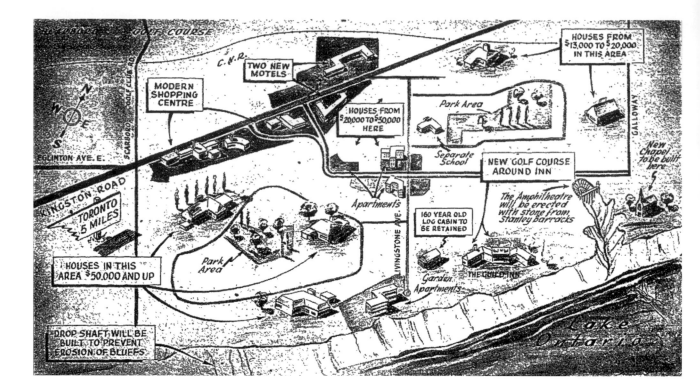

Conceptual sketch of Guildwood Village, 1955 Toronto Daily Star, April 9, 1955

E.D. Faludi, a well-known urban planner who was also involved in the development of Don Mills as North York's planning consultant, was engaged to create a subdivision plan reminiscent of England's garden city design of the late nineteenth century. Guildwood Village followed a plan of carefully laid-out streets, often turning in on themselves, with large trees and gardens prevailing in the streetscape. Wiring to the homes was buried to preserve the streetscape, and some rear-lot pathways were developed to avoid arterial roadways.

The community radiated out from the Guild Inn and grounds, which have continued to serve the local community and greater Toronto. In many ways, the Guild was the focal point for the artistic and cultural life of residents of the Scarborough shore during the years in which Scarborough changed from a township into a borough and then finally to a city in 1983. Former Scarborough Bluffs resident Kevin Brown worked at the Guild Inn in the 1970s and points out, "The Guild was something we were proud of. It was a centre for culture and the arts. It was prestigious and unusual. Many political and cultural figures attended conferences there, among them Marshall McLuhan, who gave a keynote address in the 1970s."

In 1978, shortly before his death, Spencer Clark sold his remaining lands, the Guild

Along the Shore

Inn, the outbuildings, chattels, and many architectural pieces in the sculpture garden to the Metropolitan Toronto and Region Conservation Authority and the Province of Ontario. These items and the property were later transferred to the Municipality of Metropolitan Toronto. Currently, the City of Toronto owns a remarkable collection of art and artifacts collected by the Clarks and is in the process of acquiring title to other pieces. Sadly, these treasures are now locked away in different areas of the city and are generally not available for public viewing. Many of the buildings on the Guild property have been left unoccupied in recent years, and the Studio, which once housed artists involved in metalworking, woodworking, batik, and weaving, was destroyed by fire in 2008. Other buildings, including the former Guild Inn itself, designated under Part IV of the Ontario Heritage Act in 1999, have fallen into extreme disrepair, with the Heritage Canada Foundation naming the Guild Inn as one of the most endangered historic properties in the country in 2011.

Community organizations such as the Guild Renaissance Group have worked tirelessly to revive the Clarks' vision for the property and have promoted the establishment of a cultural facility to "encourage excellence in the arts in an environment that inspires participants and audiences alike." Work is also proceeding to have the park historically designated. At the time of writing, plans for Centennial College to develop the Guild Inn and augment facilities at the site to include a hotel, restaurant, and conference centre have fallen through. Though plans for the development of the property as a "cultural precinct" have been put forward by hard-working city officials, with a chronic lack of funding, the site's future continues to be debated while the buildings fall into even greater neglect.

<hr>

INNS ALONG THE Kingston Road figured prominently in the life of the township from the earliest days. Many of these old inns eventually fell into disuse and, with the coming of the automobile age, were eclipsed by their modern equivalent, the one-storey strip motel. Author John Bentley Mays, in *Emerald City: Toronto Visited*, notes that these motels, built low to the ground and often with sleek designs and brightly coloured facades, mimicked the automobile in design and feel, just as other groupings of motel/cottage units, some designed in the pseudo-log style, harkened back to the pioneer age and its means of transportation.

At the outset, these new motels housed the motoring public — among them, families who pulled up in their station wagons for a night or more of accommodation before they pushed on to the city. Soon, however, with the coming of expressways that could lead

The Scarborough Shore

This postcard shows the Andrews Motel, "Featuring bedsitting rooms, air conditioned, sound proof, refrigerator and free T.V. in every room," early to mid 1960s Courtesy Jeremy Hopkin

the traveller directly into the downtown core, these families were no longer inclined to stop. Sadly, the motels tended to become the territory of lifestyles a world away from that of the sleepy residential streets south of the Kingston Road. Along with those other relics of the automobile age — the gas stations, the car repair shops, and the abandoned used-car showrooms — the motels are now deteriorating, although the old highway, such as it is and for better or worse, remains the single access to a reinvigorated lakefront that lies just out of sight.

Bluffer's Park, a large waterfront development begun in 1975 in the vicinity of the Cathedral Bluffs, now features a marina, restaurant, and four yacht and sailing clubs, including the Cathedral Bluffs Yacht Club, the Bluffers Park Yacht Club, the Highland Yacht Club, and the Scarborough Bluffs Sailing Club. The over half-mile-long beach, now monitored for water quality and safety according to Toronto's adopted international "blue flag" standard, has seen increased traffic of late. Torontonians from the sprawling suburbs north of the lake, as well as many others from all ethnicities, creeds, and walks of life, are finding their way down to the Scarborough shore. Nature enthusiasts and day trippers are not the only ones who have expressed a newfound interest in Toronto's eastern waterfront. The Scarborough shore has recently been the subject of a controversial study to determine the feasibility of a massive offshore wind farm development by Toronto Hydro. If the project were to go ahead, windmill towers more than 300 feet tall would extend east from the Leslie Street Spit to Ajax. Those who oppose the project argue that this proposal is shortsighted, ill considered, uneconomic, and, in the context of its overall ability to produce a significant and consistent supply of energy, frivolous and irrelevant.

Until recently, the provincial government's response to this opposition has been to frame local residents as NIMBYS (not in my backyard) and people who resent any kind of change that affects their view of the lake. And yet, Torontonians in general are waking up to the fact that the offshore windmill proposal presents a much more layered issue — one that will impact the very future of our shared waterfront.

Whatever the pros and cons, the placement of such a line of windmills directly into the source of Toronto's drinking water, in close proximity to a sensitive ecosystem, and in the pathway of several migratory bird routes will undoubtedly have an impact on the shoreline and the wildlife that inhabits the cliffs, never mind the view. At the time of writing, the Ontario government has implemented a regulation that wind farms not be placed within three miles of shore. A moratorium on all offshore wind energy projects has also been declared.

⸻ ◆ ⸻

SOME SUMMERS AGO NOW, when our children were quite young, we frequently trekked down to what remains of the wreck of the *Alexandria*, at the foot of the Bluffs near Gates Gully. We spent hours in the gully one summer, following the direction of the creek that still trickles downhill through the deep crevice and eventually empties into the lake beside a smooth pebble beach.

Near the creek's outlet, below Fool's Paradise, was one of the last-remaining natural stretches of the Scarborough Bluffs, where the breakwater still lapped at the toe of the cliff, eroding it into strange forms and patterns as it had done for thousands of years. To the east, beyond the pebble beach, the lake touched the face of the Bluffs in high water. It was in this direction that we often headed, sometimes wading right through the lake, steadying ourselves on the sticky outcroppings of clay on the surface of the Bluffs. A little farther on, we hauled ourselves up onto the unopened waterfront trail, where, just beyond the shore, we could still see the remains of the ship's boiler through the water on sunny afternoons.

Now all of that is gone. Legitimate concerns by property owners over the continued erosion of the cliffs, as well as the desire to bring more Torontonians down to the foot of the Bluffs, are behind the change. The creek my children played in is now channelled through a culvert as it flows out to the lake. The stony beach was reduced to a refuse pile, and now, after the insertion of "clean fill," a heavily fortified waterfront trail (or super highway, depending on your point of view) holds back the waves from the face of the cliff, which will in time help prevent further erosion and property loss above.

Eventually the rough pathway in Gates Gully, which has for at least three centuries brought locals down to the lake, will be formally connected to the continuous inter-regional Waterfront Trail and Greenway at the foot of the Bluffs, which follows the shores of Lake Ontario and the St. Lawrence. The Toronto and Region Conservation Authority plans to eventually link Bluffer's Park in the west with Guildwood Village and East Point Park in the east. Beyond East Point, the trail already continues, past Highland Creek and past the last remaining underwater piles of historic Port Union, until it reaches the mouth of the Rouge and the great, wild (future) national park that will run north from the lake.

Change has come not only to the shore but also to the Bluffs themselves. As geologist Nicholas Eyles has predicted, erosion control projects previously begun in many areas at the foot of the Bluffs have led to the smoothing out of the cliffs and the loss of the unique geological feature. Likewise, the installation of the waterfront trail in areas of the Bluffs not previously protected by erosion control will undoubtedly lead to similar consequences. The "white sand" cliffs first noted by Mrs. Simcoe in 1793 are already well on their way to becoming, in many sections, treed hills that lead down to the shore.

I recently walked down Gates Gully and filled my pockets with smooth stones from our lost pebble beach. They now sit on my front veranda and commemorate something lost but also something gained. More people are coming down to the water. The land on top of the cliffs will eventually be stabilized and communities will be protected. The irony is that bringing people down to the water also brings destruction. In conservation there is loss, and in development there is always change.

CHAPTER SEVEN
Renewal

The indomitable Bob McCowan still lives north of the Kingston Road on a small patch of open ground that is the sole remnant of the family farm, which in former days stretched all the way down to the cliffs and the lake. At the ripe old age of ninety-five, and in the full regalia of work pants and suspenders, he still braves the summer sun to tend an impressive bit of garden that was saved from the builders as the city closed in all around him. When I asked why he stayed on in the middle of what had become, to all intents and purposes, an alien land, he deflected the question by saying, "Well, the land was cheap," but the real answer, and I hope he won't mind me saying this, is that he has lived here all his life.

He stays because he was born here and feels a deep connection to a time and place that are now almost lost yet remain clear in his mind's eye as he says to me, "I suppose it's the way you're brought up, but to me the countryside, that's the place to be. . . . All you hear now is traffic noise, eh . . . the racket — but in those days you'd be working out there and you'd hear the meadowlarks going off and you'd hear the old crows off on the side . . . but none of that anymore, no, none of that anymore."

After the radial tracks were torn up and the Kingston Road was widened into a six-lane highway, the farms and meadows of south Scarborough seemed to disappear overnight and now are almost beyond the reach of our imagination. Yet something of what was lost can still be found along this shore and in the small communities that hug the water's edge.

One morning in late January a few years ago, I got up earlier than usual and was running along the top of the bluff in Park Hill just before dawn. It was so early that there was no car traffic at all in the quiet residential community and not even the faintest murmur could be heard from the traffic on the Kingston Road. Just as the sun broke out over the lake, a magnificent stag stepped out from the ravine, beside Jack Heron's stone house. Although aware of me, he seemed serenely untroubled by my presence and ran down the centre of the road, as if surveying his territory and quite indifferent to the houses that make up my suburban world. I followed him at a close distance. As we approached the Kingston Road, he stopped and turned to look at me. For several seconds we gazed at each other, held in this sudden conjunction of two different worlds. The honk of a horn on the Kingston Road broke the spell; in a flash my stag darted into Gates Gully and was gone.

Had I imagined him? No, he was there all right, just as his ancestors had been there before him, at a time when they were indeed the "monarchs of the glen." Then the Aboriginal peoples came, hunters and gatherers and fisher folk. Next came Mrs. Simcoe and the settlers. Trees gave way to fields and farms. Mr. McCowan's forbears would remember that. Then came the gentry, the artists, and the religious communities, seeking to live a quiet life in nature on the edge of the city. Now here is my suburban world of the twenty-first century.

It would seem that the worlds of the stag and the fisherman and the farmer have all been traded away. Has it been a fair exchange? And then again, are they really gone? Einstein said that "the distinction between past, present and future is only an illusion, however persistent." There may be some comfort in that.

The Beach

PART II

A filigree of snow graces the beach and Boardwalk,
winter 2008 Mike Maclaverty, TheAccidentalPhotographer.ca

CHAPTER ONE
The Nature of the Place

Many have heard of brothers Orville and Wilbur Wright, the two American pioneers of aeronautics who achieved the first controlled, powered, and sustained flight in a heavier-than-air machine on December 17, 1903, at Kitty Hawk, North Carolina. That flight, though just twelve seconds long, set the stage for a technological revolution that propelled the world into a new age. Canada, and by extension the British Empire, celebrated its first flight triumph five years and two months later, through the efforts of the Aerial Experiment Association, a chief rival of the Wright brothers. On February 23, 1909, association member J.A.D. McCurdy flew the *Silver Dart* out over the frozen Bras d'Or Lake at Baddeck Bay on Cape Breton Island, Nova Scotia, travelling almost three-quarters of a mile in fifty seconds.

Few Torontonians today are aware that the Toronto Beach was the setting of another pioneer adventure in the early history of aeronautics, soon after the McCurdy flight. The winter of 1909 unquestionably belonged to Baddeck Bay, but the summer that followed belonged to Toronto's Beach, when Charles Foster Willard and his *Golden Flyer* came to town.

American barnstormer Charles Foster Willard, c. 1911 CTA, F1244_it 87

In 1909, the very same year as the Baddeck flight, the Aeronautic Society of New York began the promotion of public demonstrations of flying. To build a plane and train a pilot for them, they engaged motorcycle manufacturer and flight pioneer Glenn Curtiss of Hammondsport, New York, who was also a member of the original Baddeck team. Curtiss handpicked Charles Foster Willard to be his first student and trained him on his self-made *Golden Flyer*, named for the distinctive yellow rubberized silk that covered the lifting and control surfaces.

There was no doubt that Curtiss's student was green. In the summer of 1909, while Louis Blériot crossed the English Channel, a distance of some twenty miles, Willard was achieving successive flights in the *Golden Flyer* of no more than a mile each, according to the *Globe* of August 9, 1909. Though he was inexperienced, Willard was undoubtedly a fast learner. On August 14, 1909, the *Globe* reported that Willard had surpassed, one day earlier, the Wright brothers' North American record for the longest cross-country flight by covering at least twelve miles in under twenty minutes. By the end of the summer, the Aeronautic Society was ready to take their show on the road. The first Air Exhibition would be held at the enormously popular Scarboro' Beach Amusement Park, located on the north shore of Lake Ontario in Toronto's Beach district.

The stated intention of the flight exhibition, covered in all the major Toronto papers, was to promote Willard's attempt at crossing the lake between the Beach and Niagara Falls, a distance of about fifty miles. If successful, Willard would surpass Louis Blériot's recent record crossing of the English Channel, by flying over water for almost double the distance. This was, to say the least, highly ambitious, given the young pilot's limited flight experience and, perhaps more importantly, the *Golden Flyer's* reported maximum fuel capacity of one gallon of gas.

Be that as it may, Willard and his aircraft were undoubtedly the star attractions of Scarboro' Beach's late summer season that year. Shipped in pieces by train from New York to Toronto, the *Golden Flyer* arrived on August 28 and was assembled in a tent at the centre of the park. The organizing committee, being completely unfamiliar with the requirements of flight, had threaded a truncated runway between the tent and the lake in a space so narrow it allowed a clearance of a mere six feet from each wing tip. As flight historian Frank Ellis wryly observed, "Apparently the committee intended it to take off like a bird, or swoosh up into the sky like a rocket." To increase his chances of a successful takeoff, Willard cleverly arranged for a wooden trough to be constructed down the centre of this alley, to act as a guide-track for the front wheel of his machine, with the

The Beach

trough ending on top of the three-foot breakwater, just above the surface of the lake.

The first flight on September 2 lasted a matter of seconds and landed Willard and his *Golden Flyer* in the drink, just off the beach. Joseph Temple notes in "Waterfront Dreams" that newspaper promotion for the flight changed considerably at this point to "Willard Flies." Willard himself remained undeterred. On September 7, 1909, he once again rolled his aircraft down the runway. This time he shot straight out over the lake for more than half a mile before turning to the west, then in due course north toward the shore, and then east, thereby completing a circuit of roughly two miles above the lake. In doing so he became the first person to fly across the Toronto shore at the lake, a consequential achievement, given the fact that the first recorded flight over the city by Count Jacques de Lesseps did not occur until the following summer, on July 13, 1910. Although Willard's flight was hailed as a grand success in both the *Toronto Daily Star* and the *Evening Telegram*, the aviator was denied the picture-perfect landing he had hoped to make on the beach.

According to Ellis, Willard had meant to touch down on the level sand near the amusement park. But as he approached the beach, he saw that it was packed with throngs of spectators. Although reports do vary as to how severe a dunking he suffered on this second attempt, one thing is clear: he and his *Golden Flyer* had no choice but to land in the water near the front of the park. Just a few days later, on September 11, after yet a third attempt and yet another dunking, the plucky but frustrated pilot and his flying machine packed up and left town.

This early twentieth century postcard shows Scarboro' Beach attractions by day and night

TPL, PC924

THE LANDING ON THE beach denied to Willard was achieved haphazardly some eighty-five years later by a flight that nearly went horribly wrong. The *Toronto Star* reported that on

September 28, 1994, two young men, intent
on logging enough additional hours to upgrade
their flying licences, set out early one morning
from Montreal in a 1978 Cessna 152 bound for Toronto Island Airport. The flight was
uneventful until they neared the airport from the east, in the vicinity of the Beach community. At about 2,000 feet up, all hell broke loose when the plane ran out of gas and
stalled in mid-air. One can well imagine the young hands shaking on the steering column
as the pilot radioed for help, calling, "Mayday, Mayday," while the aircraft plummeted
toward the tiny Beach homes spread out like matchboxes along a vast border of blue.

The controller's instructions were clear and unequivocal. Aim for the nearby beach
or Greenwood Racetrack and land there if you can. In those split seconds, as the plane
rushed silently through the air, the men began with amazement to make out a long,
uninterrupted expanse of sand between the houses and the lake — a clear demarcation of
not quite two miles in length, curving gently alongside the water, away from the towers
of the downtown core that were almost within reach.

The misfit pilots achieved by accident that morning what Willard had tried and yet
failed to do. They brought their plane to a textbook landing on an almost deserted

The Beach

Woodbine Beach. As the two exhilarated Montrealers tumbled out onto the hard-packed sand, a monstrous search and rescue helicopter hovered overhead, uncertain of its role in the tragedy that never happened. Later that day, the pilots-cum-heroes were whisked away from the lake and the beach to the concrete monuments of downtown Toronto. There, and no doubt elsewhere for many years to come, they would tell their story of the wounded plane and the beach that had saved them.

————◆————

THE BEACH? THE BEACHES? You say "tamaytoe" and I say "tomawtoe." Does it matter? We will consider this question later. Either way, place names *are* important. They are the newcomer's first point of contact with a community and provide clues about the spirit of a place, often with surprising accuracy. Few places in Toronto are named for the prevailing geographic feature that dominates the area. Many of the waterfront districts and communities along the shore are exceptions, and the Beach is one such, named for the long, clearly defined, and empty stretch of sand that lies between the residential neighbourhood to the north and the great blue gulf of the lake immediately to the south.

The Beach community, like the sands that border its southerly edge, is a place set apart from the rest of the city. It is a residential neighbourhood within an oasis of hidden ravines and large tracts of open parkland leading down to the shore. The community is a mishmash of professionally designed and meticulously tended homes, juxtaposed with do-it-yourself winterized clapboard cottages that recall an earlier era in the life of one of Toronto's last remaining villages.

The main boulevard and commercial thoroughfare of this village is Queen Street East, from Woodbine Avenue to Neville Park Boulevard. Its shops and amenities cater to a lifestyle that offers freedom, for the most part, from the regimentation of super-stores, though at a more demanding retail price than in years gone by. The street has a self-contained, resort-town quality, where elderly gentlemen rub shoulders with twenty-somethings in short shorts whizzing by on roller blades, all of them doing their best to avoid the strollers and dogs that seem to increase exponentially every summer. Yet the heart and soul of the place has nothing to do with all that bustle and lies instead at the village's southern edge, at the beach itself.

As Greg Stott noted some twenty years ago in "Canada Journal: The Beaches, Toronto, Ontario: Streets of Attitude," the Beach community has a complex character, a multifaceted personality that may be due in part to its evolution as a village on the shore of Lake Ontario, set within the broader hinterlands of the urban reality of Toronto.

To know and understand the Beach, you have to step onto the Boardwalk, the community's cultural key line and its most venerable public space. The Boardwalk consists of count-

Queen St. East on a summer's morning, 2012.
Whitlock's operated as a grocery store c. 1908

Keith Ellis

less wooden planks, each one approximately sixteen feet long and eight inches wide, nailed side by side across timber joists to form a smooth, flat walkway that stretches continuously across the sand, roughly from the Balmy Beach Club, located within blocks of Victoria Park Avenue in the east, to well beyond Woodbine Avenue in the west. This unassuming feat of carpentry demarcates the natural world of the lake to the south from the village that lies across the open parkland to the north.

The Boardwalk first became one continuous entity with the opening of Beaches Park in 1932. Over the years it has been much extended and occasionally re-laid. All through one winter night in the early 1970s, a blizzard raged with such force that on the following morning, bewildered residents came upon what looked like an endless concertina of crushed timbers, such had been the force of the gale. Huge willows that had stood back

Glenn Gould on the boardwalk, 1956

Jock Carroll, LAC, e011067035

twenty feet from the water now had roots hanging over a hollowed-out ledge. Some stretches were death traps, so high and cavernous were the grottoes of ice. Amazing though it may seem, this was only one in a number of violent storms that has wreaked havoc on the beach and Boardwalk over the decades.

It took some time, but eventually a broader Boardwalk was built and extended, as part of the construction for Ashbridge's Bay Park, which opened in 1977. During this time, the city imported vast quantities of sand to shape and form a deeper and more extensive beach and laid out breakwaters of rock, or groynes, at right angles to the shore to keep the sand from being carried away again.

It was on a much earlier version of the Boardwalk that the young Norman Jewison carried his cedar strip canoe in the 1940s, when his work at his parents' dry goods store at Kippendavie Avenue and Queen Street was done. Glenn Gould, also raised in the Beach, often meandered along the Boardwalk. Writers Robert Fulford and Michael Ondaatje, who have also called this place home, undoubtedly frequented the Boardwalk, as would have the late, lovable comedian John Candy, who attended school in the area. Canadian

Along the Shore

painter William Kurelek raised his children in the Beach and picnicked with his young family along the shore. Although he is best known for his poignant images of Canadian Prairie farm life, he did paint several Boardwalk scenes.

Greg Stott has mused whether "the lake and its generous view do not instill a sense of creative freedom that suits creative souls." I like to think that the community and its shore have somehow played a part in nurturing and inspiring the remarkable number of artists who have called this place home.

———— ✦ ————

DEFINING THE GEOGRAPHIC BOUNDARIES of the Beach has always been tricky because the perceived boundaries of the area have often been in a state of flux. The Beach's earliest resident and "matriarch," Sarah Ashbridge, settled with her family in the easternmost region of Ashbridge's Bay, near present-day Coxwell Avenue and Queen Street, in the late eighteenth century. A small farming district developed from there in the nineteenth century, along with a smattering of hamlets on what is now Queen Street and farther east along the Kingston Road.

In the late nineteenth and early twentieth centuries, the Beach was primarily a series of seasonal resort villages that stretched from Woodbine Avenue, east along Queen Street, and south to the lake. This led many of its earliest residents to maintain that the northern boundary of the neighbourhood was in fact Queen Street itself, from Woodbine Avenue in the west, to Victoria Park in the east, and the shoreline in the south. In the years that followed, the Beach gradually transitioned into a series of little year-round villages and communities; by the 1930s, the Beach was knit together, and the streets north of Queen were filled in. Well before the end of the first half of the twentieth century, residents conceded that the traditional northern boundary of the Beach was on the height of land at the Kingston Road, while the shore of the lake continued to define the community's southern edge.

A recent period of upheaval and change came to the tiny, perfect world of the Beach as the area was gentrified in the latter part of the twentieth century. The neighbourhood, for both good and bad, has now further evolved, as neighbourhoods do, and the traditional boundaries of the village, while upheld with religious conviction by many died-in-the-wool Beachers, have now expanded.

First, the well-designed residential streets built on the Old Woodbine, or Greenwood, Racetrack lands, west of what local police referred to for years as "the Wall," makes it virtually impossible to assert that the community now ends abruptly at Woodbine Avenue.

The Beach

Balmy Beach, c. 2008 Jane Fairburn

Likewise, few could argue that the Fallingbrook area, which lies just over the city boundary into Scarborough, does not have a strong historic claim and attachment to the village on the other side of Victoria Park Avenue.

By the 1980s it had become fashionable to live in "the Beach" or "the Beaches." This new cachet would have surprised local residents of yesteryear. Enthusiastic real estate agents began to fling the notional boundaries of the community ever wider. First they urged the public to live in the Beach as far away as Logan and Gerrard — next, the waters of the lake would no doubt lap the Danforth.

Many long-time Beach residents remember the daily commute from the downtown core, whether by the Queen streetcar or by automobile. You were almost home as you passed the raucous crowds coming and going and sometimes staggering out from the Old Woodbine, on the westerly side of Woodbine Avenue. As you crossed over coming east and passed the old Kew Beach Firehall No.17 at Herbert Avenue, you were very conscious of having moved from one area to another. That has changed. Whether in

Along the Shore

the new development west of Woodbine, up either side of Main Street, north of the Kingston Road to Gerrard, or in the long-established neighbourhood of Fallingbrook, residents in all of these quarters may well say they live in the Beach.

————•————

THE REALITY IS that the essence of the Beach community transcends these geographic limits and is rooted instead at the water's edge. I say all of this knowing that some would not consider me entitled to an opinion at all, on this or any other subject as it pertains to the Beach. Although my grandfather's first house sat on Benlamond Avenue, which is now widely considered "the Beach," my grandmother spent many years of her teaching career in one of the local schools, and I have previously lived in the Beach, and in fact still send my children to school there, by the standards of many, I am simply put, a Johnny come-lately. One of the charming things about the Beach is its continuity: some families have lived continuously in the community since the early twentieth century.

Certainly the Beach went through several significant transformations as it evolved, developing a mix of large summer homes for the moderately wealthy, with the addition of some smaller but genteel permanent residences for the aspiring upper-middle class. The majority of full-time residents, however, were by far and away the working and lower middle classes, who lived in a collection of simple, sometimes slapdash dwellings that were nonetheless charming and well cared for in their own right.

Toward the end of the twentieth century, the Beach became the fashionable, more expensive but still varied and vibrant community we know today. The constant in all of this change has been the lake. Whether it's the "Beach" or the "Beaches," the water's edge has remained central to the story from the very beginning.

CHAPTER TWO

Beginnings

The story of the Beach community is inextricably interwoven with the story of the waterfront, a story that began some 12,500 years earlier, when the Laurentide Ice Sheet that covered the Toronto region during the Wisconsin Glacial Episode began to recede for the final time. We have described in the Scarborough shore section that the melting ice sheet left in its wake a basin of water much larger than present Lake Ontario, known as Lake Iroquois. When the ice that had blocked the St. Lawrence Valley melted away, the waters in Lake Iroquois quickly drained, though it was only about 3,000 years ago that the shore, as yet unaltered by European contact, came to approximate current lake levels.

Much of the Beach community, as well as downtown Toronto, actually sits on the flat bottom of that ancient glacial lake. Going north from the shore of Lake Ontario in the Beach you will, in most places, have to climb a steep hill as you approach the Kingston Road. Under foot is a shoal of sand and gravel that was deposited near the shore in a bay of Lake Iroquois sometime after the last period of glaciation ended.

The unique geography and landscape of the Beach community, much of which is situated below the hill on the floor of Lake Iroquois, has been a key factor in the particular culture and perspective of the area that has developed over the years. Well-known author and journalist Robert Fulford, himself raised in the Beach, writes in "Memories of the Beach: The Evolution of a Village in Our Biggest City" that Beach residents, although surrounded by Toronto, don't really feel all that Torontonian. They are from the Beach and have their own perspective and ethos. This may at least in part stem from many residents being geographically "cut off" from the rest of the city by the hill and by the formerly semi-industrial and residential flatlands that lie between the Beach and the banks of the Don River. A large portion of this latter area is known as Leslieville, an area now gentrifying and reconnecting with the waterfront.

In *Accidental City: The Transformation of Toronto*, Fulford recalls climbing the steep slope of Southwood Drive as a child. As he walked away from the water, north up to the Kingston Road and toward the ancient shore of Lake Iroquois, it seemed to him that he had followed the curvature of the earth to a distinctly different land:

> When I was little, there were two important things about the beach that I fundamentally misunderstood, and the hill was one of them. As a child, I knew that the world was round; I also knew that walking north from my house for a few blocks entailed ascending a hill. I put the two things together and deduced that the hill reflected the curvature of the earth. A teacher later explained that it was an ancient sandbar, but there are still times when the idea of the earth's roundness evokes in my mind the image of nine-year-old me walking up the steep slope of Southwood Drive toward Kingston Road.
>
> My other misunderstanding was more typical of the ignorance of youth: I took it for granted that everyone lived in as wonderful a world as the Beach was for me in childhood.

— • —

IN YEARS GONE BY, living in the Beach was very much like living by the ocean in any one of a number of seaside towns. About forty years ago a friend of mine arrived from England to settle in Toronto. For a time he lived in the centre of the city and then in Don Mills, a planned urban community, located in those years outside of Toronto proper. One summer evening he was coming back to the city when he lost his way and found himself driving in along the old Kingston Road. He kept on and on past outlying motels until at last he came to what looked like a more established residential area, with a church on one

Balmy Beach, Toronto, Ont..

Early twentieth century postcard,
Balmy Beach TPL, PC 611

side of the street and a pub on the other. In sheer frustration he swung off left and came over the brow of a hill. He stopped. He was looking down on what we call the Beach, but what he *saw* was something else. He recalls:

I gazed in amazement. A vast, smooth curtain of cobalt blue hung right across the sky below the clouds and I remembered how, when I was still just a very small boy, on holiday down in southwest England, our steam train rounded a bend and what looked like this same blue curtain hung across the sky, behind a row of tiny, white cottages. I asked my Mother, "What is that?" And she replied, "It is the sea."

Now I suddenly realized that I had lately spent two years living in Toronto without ever giving a thought to the fact that it was, to an extent and in a way, a seaside town. So I spent the next few days exploring this newfound district, a homely leafy district, with as many fish and chip shops to the square mile as were in the London of my boyhood. I determined to live in the Beach and so, for the next twenty years, I did.

Along the Shore

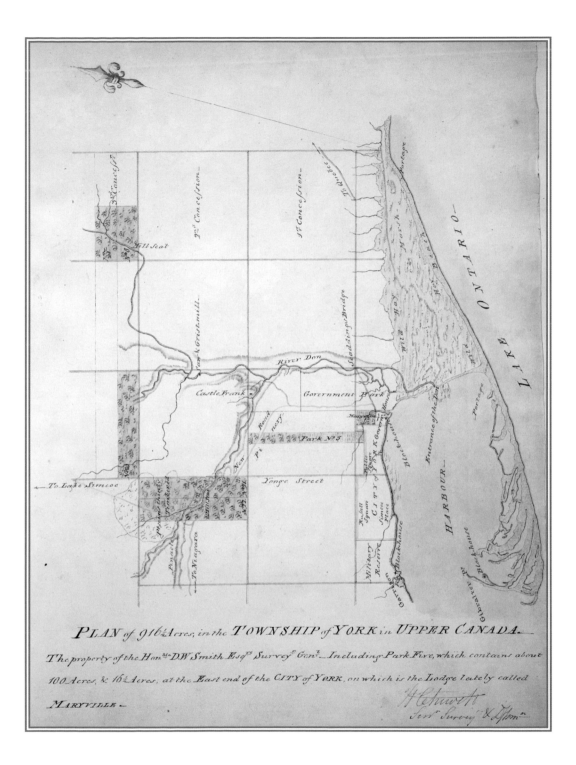

This map drawn by William Chewett in 1802 clearly shows the peninsula, Ashbridge's Bay, and their relationship to what we know in the present day as Toronto Island TPL, Ms1889.1.6

The Beach

BEFORE THE LARGE-SCALE human intervention that began after European settlement in the eighteenth and early nineteenth centuries, the landscape and natural features of the shore in the area we now know as the Beach were radically different. Likewise, the Don River that lies to the west has undergone radical and grievous change since the time of European settlement in the late eighteenth century.

After the glacial meltwater Lake Iroquois drained, the deep crevice of the Don Valley was chiselled into the earth. The wide river valley was created due to the action of the river flowing out to Lake Admiralty, a lake that was situated far to the south of the present-day shore. Likewise, the earth's crust began a process of readjustment after the massive ice sheet retreated, and this continues to the present day, causing lake levels to rise and backing up the tributary rivers and streams along the shore. As a result of this process, large deltas formed at the mouths of the waterways, including at the Don River.

Rising lake levels also caused the Bluffs to slowly erode, with currents carrying the sand and silt westward, where it settled into a beach. Continual erosion from the Scarborough Bluffs also produced a narrow sandbar that lay just to the south of the shore. Though its formation was constantly changing due to the action of the wind, waves, and erosion, it was loosely attached to the mainland at about present-day Woodbine Avenue. This sandy ridge ran in a southwesterly direction, spanning most of what is, today, the downtown core of the city. Early settlers called this land formation the Peninsula, and for the first half of the nineteenth century, it was also accessed by way of a bridge over the mouth of the Don River. The westerly reaches of the original Peninsula are known today as Toronto Island.

While the sandbar was a dynamic entity, it was generally intact at the point of European settlement, in the late eighteenth and early nineteenth centuries. For most of those years, one could travel along this natural causeway, as did Mrs. Simcoe, wife of the first lieutenant governor of Upper Canada, from what is now Toronto Island in the west, beyond the outlet of the Don River, and to the westerly regions of the Beach community in the east. David Smyth, in his 1799 *A Short Topographical Description of His Majesty's Province of Upper Canada in North America*, notes of the Peninsula that "as soon as the bridge over the Don is finished, it will of course be generally resorted to, not only for pleasure, but as the most convenient road to the heights of Scarborough."

Joseph Bouchette, who in 1792 surveyed the harbour at Toronto, described the Peninsula as "extraordinary, being a narrow slip of land, in several places not more than sixty yards in breadth, but widening towards its extremity to nearly a mile; it is principally a bank of sand with a very little grass upon it; . . . it lies so low that the wide expanse of Lake Ontario is seen over it."

Along the Shore

This unusual finger of land between the Toronto shore to the north and the open water of the lake to the south encased one of the greatest freshwater marshes to be found anywhere within the Great Lakes Basin. The wetland was named Ashbridge's Bay, after the pioneer family who were the first to settle along its easterly reaches. Ashbridge's Bay was, in fact, a series of interior lagoons created by the delta of the Don River and the sands of the Scarborough Bluffs. These lagoons provided a vast territory and natural staging ground for migratory birds and waterfowl crossing the Great Lakes. Amassing some 1,385 acres, the marsh was home to an abundance of plants, mammals, reptiles, amphibians, birds, and fish, including salmon, pickerel, and muskellunge.

Henry Scadding's book *Toronto of Old* provides us with an early snapshot of the then pristine marsh, viewed from the River Don in the nineteenth century:

> The view from the old trestlework bridge was very picturesque, especially when the forest, which clothed the banks of the ravine on the right and left, wore tints of autumn. . . . Southward in the distance was a great stretch of marsh with the blue lake along the horizon. In the summer this marsh was one vast jungle of tall flags and reeds, where would be found the conical huts of the muskrat, and where would be heard at certain seasons the peculiar gulp of the bittern. . . . Here also the blue iris grew plentifully, and reeds, frequented by the marsh hen; and the bulrush with its long cat-tails, sheathed in chestnut coloured felt and pointed upward like toy rockets ready to be shot off.

A much later description of the marsh comes from Frank Smith, who was said to be the last gunner and trapper at Ashbridge's Bay. As he recalls in *Ashbridge's Bay*, "When I saw the marsh for the first time to remember it, I think there was a blackbird on every rush in the marsh, swallows by the hundreds of thousands, small marsh wrens everywhere, rails calling to one another, coots bobbing up out of the rushes at every turn in the weeds. I was simply delighted with all this bird life. It was quite a thrill and I consider myself very fortunate having been raised so close to this lost heaven of all times."

As we'll explore in the Island section of this book, this sandy strand and marsh lying just to the south of Toronto's shore was a rich hunting and fishing ground for successive groups of first peoples who inhabited or moved through the Toronto area.

Archaeological digs conducted in the late 1990s by Dena Doroszenko of the Ontario Heritage Foundation in partnership with Martha Latta of the University of Toronto have revealed an overlapping pattern of settlement between Aboriginal people and early European settlers at the eastern edge of what was once Ashbridge's Bay, near today's Beach community. Successive digs conducted at the current Jesse Ashbridge property, near Coxwell Avenue and Queen Street, on land that was settled by the Ashbridge family in 1794, established the remains of a longhouse, as well as an in-situ hearth with pottery sherds dating to approximately AD 1100 to 1200. A large quantity of early-nineteenth-century European pottery has also been found. According to "'Down by the Bay': The Ashbridge Estate in Toronto, On," some 48,000 artifacts have been discovered in all, making the site "perhaps one of the most important archaeological sites in Toronto" and providing us with a continuous story of human habitation throughout the centuries at the edge of the bay.

Though the artifacts remain as tangible reminders of the area's past, some of the Beach's most prominent geographic features — including its great marsh and its protective sandbar — are now gone, due to the pressures of industrialization and settlement in the nineteenth and early twentieth centuries. Gone also is the potential of discovering other clues about the long history of human habitation along the shores of the bay.

———— ◆ ————

Two ceramic rim sherds uncovered at the Ashbridge Estate, Pickering tradition c. AD 1100–1200

Courtesy Ontario Heritage Trust

THE STORY THE BEACH'S lost geography begins after the arrival of the Simcoes in 1793, as the town of York was growing up along the shore of Toronto Bay to the west of the Don River. As industrialization began to take hold, it did so along the western fringe of Ashbridge's Bay, near the mouth of the Don River. Raw sewage was discharged regularly into the Bay by the early nineteenth century, and by the middle part of the century, the mouth of the Don had become little more than an open sewer.

George Fairfield, in *Ashbridge's Bay*, indicates that the condition of the bay was also greatly compromised by the operation of the Gooderham and Worts distillery at the northwest corner of the marsh. By 1843, in order to deal with the large quantities of mash that were a by-product of

Along the Shore

the distillery process, Gooderham and Worts established feedlots that housed up to 4,000 cattle near the shore. Under shameless sanitation and waste disposal practices, the untreated animal waste was simply discharged into the bay. A cut was later made in the sandbar at the westerly end of the bay to try to release some of the waste into the open water of the lake.

N. Currier's lithograph General View of the City of Toronto, U.C. *paints a pleasant picture of the westerly fringes of Ashbridge's Bay. To the right is the Gooderham and Worts windmill, which stood until 1859. Many of the mid- to late-nineteenth-century Gooderham and Worts buildings, dating back to its years as an important worldwide manufacturer and distributor of whiskey, still stand in the Distillery District today.*

Successive violent storms in the 1850s eroded the narrows in the western vicinity of the Peninsula, culminating in the storm of 1858, which tore a gap clear across the sandbar, forever separating what we now know as Toronto Island from the more easterly area that came to be known as Fisherman's Island. In the late nineteenth century, another gap, known as the Coatsworth Cut, was made to the City's specifications, at the easterly end of the sandbar, again to allow fresh water into the marsh and to flush out some of the pollution that was accumulating, most seriously in the western part of the bay. Among the contributors to this pollution was the city dumping ground that now formed small islets of garbage that straddled the government breakwater at the western edge of the bay.

Woodbine Beach, the extreme eastern portion of the sandbar, was considered an integral part of the Beach district in the nineteenth and early twentieth centuries. Woodbine Beach was probably recognized as a separate entity after the lake breached the eastern area of the Peninsula in the 1860s. It definitely became separated from Fisherman's Island with the Coatsworth Cut, which severed the sandy ridge near its eastern extremity. In any case, this easterly region of the sandbar near the present-day Beach community remained somewhat less spoiled than the rest of the bay well into the late nineteenth century. In 1894 the *Toronto World* noted, "Towards its east end the water of Ashbridge's Bay is now as pure as, if not purer than, the water of Toronto Bay. The part of the strip towards the east is excelled by no part of the Island as a healthy spot, to which the citizens of Toronto may take themselves and their families during the summer months."

Despite this, in the late 1920s the Woodbine Beach lands were expropriated and leases were allowed to lapse to make way for the city's plans for waterfront redevelopment in the east end. The Toronto Harbour Commission's Waterfront Plan of 1912 was the final death blow for the vast marsh. The plan envisioned filling the bay to allow for a further eastern waterfront industrial area, incorporating a complex system of railway lines, as well as augmented port facilities. With some westerly sections of Ashbridge's Bay by this time covered with several feet of thick, toxic muck from the raw

Nicholas Hornyansky's Ashbridge's Bay *shows an industrialized and deeply degraded waterfront in the 1930s*

TPL, 961-3-16

sewage and industrial waste that spewed out into the water, there was little opposition to this objective. The final destruction of the bay, achieved largely through an ambitious program of land filling over a number of years, dispossessed countless waterfowl, songbirds, birds of prey, and other creatures, land and water based, who nested there, as well as those birds who used the bay as a natural staging area during fall and spring migrations.

The waterfront plan also proposed an extensive park system that would exist in concert with the increased industrial and port facilities. In 1932 Beach residents celebrated the creation of a continuous waterfront park running east from Woodbine Avenue to the Balmy Beach Club, located within blocks of Victoria Park Avenue. Mary Campbell and Barbara Myrvold note in *The Beach in Pictures: 1793–1932* that the almost complete filling of Ashbridge's Bay caused "the peninsula to become merely a beach." In the years that followed, the last easterly reaches of the great marsh disappeared forever.

Today, only the Ashbridge's Bay name survives, along with the Coatsworth Cut and a tiny remnant of the waters of the original marsh that lie to the south of Lakeshore Drive near the foot of Coxwell Avenue. In an interview in 1981, then–eighty-three-year-old Florence Spencer had this to say about the Ashbridge's Bay of her youth, before it, along with Woodbine Beach, was "reclaimed" in the name of progress: "I'll tell you what there was. What they call Ashbridge's Bay today is an excuse of a bay. Ashbridge's Bay, I've been ice boating on Ashbridge's Bay. You'd have a heck of a time ice boating on that little bit of . . ." Sadly degraded by human neglect, Ashbridge's Bay and Woodbine Beach remain only in the memories of the Beach's oldest residents.

———◆———

THOUGH A NATURAL environment may be destroyed in the space of a few generations, animal instinct and the will to survive often outlast these callous interventions. As the Roman poet Horace said so long ago, "You can drive Nature out with a pitchfork, but she'll keep on running right back at you." Still, it was no less than miraculous that — even through the 1940s to the 1960s, when all but the last vestiges of the marsh had disappeared forever — some of the native birds returned during spring and fall migrations. As is noted in George Fairfield's *Ashbridge's Bay*, many species, including the Hudsonian Godwit and various species of sandpipers, owls, and plovers, returned, though in much reduced numbers. Some traded the shelter of their cattail reeds for other forms of clean and dirty fill at the foot of Leslie Street, west of what is now known as the Ashbridges Bay Wastewater Treatment Plant. Other wild areas west of Leslie Street still remained

The Beach

A Monet Morning — View From the Leslie Street Spit

John Wallace

in the 1940s, including the area that was still referred to as Fisherman's Island but was reduced, according to Fairfield, to "a long narrow shoreline of sand and gravel."

Robert Taylor reports in "Saw-whet Owls" in *Ashbridge's Bay* that local naturalists made a concerted effort during these decades to track these last remaining refugees. Among the volunteers was Frank Smith, a former Ashbridge's Bay fisherman and gunner who had shot birds for profit as well as for sport for decades. Smith was one of the few who recognized what the loss of Ashbridge's represented for Toronto and actively joined in the effort to tag these creatures that clung to their ancestral pattern of migration, despite their vanishing habitat. Among them was the dainty Northern Saw-whet Owl, which on certain days in early fall could still be found, though in drastically decreased numbers, in the dogwood brush that lined the now virtually unrecognizable water's edge.

It was also around this time, in the late 1950s, that the Toronto Harbour Commission (now the Toronto Port Authority) began the construction of the Outer Harbour East

Headland at the base of Leslie Street, in the vicinity of the former great marsh, just west of the sewage treatment facility. Commonly known for decades as the Leslie Street Spit, much of the land is now designated as Tommy Thompson Park. The structure was initially built as a breakwater that would allow the development of a new outer harbour, planned after the opening of the St. Lawrence Seaway.

The need for increased docking facilities in the harbour all but disappeared with the advent of container shipping on trucks in the 1960s, but the need for a place to dump construction waste increased exponentially with the strong post-war economy that fuelled the rapid expansion of Toronto. The lakefront on Toronto's eastern shore again filled this need, and in the years that followed, the foot of Leslie Street became a dumping ground for enormous amounts of construction rubble, notably bedrock and subsoil from the construction of subways and concrete, brick, and asphalt from the demolition of buildings and road surfaces. A 2008 article by Greg Smith in the *Toronto Star* reported that "over the past fifty years, 4.6 million truckloads of earth, gravel, old pavement, and construction debris have been dumped in the lake off the foot of Leslie St." Today, the Spit juts three miles into Lake Ontario. Still growing in extent, it now comprises some six square miles of reclaimed land.

— • —

ONE UNFORESEEN BENEFIT from the cycle of intervention, destruction, and intervention has been nature's renewal and rebirth. Over the years, the Leslie Street Spit has become increasingly well vegetated. The extensive dredging of the Outer Harbour deposited sands originally from the Scarborough Bluffs along the main headland, forming what are referred to as the inner embayments. These sandy soils became the base for the pioneer plant communities.

Remarkably, some of the plant, animal, and bird species that once thrived there, including the tiny Northern Saw-whet Owl, gradually began to return. Something like a little wilderness has resulted, one that continues to evolve to the present day, all within a stone's throw of Toronto's downtown core. Christopher Hume, in "Toronto's Accidental Treasure," describes the Spit's evolution as "a dump gone wild, an accidental nature preserve, partly industrial, partly natural, but above all, a huge civic asset."

Today visitors may spot innumerable birds and animals, including some wily coyotes that now roam freely through the park. The Great Egret and more than fifty species of butterfly may be seen, including the Wild Indigo Duskywing and the common Orange Sulphur. As in many areas of the Scarborough Bluffs, the Spit is used as a migratory staging area for thousands of monarch butterflies in late August and early September.

Along with the Northern Saw-whet Owl, other owl species may be found seasonally on the Spit, including Great Horned, Barred, Short-eared and Long-Eared species and from time to time the Snowy Owl as well. Hundreds of migratory bird species, including concentrated migrations of song birds, stop there. The Leslie Street Spit was designated an Important Bird Area (IBA) by Nature Canada and Bird Studies Canada, the Canadian partners of BirdLife International, while another area of the Spit is home to a bird research station operated by the Toronto and Region Conservation Authority.

The Northern Pike has again moved into the area, spawning in the channels near the north side of the Spit, as have other native fish species. Close to 400 plant species have also been identified, many of them nationally, provincially, or regionally rare, including the Prickly Pear Cactus, Ladies' Tresses, Bog Twayblade, and numerous grass species. In fact, Tommy Thompson Park has been designated by the Toronto and Region Conservation Authority as an Environmentally Significant Area, or ESA, with a high degree of plant, fish, and bird diversity as well as the presence of rare species in each of these categories.

While the Spit will never achieve the original marshland glory of its predecessor, Ashbridge's Bay, it is nonetheless a small miracle in its own right. In the face of destruction, an urban wilderness has risen from the ashes.

The little Northern Saw-whet Owl frequents the Leslie Street Spit in winter. This photo was taken during the Toronto annual Christmas bird count.

Jean Iron, member of Friends of the Leslie Street Spit

Along the Shore

CHAPTER THREE

Settlement

The family who gave Asbridge's Bay its name arrived in York shortly after the passing of the Proclamation of 1792, which offered free land to all who were willing to live under the authority of the British Crown. As in the Scarborough shore area, land was available to "American" immigrants from the new republic to the south, including those of Quaker and pacifist persuasions, who were in search of a new start on the north shore of the lake. One such family, headed by the widow Sarah Ashbridge, arrived from Pennsylvania in the fall of 1793 and overwintered at the garrison with Lieutenant Governor Simcoe and his family. The following spring, Sarah Ashbridge, then about sixty years old, along with her children and their families travelled into the wild and isolated land beyond the Don River and settled at the eastern edge of the bay, near present-day Coxwell Avenue and Queen Street. In 1796 the family received land patents for over 700 acres of land that fronted onto the great marsh, among other property.

Legend has it that upon first entering the bay with their boat, a member of their party blew a blast on a large conch shell, later to be used by the family as a dinner horn.

Mrs. Simcoe rendered John Scadding's Cabin *at the Don River in* 1793 AO, F 47-11-1-0-108, Simcoe family fonds, 1973

It is said that thousands of waterfowl took flight at the sound. East of the Don River, there were waterfowl aplenty but few people. William Smith, noted in Adam and Mulvany's history as one of the builders of the lighthouse on Toronto Island, observed prior to the arrival of the Ashbridges on the bay in 1793, on the east bank of the Don, "three Indian wigwams . . . one of which contained the Chief Kashago; the only white settlers then being William Peak and his family," who "had been settled there some time" and "often accompanied General Simcoe on hunting and fishing expeditions."

It is unclear why the Ashbridges took up land so far from the central hub of the garrison and the emerging town near the eastern tip of the bay. One theory is that their desire to hold adjacent parcels of land necessitated the move farther east beyond the Don. We do also know — from the favourable description contained in *Robertson's Landmarks of Toronto* of the Scadding homestead, founded on the east side of the Don River about the same time — that the lands were probably viewed as holding good agri-

Along the Shore

Jesse Ashbridge House, dating fron 1854
.Jane Fairburn

cultural prospects. Lands that fronted on the bay also provided a ready transportation and shipping route for goods and produce to both York and Kingston.

Having already spent four generations in North America, the Ashbridges proved to be highly industrious and successful farmers in their new land along the edge of the bay. Though noting the presence of "some Pennsylvanians" and German settlers east of the Don River in 1794, Mrs. Simcoe paid Mrs. Ashbridge a visit in the winter of 1796, driving out along a rough trail from York.

About sixty years later, Jesse Ashbridge, a grandson of Sarah Ashbridge, erected a house on the original homestead that still stands on Queen Street between Coxwell and Greenwood, at the outer westerly reaches of the present-day Beach community. Up to the late twentieth century, the home was occupied by descendants of the original family, who lived on the property for three centuries collectively — the longest occupation of an original homestead in Toronto. Mrs. Betty Ashbridge Burton was the last resident, her roots on the property going back five generations. Over the generations, the Ashbridge estate was enclosed, to the east and to the west, by the encroachment of Toronto, with the bulk of the land being subdivided in the early twentieth century. As noted in Doroszenko and Latta's "Down by the Bay," during this period, the Ashbridge family made the transition from pioneers to farmers to city dwellers, all the while remaining in their ancestral home.

As in the Scarborough and Lakeshore districts, many early holders of patents for the district we now know as the Beach, among them prominent residents in Upper Canada and York, including military and government officials, never took up residence in the area. One of these early patent holders was Captain J.B. Bouchette, probably a reference to Jean-Baptiste Bouchette, the father of Colonel Joseph Bouchette, who produced the *Plan of Toronto Harbour* in 1792 and the *Plan of York Harbour* in 1815.

———————•———————

BONNYCASTLE'S NOTES ON the *No. 1 Plan of the Town and Harbour of York Upper Canada*, 1833, tell us that some forty years after the arrival of the Ashbridges, a commercial fishery was established on the southern shore of the Peninsula, on what is now Toronto Island. In the decades that followed, other European settlers, like their Aboriginal predecessors, frequented Ashbridge's Bay and the sandbar to hunt and fish, providing Toronto markets, local residents, and businesses alike with a plentiful supply of fish, waterfowl, and other goods, including muskrat, live eels, turtles, cattails (used between barrel staves to stop leakage), and water lilies.

By 1860, George Lang had settled on the eastern end of the Peninsula and is said to have had the first cottage on Woodbine Beach. Lang and his family were commercial fishermen and sold their catch the same day at the markets of downtown Toronto, which they reached by boating through the marsh in dories that they kept at the foot of the beach. Though their story is not widely known, the Lang family played an integral part in the early history of the Beach and the greater history of the Toronto waterfront.

We have scant information on George Lang's earliest years on the eastern sandbar, but a copy of a fishing licence issued in his name does survive, purchased for the sum of five dollars in 1894. The licence allowed Lang the right to fish within the "public waters of Lake Ontario, lying in the vicinity of Kew Beach, near Toronto . . . with 1,000 fathoms of herring gill nets."

While George Lang's commercial fishing operation was centred on Woodbine Beach until about 1910, the Lang family photographs and papers at the Toronto Port Authority

Along the Shore

reveal that he fished the waters off Toronto from Port Union to the Humber River. Given the nature of the family's livelihood, Lang, as well as his children, came to be well acquainted with the greater Toronto shore area.

George and Laura Lang had six daughters and two sons, Hillyard Dixon and Norman Dawson Lang. Both of the sons were avid sportsmen: Norman was an amateur boxer and a trainer for the University of Toronto's hockey and football teams, while Hillyard won many Canadian middleweight and welterweight boxing championships and the North American amateur boxing title. Raised as fishermen, rowing came naturally to the brothers. Following in the footsteps of Ned Hanlan, who was raised on the Island, Hillyard won the Canadian Henley in 1908–09. He and his brother-in-law Bill Crawford also won the North American Doubles Rowing Championship on several occasions.

Despite their athletic achievements, the Langs inevitably pursued careers on the waterfront. Norman's earlier pursuits as a shoemaker and as a fisherman out of Port Union gave way to a position with the Toronto Life Saving and Police Patrol Service at Sunnyside in 1923. Norman was nicknamed "The Bamboo Kid" for his uncanny ability to find drowning victims under water. He remained at Sunnyside until his retirement in 1954 and also supervised the lifesaving boat during the many historic marathon swims in the 1920s and 1930s at the Canadian National Exhibition. These swims, culminating in Marilyn Bell's triumphant lake crossing during the year of Lang's retirement, are discussed in the Lakeshore section of this book.

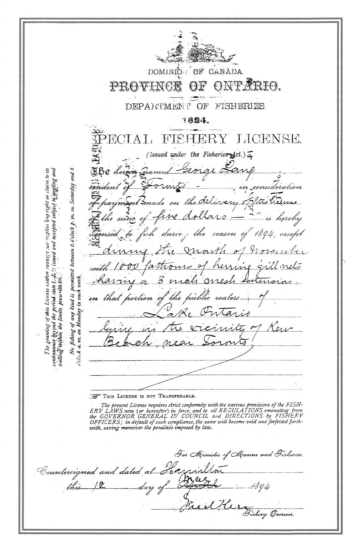

Special fishery licence issued to George Lang, 1894

TPA, SC 40/1

The Beach

The note on the reverse of this image indicates that this handsome schooner was owned jointly by Homer Smith and Norman Lang, c. 1905. Hillyard Lang is third from the far left, and Norman Lang, in the suit, is standing in the middle at the back. The picture was presumably taken in Ashbridge's Bay, near Woodbine Beach. TPA, SC 40/2

Hillyard Lang began his lifesaving career at Ward's Island. He died in 1953 while superintendent of the city's Harbour Police and chief of the Life Saving Station. Described as a man of "dash and daring" and known as "Cap Lang," he participated in many rescues and personally supervised the search for the bodies after the passenger ship the *Noronic* caught fire in Toronto Harbour in 1949, taking 119 lives. It is said that the burning of the ship took a heavy toll on Lang. The brothers were involved in many courageous rescues during their long careers as lifesavers. According to Dawson Lang's "Biographical sketches of Hillyard and Norman Lang," found in the Lang family photographs and papers, one of the rescues involved several occupants of an ice boat that had fallen through Toronto Bay in the dead of night. Due to their understanding of the currents of the Toronto shore, the men knew the location of open patches of water and were able to successfully rescue all but one of the boat's occupants.

Another miraculous nighttime rescue, some years before the deadly events of Hurricane Hazel, involved the Dier family, who were trapped at night on an "island" in the Humber River as the water rose around them. While spectators lined the shore, the

Along the Shore

brothers maneuvered their small boat through congealing ice floes with the help of only a few small flashlights, and pulled the parents and their two small children into the boat. The return trip proved to be even more precarious. The rising ice floes are said to have congealed around the boat, holding it fast and wedging it into the ice. The Langs then put their feet out onto the ice, sought footholds, and inch by inch propelled the boat back toward the shore.

———•———

IN *THE BEACH IN PICTURES*, Mary Campbell and Barbara Myrvold report that by the beginning of the twentieth century, Woodbine Beach was an integral part of a rapidly developing Beach community, boasting at least fifty eclectic clapboard cottages with names like Nufsed, Stay-a-While, and Forty Winks. Numerous makeshift dwellings could also be found there, including at least one streetcar. According to Wayne Reeves in *Regional Heritage Features on the Metropolitan Toronto Waterfront*, fifty-three adults were recorded as living on Woodbine Beach in *Might's Directory* in 1907.

One of George Lang's daughters married into the Charles Wilson ginger ale family of Toronto. Her son, Waverly Wilson, grew up in the Beach and lived on Woodbine Beach for a short period when he was a small child. In an interview in 1982, he recalled that "down at Woodbine Beach, there was no paving or anything, it was all sand. I remember some of my aunts getting married and they'd have a horse and carriage down there, a team horse and carriage and they'd leave in this carriage along the Woodbine dragging all these tins and everything along Woodbine Beach and up Woodbine Ave. and down to the railroad station. But it was quite a struggle for a horse to pull a wagon along that Beach at that time because there wasn't any road as we know a road today."

Generations of early Beach residents remember travelling from the foot of Woodbine Beach to the downtown through Ashbridge's Bay. Waverly Wilson recalls, "My father built an engine and . . . he'd put it in that boat and my mother used to take the boat up the Ashbridge's Bay to the Don and up the Don and tie it at the foot of Winchester Street and walk over to the factory." Commuting downtown from the Beach by boat, though virtually unheard of today, was undoubtedly one way of beating the morning rush in days gone by.

———•———

ALMOST FIFTY YEARS prior to the settlement of the eastern sandbar, John Small acquired lands west of present day Woodbine Avenue near the lake. Campbell and Myrvold indicate that in the years that followed, Small increased his holdings to include a large tract between Woodbine and Coxwell Avenues, bounded by the lake and Danforth Avenue. Small was appointed clerk of the Executive Council of Upper Canada in 1792, justice of the peace at York in 1796, and colonel of the York Militia in 1798. He is best known for the duel he fought on January 3, 1800, with John White, the attorney general, after White had made some disparaging remarks about Small's wife, her moral reputation, and the legality of their marriage. Small mortally wounded White in the duel, and though he was acquitted on a murder charge, he suffered considerable damage to his reputation. In the months and years that followed, he became the Beach's first gentleman farmer, eventually cultivating 472 acres.

His youngest son, Charles Coxwell Small, became clerk of the Crown and pleas for Upper Canada. He also developed his father's lands further, adding sawmills, which probably necessitated the damming of Serpentine Creek that ran through the property. The damming created Small's Pond, located north of the present-day Kingston Road and Queen Street. Until the First World War, Small's Pond was still highly visible; anecdotal evidence suggests that some residents were still fishing there before beginning their morning's commute to work in the city.

———◆·◆———

OTHER EARLY DEVELOPMENT in the larger Beach area was tied to the major east–west thoroughfare between York and Kingston, known as the Kingston Road, which in former days ran to the north of the original boundary of the Beach and then continued west, in the vicinity of present day Queen Street East, toward Toronto. The Kingston Road was the primary stagecoach route between York and Kingston, with small villages appearing along this route well in advance of the development of the lands to the south, nearest the lake.

One such hamlet was the village of Norway, which, according to author Paul McGrath, by 1837 included eighty people, a tollgate near the intersection of the Kingston Road and what is now Woodbine Avenue, a store, a hotel, and a brewery. The Norway Steam Saw Mill was established there in 1835, and the community is said to be named after the stands of red pine or, according to the *Toronto Patriot* of June 1835, "the valuable and scarce article, the Norway Pine."

"St. John the Baptist Norway: The First Quarter Century" states that Charles Coxwell Small donated three acres of land in 1850 for the purposes of building a church and churchyard in the village "to be denominated St. John's Church, Berkeley." A later

Along the Shore

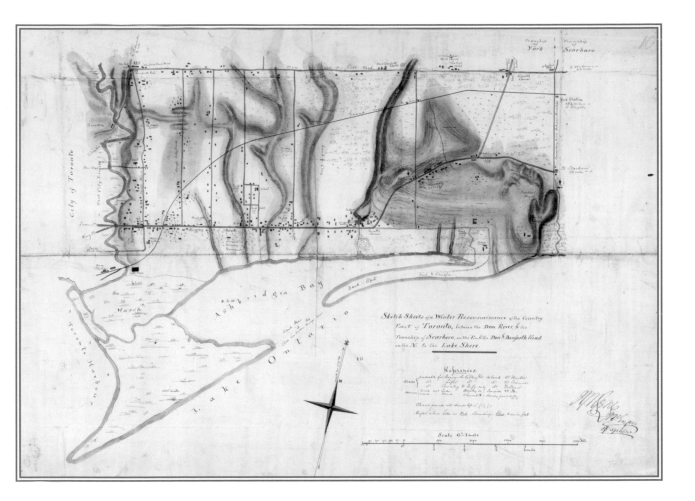

H.J.W. Gehle's Sketch Sheets of a Winter Reconnaissance of the Country E. of Toronto between the Don River; & the Township of Scarboro' on the E. & the Don & Danforth Rd. on the N. to the Lake Shore *is a detailed look at the area east of the City of Toronto, including today's Beach community. It is one of a series of military reconnaissance maps drawn between 1868 and 1869 that gave the military in-depth knowledge of the areas adjacent to the city of Toronto. Starting at the far right, the general trajectory of the Kingston Road appears to be much the same as today, with the village of Norway appearing near present-day Woodbine Avenue.* LAC, R 12567-87-1-E, NMC 20711

church, built in 1893 and now known as St. John the Baptist Norway, still stands at the corner of Kingston Road and Woodbine Avenue.

Sometime after the establishment of Norway, the Toronto Gravel and Concrete Company was begun a little to the east, beyond the hill at Kingston Road and Lee Avenues, which in those days was known as Mount Sullivan, after local inn and tavern proprietor "Gentleman Dan" O'Sullivan. In 1874 approval was given for the company to lay track for horse-pulled tramways along the south side of the Kingston Road, in order to service its gravel pits. The agreement also allowed passenger traffic on the tramways from the Don Bridge to Norway.

The village of Benlamond later took shape at today's Main Street, taking its name from two prominent landowners, Benjamin Morton and James Lamond-Smith. By 1880 these two families resided beside each other on Benlamond Avenue, with a private park to the south. Morton was instrumental in the development of the residential area of Balmy Beach to the southeast of Benlamond on the original lands of Sir Adam Wilson. He also helped bring about the incorporation of the village of East Toronto in 1888. Today's Lyall Avenue is named after his son, Edward Lyall Morton.

"Lost Villages of Norway and Ben Lamond" indicates that Lamond-Smith lived at 57 Benlamond Avenue, a grand three-storey home overlooking the ravine with a spectacular view of the lake. This building and the gardener's cottage at 35 Benlamond are presently two of the oldest surviving residences in the east end of Toronto. With elements of the Italianate and Second Empire styles, 57 Benlamond was erected between 1873 and 1876 for William Stewart Darling, rector of the Church of the Holy Trinity in Toronto. By 1872 Darling had also purchased lands on the south side of the Kingston Road that stretched down to present-day Queen Street.

Although piecemeal development had taken place along the Kingston Road by the mid-nineteenth century, the lands immediately to the south and east at the lake remained largely undeveloped. A large reason for this lay was the geography of the area. The lands near the shore were a little wilderness of marsh and sand, backed by old growth forest and fallen timber.

Joseph Williams, a former sergeant in the Second Battalion of the Rifle Brigade stationed at Toronto along with his wife, Jane, nonetheless ventured into these lands on foot in 1853. Initially acquiring property north of present-day Queen Street that is now in the vicinity of Wineva Avenue, Williamson Road, and Glen Manor Drive, they started a market garden business. According to Campbell and Myrvold, by 1854 they were producing vegetables for market under the Kew Farms label. A mere twelve years prior to Williams's arrival in the Beach in 1853, Kew Gardens, in London, England, was donated to the state and eventually became the Royal Botanic Gardens at Kew (now a UNESCO World Heritage Site).

In the mid-1860s, Joseph Williams added to his original holdings through the acquisition of lands below Queen Street that stretched south and west from what is now the corner of Lee Avenue and Queen Street to Lake Ontario. C.H.J. Snider's column "Roving with the Rover — 3: One 24th of May" describes the property as "twenty-one acres, more or less, of standing and falling timber, marsh, sand and good market garden soil," all of which had to be cleared by Williams and three of his sons, Tom, Joe, and young John (Johnny).

Williams eventually developed the lands south of Queen Street as the "Canadian Kew Gardens." Opened in 1879, it became a seasonal resort, quoted by Campbell and Myrvold as a "pretty pleasure ground of twenty acres, fifteen in bush, fronting on the open lake." Kew Gardens, or the Kew, as Joseph Williams referred to it, operated for more than twenty-five years, offering meals, accommodation for summer boarders, and tents and small camping houses to rent.

—•—

AT THE DAWN OF the twentieth century, the Beach had begun the transition from a summer resort town to a permanent community. Parklands were needed, and the City of Toronto paid Joseph Williams $43,200 for the Kew in 1907. Norah Lawson, the granddaughter of Williams, indicated in an interview in 1975 that her grandfather specified in the sale transaction that there must never be a roadway through Kew Gardens. "I think he was quite farseeing at that time," she stated. "He said that he wanted it for a picnic grounds for families and he didn't want traffic of any kind to go through it which I think is one of the nice things about Kew Gardens."

Today Kew Gardens is a generous grassy stretch of oak and maple leading down to the water, and it is every Beacher's back garden. It is a place for community celebration, for the Jazz Festival and the Canada Day festivities in summer, and for the lighting of the Christmas tree and the Menorah in winter. Year round it is a place for quiet reflection.

The legacy of the Williams family in the Beach extends not just to their pioneer efforts in the development of Kew Farms and later, Kew Gardens. The story of this early Beach family is also intertwined with the marine history of the Great Lakes, primarily through the three sons, who all sailed as lake captains in the commercial shipping industry, both in steamboats and in sailboats.

During the development of Kew Farms and Gardens, the Williams family, like many other families along the waterfront, maintained a family boat that provided additional income through trade and the movement of goods along the shore.

In his "Schooner Days" column "Roving With The Rover — 4: Little Wood Box," Great Lakes historian C.H.J. Snider described how the lumber from Joseph Williams's

Here is C.H.J. Snider's version of The Brothers, *appearing in the* Evening Telegram *in 1933*

Evening Telegram, Schooner Days, February 4, 1933

newly acquired twenty-one acres fronting the lake was chopped into cordwood and loaded onto a skiff and then floated onto their fifty-foot-long flat-bottomed schooner, the *Brig Rover*, at the marshy shore adjacent to the property. Williams, along with his sons, would set out from the beachfront for the wood markets in Toronto, inching their heavily loaded skiff through the Eastern Gap to Brown's Wharf at the foot of Scott Street or Taylor's Wharf at the foot of George Street. Snider reported that by the end of the *Rover*'s fourth year, she had made profits of more than four times her original worth.

Long-time Toronto yachtsman and writer Robert Townsend points out in *When Canvas Was King, Captain John Williams: Master Mariner* that the *Rover* was a "good carrier" and also notes that the Williams family transported other goods in her hold, including sand, foodstuffs, stone, and gravel, though as to her sailing abilities, he writes, "she couldn't sail sour apples against a headwind."

The second Williams family schooner was the *Brothers of Bronte*, sailed by Joe Jr., Tom, and John. Described by John Williams in a February 4, 1933, "Schooner Days" column

Kew Williams House, 2011

Keith Ellis

as a "fine little scow," the ship could carry "ninety tons of dead weight." The *Brothers* transported load deliveries from the north and south shores of the lake, including stone and building supplies. These efforts helped finance the development of the future Kew Gardens. The vessel carried a "home flag" of blue with a white arm and arrow on her foremast. It was not for mere family pride, for as Joseph Williams explained, "At that time it was all bush in the city, but there was a gap between the lake and our cottage, and if we were going up or down the lake I would fly the home flag, and at home they would run one up on shore in answer."

ANOTHER SCHOONER LONG associated with the Williams family was the *Highland Beauty*. It was owned and operated by Tom Williams and was said to have been kept at the foot of Silver Birch Avenue at Harris Boat House, which was built by Captain Johnny Williams. Intended originally to be a steam yacht and finished with a schooner's stern, this attractive ship was characterized as a "stepper" and as having "the habit of getting out in front and staying there." She finished her career as one of the last stonehookers on the lake,

The Beach

dragging the bottom of the water for stone that greatly assisted in the construction of the then burgeoning city of Toronto.

The *Highland Beauty* was also instrumental in construction of a more personal nature; she hauled most of the stone that clads the former residence of Joseph Williams's youngest son, Kew. This romantic stone structure, with a turret and circular staircase, is the only original building still standing in Kew Gardens and was the groom's wedding present to his bride at the turn of the twentieth century. Snider's writings, confirmed by Norah Lawson, indicate that much of the limestone for this structure was obtained from the lake bottom at Waupoose Island (now referred to as Waupoos) in the Bay of Quinte, off the shores of Prince Edward County.

Captain Johnny Williams was the best known of the three Williams brothers who sailed in the commercial shipping trade, then referred to as "the commercial." According to Robert Townsend, he retired past seventy years of age after having been a lake captain for more than half a century and having sailed everywhere from the head of Lake Superior to the Gulf of St. Lawrence. The captain is buried at the previously mentioned St. John the Baptist Norway, along with his parents, Joseph and Jane, and other members of his family.

Marjorie Howard relied on some of the personal reminiscences of the captain and his younger brother, Kew, in "The History of the Beaches District," 1938. This brief handwritten text paints a picture of the small farming community that had emerged there by about 1865, noting that at this time there were still only twelve houses in the district, with "Queen Street just a country trail with stumps of trees in its midst." During this period, Queen Street was almost impassable in some sections, with three hills between Wineva and Woodbine Avenues as well as an extensive swamp that extended "from the point where Hammersmith Avenue and Glen Manor Road meet, to the bowling green at Kew Gardens."

Though the Williams family was quite successful, their neighbours to the west, the Scantlons, lived in little more than a shanty. As Howard writes, "The animals and Mr. and Mrs. Scantlon all lived together in the same house. When the pigs were turned into hams they hung them up in a tiny smoke house and both Mr. and Mrs. Scantlon would smoke clay pipes to smoke the hams." Howard notes the presence of other farmers in the district, including Mr. Jemason and Mr. O'Neil, "the prison inspector."

In 1853, the same year that the Williams family found their way into the area, Sir Adam Wilson, then a distinguished lawyer, acquired part of Lots 1 and 2, including the broken fronts, and established his country estate. In 1876 Wilson subdivided his prop-

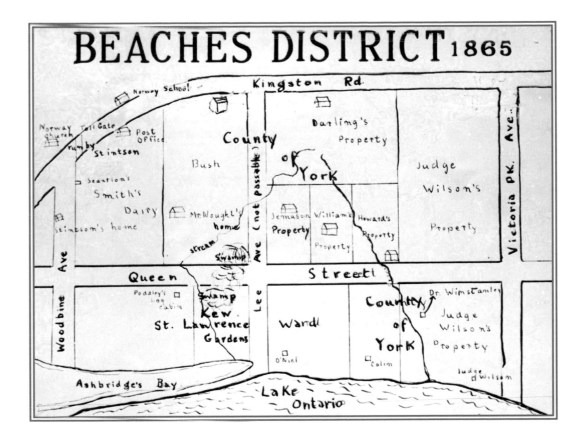

The following text labels appear on the hand-drawn map:

BEACHES DISTRICT 1865

Kingston Rd.
Norway School
Norway Church
Toll Gate
rumby
St. intson
Post Office
Scanlon's
Smith's Dairy
stimbson's home
Bush
Mr Nought's home
County of York
Darling's Property
Judge Wilson's Property
Victoria Pk. Ave.
stream
Swamp
Ave (not passable)
Jennason Property
Williams Property
Howard's Property
Property
Queen Street
Woodbine Ave
Poddley's log cabin
Swamp
Kew St. Lawrence Gardens
Lee Ave
Ward
O'Niel
County of York
Colin
Dr. Wimstanley
Judge Wilson's Property
Judge d Wilson
Ashbridge's Bay
Lake Ontario

This hand-drawn map harkens back to the earliest days of the Beach district in 1865

AO, Hand-drawn map of Toronto Beaches, S11565

erty, and reserved a private promenade near the lake for "the common use and enjoyment" of the residents. The result was the erection of the Balmy Beach Club, which survives as a fixture of the Beach community. A few years after acquiring these lands, Wilson became Toronto's first popularly elected mayor. Eventually becoming Chief Justice of the Court of Queen's Bench, he retired in 1887, and was knighted.

A little to the west of Judge Wilson was former Toronto mayor George Monro, who in 1847 established his country residence on sixty and a half acres south of the Kingston Road, including the broken front, known as Painted Post Farm. There he operated an orchard with more than 400 fruit trees as well as three acres of strawberries. In the waning days of the nineteenth century, part of the land was leased to the Toronto Railway Company for an amusement park.

The Beach also saw a seasonal influx of Toronto's rapidly growing middle class, which, with its newly acquired leisure time and disposable income, began to be drawn

The Beach

"In a way, it was like a small town. We've always had a pretty big Mick population. Father McGraw was down at Corpus Christi and he used to hear confessions for all the jockeys. So we used to ask him what was good for the fifth race . . ." — *Ted Reeve, long-time Beach resident, athlete, and sports journalist on the Woodbine* TPL, PC636

to the outlying areas along the shore, the Beach, and other waterfront locales, including the Island, the Lakeshore, and the Scarborough shore. These special places, still largely untouched by human development, were tremendously appealing for people who longed for a day in the country and respite from the city heat.

The first major draw to the Beach was a wildly successful racetrack, known as Woodbine Park or, simply, the Woodbine, whose origins date to October 19, 1875, with the "inaugural meeting of the Woodbine Riding and Driving Park." The Woodbine, which included a trotting and running track that bordered Ashbridge's Bay, was situated between what is now Woodbine and Coxwell Avenues and was formerly part of a larger acquisition made by Joseph Duggan from the previously mentioned Small family some five years earlier. Louis Cauz, in *The Woodbine 1875–1993*, mentions that visitors could access the track "by steamship or pleasure craft to the nearby docks." The park, to which a clubhouse and stables for a large number of horses were added by 1885, was also opened in conjunction with the availability of the previously mentioned Toronto Street Railway Company's horse-drawn trams. The cars arrived every half hour, reportedly carrying passengers to Toronto within twenty minutes. A description in Adam and Mulvany's history of the Woodbine Hotel, which accommodated visitors to the Park from the city, states, "The hotel is beautifully situated, and commands a fine view of Toronto and Lake Ontario, and comfortably accommodates upwards of thirty guests."

The track, though at times sloppy and in a perennial state of disrepair due to its proximity to Ashbridge's Bay, provided the venue for the Queen's Plate in 1876, the year after it opened. During the Woodbine's 119-year history, it became one of the premier centres for horseracing in North America and hosted the running of the King and Queen's Plate continuously for more than seventy years. King George VI and Queen Elizabeth were in attendance for the running of the King's Plate in 1939, with the cup and prize.

More than eighty years after the Woodbine's inauguration, the New Woodbine Racetrack opened in Rexdale in 1956. The original Woodbine was renamed Old Woodbine, so as not to be confused with the Rexdale track. In 1963 the name was changed once more, to Greenwood, to again avoid confusion with the Rexdale track. In 1963 one of Canada's greatest thoroughbreds, Northern Dancer, raced at the track.

Another early event that garnered massive attention was Buffalo Bill's Wild West Show, a circus-like attraction that featured "Indians" in traditional dress, cowboys, buffalo, guns, and re-enactments of various features of the settlers' experience in the American West. The popularity of this show in the late nineteenth century in North America and beyond cannot be overstated. On August 22, 24, and 25, 1885, the show came to the Woodbine and featured the renowned markswoman Annie Oakley and the great Sioux chief Sitting Bull.

The Lang family, who lived directly to the south of the Woodbine, just off the shore on Woodbine Beach, are said to have had some involvement with the entertainers during their time at the park. Legend has it that George Lang took Annie Oakley and Buffalo Bill out in his boat, where Annie shot snipe with a rifle. Later, she is said to have taken tea with Mrs. Lang on the sandbar directly to the south of the park.

——— • ———

BY THE LATE TWENTIETH CENTURY, business interests were becoming increasingly interested in the development potential of Greenwood Racetrack, and on December 31, 1993, the lights went out on the track forever. Soon the clubhouse was demolished and

The Beach

the track paved over to make way for a new series of residences and parklands that would in future years be amalgamated with the larger Beach community. Still, the Old Woodbine, or Greenwood, holds a formidable place in the imaginations of many older Beach residents. It was the forerunner to the amusement park era that would define the Beach community for decades to come.

CHAPTER FOUR
A Resort Town

With the influx of day trippers into Woodbine Park, the stage was set for the beginning of a new era in the Beach, one that would see the opening of various other pleasure gardens and amusement parks. Though the earliest of these incarnations lacked the excitement of the modern midway and were virtually unrecognizable in comparison to our present-day Disney World and Wonderland extravaganzas, they were, nonetheless, the grand social venues of their time, where ladies in parasols and gentlemen in top hats strolled along the promenade on the beach while their children frolicked in the water offshore.

Victoria Park, established in 1878 and situated near the southeasterly end of present-day Victoria Park Avenue in the Beach, was such a place. In the early years, no street railway service existed to the park — the most popular mode of transportation was therefore the steamers that departed from the downtown docks of the Toronto Harbour.

Upon arrival, patrons could partake in popular diversions of the Victorian era, including a multi-storey leaning lookout tower at the northerly edge of the property. It was

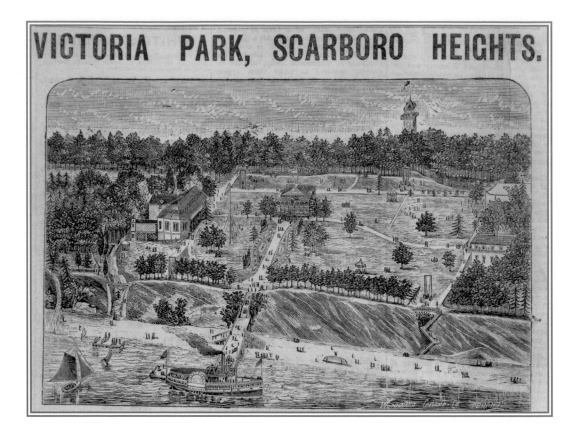

VICTORIA PARK, SCARBORO HEIGHTS.

nicknamed the Sway for its tendency to move with the wind. According to Barbaranne Boyer's *The Boardwalk Album*, it provided excellent views of the lake and the surrounding Beach countryside, until it was toppled by a tremendous storm and never replaced.

One of the main features of the park was, according to Marjorie Howard, a "quaint rustic pavilion" where dances were held. Sir John A. Macdonald reportedly made a six-hour speech, which was sent by wireless transmission across Canada, at the park in 1878.

One year after the opening of Victoria Park, Joseph Williams had successfully developed his lands, which reached down to the marshy waterfront near the edge of Ashbridge's Bay, as a seasonal resort and recreational area for city dwellers wanting to escape to a simpler life in the country. Kew Gardens then became a summer resort, a place where city folk could camp by the lake or take advantage of the overnight accommodations on site and enjoy cooked meals made in large measure from the garden's produce, not to speak of "innocent amusements in great variety, including dancing,"

according to a brochure that advertised the park in the nineteenth century.

"Linger-Longer," pictured above, was one in a row of cottages that fronted onto Kew Beach

With the presence of the well-established Kew Gardens and Victoria Park, and the extension of the Toronto Street Railway Company's tramway east to Lee Avenue in 1889, visitors now flocked to the Beach by the thousands each summer. During this period, many hotels and rooming houses were established in the area to cater to the summer visitors. One of the earliest was the Scarboro' Heights Hotel Co., in the vicinity of Beech Avenue and the Kingston Road, which opened in 1879. Though it has not survived, we can see glimpses of the era in the renovated Alexandra Hotel Annex, now a private residence, located near Balsam Avenue below Queen Street. Pieces of another structure, Pine Terrace, though now extensively renovated, may be found north of Queen Street near Beech Avenue. Pine Terrace was part of a larger summer hotel called the Pines. Long-time Beach resident Olga Marie Porter Commins describes the Pines in *Ward 9 News* as having "verandas all around the first and second floors, and a tennis court on the south. . . . Guests came over to the main building for meals, and you could hear the big dinnerbell ringing three times a day."

155

The Beach

Distinct from the hotels and amusement parks, a summer cottage community was firmly established in the Beach by the last decade of the nineteenth century. Like the Lakeshore in the west and, to an extent, the Scarborough shore in the east, the summer cottage colony presaged the development of further suburban growth along the lakefront. Legendary athlete and sportswriter Ted Reeve remembers in *More Beach Reminuisances* the row of cottages at the lake he knew as a child, which extended from east of Leuty Avenue to the tip of Woodbine Beach before they were expropriated to make way for the continuous boardwalk and Beaches Park, established in 1932. With names like Linger-Longer and the Merry Widower, these were holiday places "in the old summer resort style, and housing groups of lively men who lived a happy life, sailing, canoeing, singing, swimming and such, and they came home from the city each night; doing their own cooking too much, to the added prosperity of the beach butchers. We would sit on the little boardwalk outside these carefree habitations until it was time to report home for bed and it was there we developed our liking for 'summer cottage piano' or the sound of an old victrola or a mandolin being played somewhere out on the lake in a canoe."

A little farther east were Balmy Avenue's summer residents, who organized idyllic evenings of their own. As the *Globe* reported in August 1901: "The weekly hop of the Balmy Beach Recreation Association was held last night at 'Bohemia,' Balmy avenue, . . . and proved a most successful affair. . . . Rows of Chinese lanterns were strung around the spacious verandah. Light refreshments were served by the ladies during the evening." According to the "Balmy Beach Heritage Conservation District Study: Balmy Avenue," the street also sported a small hotel, Shandylands.

Tenting had also become a popular option in the last decades of the nineteenth century, primarily geared to the vacationer who wished to stay for a number of weeks, or even months, in the Beach during the summer. In the Beach and throughout the other waterfront jurisdictions, including the Island, landowners constructed solid platforms near the waterfront to accommodate large canvas structures capable of housing an entire family. Campbell and Myrvold point out that by the summer of 1900, the Beach's overall summer tenting community exceeded that of the Island's, with ninety-one tents reportedly established on the lakefront east of Woodbine Avenue according to the *Toronto World*.

Even a non-denominational summer tent church was started in about 1894, located on the south side of Queen Street near Balsam Avenue. This structure was described in *Robertson's Landmarks of Toronto* as "supported on tall cedar pillars, stripped of their bark, and there are none other than canvas walls. . . . There is no boarded floor, simply loose tan bark on the ground . . . Handsome oil lamps are suspended from the open roof, and

Along the Shore

these during August and September have always to be lighted for at least a portion of the service." Regardless of the temporary nature of the structure, the church community, like the Beach itself, was built on firm foundations that would last. Saint Aidan's Anglican Church has remained a pillar of the Beach community for many generations.

While the amusement parks were the early drivers that brought throngs of visitors to the Beach, the lake remained a major draw to day trippers and summer cottagers alike. In an interview in 1967, Mrs. Alice Keys recalled the swimming ritual that was endured by every child prior to getting into the water at the Beach:

> Down the hill we went, my sister and I, in scratchy luster bathing suits, bloomers attached to a blouse with sailor collar (always the British naval touch), skirt of decent length, stockings were held up by round elastic garters, always too tight, one usually missing, and running shoes. . . . These immodest garments were well and truly concealed beneath heavy old raincoats, buttoned right up. Going down the hill was bad enough, but the climb up was Turkish bath torture. But it was worth it — clean water — cold indeed, but a good stretch of clean hot sand to warm us — which always involved one more dip to rinse.

Around Labour Day weekend, the mass exodus to the city began, with the children taking their final luxurious dips in the lake before returning to school and the city on the other side of the Don River. As the tents were folded up and the shutters nailed down on the summer cottages, the Beach returned to its full-time residents who were, despite the lack of continuous streetcar service on Queen Street, steadily increasing in number by the last decade of the nineteenth century.

These girls, though on the sandbar at Fisherman's Island farther west, were certainly enjoying the warm near-shore waters of the lake, c. 1907
CTA, Γ1244_it0177

The Beach

Glen Stewart Ravine, 1912

CTA, S372_ss53_it40

A SIGNIFICANT, ALBEIT SMALLER, group of Toronto's wealthy also enjoyed the Beach district during the summer resort period. A few spacious wooden clapboard homes constructed in the New England tradition during this era still stand in the community. One such residence is Pine Crest, which dates from 1902 and was designed, according to Gene Domagala in "A History Tour of the Beach," by well-known architect Charles Frederick Wagner, who also designed Inglenook, located on Waverly Road in the Beach. After Adam Wilson subdivided his Balmy Beach property in 1876, a more affluent group of wooden clapboard cottages was also eventually erected near the lake on Balsam Avenue. Other elegant homes include the former residence of Henry P. Eckardt on Fallingbrook Road as well as, nearby, the more elaborate Château des Quatre Vents on Rockaway Crescent.

One of the most impressive estates during the latter years of the nineteenth century and the early twentieth century was undoubtedly Glen Stewart, a name that is still attached to the formerly mentioned ravine that runs from the Kingston Road down to Queen Street in the Beach. Glen Stewart was begun by the Reverend William Stewart Darling, an Anglican priest. Darling had ministered to several country parishes within the Township of Scarborough between 1843 and 1853 before becoming the rector of

Church of the Holy Trinity in Toronto. In 1872 he and his wife, Jane, acquired lands south of the Kingston Road to which he quickly added other property and built the gracious estate known as Glen Stewart. Darling's son Frank, a renowned architect, sold the property in 1900 to Alfred Ernest Ames, a Toronto stockbroker who for many years generously allowed the community to use the grounds, ponds, and trails that wound through the delightful country property.

The Glen Stewart estate still stands just south of Kingston Road on Glen Stewart Crescent, though it was later altered and divided into apartments, as were many of the larger Beach residences, after the resort era at the Beach ended and the area transitioned into a full-time community early in the twentieth century. By 1923 the estate lands were already well under development by the Provident Investment Company, which developed the area as a higher-end garden suburb. Despite the intense building that occurred in the earlier part of the twentieth century, a portion of the original grounds of the property remain in the heavily oak- and pine-forested Glen Stewart Ravine, which was originally identified by the Toronto and Region Conservation Authority as an Environmentally Significant Area (ESA) in 1982.

Another impressive estate built in the early twentieth century was Sir Donald Mann's Fallingbrook. Ted Reeve, in comparing the forest of Glen Stewart to Fallingbrook, noted that, "Mann's Bush, was deeper and wilder, almost weird in its further recesses, along the top of the great bluffs that start to ascend at Fallingbrook." The estate of Alan McLean Howard, located in the vicinity of today's Queen Street and MacLean Avenue, was also noteworthy for its pond adjacent to Queen Street, replete with swans and Peking ducks. Though its grounds have virtually disappeared, it is said that the impression of the pond may partially be seen (and a glimpse of the past imagined) in the gully that remains at Queen Street and Glen Manor Drive.

<hr>

THE ELEGANT RETREAT properties of Toronto's upper class played a small but significant role in the story of the Beach in the nineteenth and early twentieth centuries. By the 1890s, while the Ameses and Howards of the Beach surveyed their manicured lawns from sheltered porches, the middle and lower classes got on the electric streetcar and travelled east to the amusement parks. In 1896 the heirs of the former Toronto mayor and gentleman farmer George Monro leased the most southerly portion of the property to William Mackenzie's Toronto Railway Company (TRC) for the development of an amusement park. In the coming years, patrons were brought directly into Munro

Open car and trailer, Munro Park line, c. 1900

CTA/TTC F16_s71_it3379

Park by the addition in 1898 of a stump line that ran along Queen Street in the summer months. Until 1907, crowds of Torontonians gathered at Munro Park for vaudeville shows as well as many other attractions, including an enormous 150-foot Ferris wheel, moving pictures, and a large performance stage that in 1901 seated 5,000 people. The grounds of Munro Park were eventually developed as a small subdivision of homes, designed primarily in the arts and crafts tradition. With a beautiful tree canopy and splendid views of the lake, Munro Park Avenue remains one of the most idyllic residential streets in Toronto.

The introduction of continuous, though spotty, electric street railway service to Munro Park in 1898 meant that, for the first time, all of Queen Street was accessible to the general public during the summer months. With that came the notion that it was possible to work in one jurisdiction and live in another. Like the Lakeshore district farther to the west, street railways encouraged large-scale permanent settlement in the Beach. In the years that followed, the Beach would become one of Toronto's early street-car suburbs.

BY THE FIRST DECADE of the new century, a series of permanent districts and villages had emerged from the summer resort communities and pleasure grounds that had begun decades earlier. Woodbine

Beach was the farthest west, with Kew Beach in the middle, situated around the Williams family's holdings, and Balmy Beach in the east, built on Sir Adam Wilson's former estate and other lands adjacent to that property.

The Beach's transition to a full-time community actually came about through a slow, piecemeal process rather than a purposeful design. First, part-time summer residents who decided to stay winterized their whimsical frame cottages, adding plumbing and heating when they could afford them. More affluent Beachers bought multiple lots and built their own home and often two or three more that they sold off as demand increased for year-round properties. Small and large-scale land developers built up the remaining land, as in the case of the Glen Stewart estate.

Campbell and Myrvold indicate that by the turn of the century, Kew Beach had its own post office and a stated population of 250 families, while Balmy Beach, farther to the east, claimed 150 families in 1899. These two areas were becoming quite competitive, with rivalries playing out in sporting events focused squarely on the lake and the out-doors: sailing, rowing, swimming, and lawn bowling in the summer, and curling, hockey, and skating in the winter. In the first decade of the new century, both Kew and Balmy Beaches constructed their own clubhouses at the lakefront.

In an interview in 1982, Waverly Wilson describes the two Beach areas: "Kew Beach was like a foreign section to Balmy Beach. They were two separate towns. Leuty Ave. divided it. Even the money was different here than it was there. They were very jealous about their area."

With a sizable number of residents living year-round in the Beach by 1900, there was an increasing need for services. In the early decades of the century, fire halls, recreation centres, libraries, and places of worship were erected, many of which are still present in the community today. With most people living in wooden houses, a number of Kew Beach residents formed a volunteer fire brigade as early as 1891. In 1906 Kew Beach got its new Firehall No.17. City architect Robert McCallum designed it in the Queen Anne revival style, and it is said that local carpenters and masons, some of who lived on Lee Avenue, built it. As Barbaranne Boyer notes, old-time residents remember the horses that drew the water tank being exercised at the back of the station off Herbert Avenue right up to the 1930s.

Kew Beach Fire Hall, 2011 Keith Ellis

In later years, the fire hall's tower roof served as the local community hall and rooming house for the bats of the area. They flocked out at dusk to pay nocturnal visits to the residents of Herbert Avenue, not in huge numbers but enough to be a bit of a nuisance in summer when bedroom windows were open.

Today, the Kew Beach Fire Hall is one of the more popular excursions for local school children. Teachers and children alike marvel at the two-storey floor-to-ceiling brass pole,

Along the Shore

the wall-mounted fire bell, and the narrow staircase that leads you to the clock tower, which affords excellent views of the area. Carved into and scrawled over the walls of the clock tower are the names of the fire fighters who for generations have watched over the Beach.

Another major addition to the communities of Woodbine, Kew, and Balmy Beach was the Beaches Branch Library, which opened in 1916. This library was one of three libraries in Toronto designed by architect Eden Smith. Designed in the arts and crafts tradition, the library and its Wychwood and High Park counterparts are often described as being in the English cottage tradition, given their quaint exteriors that recall the collegiate grammar schools of seventeenth-century England. The library was, however, quite progressive in its day, being, as Mary Campbell and Barbara Myrvold point out in *A Walking Tour of Kew Beach*, one of the first libraries in Toronto designed to permit public access to the stacks. The Beaches library, complete with a fireplace on the second floor, survives and is well remembered by many long-time Beach residents, including one of Canada's premier film directors, Norman Jewison, who was raised in the Beach in the 1930s and early 1940s. In a 2009 interview, Jewison told me, "It was the only library that I can remember where there was a fireplace. It was so cozy and warm and intimate. When I was six or seven years old I used to go to the library. I remember the kids all sitting in a circle with somebody, I guess the librarian, reading, introducing us to books. The atmosphere was unlike any library I've ever been in since . . . there used to be a roaring fire there in the winter and it was so sweet."

ELEVEN YEARS PRIOR to the opening of the library, Balmy Beach got its own clubhouse on land Sir Adam Wilson had set aside as a private promenade for Balmy Beach residents. In 1903 a provincial act passed by the legislature of Ontario designated the land as Balmy Beach Park: a "place of recreation" essentially for residents, and visitors to the town of East Toronto. (A significant portion of the area of the present-day Beach community, including the private promenade, fell within the jurisdiction of East Toronto, and was not officially part of the city of Toronto until 1908. The lands farther east, between East Toronto and the Township of Scarborough, were annexed in 1909.) A board of management was also established to oversee Balmy Beach Park that continues to this day. A separate executive governs the affairs of the clubhouse, which was constructed in 1905.

Over its more than 100-year history, the Balmy Beach Club (BBC) has been razed by fire and rebuilt twice and holds claim to the being one of the oldest surviving community institutions in the Beach. Today the BBC is run as a not-for-profit organization and is

the hub of community, social, and sporting events in the Beach. Norman Jewison fondly remembers the club and recalls it as "a centre of teenage activity — where everybody wanted to be." Since its inception, the BBC has been at the forefront of the development of amateur sports in Toronto.

In its golden years in the first half of the twentieth century, it produced several Olympic paddlers, including the legendary Roy Nurse, who captured two gold and four silver medals at the 1924 Olympics in Paris. The Balmy Beach Club has sent competitors to seven different Olympics in all and won the Grey Cup twice, before the latter was the purview of solely professional athletes. More recently, the men's rugby team has won eleven Ontario championships since 1968. The BBC has also made a major contribution to beach volleyball in Canada: coach John May and athlete Mark Heese won a bronze medal at the Atlanta Olympics in 1996.

The ladies teams have also fared very well, with Glenna Boston and Doreen Creaney winning the Canadian championship in ladies doubles lawn bowling in 2008. In 1999 Doreen Creaney went on to win the Canadian ladies' singles bowling. In 2011 club member K.C. Fraser won gold in the K4 five-hundred-meter kayak race at the Pan American Games.

Ted Reeve, who was instrumental in capturing the 1930 Grey Cup for Balmy Beach in spite of a broken collarbone, is said to have created the slogan "Dance Where the Balmy Breezes Blow" during the big-band era at the BBC. With names like Red Humphries, Red Heron, and Jimmie Sinitan appearing at the club, dances ten cents a piece out under the stars, and the canoes snugged tightly away under the dance floor, it soon became one of the hottest dance spots in Toronto. The BBC even created its own dance, the Balmy, a slower, sultrier version of the two-step.

THOUGH THE BALMY BEACH CLUB earned a great deal of attention with its sporting heroes and flashy musical guests, nothing is more symbolic of the Beach than the Leuty Lifeguard Station. Designed in 1920, it is a simple clapboard cottage with a cedar-shingled roof and lookout tower and rests on the beach at the foot of Leuty Avenue. It was designed by the Toronto architectural firm of Chapman and Oxley, the same architects that designed the Sunnyside Bathing Pavilion, the Palais Royale and the Princes' Gates at the CNE — grandiose designs that only amplify the station's sweet simplicity.

The Leuty building was not unlike other lifesaving stations that dotted the busy Toronto shoreline at the beginning of the twentieth century. The Cherry Beach Lifeguard Station (now renovated), to the west of the Beach community, was in fact built to the same specifications as the Leuty facility. Rather than being left to rot away in obscurity, as were so many of the other stations, the Leuty station was designated a historical site in 1993 and was restored through a vigorous community fundraising campaign.

Leuty Lifeguard Station, 2006 Jane Fairburn

About the same time that the Leuty Lifeguard Station was designed came the Beach Hebrew Institute. Walk south on Kenilworth Avenue at Queen Street toward the water and you will find it there, established to meet the needs of a small, vibrant Jewish community that had been in the Beach since the late nineteenth century. According to "Toronto's First Synagogues: The Beach Hebrew Institute," "The synagogue played a central role in helping Jewish residents of that area feel a sense of community." During this early period in the Beach, Jewish residents were among the tailors, pharmacists, storekeepers, and even tavern keepers that contributed to the evolution of the permanent community.

The building on Kenilworth initially fronted onto Queen Street and actually began life as a Baptist church, but that congregation outgrew the facilities and vacated the property before 1910. In 1920 the premises were moved south onto Kenilworth and remodelled in the style of a small synagogue, or shul, reminiscent of those in the villages of Eastern Europe. The Institute, now commonly referred to as the Beach Synagogue, is one of the oldest synagogues in Toronto and was designated a historic site in 1982. Though the number of Jewish families in the Beach sharply declined in the late 1930s and 1940s, and then again in the 1960s, the shul never closed its doors. It experienced a resurgence in the 1970s, and as late as 1970 it was the only synagogue east of the Don River within the old city boundary. The Institute is highly valued within the Beach community, so much so that its former president, Arie Nerman, was named the Beach Citizen of the Year in 2005.

The Beach Synagogue, formally the Beach Hebrew Institute, 2011 Keith Ellis

EVEN AS THE YEAR-ROUND community took hold, day trippers continued to pour into the area, with the opening of the largest and most successful of all the Beach amusement parks, Scarboro' Beach. Scarboro' Beach Amusement Park was formally opened on Saturday, June 1, 1907, on the lands bounded by Leuty and MacLean Avenues and the lake. This property was previously the House of Providence Farm, owned and operated by the Sisters of St. Joseph. The farm supplied dairy and produce for the sisters' downtown House of Providence, established in 1857 to serve the needy, poor, and elderly. After selling their property in the Beach to the president of Toronto Park Co., Harry A. Dorsey, and his wife, Mabell, the sisters re-established their community and agricultural operations at present-day St. Clair and Warden Avenues. Today the site is known as Providence Healthcare, a geriatric and rehabilitation centre.

In 1913 the Toronto Railway Company took over the Scarboro' Beach Amusement Park that had been developed on the sisters' old farm. Until its closure in 1925, it was the grandest and longest running of all the parks in the Beach, opened fifteen years before the well-known Sunnyside Amusement Park, located on Lake Ontario at the foot of Roncesvalles Avenue east of the Humber River. With its Coney Island atmosphere, midway, athletic fields, dance halls, and throngs of visitors, the *Evening Telegram* reported that Scarboro' Beach had a record-breaking attendance of 32,000 people on August 15, 1920.

The park had a decidedly spicier flavour than some of the Victorian parks that had preceded it. Included in the attractions were shows that featured simulated natural disasters, including the San Francisco earthquake of 1906, and a burlesque show featuring the Tipperary Girls. It was even a honeymoon destination for

Crowd at the Scarboro' Beach Park midway, 1907
CTA, F1244_it0149

those pressed for time and money. Remembering this, resident Waverly Wilson quipped, "I've heard of people getting married in Toronto and going down to Scarboro' Beach and spending the day for their honeymoon and going back and starting in to work. One trip through the tunnel of love and the swings and they've had it."

From the living room where she had been born some ninety years earlier, lifelong Beach resident Edna Houston chuckled as she reminisced about breaking into Scarboro' Beach Park with her friends on the days when the grounds were closed. She recalled climbing under the lifeboat ramp at Little Leuty (Leuty Lifeguard Station) and the illicit thrill of running through the boarded-up concessions. There the youngsters climbed the steps to the top of the Bumps, an enormous slide of polished wood, and flung themselves over the crest of the slide into the darkness. Soon after that they would run home through the Leuty Forest to Lee Avenue, which was still no more than a series of wooden boards over broken earth.

During the years of the First World War, the Beach community closed down on Sundays but relaxed the rules in the evenings, when the children were taken in their Sunday best to hear live concerts at Scarboro' Beach. Courting couples routinely listened to the big bands off Scarboro' Beach from their plush canoes, complete with electric light and which were, according to Waverly Wilson, "varnished up to the hilt, a nice red carpet down the middle, . . . and cushions for the girls to sit on." Much anticipated was the nine o'clock swell, when the *Cayuga* and *Chippewa* steamers entered the Eastern Gap from Niagara, their wakes creating waves that rocked the boats while the band played on.

———————— • ————————

THE VILLAGES OF Woodbine, Kew, and Balmy Beach were entirely different places in winter, especially during the first two decades of the twentieth century. Once the influx of Toronto "tourists" had abated in September, these places reverted to the permanent residents, many of whom were from the working class. Times were hard, especially during the First World War and the years that followed. During this time, it was not uncommon for Beach residents, like other Torontonians, to hold down several jobs at a time out of financial necessity. J.M.S. Careless, in *Toronto to 1918: An Illustrated History*, writes that between 1915 and 1919, inflation soared to more than fifty per cent while the cost of food climbed by nearly seventy-five per cent.

Toronto's contribution to the First World War was immense. Approximately 70,000 of the city's men joined the forces, which constituted the weight of the younger adult male population. Participation in the war effort from the Beach was at least as high as in other jurisdictions in the city, with many students and graduates from the local high school, Malvern Collegiate Institute, enlisting. According to an article in the *Malvern Collegiate Institute Centennial Book*, about 122 students and graduates of the school signed up, including one of their teachers, Mr. Wood. Of those who enlisted, more than one in five were lost in the war.

With the local men already sacrificed in great numbers to the killing fields of Ypres and Vimy Ridge, the numbers of widows and fatherless children were mounting almost daily. There were also the shortages, particularly of coal, the price of which skyrocketed so much so that many folks simply could not keep themselves warm through the unusually cold winter of 1917–18. Some of those people huddled together under blankets through the long winter nights as the wind cut through their homes, many of which were no more than clapboard cottages.

These dire circumstances attracted the attention of Dr. William D. Young, an Ottawa-born family physician who made his home in the Beach. He administered to the rich and poor alike, but it was for his service during the dark days of the war that he is best remembered — as the hero who stayed home.

He is known to have ordered coal to the homes of poor families at his personal expense. Ten dollars was left under the pillow of a sick child when Dr. Young discovered that the family could not afford food — a simple act of kindness in a war-weary world. Families who never received a bill from the doctor and who could pay began sending him victory bonds to contribute to the war effort.

Local lore attributes Dr. Young's own death in early January 1918 to the influenza pandemic that swept the world at the end of the First World War, claiming at least twenty million lives — vastly more than were lost in the war itself. However, a report from the Toronto medical officer of health confirms

Dr. William D. Young Memorial, designed by Maurice D. Klein in 1919, as it appears today

Keith Ellis

The Beach

that the influenza did not strike this city until October, eight months after the doctor's demise, and his death certificate clearly indicates that he died of acute nephritis.

Although he had been virtually unknown to the rest of Toronto, the entire Beach community shut down on the day of his funeral and lined the streets to St. John the Baptist Norway's cemetery in honour of him, not for his medical advancements or scientific breakthroughs but for his overwhelming capacity for goodness. Within days of his passing, the community's grief inspired a move to recognize his deeds with a fountain and statue in his memory. Designed by the architect Maurice D. Klein, it was unveiled two years after the doctor's death before a throng of 2,000 people. At the dedication ceremony, Mayor Tommy Church said that Dr. Young had, in his life, displayed "the spirit of a divine healer" and assured, "His memory will live in the hearts of the people of the Beaches and of Toronto."

You will still find his memorial among the maples near the east entrance to Kew Park, just off the side of Lee Avenue. Framed at the heart of the Italianate stone structure stands the statue of a child, honouring a healer and a hero from some of Toronto's darkest years.

<hr />

AFTER THE END of the First World War, Scarboro' Beach Amusement Park continued, though with dwindling numbers after the opening of the popular Sunnyside Amusement Park in the Lakeshore, in the city's west end, in 1922. At the end of its summer season in 1925, Scarboro' Beach closed for the final time, signalling the end of the resort era at the Beach.

In September 1926, the *Toronto Daily Star* ran an advertisement for a new residential subdivision to be located on the former grounds of the Scarboro' Beach Amusement Park: "The old Scarboro Beach Amusement area . . . 25 minutes on Beach cars to Yonge St.; on the lake with the finest stretch of beach around Toronto . . . right in the city with all the improvements, but with the desirable features of a beautiful suburban district. You remember how nice it was down there; now see it with its wide streets and attractive new homes."

By the early part of the 1930s, Scarboro' Beach was only a memory, having made way for housing that extended down to Hubbard Boulevard near the lake, linking the otherwise psychologically distant worlds of Balmy and Kew Beaches. Likewise, the majority of the district's streams had been buried underground and the ponds drained, including Small's Pond. In 1932 a continuous waterfront park was opened, necessitating the

Along the Shore

removal of 211 cottages and an unspecified number of boathouses from the lakefront. According to Ted Reeve in *Beach Reminuisances*, some of these dwellings were simply removed from their foundations and floated over to Hanlan's Point, where they began a new life on the Island. With the Beach's resort past literally floating away, the transition to a full-time community, steeped in history and charm, was now complete.

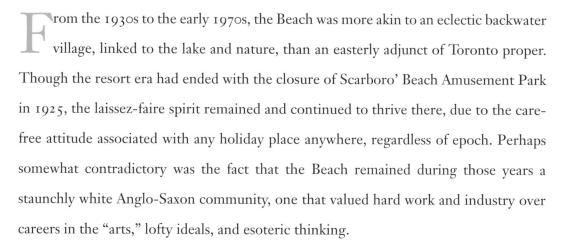

CHAPTER FIVE

The Village

From the 1930s to the early 1970s, the Beach was more akin to an eclectic backwater village, linked to the lake and nature, than an easterly adjunct of Toronto proper. Though the resort era had ended with the closure of Scarboro' Beach Amusement Park in 1925, the laissez-faire spirit remained and continued to thrive there, due to the care-free attitude associated with any holiday place anywhere, regardless of epoch. Perhaps somewhat contradictory was the fact that the Beach remained during those years a staunchly white Anglo-Saxon community, one that valued hard work and industry over careers in the "arts," lofty ideals, and esoteric thinking.

Given that the Beach, and for that matter Toronto, during those years was hardly a centre for intellectuals or culture, it is initially difficult to reconcile that the community was home to a disproportionately large number of people who would go on to achieve international recognition in the fields of the arts, industry, and finance. Yet as author Kevin Bazzana points out in relation to one Beach resident, pianist Glenn Gould, it was perhaps the distinctive characteristics of the Beach prevalent during this time — in particular its village mentality and ties to nature and the outdoors — that provided fertile ground for the development of creative minds.

Norman Jewison certainly had a childhood shaped by those two factors. He told me, "[The lake] had a pull for me and I really loved spending time on the water. You didn't feel like you were living in a major metropolitan city, ever. You felt like you were living in almost a cottage-like area. It was pleasant."

The full-time residential community that followed the resort era was a very different place from what the Beach has become since. Until then it had primarily been home to a close-knit community of plain but rooted working- and middle-class folk who never expected that life should offer them the best of everything, cachet and privilege, fashion and far-flung choices. The majority of the old inhabitants could afford no such aspirations. On the whole, the people of the Beach were plain and ordinary folk, a tough but warm and undemanding lot. They knew who they were and were proud to be who they were, and they certainly loved their Beach.

Rather than the million-dollar homes prevalent in the Beach today, many residents were likely to live in small, modest homes, many no more than converted wooden cottages of another era. Others rented rooms or small apartments in what had been the rambling summer homes of upper-class residents who had abandoned their Beach properties for summer mansions in Muskoka. Norman Jewison told me in 2009, "Nobody wanted to live in the east end. It was kind of a working class area, and the people were kind of rebellious and they were kind of suspicious of foreigners and all of that . . . but they had the Lake — and they had the Boardwalk and they had Kew Beach Park and they had the racetrack. And these things were all very important to them. . . . The people in the Beach always stuck together. They considered themselves a very special area."

While middle-class folk could be found at the new subdivision at Scarboro' Beach by the early 1930s, this was also the decade of the Great Depression. Even if these middle-class residents were lucky enough to hang onto their jobs, it was unlikely that they had much disposable income. A smaller number of the well-to-do populated the lands of the previously discussed Glen Stewart estate.

Though the place was rich in charm and beauty, it was rough and ready and quite the contrary of chic, but that did not matter in the least. A newcomer might say to his neighbour, "That's a lovely lilac tree you have there," and she might reply, "My grandfather planted that." Quite simply, the Beach was family. The Beach was home.

————— ◆ —————

The Beach

LIKE MANY OTHER areas of Toronto, the Beach had a profusion of little cinemas, or "nabes," that were at the heart of community life and entertained a mainly local clientele. The popularity of these cinemas only increased after the closing of Scarboro' Beach Amusement Park in 1925. For ten to twenty-five cents you could experience a serial, a cartoon, and two features as well as the news, which, while seeming hopelessly corny from our modern point of view, brought the reality of the outer world to the still relatively remote world of the Beach. These theatres included the Manor, the Family, the Scarboro, the Beach, and the Prince Edward (renamed the Fox Theatre in 1937), all located along the streetcar lines of Queen Street and the Kingston Road.

One can well imagine the fascination such an experience would hold, especially for an impressionable child whose father was on "relief" during the Depression. These years were marked by a considerable degree of social unease, and with no access to television or the numerous media choices of today, the movies were an escape. Later, during the 1940s, for as little as a dime, you could relive the invasion of Poland or see the bombing of London during the Second World War, the elections in the United States, Hollywood stars, and the high action of the Wild West. The pluckiest ducked down under the seats as the theatre cleared out, reappearing only as the projectionist began to play it all over again.

Typical of the people of his time, former Beach resident Norman Jewison was enthralled with the movies at the local picture houses. Born in 1926 in his grandmother's house on Lee Avenue, Jewison was raised above his parents' dry goods store and Sub-post Office Number 10 during the Great Depression. In describing his experiences to me he said, "I grew up in a village. Everybody knew each other and my parents had a store and a sub-post

The Fox Theatre still stands today on Queen Street East, near Beech Avenue Wayne LeFort

office, which meant that we were a centre. If you wanted stamps, you wanted to mail a letter, you wanted to mail a parcel and you lived anywhere between Woodbine and all the way over to I'm sure past Lee Avenue somewhere, everyone came to our store, at Kippendavie and Queen."

Jewison's Dry Goods Store and Post Office, with Norman Jewison's mother Dorothy (née Weaver) standing outside, late 1930s
Courtesy Norman Jewison

Jewison also displayed a flair for the dramatic, whether it was reciting poetry to the Orange Order and the Ladies of the Eastern Star or, in later years, producing, directing, and acting in many plays at Malvern Collegiate Institute, the local high school. As Jewison writes in his autobiography, *This Terrible Business Has Been Good to Me*, "I believe that those years in the Kippendavie Store and my adolescent love of performance prepared me for my future career."

In his spare time, Jewison went to the movies. These were tough and volatile times during the Depression, and the dime entrance fee was still prohibitive for many of the local children. From a young age, little Norman would act out the parts of the movies he had seen to the captive audience of children waiting outside the theatre, often finishing the act with a flourish that included a dramatic death finale that could last several minutes.

From the early twentieth century, and in fact right up to the 1960s, there was an

The Beach

undercurrent of anti-Semitism in the Beach that bubbled to the surface from time to time. Despite being born to parents of Protestant British heritage, the name Jewison implied difference in the Beach, and Jewison was subject to the same taunts and bullying that the small number of Jewish children experienced in the neighbourhood during that era. Later in life, these early experiences contributed to the strong current of social justice that runs through many of his greatest works.

Known for compelling story lines, Jewison remains a storyteller with a strong social message who has produced consistently high quality movies, many of which have become classics, including *In the Heat of the Night*, *Fiddler on the Roof*, *The Thomas Crown Affair*, and *A Soldier's Story*. Jewison founded the Canadian Institute for Advanced Film Studies (renamed the Canadian Film Centre), and in 1992 was made a Companion of the Order of Canada. In 1999, he received the prestigious Irving G. Thalberg Memorial Award for lifetime achievement from the Academy of Motion Picture Arts and Sciences. Though now a citizen of the world, his earliest life experiences remain centred, first and foremost, in the Beach.

———————◆———————

WRITER AND JOURNALIST Robert Fulford was also raised in the Beach in the 1930s and 1940s. Though six years younger than Jewison, Fulford also remembers the Beach of his youth as primarily a community of lower-middle-class and working-class folk who lived in small, confined homes. Fulford says that with space often at a premium indoors, Beach residents tended to see the community's open spaces and the beach as almost an extension of their own private living space. They were extremely protective of that space — a feeling that persists today.

Since the very beginning, Beach residents have carefully guarded their neighbourhood from outside "intrusion" that has been perceived, sometimes rightly and sometimes wrongly, as a threat to the essential nature and character of their village. As early as 1907, plans were underway to run the Grand Trunk Railway along the edge of the lake. Citizens rallied and raised a hue and cry that involved four levels of government and a delegation sent to Ottawa. Needless to say, the plans for the railway were changed.

When East Toronto, including a portion of the Beach east of Lee Avenue, was annexed to the city of Toronto in 1908, community pressure led to the adoption of a rudimentary zoning condition that influenced the development of the district in years to come. Campbell and Myrvold note that the term stipulated that the area south of the Kingston Road was to remain residential in character, without factories and hotels.

Along the Shore

In the early 1970s, Beach residents successfully fought off a proposal for a Scarborough Expressway that would have seen a major east–west freeway threaded along the path of the Kingston Road. Since then, and recurrently, proposals for the expansion of the Toronto Island Airport (now the Billy Bishop Toronto City Airport) have brought the prospect of increased passenger aircraft flying out along the lake, parallel with the shoreline and thereby disturbing the peace of the Beach. Conservation efforts have not neglected even the smallest details. In the mid-1980s, a couple of young shopkeepers on Queen Street chained themselves to a tree after the city threatened to chop it down.

The sense of protectionism alive in the Beach did turn truly ugly once, in the 1930s, when some members of the community indulged in their own flirtation with fascism and racial discrimination. A group of young men from the local Orange Order formed a branch of the Swastika Club and began "patrolling" the Boardwalk, ostensibly against "intruders," those who were coming from "outside" and "littering" the Beach. In the 1920s and 1930s, anti-Semitism reared its ugly head in Toronto, and it is no surprise that discrimination against Jews could be seen across the waterfront during those years. By no means was it restricted only to the Beach.

According to "Toronto's First Synagogues: Beach Hebrew Institute," there were some forty Jewish families living in the Beach in the 1920s and 1930s. Ben Orenstein, a youngster at the time, recalls being asked by his friends to join in the protest against the Jews. When he informed his friends that he was in fact Jewish, his friends told him that the protest did not apply to him because he was part of the community. Though the protest was short-lived, it remains a regrettable blot on the story of the community. Membership at the Balmy Beach Club was also unofficially restricted to non-Jews in the first half of the twentieth century.

Despite periodic incidents of anti-Semitism, Jewish families generally lived very peaceably with their neighbours in the Beach. Avrom Siegel grew up in the Beach. As he recalled in an interview in 2006, "I made good friends . . . I was welcome in their church because I knew so-and-so. We had a good life there."

Today it is the unwitting tourists and day trippers who are most likely to face the ire of overprotective Beachers. In the 1990s, a small coalition of disgruntled residents, tired of the constant traffic congestion and of visitors traipsing across their lawns on their way to the beach, formed the Beach Residents Against Tourists Association. The message on the T-shirts printed by the organization — "Welcome to the Beach, Now Go Home" — said it all. This aspect of the Beach personality, still subtly evident today if you care to look for it, is rooted in community protection and is as old as the Beach itself.

"Harris had dreamed the marble walls, the copper banded roofs. He pulled down the Victoria Park forest and an essential temple swept up in its place, built on the slope towards the lake."
— In the Skin of a Lion, *Michael Ondaatje. R.C. Harris Water Treatment Plant —*
service building and alum tower with pumping station behind, 2011 Natalia Shields

Misguided community protection aside, the desire to maintain the village-like character of the Beach is a testament to the strength of the community, which has succeeded, where other communities have failed, in maintaining a close connection with the lake. The historical buildings that stand at or near the water's edge attest to this enduring connection. We have already discussed the history of the humble Leuty Lifeguard Station. Farther to the east, on terraced lands above the lake at the foot of Victoria Park Avenue, stands a stately building that was conceived by public works commissioner and local resident Roland Caldwell Harris. The R.C. Harris Water Treatment Plant (informally known as the Waterworks) was constructed in the 1930s and opened in 1941. It is a notable example of the art deco style of architecture and is one of the principal sources of Toronto's drinking water. The Waterworks also has a place in popular culture, being one of the primary settings for author Michael Ondaatje's novel *In the Skin of a Lion*. Yet the significance of this building extends far beyond this. As previous authors have noted, high on the shore, facing out to the water and so to the horizon, it may be seen as a metaphor for the connection between Lake Ontario and the living city.

In the span of just twenty years, between 1901 and 1921, Toronto had grown dramatically with the annexation of many districts; during this time the city's population more than doubled. As a result, Toronto lacked form, coherence, and integration. It was in desperate need of infrastructure to sustain its growth and to allow its continued expansion. In the late nineteenth and early twentieth centuries, Toronto had suffered through two separate outbreaks of typhoid, with some losing their lives. In the most recent incident, Torontonians drank raw water out of Toronto Bay, after the main pipe to the Island Filtration Plant had become disabled. As public pressure mounted, a duplicate Waterworks system was recommended in a report submitted to Public Works in 1912.

Into this chaos came Roland (Roly) Caldwell Harris. Rising through the ranks of the city bureaucracy, he became commissioner of Public Works in 1912, the same year as the release of the first Waterworks report. Harris championed Toronto's need for a unified core of services and implemented an elaborate plan for their development. One of his first achievements as commissioner was the completion of the Prince Edward Viaduct, which still gracefully spans the chasm of the Don Valley between Danforth Avenue and Bloor Street.

As to the duplicate Waterworks system, Harris favoured the lands just beyond the city boundary at the Victoria Park site. A hardwood forest of some twenty acres still stretched down to meet the lakeshore on what were formerly the grand old pleasure grounds. It was on this site that Harris planned to build the Victoria Park Filtration Plant, a palace of grand proportions that would service the city throughout the twentieth century and beyond. Its purification system would introduce state-of-the-art technology, employing super chlorination and dechlorination equipment that was heralded at the time as the most innovative in the world. Most importantly, Harris's plant would celebrate water.

By 1912 it was already clear that Harris envisioned a series of elegant buildings arising out of the little escarpment. Steven Mannell quotes Harris's 1913 Toronto Waterworks extension project report as envisioning the erection of "handsome buildings

*The marble and bronze signal pylon is situated
in the middle of the filter building's rotunda*

Keith Ellis

[at Victoria Park], which, in conjunction with the park section and the Beach, will constitute one of the most beautiful areas in Toronto." In 1915 he came to live in the Toronto Beach community to better ensure the realization of his dream.

Gore Nasmith & Storrie was appointed consulting engineers for the Victoria Park project. The engineering assistant assigned to the project was the little-known Thomas Canfield Pomphrey, a native of Wishaw, some twenty miles south of Glasgow, Scotland. Pomphrey's firm, Ferguson & Pomphrey, had recently designed the cenotaph that still stands in front of Old City Hall, which may have caught the eye of Harris. Before immigrating to Canada, Pomphrey had taken classes at the Glasgow School of Art, and he would also have been well schooled in the emerging modernist ideas of another Glaswegian, the renowned Charles Rennie Mackintosh.

In any case, Pomphrey's first set of preliminary drawings was rejected by Harris, whose vision for the plant could not be satisfied by the everyday utilitarian structures of water purification. When Pomphrey offered a more elaborate alternative, Harris was so pleased with the design that he specified that Pomphrey, and not the city architect, would make all future decisions on materials, details, and interpretation of specifications.

Pomphrey and Harris spared no expense in achieving their now mutually held vision. The three buildings that comprise the Waterworks are finished in yellow brick and Queenston limestone with copper roofs and ornamental

Frigid water is sucked into the mouth of a tunnel from more than a mile out into the lake, and is eventually channeled up to filter basins for purification. The deep cold of the lake makes it a pleasant place to be on a hot summer day. Keith Ellis

bronze. Classical and Romanesque influences may be found throughout, along with decorative relief carving that focuses on machine iconography. The interiors of the three buildings are similarly generously appointed with marble, terrazzo floors, herringbone tile, and bronze hardware.

The interior space of the pumping station has been described by George Baird in "Waterworks: A Commentary" as suggestive of a basilica. At its "apse" are the pump controls, which have an art deco motif and span the height of a two-storey building. The filter building that faces out onto Queen Street is no less grand and is constructed as a series of forty serene reflecting pools. Reminiscent of Roman baths, the pools house two hundred million gallons of water, each pool resting on a bed of fine sand and gravel. Instead of a concrete tank to house the alum, a substance that is one of the main ingredients for water purification, Pomphrey designed a tower with a belvedere.

The buildings were completed in 1937 and were fitted out with pumps and other equipment over the next three years. For a year after that the Waterworks sat unused, and it was during this time that a local mythology developed around supposed secret balls and clandestine meetings said to be taking place within the walls of the "palace." At last and amidst all this speculation, the water began to flow in November of 1941.

Harris died while still commissioner of the Public Works Department four years later. Though work on his Toronto Waterworks extension continued, along with the addition of the east wing of the Victoria Park site in 1955–1956, his passing signalled the end of an era in the life of Toronto. By the end of his tenure, public works had transformed Toronto from a muddle of unserviced hamlets and villages into a coherent, industrialized metropolis with a safe and sufficient supply of fresh water.

Perhaps not surprisingly, the completion of the Waterworks was met with great criticism in the still provincial Toronto of the 1940s. Torontonians were scandalized by what was seen as a lavish waste of money on materials and construction (the Waterworks was nicknamed the Palace of Purity by local residents). It was a well-known subject of gossip in the Beach that Roly Harris's front door on Neville Park Boulevard cost $100 — an unimaginable amount for most local residents at that time. The fact that Harris had extended such extravagance to the building of the plant, as when he approved the outlay of twenty thousand dollars for an iron railing along the expansive promenade overlooking the water, only fuelled the outrage.

Sadly, the cultural significance of the Waterworks was lost on most Beach residents and the people of Toronto as a whole. Wayne Reeves points out that as late as 1974, a guidebook by the Toronto Chapter of Architects described the buildings as "disasters both inside and out, [with] not even the end-of-tour enticement that a candy factory or a brewery offer." It was only in the later decades of the twentieth century that Torontonians began to realize the deeper significance of the plant. During the years of great fiscal restraint that preceded the Second World War, Harris lavishly celebrated the city's connection with the lake, the source of our water, and the principal reason for the city's existence. Rather than an indulgent expression of ego, the construction of the Waterworks may be viewed as an accomplishment of courageous vision and abiding faith.

It is rumoured that Harris kept a secret office at the top of the alum tower, overlooking Lake Ontario. On a sultry summer day, it is not hard to imagine him there still, standing in the belvedere staring out at the emptiness of Lake Ontario. As he drinks in the horizon, he is still building a vision for a city that is inextricably linked to the great lake resting silently at his feet.

ONE FORMER BEACH resident who maintained a lifelong connection to water and open spaces was the brilliant pianist Glenn Gould. Born in 1932, Gould lived with his parents on Southwood Drive until he was almost thirty years old. While living at home, he frequently wandered the Boardwalk at the community's southern edge.

Gould's ramblings along the beach were captured in a series of iconic images taken by writer-photographer and fellow Beach resident Jock Carroll in *Glenn Gould: Some Portraits of the Artist as a Young Man.* In one such image, the young Gould may be seen on a raw, snowless, leafless Boardwalk staring out at the water with the raised promenade of the R.C. Harris Water Treatment Plant clearly visible in the distance. After wandering the Boardwalk, Gould would turn northward and make his way home to the unassuming brick two-storey that still stands south of the Kingston Road on the grounds of the former Glen Stewart estate. As he walked uphill, away from the lake, he was perhaps only half aware of his surroundings, humming a Bach canon or fugue. This was the music that the immediate neighbours of the Gould family already knew by heart. For well over a decade, Bach, Beethoven, Haydn, and Brahms had been wafting out of the family's living room, as local residents peeled potatoes for dinner on the back porch or walked down the hill of the quiet tree-lined street from the Kingston Road trolley.

Gould's parents, Russell (Bert) and Florence Gould, personified Toronto the Good and, in turn, the ultra-Anglo-Protestant Beach community of those years. As Kevin Bazzana notes in *Wondrous Strange: The Life and Art of Glenn Gould,* they were kind, decent people — good neighbours who read the Bible and minded their own business. Though financially secure and living well beyond the means of many fellow Beachers, they eschewed ostentation, living an almost banal existence with one notable exception. From an early age, their son Glenn showed signs of being a musical genius. Now, almost thirty years after his death, groupies and tourists from all over the world still make the pilgrimage to the modest house in the Beach where Gould began.

In the first half of the twentieth century, Toronto and its Beach were by no means founts of inspiration, let alone places of pilgrimage, for lovers of classical music. The Beach, much like the city itself, maintained a strong Protestant work ethic, which favoured hard work and industry over the perceived frivolity of artists and intellectuals.

It was nonetheless into this world that Gould was born, becoming one of the most admired and celebrated musicians of the twentieth century. As Bazzana notes, his influence on classical music was so profound that his recording of Bach's Prelude and Fugue in C, No. 1, from Book 2 of *The Well-Tempered Clavier*, was one of twenty-seven samples of Earth's music included in the *Voyager* spaceships, launched by the United States in 1977. The ships are still out there, exploring the outer reaches of the galaxy.

Gould's international concert career began on January 2, 1955, at the Phillips Gallery in Washington, D.C. A year later, and while still living in the Beach, he produced his debut Columbia Records recording of Bach's *Goldberg Variations*. It remains one of the most popular classical music recordings ever made, perhaps only succeeded by the second, radically different, recording of the variations he released just days before his untimely death in 1982. The second recording, filled with barren space and sadness, has been described as "elegiac," only heightened by the fact that the closing iteration of the aria, the theme of the work, was played at Gould's own memorial service on October 15, 1982. In the recording, Gould may actually be heard humming along.

Glenn Gould, Fort Montagu Beach Motel in the wee morning hours, Bahamas, 1956

Jock Carroll, LAC Canada, e010865579

Yet part of the magic of Gould is that he was so much more than a musical genius. He was also an innovative radio and television broadcaster, writer, and composer. In the first half of the twentieth century, success in the classical music world demanded a gruelling round of concert performances — a way of life that eventually became intolerable for the emotionally sensitive Gould, who suffered from a fear of crowds. He ceased live concert performances at about the age of thirty-two and turned to the emerging field of music recording, becoming one of the first modern classical performers.

Reclusive by nature, Gould lived an almost monk-like existence in Toronto and liked to refer to himself as "the last Puritan," a subtle reference to the Anglo-Protestant culture in which he was raised. After moving from his parents' home on Southwood Drive, he obtained an apartment penthouse in mid-town Toronto, on St. Clair Avenue West. From the 1970s, he also kept a studio in the now demolished Inn on the Park, which

Along the Shore

then stood on the southern edge of the rapidly expanding suburbs, near the Don Valley ravine system and the well-established Edwards Gardens.

Gould cultivated this image of the outsider in later life, although this characteristic appears to have developed unconsciously as a child, growing up in the Beach. Sal and Ross Azzarello ran a grocery store near the corner of Kingston Road and Main Street, which operated in the larger Beach area for almost sixty years. Glenn's mother frequented the store for many years. Sal Azzarello recalls of the family that, "They were great customers and wonderful people . . . [Glenn] always wore gloves, didn't want anyone to touch him, and he always had a coat and hat . . . all year round he was dressed warm like that." One ubiquitous picture of the adult Gould shows him wearing a long woollen overcoat, galoshes, cap, and scarf and seated alone on a Toronto park bench in the middle of July.

It is initially difficult to place Gould's accomplishments and innovations in the context of the culture in which he lived. Bazzana points out that many earlier biographies of Gould simply do not acknowledge where he was raised, the place and the landscape that inevitably got into his bones and profoundly influenced his art. His biography references the Beach's nurturing quality, arguing that Gould developed into the artist he became not *in spite of* being raised in the Beach but to an extent *because* of where he was raised. He writes, "Gould, given his particular talent and temperament, *needed* a sheltered upbringing in which to thrive. Or at least, had he been brought up in different circumstances, he might have been a very different, and perhaps less interesting, artist than the one we knew."

Gould guarded the details of his personal life very carefully, and we are left with a scant record of his years in the Beach, though he did say in an essay entitled "Toronto" that "[it] does belong on a very short list of cities I've visited that seem to offer me, at any rate, peace of mind — cities which, for want of a better definition, do not impose their 'cityness' on you." He also acknowledged, "The only Toronto I really know is the one I carry about with me in memory. And most of the images in my memory-bank have to do with Toronto of the forties and early fifties when I was a teenager."

Perhaps more telling, he also says, in John McGreevy's TV film *Glenn Gould's Toronto*, that Toronto had "always been rather like a collection of village neighbourhoods." At his core, Gould, like Norman Jewison, six years his senior, was a small-town boy raised in a village, Toronto's Beach. As a boy he knew many of the shopkeepers by name. Even after moving to midtown Toronto when he was almost thirty, he frequented the same neighbourhood pharmacy in the Beach for most of his adult life. He could fit into the tightly knit community and yet could be alone.

Trees and mist, Kew Gardens Marley Adams

Throughout his life, Gould actively sought the psychological freedom of open spaces and water. Though Gould spent many hours at his family's cottage by Lake Simcoe and later on the North Shore of Lake Superior and beside the Mediterranean Sea, there was also Lake Ontario, the lake he first experienced as a child, growing up in Toronto's Beach.

In an autobiographical essay that he began in the last year of his life, Gould writes that "his earliest first dream-like images of childhood" were "images exclusively of trees — trees shrouded in the morning mist, trees heavy with snow on a winter afternoon, trees, above all, whose branches served to filter the waning twilight of a summer evening." Farther down the page he scribbled, "Acc[ording] to my own evol[utionary] scheme, God first invented trees and then the sunless states of fog and snow and the sun-defeating purple wash of twilight — it was several y[ea]rs before human beings and the sounds they produced took their place in my world."

Gould's notes reveal that his appreciation of nature, and its paramount significance in his worldview and his art, developed very early, even before his appreciation of sounds and music. One of the primary places for this development was the leafy community in which he was raised. On a cloudy day in late autumn, the trees hugging the edge of the Boardwalk are bare and the sun is held hostage by the impending gloom of winter. If you stand very still and look out at the lake toward the horizon, you may hear Gould's *Aria in the Goldberg Variations* as our anthem, its achingly beautiful melody unfurling on the surface of the grey November water.

———— ◦ ————

IN THE LATE 1940s, my Aunt Mary Ann's grade 12 class at Malvern Collegiate Institute in the Beach was struggling with the elements of a three-part Bach fugue. Their teacher, Roy Wood, employed a rather unconventional strategy to impart the wisdom of Bach. At the appointed hour, a gangly student, Glenn Gould, appeared at the doorway to the classroom, slouched over to the piano, and then sat down while the class waited in awed silence. Then he began the serious work of deconstructing the fugue, playing the intricate parts from memory, over and over again with unprecedented passion and precision.

Gould actually made his professional debut as a performer at the age of thirteen on the organ with the Malvern Collegiate Choir, conducted by music teacher Roy Wood, at the Eaton Auditorium. For the first fifty years of its existence, Malvern remained a tight-knit, conservative community that mirrored the Beach itself. Up to and including the Second World War, many of the teachers spent their entire career at Malvern and lived locally. Accordingly, they took an unusual degree of interest in the lives of the students, both inside and outside the school.

Founded in 1903, Malvern Collegiate continues to be a cornerstone of the Beach community and is fondly remembered by many graduates. Despite Gould sometimes being quite negative about his school experience in general, in a letter to Mr. Emid in 1961 he wrote, "It is ten years now since I left Malvern . . . the strongest impression that I retain from my years at Malvern is of the enormous goodwill and generosity of the staff." Robert Fulford, another Malvern alumnus, remembers the school somewhat less favourably, describing it as "a school of dourly limited ambition."

Senator Irving Gerstein, who lived around the corner from his chemistry teacher, Robert Philp, on Glen Oak Drive, had this to say about his history teacher, Mr. Gilmore: "I'll tell you, he was an old curmudgeon. I went to the Warden School of Finance, which isn't a bad school. I went to the London School of Economics, not a bad school. You want to know who sticks out in mind as the best teacher I ever had? *Gilmore*."

Likewise, Norman Jewison recalls in *This Terrible Business Has Been Good to Me* that his early performance skills were honed in the Beach and at Malvern. In high school he wrote and directed comedy sketches for the annual Christmas events and even appeared on stage once in a toga, where he invited students to a dance in broken Latin, "a feat that made even the sternest of our teachers howl with laughter."

There is no doubt that Malvern has produced a disproportionate number of successful and creative minds over the course of its more than one-hundred-year history. Aside from Gould, Jewison, and Fulford, other notable Canadians who attended Malvern in its first fifty years include mathematician and social activist Israel Halperin, landscape painter Doris McCarthy, entrepreneur Jack Kent Cooke, opera diva Teresa Stratas, and Senator Irving Gerstein. More recent Malvern attendees include Olympian Bruce Kidd, gold-medal Olympian Mark Heese, and members of the popular rock band Down with Webster.

———◆———

AS FAMILIES REUNITED at the end of the Second World War and immigration to Canada picked up its pace, the Beach faced the unprecedented challenge of integrating thousands of newcomers into the city. Along with this challenge came a serious housing shortage, the likes of which Toronto had never seen. While areas of the city to the north, east, and west of the Beach experienced unprecedented change in the post-war years and into the 1960s, the Beach remained seemingly untouched by such transformations. While absorbing its share of newcomers, it still remained the quintessential small town, although during the 1960s it began to include a slightly more bohemian population than in some of its previous incarnations. By the 1960s and 1970s, artists and other creative types, attracted to the area's relatively low rental and housing market, were now living in the subdivided old holiday homes of yesteryear alongside long-time working- and middle-class residents.

One such artist, William (Bill) Kurelek, moved his family into a modest, newer home on Balsam Avenue in 1965 at the suggestion of his friend and well-known Toronto sculptor Bill McElcheran, who also lived on Balsam Avenue back in those days. He remained there until his untimely death at the age of fifty in 1977, but unlike fellow artists Gould and Jewison, who were raised in the then tight Anglo-Saxon community, his early influences were entirely different.

Kurelek came of old-world Ukrainian parentage. Born in Alberta and reared in Manitoba during the Depression, he is best remembered for his innocent and naturalistic scenes of rural Prairie life. In 1976, one year before his death, Kurelek was made a

member of the Order of Canada. He died as one of Canada's best-loved artists.

Kurelek also painted many Beach scenes, although this body of his work is less well-known. Among these paintings are *Balsam Avenue After Heavy Snowfall*, which actually includes the artist and his four young children as figures in the setting. It was composed as it would have been seen by his wife, Jean, were she to look south from their home on Balsam Avenue. A scene at the beach was captured in his painting *The Board Walk at Toronto's Beaches*. It was preceded by another intimate portrait of the Kurelek family on the present-day Toronto shore, *Family Enjoying the Beaches*.

The Beach

It is often overlooked that Kurelek's most prolific painting period was during the years he lived in the Beach. Much of Kurelek's work, including a multitude of his Prairie images, were painted in the austere inner sanctum of his basement studio at his Balsam Avenue home. What remains unexamined is the influence of the Beach on Kurelek and, in turn, how the artist chose to interpret this unique place in his art.

———•———

KURELEK WAS A sensitive child, ill suited for the rigorous demands of farm life in the Prairies. His interest in creative pursuits and, later, his desire to become a painter met with harsh discouragement from his father, which implanted in him a sense of alienation and suffering that persisted to some degree for the rest of his life.

In 1952 Kurelek was admitted to the Maudsley Psychiatric Hospital in London, England, and treated for schizophrenia. Ukrainian Orthodox by birth, Kurelek credited his emotional recovery to his conversion to the Roman Catholic faith. Kurelek's long-term art dealer and friend, Avrom Isaacs, maintained that all Kurelek's work was "a religious act." Each piece, whether a whimsical Beach snapshot, a Prairie reminiscence, or a moralistic parable, has a feeling for the divine and is a way of teaching, of exposition, and of homily.

Kurelek's art also reflected the darker side of his personal struggles, as may be seen in a lesser-known painting of the waterfront in the Beach. After his religious conversion, he had, in the words of his son Stephen Kurelek, "become preoccupied with an apocalyptic world view focused on the traditional Christian themes of judgment and redemption."

Meanwhile, within three years of Kurelek's return from England, he married Jean Andrews and began to paint full time. Jean, who was raised both in East Toronto and Gravenhurst, Ontario, wanted to bring their children up in an urban environment. Kurelek, on the other hand, adored nature and yearned for the wide-open spaces of his childhood. The Beach in the mid-1960s represented a compromise for the couple, offering all the conveniences of a small town and plenty of access to nature. From time to time, Kurelek escaped into the thickly wooded Glen Stewart Ravine for quiet contemplation. In fact, that is where he depicts Toronto mayor David Crombie envisioning the ideal city in *The Dream of Mayor Crombie*. Undoubtedly, Kurelek's happiest years were in the Beach, where, in the words of his son Stephen, "he had extricated himself from his overbearing father . . . and was also doing what he wanted to do. He wasn't searching. He'd found his vocation."

———•———

Along the Shore

AN ARRANGEMENT WITH Avrom Isaacs allowed Kurelek to sell and barter his paintings from the cramped basement studio that doubled as a recreation room for his growing family. After Kurelek's untimely death in the late 1970s, the space served as an apartment for one of their older children and as a multi-purpose storage area for the family. Until 2009, the space remained largely unrenovated. I had the privilege of visiting Kurelek's studio in April 2009, shortly after the death of Jean Kurelek and before the house was sold.

Inside the front hall of the Balsam Avenue house was a weathered sign that had hung for years outside the main entranceway. It directed me to a side-alley entrance, where I descended into the world of William Kurelek. A religious icon, harkening back to Kurelek's early roots in the Ukrainian Orthodox tradition, hung on the south-facing wall. While the floor was covered in dark linoleum, Ukrainian decoration, in bright blues and reds, was lavishly applied to the storage cabinets, doors and some of the walls. Handmade wooden slats for displaying his paintings still hung from the ceiling. Kurelek had cleverly stored his paintings in storage ports that he had installed in the ceiling, above the showroom space.

But Kurelek did not paint in this room because painting for him was an intensely private affair. The basement was divided into two compartments by a sturdy wall and door more befitting a bank vault than a home workspace. The workspace was minimalist in the extreme, filled with bright light and covered in white and pale blue mosaic tile. In this sacred space, within the confines of a four-foot by eight-foot cell carved out of the former coal storage area, Kurelek locked himself away and painted. A bunk bed was installed above his desk and the heavy, fireproof door blocked off the space from the bustle of the household. Many visitors were nonetheless scandalized by the conditions in

Kurelek's workspace door and inner studio

Jane Fairburn

The Beach

Detail of side altar mural at Corpus Christi Church, showing a storm gathering over Lake Ontario at Woodbine Beach William Kurelek, © The Estate of William Kurelek, courtesy of the Wynick/Tuck Gallery, Toronto and the Archives of the Roman Catholic Archdiocese of Toronto (ARCAT)

which Kurelek painted. He only installed a vent in his workspace on the urging of his physician, a short time before his death.

The studio, however, served a dual purpose. It was also a bomb shelter, should Toronto be struck by a nuclear attack. Kurelek believed this event would signal the beginning of the apocalypse, in which all the iniquities and sins of the world would be cleansed, in fulfillment of the biblical promise. In his own words, he had "an intuitive premonition of what the world is heading for." Eventually, plans were drawn up for an enlarged bomb shelter that would extend from the east wall of his studio underneath the back garden. In the end, Jean, herself a devout Catholic, would have nothing of it and the plans were never executed.

Lake Ontario and its horizon must have had, in part, a foreboding aspect for Kurelek, one that was tied to his deeper worldview. Kurelek never learned to swim and had an uneasy relationship with water throughout his life, his only experiences as a child being in the bog ponds that lined the fields of the Canadian West, which he featured in some of his Prairie paintings. His children remember his extreme timidity in the water and his constant reminders not to stray beyond where he could reach them.

Months before his death in 1977, Kurelek painted a mural at the side altar at Corpus Christi Roman Catholic Church in the Beach, offering another vision of the Boardwalk and Lake Ontario. This work is a glimpse into his foretelling of the apocalypse, a vision he does not overtly feature in his otherwise light-hearted paintings of the Beach. In the lower part of the mural, Lake Ontario provides the backdrop of a storm gathering off-shore, near Woodbine Beach, while residents walk idly by, unmindful of the impending doom. Out in the water, a swimmer moves toward the jaws of a great whale, an obvious reference to Jonah, announcing in Kurelek's words in a pamphlet that describes the mural, "the big time of trial." The scene includes the priests and parishioners of Corpus Christi, who are rendered in the same style as appeared in the artist's earlier waterfront paintings.

Some may wonder how this artist could so often paint the Beach cheerfully and simply, as in the sunny strand at the community's southern shore or the leafy Glen Stewart Ravine, and then, so close to his death, envisage the end of the world and the Day of Judgment in the same familiar setting. Yet there is no contradiction. He had known what it was to be cast out into mental and spiritual chaos. After his religious conversion and overcoming schizophrenia, he left us a little parting gift. He looked on the Beach and, from his unique perspective, set down what he saw, in paint.

CHAPTER SIX

Destruction and Loss

In contrast to the upheavals that came about elsewhere in Toronto during the post-war years, the Beach, as late as the 1960s and very early 1970s, remained outwardly like a forgotten small town. Nevertheless, change was afoot. After the general drift to the suburbs that occurred in the years following the Second World War, many of the homes that had been built up on the hillsides from Queen Street, some grand and stylish, others rustic and quaint, had been converted into rooming houses.

In the 1960s and early 1970s the Beach began to display an increasingly diverse social and cultural mix, with its share of major eccentrics and bohemian "roomers" living alongside the staid Anglo-Saxons of yesteryear and newly arrived families who were finding their way back into the community. Too often what was behind the pillared porch proved to be a challenge for the recently arrived, unwary new homeowner. Tenants had to be bought off. Then came replacing what was behind the crumbling, plastered walls — usable sanitation and non-combustible wiring — as well as ridding the structure of unwanted four-footed friends, including the dead raccoons under the porch.

Lick's Homeburgers & Ice Cream,
formerly the Seaway Market, 2011

Keith Eliis

The Queen Street of the 1960s and early 1970s was a very different place than it is today. East of Woodbine Avenue was Tony's Fruit Market. As you walked east, you came upon the Seaway Market, which was in that era an old German butcher shop with sawdust covering the old wooden floors. The popular Lick's Homeburgers & Ice Cream restaurant (later franchised with many other locations) took over the Seaway. At the time of writing the current Lick's location is soon to be converted into a multi-storey condominium complex. Farther east was a place called English Style Fish and Chips, distinct from Nova Fish and Chips, one of its main competitors. Two IGA grocery stores carried on business within a block and a half of each other.

As in some other parts of Toronto during the 1960s, it was virtually impossible to find an establishment in the Beach or surrounding area that served alcohol. The exception was the Orchard Park Tavern, located across from Greenwood Racetrack. This establishment had long been associated with the bookmaking crowd at the track and is believed to have been licensed since the repeal of prohibition.

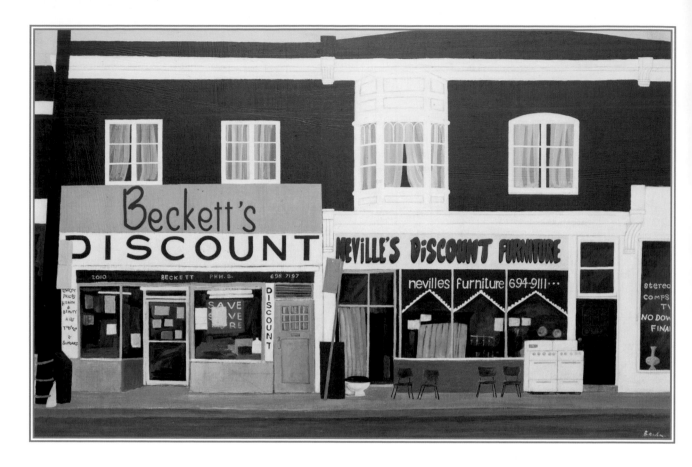

Neville's Discount Furniture, 1973

Roger Boulton

Then sometime in the late 1960s or early 1970s, Alex Christie, a well-known Beach community supporter and local businessman, obtained the first liquor licence for a restaurant in the greater Beach area. Patrons of the Meca Grill at Coxwell and Queen could then have a beer with their sandwich at lunch (and perhaps at the same time place a bet on the trots at Greenwood, but that is another story). A similar licence was granted in 1975 to the Chalet, a restaurant in Balmy Beach. By the mid-1970s, the Palm Restaurant had opened next to Vic Jenkins's post office (now Whitlock's) on the south side of Queen. According to former Beach city councillor and local resident Tom Jakobek, the Palm was an upscale breakfast place, not a ma-and-pa greasy spoon operation like so many of the others, and it was somewhat expensive. It was bright and trendy and different from anything else in the community. The commercialization of Queen Street had begun.

The change that came to Queen Street and the Beach coincided with Toronto's self-styled urban renaissance, which saw many puritanical values and restrictions that had previously defined the city melt away. Toronto the Good was about to become, well, not quite so good. Younger middle-class families started to look into older city areas rather than at the suburbs that had typified the lifestyle of the post-war years. With this transition also came an influx of moneyed, upwardly mobile urban professionals who sought to gentrify various areas of the city, including the Beach.

All of which meant the end of an era was at hand for the long-established businesses, many of them family-run, including the butcher, the greengrocer, the shop where you could get your old brass hanging lamp repaired, the Woolworth's at the corner of Queen and Lee, and the discount furniture store where Neville, a Yorkshire giant with a huge black beard, would buy or sell anything, including old mattresses and unwanted lavatory pans, which, if there was no room inside, might simply sit beside the telephone pole on the sidewalk. Of the utmost cultural importance was the beloved Goof, a diner of

such drab and worn antiquity as to make a movie location scout faint for joy. This establishment was known as the Goof because the neon sign promising "Good Food" had lost a few letters so far back in time that nobody could remember exactly when.

The upscale Palm Restaurant was soon followed by other higher-end eating establishments, chain stores dedicated to lifestyle and personal fitness, and, to adapt the words of one former resident, "more coffee shops between Woodbine and Beech than in all of Buenos Aires." As Robert Fulford was to say years later in *Accidental City*, for Beach residents, "the 1970s were a kind of cultural nightmare. It was like going to sleep in your home town and waking up in a garish Hollywood movie set."

⁕

THEN AT LAST THE stage was set in the 1980s for the über-battle of the Beach that pitted the old-time granny and the Nevilles against the newcomers, perceived by some of the locals as immigrants from latte-land, the self-appointed standard bearers of the smart and the new.

The Garden Gate Restaurant, better known as The Goof, 2011 Keith Ellis

Their battleground was the name of the place. The conflict was sparked when local merchants successfully lobbied for signage along Queen Street that would refer to the place as "the Beaches" rather than the more traditional "the Beach." A case could be made for the former, given that the community had evolved from at least three definable beaches: Woodbine, Kew, and Balmy. While there was at least some acknowledgement of the mutual use of the terms in public signage, most notably at the Beaches Branch Library, opened in 1916, these were only meaningless technicalities to the dyed-in-the-wool Beacher and did not address the heart of the matter.

Many old-timers had simply had enough of the wrecking ball and the smart and the new. Like the Day of the Bridge on the Island some years earlier, long-time residents protested a perceived virtual eviction of another sort — their own — and wrote into the local newspapers with rage, condemning what they saw as a spiral of decline. One such letter, from a resident quoted by Fulford, commented on the glut of restaurants and pubs that had recently come into the area and noted, with sadness, that the signs "demean the district, just as the preponderance of eating houses and drinking parlours do . . . I grieve for the younger generation, their children, and their paradise lost."

Of the battle that ensued, Tom Jakobek said to me, in an interview in 2011, "I can tell you in no uncertain terms that I realized that every long term resident who lived in the area took offence to the name Beaches. There was no logic to it, it was just, you know what? I am not agreeing to this. Transitional resentment manifested itself in a sign."

The signs were just the tip of the iceberg of the multitude of other changes proposed for the community. Local merchants were also seeking to capitalize on the new slick look of the Beach by having it recognized as a tourist area within Metropolitan Toronto. This possibility was slammed shut by local politicians, who by this time were sensing that Armageddon was at hand. In the end, the signs were removed and replaced with the original street names.

After a cooling-off period of some twenty years, the issue of what to call the newly configured village surfaced again in the early spring of 2006. This time the matter was handled democratically, with residents being invited to vote on whether the community should be named the Beach or the Beaches. The older name, the Beach, carried the day, but only by an eight per cent margin, and probably both names will continue to be used interchangeably to define the area. As recently as the spring of 2009, new signage was gently introduced on Queen Street, with "The Beach" ever so delicately indicated in the upper left-hand corner.

Along the Shore

CHAPTER SEVEN

Renewal

In January 2011, my daughter and a group of her friends were given an assignment in their grade eight extended French class in the Beach. The teacher asked the girls to apply the urban design principles they had learned in class to create an ideal neighbourhood. Perhaps it is of little surprise that they drew a village bisected by a commercial sector, or Main Street, that ran from east to west. Radiating north and south from Main Street were a series of tree-lined streets dotted with modest homes and generous porches and interspersed with leafy ravines. At the bottom of their rendering was a lake bordered by a sand beach and a boardwalk, which they aptly entitled the Promenade.

I was struck by the fact that the girls had unconsciously drawn what was, in their world, a microcosm of their own experience of Toronto's Beach. What their drawing didn't reveal, however, were the stark and definitive changes that have come to the community over the past thirty-five years. By the mid-1970s came the commercialization of the area's "main drag," Queen Street, and with it, the notable gentrification and social reorganization of many areas of the Beach. The development of the racetrack lands, whose homes duplicate the earlier residential patterns seen on Kippendavie and Kenilworth Avenues and Waverly Road, has increased the overall density of the area and added yet a further vibrant dimension to the community. The Goof, though primped, remains.

The Beach has, in fact, undergone many incarnations in a history that spans three centuries, from the wild Ashbridge marsh of the eighteenth century to the pioneer out-post of the Williams and Lang families to the carefree resort community of the late nineteenth and early twentieth centuries and finally to the slightly shabby and forgotten village that disappeared in the 1980s.

At first blush, the Beach residents of today have little in common with these ear-lier residents. For one thing, the community is more ethnically diverse and far more upwardly mobile than it was in years past. Some thirty-five years ago, the Beach became desirable and continues to be, year after year, one of the hottest real estate markets in the city. And yet, despite all the changes, the Beach remains, on some level, a village. Or perhaps more accurately, the Beach retains many village-like qualities. At its most fun-damental level it reminds us of a time in Toronto that is all but forgotten. This is at least partly why the area resonates with so many of us and makes it so lovable.

Many local community groups foster this connection with the past. Pre-eminent among them is the Beaches Lions Club. Established in 1935, the Lions sponsor and stage a multitude of events, including the annual Easter parade, Christmas tree lighting, Canada Day and Labour Day celebrations, and the Terry Fox Run. The Balmy Beach Club con-tinues to be the local gathering place, while community groups like Centre 55, Seniors Link, churches of various descriptions, and the local shul (the Beach Hebrew Institute) round out the picture, providing services to many Beach and East Toronto residents.

Retention of this small-town flavour will no doubt be challenged in the years to come. The next round of development threatens to narrow yet further the spread of income groups who live in the Beach. While the area is today predominantly upper-middle class, there remain pockets of original working-class residents in the Beach, with the middle class still well represented. It is this mix of income groups that contributes to the unique character of the community.

Pressure continues relentlessly for the building of higher-density residential condo-minium developments, both on the Kingston Road and back and forth along Queen Street, as well as closer to the lake. While some areas of the Beach have now been desig-nated by the city as Heritage Conservation Districts, there is now a desire among some residents to consider a heritage designation for Queen Street proper, there being little doubt that unchecked development will bring unprecedented and irrevocable change.

Storm Over Little Leuty, **painted by Ms. Rosanna Mitchell's grade eight children at St. John's Catholic School,** 2012 Courtesy Doerksen Smith family

Like in decades gone by, with the railway and then with the Scarborough Expressway, Beachers are mobilizing. Petitions are being signed for what they see as a threat to the village-like character of their neighbourhood. To this end, Toronto City Council has recently adopted urban design guidelines for Queen Street in the Beach that in general terms cap development at six storeys between Woodbine Avenue and Neville Park Boulevard, with an "apparent height" qualification that is not to exceed four stories. Many Beach residents see height as only one of a number of issues that threatens the small town atmosphere of their village. Local historian and community activist Gene Domagala states, "These larger glass structures you see down at Queen and University . . . there's nothing wrong with them architecturally, but they *do not* fit in with the nature and character of the Beach." The urban design guidelines do address "glass curtain walls" in the Beach, but how far they will go in meeting the community's concerns remains to be seen.

While residential density along Queen will undoubtedly see at least some intensification in the years to come, new multi-storey condominiums down by the Lake would seem to be even less welcome. Not surprisingly, residents see this sort of development as a threat to the waterfront itself and *their* beach.

NEIGHBOURHOODS DO CHANGE. The Beach changed in the 1970s and 1980s. Yet despite the identity crisis of those years, the community not only has survived but, on the whole, has flourished and prospered. Paradise was not lost. The Beach, though perceived by many as having been invaded, can also be said to have been rediscovered, if the early history of the area is taken into account. The fact remains that despite the confusion over names, the continuous reshuffling of storefronts, the profusion of condominiums along Queen Street, the elbow-to-elbow congestion of summer Sundays, the wild escalation of real estate prices, and the fiction that anything south of the Danforth, not to say Eglinton or the 401, is or soon will be prime Beach real estate, the identity of the place remains elsewhere.

The heart of the Beach is down at the southern edge, where the water laps at the shore, the one constant in an inconstant little village world. It was here that Glenn Gould sought quiet contemplation and here, perhaps, where the great John Candy came up with his first funny lines. And it is here that a creative spirit, a certain carefree abandon, will be inspired in future generations, whatever they may choose to call the place.

The Boardwalk after a heavy rain,
2010 Marley Adams

The Island

PART III

On the lagoon, 2007 Jane Fairburn

CHAPTER ONE

The Nature of the Place

Torontonians are very lucky. Whenever the crush of humanity becomes too intense, whenever the pressures of Bay Street become too overwhelming, whenever the demands of urban living become too exhausting, the possibility remains of leaving all of that behind. On any given day in the downtown core, you can walk south, through the noise, the traffic, and the congestion, board a ferry at the water's edge, and cross a little stretch of water to the faraway world of Toronto Island. The Island is the alter ego to the skyscrapers of concrete and glass that stand shoulder to shoulder along the edge of the harbour, and is more accurately described as a series of "islands," or sandbars, that form the southern perimeter of Toronto's Inner Harbour. Collectively they constitute a place that is in equal parts captivating and unique, silent and dishevelled, romantic and isolated — a place seemingly disconnected from the metropolis yet nevertheless deeply entwined with our cultural identity as Torontonians.

Perhaps it is the very nature of the place, its wide-open spaces and its solitude, that invites us to reflection, self-examination, and introspection, for it is in the quiet corners

Gazing back at the metropolis, 2007

Jane Fairburn

of the Island that we can begin to ask the difficult questions about who and why and what we are, both as a city and a people. If we are patient, we may find that at least part of the answer is revealed not in the commercial towers of the financial district, nor in the elegance of Rosedale, nor even in the raucous exchanges on Yonge Street, but a mile offshore on a sliver of willow and sand — our Island, that beguiling oasis of mystical imagination, overlooking the empire.

The allure of the Island is heightened by the fact that it is mostly hidden from the mainland by the rampant growth of waterfront towers and condominiums that occurred in the late twentieth century. Now, in the present century, Torontonians are often afforded their best views of the Island from above the city centre, whether it be from our cars on the Gardiner Expressway, as we peer between the massive buildings that hug the shore, or from the highest reaches of glitzy downtown office towers. In any case it is from above that one is most struck by the size of the Island. Helped along by massive infilling projects that occurred primarily in the twentieth century, it is today more than

This Island home has overlooked Toronto Bay since the 1930s April Hickox, Katzman Kamen Gallery, AprilHickox.com

800 acres in overall area, seemingly only a stone's throw from the city centre.

The Island is best known to Torontonians as a popular tourist destination and a place for cheap and cheerful summer day trips, when crowds wait to bustle aboard the crowded ferries, lugging with them their children, their dogs, their picnic baskets, and their bicycles. But there is also a population of very much "other" people who make that same journey but in the reverse direction, and not just once or twice in the holiday season but day after day throughout the year, and not only when the water is as bland and blue as the French Riviera, but occasionally when it comes crashing up over the bow and drowns the decks, so that it's safer to seek shelter in the cabin.

On just such a day in the middle of February, I stand shivering at the Island ferry docks behind the towers of the Harbour Castle Hotel, waiting for the Island ferry to take me across to Ward's Island. As the wind whips around the ferry gates, survival mode kicks in, and we passengers huddle together for warmth and company. We are an oddly diverse

The Ongiara cruises into Ward's Island on a bracing February morning, 2013 Wayne LeFort

collection of Torontonians: school children burdened with snowsuits and backpacks alongside a cadre of intrepid winter cyclists, mostly middle-aged Island residents who are in turn weighed down with a week's groceries strapped to every possible place on their bikes and bodies.

The gates of the ferry terminal are hauled back as the old *Ongiara* bumps up with a thud against the harbour wall. We step onto the solid little ship and haul open the ice-encrusted door to the cabin, settling down to relax, cocooned by the sudden warmth. Choppy waves lurch up and down outside the frosty windows as the boat churns away from the dock. Seemingly so far off at first, the Island begins to emerge from the far tree-lined shore.

At the Ward's Island landing, the creaky ferry platform eases into place, and the crowd moves away from the ship in all directions, only to be slapped back by a blast of arresting Arctic cold. The Island always seems at least ten degrees colder than the mainland in winter.

Along the Shore

Down on the beach by the ferry landing the sun comes out from behind the clouds. Shining through the ice cakes that have stacked up on the hard-packed sand, it turns them as transparent as glass. Farther down the beach, an old rowboat lies at the water's edge. Someone has forgotten to take it in for winter. Frozen in time, it remains poised at the water's edge, patiently awaiting its launch toward the towers of the emerald city.

Now all the people have gone from the landing place, off on their various paths, and I am left alone to follow mine, which is to be of a rather different nature. First I am going to pause at a place called "myth." It has been often said that "as the mountain is to Montreal, so the Island is to Toronto." Former Islander John McLarty told me a story many years ago about another long-time Island resident, Dick Oldershaw, that should illustrate the point. When Oldershaw took part in the liberation of Holland during the Second World War, he became friendly with one of his German prisoners. As the war-weary twosome whiled away an afternoon together, the German prisoner asked him where he came from. Oldershaw replied that he was from Ontario, Canada, but that he lived on a little Island close to the city of Toronto, an island of which his prisoner could not possibly have heard. In halting English, the German asked in reply, "Would that be Ward's or Centre?"

How is it, one wonders, that while Muskoka, Algonquin, the shores of Georgian Bay, and the rocks and waters of the Canadian Shield are seen as central images of prime importance to the imagery of Ontario, the seemingly inconsequential island lying off Toronto's shore is also to be found not only in local memories and imagery near at hand but also in thoughts far removed from those other places? What gives the Island such universality? Is it the classical appeal that the ancients spoke of as *rus in urbe*, the "countryside in the city"?

———— ·•· ————

WHILE THE ISLAND is without doubt the enchanted garden of Toronto's highly urbanized downtown core, it also has a remarkable history, linked to the first peoples, the French, and the European settlement that began some years after the arrival of Lieutenant Governor Simcoe in 1793. From its golden years as a venue for pleasure seekers and as a seasonal resort town, and then to the village and cherished urban sanctuary that it is today, the Island has been a retreat and an escape, a place paradoxically of both repose and revelry, at times called our collective Shangri-La.

For the Aboriginal peoples who established encampments, and villages for a brief period in the seventeenth century, at the river mouths on the mainland along the shore,

Toronto Bay with Rainbow; Dredging the Bay, *1890, watercolour on wove paper*

William Armstrong, with permission of the Royal

Ontario Museum © ROM, 972.408

the Island was also undoubtedly a place of plenty — a valuable resource for both fishing and hunting. Later, the Island was of central importance to the Mississaugas as a sacred place of healing and a place in which to be born and to die. The French presence formally began with the building of a series of eighteenth-century forts on the mainland, at the mouth of the Humber River, and, later, beyond the western tip of the Island, on the present grounds of the Canadian National Exhibition. This was followed by European habitation that began early in the nineteenth century and has continued right on up to the present time. Today's community, though much reduced in numbers from its population peak in the 1940s and 1950s, is set within the framework of a massive city park that is visited by well over one million people a year. These residents, many of them having multi-generational ties to the community, live in a diverse collection of homes now located on the eastern end of the Island and run the gamut from whimsical to ramshackle to newly renovated houses with all the modern conveniences.

The community is the antithesis of the suburban cookie-cutter society; it is a place where anything goes — anything but cars, that is. The Island is said to be the largest car-free zone within North America, and Islanders of necessity walk or bicycle to where they want to go. This lack of cars keeps them exposed to nature and each other, and it may inspire a noticeably more active civic culture among residents who, given also the

Along the Shore

lack of services like grocery and convenience stores, are more likely than your average mainlander to borrow a cup of sugar or to ask for help in pruning an overgrown hedge.

The sense of neighbourliness on the Island today has a long history. The first Island resident was J.P. Radelmüller, who was appointed keeper of the newly erected Island lighthouse in the summer of 1809. The isolation that he must have felt would have been formidable, particularly in the winter, with the ice frozen in around him in all directions and the damp wind howling under his cottage door.

After Radelmüller's untimely death, several fishing families banded together on Island shores in the late 1830s and 1840s. Some of these families were later among the sandbar's first hoteliers, as the area transitioned to a venue for pleasure seekers and a summer cottage retreat for Toronto's wealthy elite. In the twentieth century, many other Torontonians of more modest means started to call the Island home in summer, and as the century progressed, many of these folks decided to stay year round — their numbers augmented by returning Second World War veterans and others seeking shelter during the ensuing housing shortage of the 1940s.

The Island community of the twentieth century was sometimes referred to as "the only unfenced asylum in the world." It is certainly true that living away from the mainland and surrounded by water on all sides, Islanders have always exhibited a strong "island" mentality, one that manifests itself in an individualistic and idiosyncratic nature — with a disproportionate number of larger-than-life characters. At the wake for

The Lighthouse, Toronto Island, as it appeared c. 1907 TPL, Owen Staples, JRR 472

The Island

Five ladies and a tent, Ward's Island, c. 1913

CTA, F1047_s 1825_f136 (image originally held in Toronto Island Archives)

critically acclaimed, avant-garde painter and former Island resident Tom Hodgson, one the guests, seemingly moved by the speeches, chose a rather unconventional way to honour his dear and now deceased friend. He threw off all his clothes and ran naked around the assembled crowd, yelling, "Here's to Tommy!"

While not an Islander himself, he was in good company: the eccentricities and diversity in interest and temperament displayed by many Islanders certainly ran counter to the conservative "norms" of a puritanical Toronto that is almost lost on us now — "norms" that were evident until well into the middle decades of the twentieth century. Some Islanders, rather than trying to "fit in," opted for life on the sandbar a mile offshore, where they were free to develop their own unique sense of culture and community that remains to this day. As former Island resident Michael (Mike) O'Shea told me, "It was such a difference to living in a row of faceless houses in the city. You don't realize it — living on the water — it's somewhere deep in your subconscious. We were a community totally apart from the city and we were more adventuresome and much happier. We stuck together."

Along the Shore

Since the very earliest days of Toronto, the Island's development has followed a distinct and different path from that of the mainland. Never having been subject to "city planning," the community has grown organically and today is the alter ego of the built, purposeful "other" Toronto that sprawls along the shore of the mainland. Although in present times it is often used as a location for movie sets, there is nothing false or contrived about the Island; it is real, and it defies any attempt at characterization or duplication. Likewise, there is nothing false or contrived about Islanders; they are originals, and, like the place itself, they have displayed a remarkable will to survive and to change over the decades as change has come. Their anecdotes and remembrances, grounded in history and occasionally elevated to myth, animate this special place, giving the Island a reality that extends far beyond its official status as a city park.

CHAPTER TWO

Beginnings

It may be geology that formed the Island, but myth delineates it in our mind. In an article that appeared in the *Globe and Mail* on December 18, 1954, Mohawk historian William Smith recounts the legend, generally shared by the Iroquois, that in a far-off time, long before the white man came, the Great Spirit was moved to anger by his children and was so provoked that the curse of a terrible storm was inflicted on Lake Ontario. Smith relates, "Thunder rocked the earth and lightning split the darkening sky with whiplike fury, booming and crackling. . . . Along the lakeshore a collapsing movement . . . began, and the land started sliding into the water, submerging, thrusting up, sinking again." The intensity of the storm "laid the forests flat as matchsticks, whipped the waves as tall as treetops on Lake Ontario and made the earth tremble with their violence. . . . There was then no Island off the northern shore of Lake Ontario but, when the sinking and upheaval finished and the storm had ended, an island had been formed and that island is now Toronto Island."

Until the middle of the nineteenth century, the Island was not an island at all but

Toronto Daily Star *artist George Paginton was fascinated with the changing colours and moods of Lake Ontario and captured the power of this winter storm, as seen from his living room window in New Toronto, c. 1960*

a peninsula, and it was referred to as such by York's first residents. This narrow sandy ridge, the configuration of which was constantly changing due to the vagaries of the wind and waves, was loosely attached to the mainland much farther east, in the vicinity of Woodbine Avenue, and in the west by a strip of marshy land bisected by the outflow of the Don River. Continual wave action, helped along by a number of storms that took place in the mid-nineteenth century, eroded the narrow neck of this sandbar, so that by 1858 the Peninsula in front of what is now downtown Toronto became an island.

Sir Sandford Fleming, the Scottish-born Canadian engineer and inventor, and Professor A.P. Coleman, scientist and geologist, first put forward the scientific version of the origin of the Peninsula in the nineteenth century. The formation of Toronto Island began several thousands of years ago, when sediment from the sand and clay deposits of the

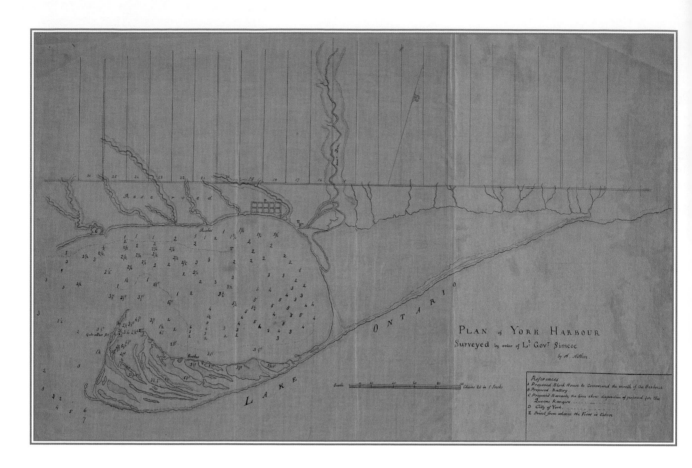

Alexander Aitken's Plan of York Harbour Surveyed by order of Lt. Govr Simcoe, *1793 clearly shows the extent of the Peninsula and the "City of York," which is smaller and situated nearer to the Don River than in his earlier* Plan of Toronto, *1788 (see page 25)* TPL, Toronto 1793 (col. copy)

Scarborough Bluffs gradually began to erode into the lake, carrying sediment away to the west. Along with the outflow of the Don River, these deposits formed in time an immense recurve sand spit: a peninsula of some five and a half to six miles in total length that extended from present-day Woodbine Avenue in the east, in the vicinity of the Beach, all the way over to the Island in the west, where it was best described as a series of narrow interconnected sandbars, lagoons, marshlands, and ponds, fanning out like an arc in front of a deep, sheltered harbour.

In an 1833 report entitled "York Harbour," Harbour Commissioner Hugh Richardson offered a more lyrical version of the birth of the Island, stating that the Scarborough promontory was "torn periodically by the easterly gale . . . and sprinkled its first deposit in the direction of the wind, laying the foundation of the peninsula as simply as a pail of

Along the Shore

sandy water thrown into a clear pool would deposit the sand in the direction in which it was thrown. And thus has fallen from the charged wave of the storm, deposit on deposit, until, from the bosom of the Lake, up rose the peninsula, the work of ages of repetitions, and the monstrous index of the ravages of countless easterly storms upon the highland of Scarborough."

———•———

THE PRESENCE OF human beings in the Toronto region extends back in time some 11,000 years ago, long before there was even an island and when the shore extended far out into the present-day lake, beyond what would become the Peninsula. In his book *Toronto: An Illustrated History of Its First 12,000 Years,* Ronald F. Williamson notes that east of Hanlan's Point, in 1908, city workers made an astounding discovery while tunnelling in Toronto Bay. At a depth of seventy feet below the water and immersed in a six-foot-wide layer of blue clay were more than 100 perfectly preserved human footprints of all shapes and sizes, some on top of each other. The construction company foreman described the footsteps as being "clear as those made by a man's moccasined foot stamped into the stiff mud."

After the Peninsula began to take shape, it was used, no doubt, by indigenous peoples, among them the ancestral Huron-Wendat who left the north shore of the lake at Toronto and migrated into the Lake Simcoe and Georgian Bay areas in the late sixteenth century. Though we have an incomplete knowledge of their uses of the Peninsula, we know it was an abundant hunting and fishing area and no doubt also served as an important landmark, situated as it was in close proximity to the Carrying Place Trail. As we will read in the Lakeshore section, the western branch of the ancient portage route of some twenty-eight miles began about a mile and a half upriver from the mouth of the Humber, near the short-lived Seneca village of Teiaiagon, and provided a convenient shortcut into the hinterlands north of Lake Ontario.

Likewise, the Island was also a familiar marker for French explorers, who called the Peninsula the Presqu'île of Toronto, which literally means "Almost Island" of Toronto. Among them was Father Louis Hennepin, who, as we shall read in the Lakeshore section, gives us one of the first European accounts of Teiaiagon. Likewise, the French explorer René-Robert Cavelier de La Salle sailed up the lake from Fort Frontenac and accessed the Carrying Place Trail on his way to exploring the Upper Great Lakes region and the Mississippi River Basin.

Sally Gibson in *More Than an Island* notes that the original isthmus (the narrow neck of the Peninsula), located near the mouth of the Don River, was a key shortcut to the mouth of the Humber River and all that lay beyond. The isthmus was used, especially in bad weather, to avoid foundering on the sandy shoals along the western reaches of the Peninsula. Many coureurs de bois, explorers, and military men hauled their vessels out of the water and rested on the Island before travelling up the Carrying Place Trail or visiting the Magasin Royal, built by the French near the mouth of the Humber River and operating between 1720 and 1730, or, later, Fort Rouillé, established by 1751 off the western tip of the Peninsula, on the grounds of today's Canadian National Exhibition.

The Peninsula may well have looked like a group of trees standing in water to these Europeans, given the low-lying nature of the sandbar. Interestingly, the Mohawk meaning for the word "Toronto," defined as trees standing in water, is now the more favoured translation, replacing the well-known "meeting place" definition that was previously proffered by Henry Scadding, author of *Toronto of Old*. It may be tempting to view the Island as the original source of the translation, but recent thinking by historians now suggests otherwise.

A variation on the word Toronto, "Taronto," appears in reference to Lake Simcoe on a map attributed to the explorer Louis Joliet, drawn about 1675, during the years that the Seneca had migrated into the Toronto region from the south shore of Lake Ontario. It is generally accepted that the words "trees standing in water" refer not to the Peninsula but to the fishing weirs of the Aboriginal people who occupied the lands at the narrows between Lake Simcoe and Lake Couchiching around this time. Variations on the name "Toronto" gradually began to appear on successive French maps of the period, and in time the name came to be associated with the entire region immediately above the Carrying Place Trail. Eventually, the name was also used to describe the entrance to the Carrying Place Trail itself, namely the vicinity of the mouth of the Humber River, including the peninsula that lay just off the shore.

Though the name Toronto may originate with the Iroquois, it is from the Mississaugas, previously discussed in the Scarborough shore section, that we gain our initial snapshot of Island life. According to Donald Smith's history of the Mississauga Chief Kahkewaquonaby (in English, the Reverend Peter Jones), the Mississaugas (a branch of the Anishinabe nation) practised a way of life that involved mobility and seasonal shifts in resource harvesting. Though concentrated at the mouth of the Credit River during spring and fall, the Mississaugas frequently camped on the Peninsula, which they called "Menecing," or "Minnising," literally translated as "island," according to the *History of the Ojebway Indians; etc.* or "on the island."

Some seventy years after the Mississaugas had moved into the Toronto region came

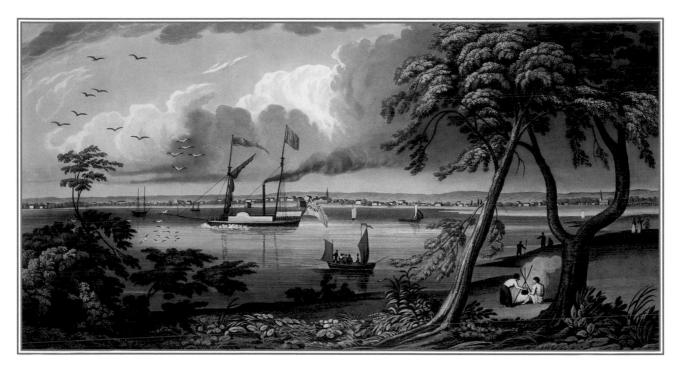

York from Gibralter Point, 1828, *aquatint based on a drawing by James Gray. The image is rendered from the perspective of the Island — note the Aboriginal people depicted under the luxuriant foliage.* TPL, JRR 195

the end of the French régime at Toronto with the burning of Fort Rouillé in 1759. During this period, the Mississaugas witnessed Toronto's transition from a backwoods fort to a fledgling town with the founding of York by the English in 1793. Participating in the defence of York during the War of 1812, the Mississaugas, along with other Anishinabe, were the first to fall as the Americans approached the beach about a mile west of Fort York, near present-day Parkdale. In later years to come, they were present as the foundations were laid for the development of the great postmodern city of today. Along the way, through the ages and stages of this transition, the Island would play a central part in this story.

We have said earlier on that the Island served as a geographic marker for Aboriginal people and Europeans travelling into the Toronto region. The Island certainly served a similar purpose for the Mississaugas, who saw it as a significant landmark within the easterly reaches of their territory. The Peninsula was also from earliest times a bountiful fishing and hunting ground for the Mississaugas, as it had been for the first peoples who had preceded them, the shallow offshore waters containing, among other species, herring, salmon, whitefish, and muskellunge. *The Diary of Mrs. Simcoe*, written by the

The Island

wife of John Graves Simcoe, the first lieutenant governor of Upper Canada and founder of York, includes many first-hand accounts of the local first peoples engaged in everyday activities on the Island at Toronto. She writes in her diary that on the evening of November 1, 1793, "We went in a boat to see salmon speared. Large torches of white birch bark were being carried in the boat, the blaze of light attracts the fish, when [*sic*] the men are dexterous in spearing. The manner of destroying the fish is disagreeable, but seeing them swimming in shoals around the boat is a very pretty sight."

In close proximity to the Peninsula was a great river that the Mississaugas referred to as the Wonscotonach, translated, according to Augustus Jones' 1796 list of "Names of the Rivers and Creeks, as they are called by the Mississaugas," as "back burnt grounds." Trout, bass, and salmon were in ample supply on the Wonscotonach, now known as the Don River. According to the Reverend Peter Jones, the Mississaugas had once maintained campsites along the river, as well as in the vicinity of what we know today as Riverdale Park.

The Peninsula was not only a bountiful fishing and hunting ground, it also served as a sacred healing place, confirmed by Mrs. Simcoe when she writes, "The air on these sands is peculiarly clear and fine. The Indians esteem this place so healthy that they come and stay here when they are ill." As a sacred place it was a fitting location for births. The marriage record of Mississauga Chief George King (great-grandfather of Mississauga community and political activist Lloyd King), held at the Ontario Archives, indicates that he was born on the Island in 1815. Likewise, a sworn statement of his contemporary, James Tobico (Etobicoke), from 1888, indicates that he was also "born on the Island in front of Toronto" in 1820.

The Island was also a final resting place for the Mississaugas. After dining on the sandbar in early November 1793, Mrs. Simcoe wrote, "I passed a spot on the peninsula where it was supposed an Indian had been buried lately. A small pile of wood was raised, a bow and arrow lay on it, and a dog skin hung near it." Despite the presence of the Mississaugas on the Peninsula at the time of the arrival of Lieutenant and Mrs. Simcoe in 1793, and the strong likelihood that other earlier Aboriginal peoples would have accessed the same sandy spit, very few artifacts have been uncovered. By the turn of the nineteenth century, European settlement was about to begin — a process that would bring great change to the Island and contribute to the loss of much of this archaeological record.

CHAPTER THREE
Settlement

Geography is one of the key determinants in the origin of any great city. So it was with founding of Toronto, which is situated in the lee of a natural sheltered harbour formed by the Peninsula. After Lieutenant Governor Simcoe arrived in Upper Canada in 1792, his first order of business was to secure the province's defences against the prospect of an American attack, and to this end he toured Toronto Bay by bateau in May of 1793. While initially envisioning the site as an ideal location for the establishment of a naval base, it would soon, in 1796, be chosen as the location for Upper Canada's capital. Simcoe viewed the Toronto site as advantageous not only due to its proximity to the Carrying Place Trail but also because he believed the harbour to be highly defensible, offering, at that time, only one point of entry around the western tip of the Peninsula. So confident was he in the impregnability of the harbour that he began referring to the northwestern tip of the Peninsula as "Gibraltar Point," in respect to the blockhouses he would eventually erect there for the defence of the bay.

Governor Simcoe's enthusiasm for the harbour was shared and in fact surpassed only by that of his wife, Elizabeth. After the Simcoes had set up camp near what became the foot of Bathurst Street, the lively Mrs. Simcoe began taking frequent outings to the Peninsula, which she referred to as her "favourite sands." In weather conditions that would make the modern Torontonian shudder, she filled her days there with experiences of nature, whether through ice skating or horse racing, picnicking by the water, or observing the Mississaugas, who hunted, fished, and camped along the shore.

Given the tight constraints placed on women in the eighteenth century, one can hardly imagine the freedom she found there, a place where she was able to explore nature, to paint, and to be alone with her thoughts. Her diary has become a valued document of early Ontario history, with many pages devoted to her experiences on the Island and along the present-day Toronto shore.

Mrs. Elizabeth Posthuma (Gwillim) Simcoe, 1762–1850 *Mary Anne Burges, 1790* TPL, JRR 3264

Of the Peninsula she writes on August 4, 1793, "We met with some good natural meadows and several ponds. The trees are mostly of the poplar kind, covered with wild vines, and there are some fir. On the ground were everlasting peas creeping in such abundance, of a purple colour. . . . The diversity of scenes I met with this morning made the ride extremely pleasant. The wooded part of the peninsula was like shrubbery. The sands toward the lake reminded me of the sands at Weymouth." In a letter to a Miss Hunt, at York, dated August 3, 1793, she spoke of the Peninsula being "intersected with numberless ponds, so that if you ride thro the internal or middle part . . . a stranger cannot find the way out."

The Island, though vastly changed since the days of Mrs. Simcoe, retains a recently affirmed provincially significant wetland complex of thirty-four sites, many of which are also identified by

Along the Shore

Snug Island lagoon, 2011 — if you look closely, you might be able to make out the Blue Heron resting on the tree branch above the hammock April Hickox Katzman Kamen Gallery, AprilHickox.com

the Toronto and Region Conservation Authority as Environmentally Significant Areas (ESAS). The province has also designated some parts of the Island as a Life Science Area of Natural Scientific Interest (ANSI). Wandering through hardwood and shoreline marshes as Mrs. Simcoe did, naturalists can spot water lilies on the Lighthouse Pond at Centre Island, as well as many important species of plants, including the Canada Bluejoint and the Nelson's Horsetail in the meadow marshes. The Island also has no shortage of important bird species, including the Least Flycatcher, the Yellow Warbler, and the Blue-grey Gnatcatcher, all which may be spotted in the treed swamps that line the shore.

———◆———

WHEN MRS. SIMCOE left Toronto Bay forever in July of 1796, she sketched one final drawing of the Peninsula from Gibraltar Point and inscribed in her diary, "Cried all day." She was, beyond doubt, an Islander at heart. Within a month of her leaving, the Peninsula figured prominently in the events surrounding the death of the much-loved head chief of the Mississaugas, Wabakinine, who spent some of his final hours there after suffering a vicious, unprovoked attack by a British soldier, Charles McEwan (also spelled McCuen).

Fearing a Mississauga uprising, a murder charge was laid against McEwan, though the charge was later scandalously dismissed due to a lack of evidence. The years following the death of Wabakinine proved to be unsettled ones with respect to relations between the British, the Mississaugas, and the larger Aboriginal community. In 1803, United Empire Loyalist Samuel D. Cozens allegedly murdered a Mississauga man, Whistling Duck. Brendan O'Brien surmises that it was largely due to Cozens's influence and connections that the matter had never been brought to trial.

About a year after the crime had been committed, and still in the absence of the arrest of Cozens, Whistling Duck's "brother," Ogetonicut, allegedly killed fur trader John Sharp in retaliation for the death of Whistling Duck. The murder, while undoubtedly callous when judged by our standards, was in accordance with the Anishinabe code of conduct, which allowed for retaliation against the tribe who had been the first to kill.

After the alleged murder of Sharp, Ogetonicut, along with several other band members, travelled south to the shore of Lake Ontario and repaired to the Island. Outraged York citizens demanded that the "Indian" murderer now in their midst be thrown into leg irons and prosecuted to the full extent of the law, while paying little or no attention to the fact that Cozens, the white man implicated in the death of Whistling Duck, remained at large. Ogetonicut was arrested on the Island a short time later. Meanwhile the *Speedy*, the ship that would transport him to his trial and probable public execution in Newcastle, underwent repairs in the harbour.

The *Speedy* was part of the Provincial Marine. Like many of the other vessels built for the marine during this period, she was constructed of green timber from the virgin forest that hugged the north shore of the lake. Built in 1798, she was some six years later rapidly reaching the end of her life expectancy and was filled with dry rot. Regardless of the dubious safety of the vessel, Ogetonicut, along with several prominent members of York society and Upper Canada's justice system, boarded the schooner in York Harbour on October 7, 1804, bound for Newcastle.

O'Brien notes that prior to setting sail, the captain of the *Speedy*, Thomas Paxton, implored Lieutenant Governor Peter Hunter to postpone the voyage due to the

H.M. schooner Speedy *(Lake Ontario), c. 1800* C.H.J. Snider, coloured with water colour by Owen Staples, TPL, JRR 1199

unseaworthy condition of the vessel. Hunter would hear nothing of it and ordered Paxton out of the harbour under threat of court martial. It is said that before the ship set sail in the harbour, Ogetonicut's mother retreated into the woods and waited at the top of the Scarborough Bluffs for the vessel to pass by on its journey eastward. With her son now in leg irons, deep within the ship's hold and on his way to almost certain death, legend has it that she cursed the *Speedy* and its crew as it sailed on to Newcastle.

Some time after the vessel passed the Bluffs, a violent storm arose, creating raging seas and hurricane-like conditions. Variances in the magnetic field in this area of the Lake, which have been reported by sailors even up to the present day, may have been at play.

The Island

An emergency bonfire was lit to alert Paxton to the entrance of Presqu'île Harbour, but the ship, along with all its passengers and crew, disappeared that night, never to be seen or heard of again.

There is now evidence to suggest that the *Speedy* lies in deep water at the bottom of the lake, many miles south of Brighton Bay, just east of Presqu'île Point. In 1990, the remains of a pre-1820 shipwreck, complete with cannonball and consistent in design with ships built for the Provincial Marine, were discovered in this area. One theory is that the ship, which constitutes a significant piece of our early marine history in Ontario, struck Dobbs Bank, the theorized site of the fabled Devil's Horseblock, a gigantic limestone shoal that was said by early sailors to extend up from the bottom of the lake to within a short distance of the surface of the water. For a ship caught in a blinding storm without the help of modern navigational aids, a nightmare waiting to happen. Perhaps Ogetonicut's mother got her wish.

———— •◦• ————

ENCROACHING SANDY SHOALS around the westerly edge of the peninsula made negotiating the entrance and egress to Toronto Bay increasingly difficult and treacherous in the late eighteenth and early nineteenth centuries. The *Speedy*, upon leaving York Harbour in 1804, initially ran aground in the bay, while a government yacht, the *Onondoga*, had previously foundered off Gibraltar Point (now Hanlan's Point). Given that York relied almost exclusively on water transport during this period, it was clear that a lighthouse had to be built on the Peninsula.

In 1809, a distinctive fifty-two-foot-high hexagonal tower of grey Queenston limestone was completed. Originally standing less than twenty-five feet from the water on the southern shore of the lake, it remains one of Toronto's oldest landmarks. Today the lighthouse is located somewhat inland due to the accumulation of sand along the southern edge of the Island from the erosion of the Scarborough Bluffs. (The construction of the Leslie Street Spit and the shoring up of the Bluffs are now having the opposite effect: the Island sands are now actually eroding.) The lighthouse stands at what is currently referred to as Gibraltar Point, although that place name was originally associated with the northwestern tip of the Island.

While Mrs. Simcoe may have been the first European Islander in spirit, the first resident was lighthouse keeper J.P. Radelmüller. According to Sally Gibson, Radelmüller lived near the lighthouse in a shuttered plank cottage with nails and door latches forged by the military blacksmith at Fort York. Sarah Hood, in a number of articles, including

"J.P. Radelmüller Arrives in Canada," gives us a more fulsome picture of the background of this interesting character. In a letter dated January 1, 1808, Radelmüller describes the circumstances of how he arrived in Upper Canada, indicating that he was born in Anspach, in present-day Bavaria, Germany. After moving to England, he became a high-ranking servant for the British royal family, and in his official capacity he made his way to Halifax. Later, he travelled to Upper Canada on his own and was eventually appointed the lighthouse keeper on Toronto Island on July 24, 1809. He married Magdalen Burkholder in 1810, and they presumably lived together on the Island, at least until his demise in 1815.

Radelmüller's life was cut short by a series of events that remain shrouded in mystery. According to an account in the *York Gazette* of January 14, 1815, "there is every moral proof of his [Radelmüller] having been murdered. If the horrid crime admits of aggravation, when the inoffensive and benevolent character of the unfortunate sufferer are considered, his murder will be pronounced most barbarous and inhuman."

As legend would have it, the murder is connected to Radelmüller's unofficial occupation: he was the first local bootlegger on the Island, serving liquor to the British soldiers stationed at Fort York. While details vary, the story goes that two or three of these soldiers "got away" to the Island one night in January 1815 and were served generous amounts of alcohol by Radelmüller. When the intoxicated soldiers became unruly, Radelmüller refused them any more libations and paid the ultimate price for his decision. Though accounts vary, legend has it that soldiers John Henry and John Blowman, now in

Gibraltar Point Lighthouse, Toronto Island, c. 2007
Jane Fairburn

The Island

a drunken stupor, beat Radelmüller to death and then, as some versions suggest, carried him off to the lighthouse. After dragging his body to the top of the lighthouse and tossing it over the side, they buried it somewhere nearby.

Research conducted by Gibson indicates that John Blowman and John Henry were in fact arrested, jailed, and indicted for the murder of Radelmüller, though court records indicate that they were acquitted on March 31, 1815, possibly because no body had been found. *Robertson's Landmarks of Toronto* reveals that a subsequent keeper of the light, George Durnan, discovered, in 1893, parts of a coffin and a human jawbone close to the lighthouse. In another report, he maintained that he had heard a lone male voice moaning during the early hours of the morning in the vicinity of the lighthouse.

Although the mystery of the death of Radelmüller remains unsolved, the story, like many Toronto Island legends, persists to the present day. In the 1990s Island resident and photographer Glenn McArthur, while shooting the lighthouse, had his camera jam on the thirteenth step. Having never had his camera jam in his fifteen years of professional photography, he anxiously awaited the negatives from the developers, which revealed that the thirteenth exposure of the thirteenth step was blood red. While we may never fully unravel the events that took place on that dark night in January 1815, it nonetheless makes for another spooky tale to tell over drinks.

Three years before the death of Radelmüller, another notorious incident occurred on the Peninsula, one with an outcome of provincial, if not national, significance. On a bleak morning in the spring of 1812, two prominent members of York society, John MacDonell and William Warren Baldwin, met on the Island to fight a duel.

Emigrating from Ireland in 1799, W.W. Baldwin was an ambitious and talented lawyer, doctor, and architect. He belonged to the privileged class of York society, where promotion and success were largely dependent on personal friendships and political patronage. Competition for the limited positions within this closed circle was fierce.

The dashingly handsome John MacDonell was also from the upper class, and he was rapidly ascending the ranks of York society. (MacDonell was the nephew of Alexander McDonell, whom we met in the Scarborough section.) At the age of twenty-seven, he was expected within days to be named the new attorney general of Upper Canada, a position that Baldwin coveted. Furthermore, MacDonell was a Scot, and, as such, Baldwin assumed he had a natural advantage within the tight clique that governed the administration of the province. As to the personal qualities of MacDonell, Baldwin described him, in a letter to William Firth in April 1812, as "such a paragon of excellence that he leaves no virtue no commendable qualification to found pretensions on . . . the field, the cabinet and the Forum are all to be the scenes of his Renown — his honors not rain upon him, they come in tempests."

The final outrage to Baldwin, however, was MacDonell uttering "wanton and ungentlemanly expressions" against him. Though the details of the insult are unknown, Baldwin flew into a rage and demanded an apology. When it was clear that none was forthcoming, Baldwin challenged him to a duel. Baldwin's honour would be satisfied, over risk to family, reputation, and even his life. The night before the duel, Baldwin wrote to his devoted wife, Phoebe, "My soul, I beseech you to pardon this step which I am now about to take not to indulge a rash or resentful spirit but to protect me from insults which, as a gentleman I cannot submit to . . . Farewell — perhaps forever."

On the morning of April 3, 1812, Baldwin arose at daybreak. With his second, Thomas Taylor, he walked in silence along the shore of the windy, frozen bay, stopping at the Blockhouse near the Parliament Building to execute the will he had prepared the night before. Although the exact location is unknown, it is possible that the combatants and their seconds met on the sands of the remote southern shore of the Island. Beyond them was the great expanse of the open lake, pounding against the beach. Taylor's hands undoubtedly shook as he loaded the flintlock pistol for Baldwin. MacDonnell's second, Cameron, placed the opposing pistol in the hand of his friend, who gave no forewarning of what was to come. The combatants placed themselves back to back, and at Taylor's command, the duellists took their ten paces and turned to fire.

Baldwin raised his pistol and locked eyes with his opponent. To his astonishment, MacDonell stood stalwart on the icy sands with his weapon held tightly at his side. Cameron yelled to Baldwin over the crashing waves, "He wants you to fire!" Baldwin, a gentleman to the end, had decided not to fire on MacDonell. He chose to see MacDonell's gesture as a sign of contrition, and the affair ended with a handshake on the Peninsula.

Baldwin's split-second decision on the blustery Peninsula in 1812 had far-reaching consequences. William Warren Baldwin became a leading proponent of reform policies that eventually led to the transition to responsible government in the United Province of Canada in 1848. Under his influence, followed by the contribution of his son, Robert Baldwin, these reforms paved the way for the evolution of the democratic process in modern Canada.

Six months after the duel, John MacDonell became one of Canada's almost forgotten heroes in the Battle of Queenston Heights, the first decisive battle on Canadian soil in the War of 1812. After Major General Sir Isaac Brock had been killed by an American

Where General Brock Fell, Queenston *(Niagara-on-the-Lake, Ontario)* Owen Staples, TPL, JRR 1299

Along the Shore

sniper, the general's own aide-de-camp, Lieutenant Colonel John MacDonell, rallied the York volunteers and led them in a second charge up the heights. In the course of the assault MacDonell was shot, dying the next day. Yet his sacrifice was not in vain; the arrival of further British troop reinforcements led to the total defeat of the American invading forces. Half a year later, the Americans would settle the score, after landing west of what is now Sunnyside Beach, and sack the town of York.

———•———

BY 1832 JAMES DURNAN began his tenure as the Island's lighthouse keeper, first taking up residence in the same plank cottage first occupied by J.P. Radelmüller. Later in the 1830s, *Robertson's Landmarks* indicates that the Durnan family moved to a one-storey frame cottage erected nearby. When exactly others came to live on the Island is unclear though the Wards, Island fishermen, appear to have been established there by the early 1830s. Captain R.H. Bonnycastle's 1833 *No. 1 Plan of the Town and Harbour of York Upper Canada* and other sources indicate that a substantial fishing industry had been established on the Island by at least 1833. In time, other fishermen, rugged pioneers who harvested the plentiful bounty of the southern shores and lagoons of the Peninsula, also made the Island their home, constructing their cabins from loose timber and driftwood from the beach. The names of these families — the Strowgers, the Hanlans — came to be the backbone of the Island way of life, a life that was hard, demanding, and often dangerous. In centuries gone by, the lake took lives and changed lives, destroyed people and made others what they were. So it was for the family of William Ward.

William's father, David Ward, was a North Sea fisherman who emigrated from Yarmouth in England in 1830 and later built a small cottage on the easterly narrow neck of the Peninsula, at what was then referred to as the Marsh Shore. William was born there, and from the age of five or six helped his father haul laden nets out of the water south of the Island. The pair would then row their daily catch to market, earning a single York shilling for a salmon or a dozen whitefish. In an article in the *Star Weekly* from 1912, "65 Years a Dweller on Toronto Island," William tells of scaling the trees that lined the water's edge to scan for the herring schools offshore, a skill his father had learned from the "Indians." When a school was spotted, the "Indians went out in canoes and splashed the water to drive the fish to the seining ground . . . they loaded 380 barrels, and left a lot on the beach even then."

In those days the bay, while yielding a good living, was no placid stretch of water. In our time of GPS tracking devices, navigational aids, and Harbour Police, it is difficult to

This version of the Fish Market at York appears in James Timberlake's Illustrated Toronto Past and Present *Based on a drawing by W.H. Bartlett, 1838, Courtesy D&E Lake Ltd., Toronto*

imagine that the vagaries of wind and wave in Toronto Bay, so close to the mainland, had the potential to be life threatening. It was into that bay that fourteen-year-old Ward set out for a sail on Sunday, May 11, 1862, taking along his five sisters, Phoebe, Mary Ann, Jane, Cecilia, and Rose Ellen, who ranged in ages from four to thirteen.

According to various reports, a strong breeze was blowing out across the bay that day, and William's father objected to them venturing out onto the water. (The family had already lost three other daughters to scarlet fever on a single night some years earlier.) William ignored his father, being himself a strong swimmer and an avid oarsman. (Accounts of the event in various newspapers decades later do offer alternative explanations as to why the Wards were out in the bay in the first place, including returning from church and school, rather than a pleasure sail.)

For an hour or more the Ward girls and big brother William sailed up and down, enjoying the mild spring weather. Only about half a mile from their cottage, turning the boat for home in the face of a stiff breeze, William sat on the gunwale, in the stern of the

Along the Shore

boat, to better grip the steering oar. He was probably trying to manage all the tasks of sailing the
boat, rather than delegating responsibility to the
girls, and in the circumstances, the rope for the sail

William Ward and his sisters out for a sail
on the bay Laurie Jones, first appeared in
William Ward: Island Hero by Joanna Kidd

was run through a hole on the side of the vessel, so he could steer at the same time. At that
very moment a strong gust caught the sail and the rope jammed, flinging William and his
sisters into the water and capsizing the boat. Unable to swim and dragged down by their
dresses, all of the girls were drowning.

William struggled to right the boat and drag his sisters in one by one. Just as he pulled
a third one aboard, the fourth, barely alive, crawled over the gunwale while the fifth sister
clung to the boat in the water. The sail again filled, capsizing the boat for a second time.
His cries for help were swept away by the wind and the sound of the waves. Clinging to
the upturned boat, he watched in horror as his sisters drowned. The *Globe* reported that a
young man heard him from the Esplanade and set out to rescue him. For the girls it was
too late. Four of the bodies lay for four days in the cottage while men dragged for the
fifth. It was not recovered until some days later. An inquest determined the girls' deaths
had been an accident, and immediately following, they were laid in St. James Cemetery.

Sometime after the tragedy, the Wards and their two surviving children abandoned their first cottage. Sally Gibson notes that by the mid-1860s the family had moved west, "toward the centre of the Island, to the edge of what became Ward's pond." Although David Ward went on to establish a sizable and productive homestead on this second site, legend has it that William's mother, unable to recover from the tragedy, walked the Island shore to the end of her days, staring out at the water that had taken five of her daughters.

The burden that William Ward carried was heavy, in view of his father's warning, his sisters' death, and his mother's grief. But he was given a chance to redeem himself six years later, on December 7, 1868, when the *Jane Ann Marsh*, a heavy schooner from Port Hope that was loaded down with cordwood, ran aground in a blinding snowstorm off the southeast shore of the Island.

The timbers washing up onto the beach alerted fishermen on the Island. As Ward himself recalled some forty-four years later in "Snatched from Death," "through the whirling snow clouds they made out the loom of her spars. It was so thick you could hardly see the water or the hull of the vessel. The crew was hanging to the rigging." Young Ward was faced with a choice: he could stay on shore and watch while the sailors died as his sisters had, or he could get out into the water and try for the wreck.

Ward chose the latter, and with the great black champion oarsmen and boxer Robert Berry and a lifeline tied fast to their skiff, Ward climbed the rigging of the *Jane Ann Marsh*. Ward recounted that with breakers crashing overhead, Ward and Berry pounded the ice off the benumbed crew, some of whom were, according to Ward, frozen in place by ice up to six inches thick. It took seven trips to rescue the crew, who were rowed ashore two at a time. In between trips, the fishermen onshore prepared their skiff for the next foray into the lake, while the two men raced up and down the beach in snow up to their knees so as to bring back their circulation. All hands were saved, including one man so helpless that he slipped between the schooner and the boat as the waves burst over the rescue vessel. Ward recalled that the ice on his limbs kept him afloat and they got him in again.

Ward received the Royal Humane Society's silver medal for his efforts in saving the crew of that ship, a medal that had never before been presented in Canada for heroic efforts in saving the lives of others. But this was only the first of successive awards he'd receive and rarely display. Though accounts do vary, Ward would go on to save the lives of at least 160 off the shore of Toronto Bay during the course of his life.

Another severe winter storm in 1875 brought the *Olive Branch*, a schooner from Oswego, aground within 200 to 250 feet of the shore. Island fishermen were unable even to launch a boat to attempt a rescue due to the breakers crashing over the beach. The

Along the Shore

Sometime after the tragedy in the bay, the David Ward Sr. homestead was located on Centre Island, pictured here in 1885

Owen Staples, TPL, JRR 727

terrified crew, hanging from the foresail, had thrown a hatch cover from the ship on a rope out toward the beach in hopes that someone would be able to grab hold of it and pull them to shore.

As William recounted years later, his father, David Ward, said, "Will . . . make a line fast round your waist and have a try for that hatch." Ward did and later recalled, "I made the line fast and plunged in. One sea reared up fourteen feet of solid water above me." Miraculously, Ward again made the boat and was credited with saving the entire crew of ten, including the female cook, who was lashed to the line and slid down from the mast-head to the shore. On this occasion Ward received the Royal Humane Society's gold medal, the highest honour for an act of bravery given in the British Empire. His greatest prize, however, was not the medal but a lifesaving boat, donated by the Dominion Government, for use on the Island. According to a report in the *Globe* in January 1912, Ward was made captain of the Dominion lifesaving crew in 1881, a position that he would hold for the next thirty years.

Sometime long before, out amidst the heaving, crashing waves, William Ward decided that no one would drown in the bay again, not if he could prevent it. A personal loss to the lake that would have broken men of lesser resolve had transformed him into a hero. During the years to come, Ward threw himself into the water whenever others were in danger, regardless of the risk to his own life. By the time of his own death in 1912, Toronto Bay was an entirely different place. Steamers now ruled the waters and with them came better navigational and tracking devices, leading to a steady decrease in shipwrecks and drownings. However, the courage of one man, forged out of suffering and loss, has not been forgotten.

———•———

DESPITE THE IMPROVED navigational and safety equipment that was in use by the late nineteenth and early twentieth centuries, the sandy shoals off Island shores still made navigation a challenge. This was particularly true of the Western Gap, owing to the shallow rocky bottom that for long was thought impossible to excavate. Conditions in the Western Gap led to many tragedies, among them the foundering and sinking of the steamer *Resolute* in 1906. Unable to navigate either entrance to the harbour in a fierce fall storm, the captain made one last try for the Western Gap but struck bottom. Six men drowned in the bay, despite their being within clear sight of the mainland.

Countless other ships were driven aground on the sandy shoals of the Island by winter and summer gales. Such was the fate of the three-masted schooner *Reuben Dowd*, which struck bottom the same year as the *Resolute*. While several members of the Ward family and a collection of other Islanders managed within hours to rescue the terrified crew, coal from the *Dowd*'s hold washed up on the beach and undoubtedly provided some Islanders with a steady source of fuel in the winter months to come. As was the case with the *Alexandria* (which foundered off the Bluffs), shipwrecks off Island shores provided local residents with a treasure trove of food, fuel, and household goods that lasted for weeks and sometimes even for months.

Given the vast number of shipwrecks recorded along the shores of the Island, it may seem strange that so few traces of them remain today. As early as the mid-1800s, many previously foundered boats were becoming a hindrance to navigation in the relatively shallow waters of the bay, so contracts were tendered for their removal. The *Resolute* was hauled away in the early twentieth century, as was the *Queen City Royal Tar* in the mid-1850s.

While no dedicated boneyards existed along the Toronto waterfront, old wooden-hull derelict ships could be found all over the undeveloped eastern end of the bay, including to the south of the present-day St. Lawrence Market. There was simply no money in their salvage like there is in the steel-hulled ships of today. Many other ships fell victim to the shifting sands of the Island itself and were buried over time, helped along by the several harbour reclamation projects that took place in the twentieth century, both at the Island and on the mainland. What's left of the previously mentioned wreck of the *Reuben Dowd* is in fact now buried off Ward's Beach. Knapp's Roller Boat, a unique tubular ship that "rolled" over the water rather than plowing through it, is said to lie under the Gardiner Expressway, having been simply buried under landfill at the foot of Parliament Street in the late 1920s, as the Toronto Harbour Commission extended the shoreline southward into the lake.

A few heritage shipwrecks have nonetheless been identified in the harbour, a little to the west of Hanlan's Point in Humber Bay. The most intact of these is the *Sligo*, built as a three-masted barque in St. Catharines in 1860. Early in the twentieth century she was cut down and converted into a towing barge, but she sank in Humber Bay during a fierce storm in 1918. Humber Bay also serves as the graveyard for some of the last of the Great Lakes schooners, the *Julia B. Merrill* and the *Lyman M. Davis*, which were burned as spectacles at Sunnyside Amusement Park in the 1930s.

If you lie very still and press your face upon the frozen surface of the Island lagoon in winter, you may see what remains of the *Baltic Belle*, a North Sea fishing boat owned by Islanders Ron and Alida Turner in the 1950s. A storm sent her to the bottom of the lagoon as the Turners were in the process of refitting her. Bits of the old ship are now dispersed around the Island, incorporated into the homes of local residents and used as furniture, or simply kept as remembrances. While the *Baltic Belle* never plied the waters of the Great Lakes, these souvenirs remind us nonetheless of the rich maritime heritage of Toronto.

Coinciding with the earliest families who had established small cottages on the Island by the late 1830s and early 1840s was the erection of the Island's first hotel, the Retreat on the Peninsula, which was opened in 1833 by Michael O'Connor on the narrow neck of land at the easterly end of the bay. The hotel ferried patrons to the far Island shore on a horse-powered ferry named the *Sir John of the Peninsula*. Despite the relative ease with which patrons could now access the Island, the hotel never flourished under O'Connor's ownership because of its reputation as a heavy-drinking, disorderly establishment. Its presence, however, along with the subsequent erection of a couple of other modest establishments, ushered in another era in the life of the Island.

In order to escape the cholera epidemics that periodically swept through York and

The Island

This watercolour by Owen Staples (after a pen & ink drawing by W.J. Thomson, 1893) depicts the Peninsula Hotel as it appeared in 1850 TPL, JRR 916

then Toronto in the nineteenth century, the lieutenant governor of Upper Canada, Lord Sydenham, erected a house on the Island in 1839. According to *Robertson's Landmarks of Toronto*, Louis Privat converted this home into the Peninsula Hotel in 1843, and he was joined by his brother the following year. The brothers ran a similar horse-powered ferry boat service between the hotel, which was situated at the aforementioned narrows, and the mainland. At about 1850, the Privats replaced their two successive horse boats with a steamer that ferried passengers across the bay. The Privats also established what has often been described as Ontario's, and possibly Canada's, first, though modest, amusement park, opposite the hotel. They also maintained a small zoo and shooting gallery (the targets were live animals).

The 1850s was the decade of fierce storms around Toronto Bay. This storm activity, coupled with the ongoing removal of sand from Island shores that facilitated the building boom taking place in Toronto, contributed to significant erosion at the narrows where Quinn's Hotel (formerly Privat's) was situated. In time, a foreboding trickle of

Along the Shore

water began to build to a stream that washed across the Peninsula just east of the hotel. The breach later filled in but was undoubtedly the harbinger of things to come.

Sally Gibson's *More Than an Island* tells us that on the evening of April 13, 1858, the proprietor of the hotel, John Quinn, ferried his work crew back to the mainland as yet another storm broke over the Peninsula. While Quinn battled his way back to the Peninsula, water was rushing through his hotel, ripping it apart. Upon reaching the hotel site, virtually all that remained of the structure was the timber on which his terrified wife stood with her children clinging to her skirts. Gibson reports that by the early morning hours of April 14, the storm had washed away all vestiges of Quinn's Hotel, creating a channel four to five feet deep through the neck of the Peninsula. By May 30, 1858, the channel had widened and deepened enough to accept some boat traffic. The Peninsula was now truly an island and was poised to become the premier resort area for burgeoning Toronto — our own Riviera.

CHAPTER FOUR

A Resort Town

We have said that the Island's development, from the very beginning, was never planned or contrived. This is also true of how the resort community, amusement park, and other pleasure facilities that were established there in the 1880s and 1890s began. By the dawn of the twentieth century, the Island was easily one of the most popular destinations for fun seekers in Toronto, if not the entire country. The roots of this unique chapter in Island history began in the 1830s, with the establishment of O'Connor's Retreat on the Peninsula and, later, the Peninsula Hotel and amusement park, operated by the Privat brothers. Some of the other facilities were begun by Island residents themselves, who faced their fair share of adversity while eking out a living on Island shores.

Some seven years after the opening of the Eastern Gap in 1858, another storm ravaged the Island, wreaking havoc on the shanties located near the newly created channel. It was during this period that the family of Irish fisherman John Hanlan floated down to the westerly end of the Island on salvaged beams from their destroyed cottage.

240

By the mid-1860s the Hanlans had started a modest hotel business on the part of the Island that would eventually bear the family name, now known as Hanlan's Point. There was nothing at all out of the ordinary about this little establishment, which largely catered to hunters and amateur fishermen, who at the end of the day dragged their boats and muddied bodies onto the beach for a good night's rest on the almost deserted Island — nothing that smacked of the stately mansions, raucous laughter, and sights and sounds of the halcyon years to come.

Into this scene a small boy, not more than ten or eleven, would quietly row himself back and forth to school across the bay in a small handmade shell. This boy, Ned Hanlan, would go on to become Canada's first internationally renowned athlete and personality, who at the height of his fame in 1880 was granted permission by city officials to build a grand hotel near his childhood home at Hanlan's Point.

Given that Canada may well have more lakes and rivers than any other country in the world, it is no wonder that from very early on these bodies of water were a setting for championship sports, whether on the water or, in winter, on the ice. Whereas hockey captured the popular imagination in the twentieth century and holds it to this day, in the nineteenth century sculling was the sport of choice. Crowds of enthusiastic spectators would line the shores of the bay, all straining for a clear view of the water that was thronged with countless needle-shaped racing craft, or "shells," each rowed with two oars per man. One such man was a local teenaged fisherman by the name of Ned Hanlan, who was already becoming something of a sensation.

The indomitable Ned Hanlan beat the Americans, the Australians, and the British at their own game, claiming the single scull championships both of America and of England, and he then went on to become the Champion of the World for four consecutive years. Known as the Boy in Blue because of his racing colours, he is still regarded by some as the greatest sculler ever, an oarsman who won 300 consecutive races without a loss.

His training grounds were the waterways of his Toronto Island home. Ned Hanlan was virtually raised on Toronto Bay, and so, quite simply, he knew how to row. Throughout those early years, Ned rowed the mile and a quarter across the bay for school and for errands, and he rowed to fish.

With former Islander David Ward (William's brother) as one of his original backers, Hanlan was among the first to adopt and certainly the first to perfect a new sculling device, the sliding seat. This mechanism made for a longer pull on the oars, as the body moved forward and back with the stroke, thus enabling a faster and harder thrust against the water. It was said that in his sliding seat he rowed like "a small steam engine," though

Hanlan Beating Plaisted, Toronto Bay, *May 1878, watercolour, touches of gouache, over graphite on wove paper* Frederick Marlett Bell-Smith, with permission of the Royal Ontario Museum © ROM, 976.203.1

in the eyes of many commentators he seemed to row all wrong, with a bizarre "knees to nose" style that had never been seen before.

Hanlan was not a big man, never quite reaching five foot nine and weighing no more than a 150 pounds. It is easy to see why the odds were so stacked against him on November 15, 1880, when he met the self-confident six-foot-five Australian giant Edward Trickett for the World Championship race on the River Thames in London, England. Trickett — who, along with his team of supporters, had been mocking the Canadian's chances — was completely surpassed by Hanlan, who played with his opponent all along the same four-mile championship course that is the setting for the Oxford–Cambridge Boat Race.

As Pierre Berton writes in "The Greatest Oarsman of All Time," from time to time throughout the race, Hanlan actually stopped rowing, and at one point feigned a seizure, only to pick up his oars and row furiously away again as soon as the heavy, labouring Trickett began to make up the distance. One observer remarked, "I fully expected him to stand up and dance the Highland fling." Trickett fared no better in a rematch, when Hanlan finished the race well ahead but went back and crossed the finish line for a second time, thus in some sense beating his opponent twice.

While the "little Canuck" Hanlan was widely loved and admired in Canada and abroad, he was no angel in his personal dealings on the Island. Like other Island hoteliers during that period, he was known to have sold liquor outside his father's hotel without a permit. The story goes that the police were hot on his trail just days before he was to leave for

Along the Shore

This photo shows the Hanlan's Hotel in the late nineteenth century City of Toronto Archives, F1478_it13

the Philadelphia Centennial Regatta of 1876, an occasion that would launch his international career. After receiving a tip that the police were nearby, Hanlan slipped out the back door of the Toronto Rowing Club, jumped into a skiff, and took off like a bat out of hell into the lake, from which he climbed aboard a ship travelling stateside. A few days later, he won the cup and returned home to a victory parade while the band played "See the Conquering Hero Comes." Presumably the bootlegging charges were filed away somewhere. Torontonians, it seemed, had other priorities, or perhaps, however strait-laced they were, they knew when to forgive and forget.

After holding the World Championship title for four years, Hanlan travelled to Australia to defend his title against another physically imposing 200-pound Australian giant, William Beach. This commonsensical blacksmith was not in the least bit intimidated by Hanlan's well-known psychological tricks and antics. Hanlan was out-rowed. He remained competitive, drawing great crowds wherever he appeared, but while he met Beach three more times over the years, he was never able to regain his title. Australians rejoiced in their new champion, yet they never lost their admiration for the Boy in Blue. Indeed, it was by way of honouring an earlier commitment to Hanlan that a lakeside town in New South Wales was named after his much beloved Toronto.

Once his racing years were over, Hanlan repaired to the Island, where he had earlier been granted a free lease and had built an elegant hotel in the Victorian "stick" style in 1880, replete with balconies and pagodas. The amusement park and the stadium that followed would become key features that would draw pleasure seekers from Toronto and beyond to the Island for years to come.

Subsequently Hanlan briefly served as alderman for the Island and coached both the Ottawa Rowing Club and the University of Toronto team. Then, unexpectedly, on January 4, 1908, at the age of only fifty-two, he died from pneumonia. Ten thousand people passed by his coffin, and his funeral cortège extended for more than a mile into the city streets.

At the height of his racing career, international news media had expended much time and effort in trying to claim a piece of Hanlan as their own. While American newspapers did not hesitate to call him American, the English reminded themselves that he was, after all, "a citizen of the same vast empire." As for Ned Hanlan himself, to be sure he asserted that he was nothing other than Canadian, yet at some deeper, more personal level, we may assume that he well knew himself to be, first and last, a man of that small, distinct and independent breed, a man born and raised to be a Toronto Islander.

⸻ ◦ ⸻

IN 1867, ABOUT A decade before Ned Hanlan's glory days, the City of Toronto had acquired ownership of the Toronto Island from the federal government and had earmarked the Island for development as a resort area. They offered a number of lots for lease, with modest success and only a few cottages erected. But in the months and years that followed the completion of Hanlan's Hotel in 1880, Island development began to take off. In November of that same year, the city announced plans to begin construction of a public park on Centre Island. In 1881 the Royal Canadian Yacht Club built its clubhouse on the Island, and to this day it is Canada's most prestigious yachting organization. By 1888 the Island had a thousand summer-time residents, many of them living in luxurious homes overlooking the lake at Centre Island.

Yachting was a popular pastime among these upper-crust residents and certainly a draw to the Island. *Robertson's Landmarks of Toronto* indicates the origin of yachting in Toronto goes back to 1850. By 1852, several enthusiasts — among them a physician, Captain W.H. Fellows, H.H. Harmon (a future city treasurer), E.M. Hodder (a city coroner), and William Armstrong (a civil engineer and painter) — changed their name from the Toronto Boat Club to the Toronto Yacht Club. In 1854 the club was granted by Queen Victoria the privilege of becoming the *Royal* Canadian Yacht Club, a title it holds to this day, though it's more commonly called the RCYC. The royal associations continued in 1860, when Edward VII, at that time Prince of Wales, visited Toronto and donated the Prince of Wales Cup to the RCYC. Prominent RCYC member William Armstrong recorded the visit in paint. He later established a summer home on the Island and completed many other images of the bay. In 1919 the club hosted a garden party for another Prince of Wales (the future Duke of Windsor).

As discussed in *Robertson's Landmarks of Toronto*, the RCYC's earliest clubhouses were old boats docked along the central downtown waterfront, the first being a disused scow and then, in later years, a lake steamer, the *Provincial*, both of them stark contrasts to the elegant mansion on the Island that houses the club today. In 1869–70, the RCYC built its first clubhouse on the Esplanade, at the foot of Simcoe Street and to the west of what was then known as Rees' Wharf. However, during the next ten years, with the unprecedented growth of industry, the downtown waterfront was increasingly given over to industrial

use and the recreational boating community had to consider other options offshore. The Island offered a bucolic setting within minutes of the mainland.

In 1881 a decoratively trimmed clubhouse with extensive waterside verandas was opened on a narrow point of land overlooking the city. By that time the club had a membership of more than sixty yachts and was developing an active social life. Several of Toronto's leading families decided to establish residences on Centre Island, to escape the city heat in the summer and be closer to the club. As a result, the RCYC move to the Peninsula was a factor in the creation of the Island community itself.

The present RCYC clubhouse, designed in the elegant plantation style with pillars two storeys high, a double veranda, and sprawling lawns, was actually built in 1922 and is the third clubhouse to overlook the downtown waterfront from the Island location, the two previous buildings having been razed by fire in 1904 and 1918 respectively.

The establishment of the RCYC on the Island prompted the formation in 1889 of another prominent yachting organization: the Queen City Yacht Club (QCYC). Initially comprised of RCYC members who opted to stay city-side when the club moved, for decades the QCYC remained at the foot of York Street. Extensive water reclamation work in the central waterfront area loosened the moorings of the clubhouse and, in 1920, caused the building to sink into the lake, hastening the Queen City Club's intended move to Sunfish Island (now Algonquin Island), where it has remained ever since.

Many other boating facilities and yacht clubs may be found on the Island today, including the Toronto Island Marina, a privately owned facility where boats can be moored,

the Island Yacht Club, established in 1950 by
members of Toronto's Jewish community, and
the Harbour City Yacht Club, established in
1972. Together these clubs enrich and sustain
one of Toronto's earliest recreational traditions.

*This 1910 postcard features the death-defying
Hurgle Gurgle slide at Hanlan's Point* TPL, PC 791

———— • ————

WHILE THE ERECTION OF Hanlan's Hotel and then the RCYC clubhouse undoubtedly
stimulated growth on the Island, the biggest change in the nineteenth century was the
building of Hanlan's Point Amusement Park, which was in full swing by 1888. Operated
by the Doty brothers, it had attractions to suit all tastes and budgets: a midway, a 510-
pound lady from South Africa, a "real live Zulu with an Irish accent," and, years later, a
famous diving horse.

In order to understand the enormity of the Island's change from an insular fishing
community to a grand summer resort town, one has to consider the times. The Island
came of age in the late Victorian and early Edwardian periods, in a time that is typified in
A Tearful Tour of Toronto's Riviera of Yesteryear as "a precious quantum of civilized history."
Toronto was booming in the last two decades of the nineteenth century, and after 1896 the
city experienced an unprecedented period of growth. The middle class had emerged from
the factories and drudgery of an earlier era and had discovered leisure. Dressed in their
finery, they flocked to the lakeshore to promenade on the boardwalk or politely exchange

The Island

This whimsical postcard, stamped in Hamilton on May 24, 1907, shows a family eagerly approaching the ferry docks, on their way to a day of fun and frolic on the Island

City of Toronto, Museum Services, 1996.18.69.132

pleasantries over a picnic taken on china under the shade of a willow tree. Ladies would dip their toes into the cool water of the bay, boldly revealing an un-stockinged ankle.

While merrymakers could go to Victoria and Kew Parks in the Beach, John Duck's Wimbledon House at the mouth of the Humber, and, by 1887, Long Branch Park near Etobicoke Creek, Hanlan's was far and away the most elaborate of these early amusement parks and pleasure gardens. Visitors, residents, and city officials alike began referring to it as the Island of Hiawatha, after the romantic poem *The Song of Hiawatha* by Longfellow, which harkened back to an escape to another perfect, natural world.

While the Island provided an escape for the upper and emerging middle class, it also provided welcome respite for those less fortunate. In the late nineteenth century, Toronto still suffered from alarming outbreaks of contagious diseases, among them tuberculosis, with the city's children often the hardest hit. In 1883 John Ross Robertson, founder and publisher of the *Evening Telegram*, provided $2,000 for the erection of the Lakeside Home for Little Children on a four-acre site on Hanlan's Point. This provided a quiet, restful place for Toronto's sick children to convalesce and harkened back to the Mississaugas' earlier use of the Island as a sacred healing ground. Burned to the ground in 1915 and later rebuilt, it served as quarters for the Royal Norwegian Air Force during the early 1940s.

Most who wanted to travel to the Island (or even farther afield) boarded steamer ships and ferries, many of which were built close to home. Though possibly the first Upper Canadian steamer, the *Frontenac*, was built near Kingston in 1815, some, like the *Canada* or the homely "basket boat" *Toronto*, were built locally at the water's edge. By and large the steamers were well suited for passenger service on the lakes, given that they could keep to a schedule more closely than could ships under sail.

Just as steam was outmoding sails, the age of the railways began, their lines often running parallel to the water routes and alongside the ports of call frequented by water-going vessels. As rail became the most efficient way of moving goods and people, a pleasure craft industry found a niche and was on the rise. Luxurious passenger steamers, often referred to as "floating palaces," began to ply the lake, stopping at the same ports of call as the freighters and passenger steamers of previous decades. Toronto became a centre of such activity, with daily runs to Port Dalhousie, Hamilton, and Niagara while longer, overnight voyages were made to destinations in the United States and the rest of Canada.

Though few such luxury steamers ever docked at the Island, the pier at the Eastern Gap being unable to bear the weight of such heavy ships, Islanders would sometimes gather at the landing stage to greet the passenger ships on their daily runs in and out of the bay. Local steamers, among them the *Chicoutimi* and the *J.W. Steinhoff* as well as the steamer *Greyhound*, plied to and fro between the greater Toronto shore area and other nearby ports of call, pleasure grounds, and amusement parks, including Victoria Park in the east and Long Branch in the west.

Among the best loved of these local ships were the wooden-hulled Island ferries that brought throngs of Torontonians to Island shores. These ships were a substantial improvement over some of the oddities that had plied, or attempted to ply, the waters of the bay in the past, such as O'Connor and Privat's horse-driven paddlewheelers and the ill-fated Knapp's Roller Boat. Many of these wooden vessels were built by the Toronto Ferry Company, and some made an inglorious end as the steamship era was drawing to a close, when a few of the once-admired ferries were burned as spectacles just off the shore of Sunnyside Amusement Park. Today, the only steam-powered Island ferry still

The Island

The Cayuga *(1907–60) leaving Toronto through Eastern Gap, c. 1920* TPL, 964-6-45

running on the bay is the steel-hulled paddle-wheeler the *Trillium*, rescued from the Island lagoon and refurbished some three decades ago.

Many say that the true finale of the passenger steamer era came in 1949, when a tragic and horrific fire aboard the Canada Steamship Line's *Noronic* took at least 118 lives at Pier 9 in Toronto. It was said that the screams of the trapped and dying passengers drowned out even the uproar of a rescue effort that came too late for the ill-equipped, aging ship that had once been known as "the Queen of the Lakes." The smell of burnt human flesh hung in the air as the ship sank to the bottom in the shallow water. The romance with the lake steamers had come to an end.

———— • ————

LOOKING BACK AGAIN to the 1880s and the years that followed the construction of Hanlan's Hotel and Amusement Park, as well as the newly erected RCYC, it's not surprising that many of the leading families chose to lease Island lots from the city and become Islanders for the summer. The great old Toronto families — the Masseys, the Gooderhams, the

The burning of the Noronic, *September 17, 1949* CTA, F1244_it1518

Jarvises, and the Oslers — boarded wooden-hulled ferries and made their annual pilgrimage across the bay with their children, servants, and provisions to elegant summer cottages — mansions of another era with names like Cloverlawn, Floreat, Belvedere, and the Breakers. As *A Tearful Tour* relates, "There were beautiful homes with beautiful people sitting in beautiful gardens."

Up until the late 1950s, many of these grand old ladies still stood on Centre Island, overlooking the lake near the present site of the boardwalk. These summer homes were complete with butler's pantries, servants' quarters, spacious verandas, and green lawns overlooking sandy beaches. They are all gone now, victims of "progress" in the dark days of Island life that preceded its stabilization in the 1980s and 1990s.

There is an old saying that "the Island is not just for the Masseys but also for the masses," and this was certainly as true in the decades that spanned the late nineteenth and early twentieth centuries as it is today. On July 22, 1882, Winman Baths was opened on Ward's Island. This facility was a large and somewhat elaborate change house for

The Massey House on Centre Island as it appeared to Island resident Lorraine Surcouf, shortly before its demolition, c. 1960 TPL, 961-2-2

bathing and was adjacent to the bathing grounds that overlooked the city. The opening of the baths, catering to Toronto's less affluent citizens, was closely followed by the erection of a hotel, built by William Ward and located near the ferry docks facing out to the city. With a four-storey tower and sixty-foot-long balconies, it was still a more modest structure than Hanlan's Hotel, its contemporary.

In contrast to the sprawling mansions of the upper class on Centre, a summer tent community of those of modest means began to develop at Ward's shortly after the turn of the century. Sally Gibson, in *More Than an Island*, points out that by 1912, the community had grown to 685 campers. A request to occupy a summer tent site on the Island by fourteen-year-old David Scott best sums up the spirit of the place. In a letter dated March 10, 1909, he wrote, "We beg to apply for permission for spaces at Centre or Ward Islands to erect a tent 9 feet by 9 feet. . . . If you give us permission we will neither harm

Along the Shore

the ground or trees, or anything that does not belong to us. Kindly state if there is any charge. Hoping to hear from you at your earliest convenience." The original Ward's Island tent sites were later converted into forty-by-forty-five-foot city lots upon which permanent residences were built, and even in the present day the community retains something of its original camp-like atmosphere.

Meanwhile, at the other end of the Island, Hanlan's Point Amusement Park had expanded its grounds with an ambitious landfill project and facilities, which included the addition of Hanlan's Point Stadium in 1897. With the park and hotel under the managing directorship of prominent Toronto businessman Lawrence (Lol) Solman, the facility became the largest of its kind in Canada, with service to and from the mainland provided by the Toronto Ferry Company every twenty minutes.

Despite two successive fires in 1903 and 1909 that laid temporary waste to the amusement park and ultimately destroyed the hotel, throngs of Torontonians boarded a ferry for a day on the Island, where for fifteen cents they could take in the midway and then watch Lol Solman's Maple Leafs of the International Baseball League, Toronto's first professional baseball club, play ball in the newly constructed stadium. There soon-to-be American baseball legend Babe Ruth hit his first professional home run in 1914, allegedly sending the ball far out into the bay. In 1926 the Toronto Maple Leafs were moved to Maple Leaf Stadium on the mainland at Bathurst Quay, four years after Sunnyside Amusement Park opened in Lakeshore.

Though attendance had waned at Hanlan's Point Amusement Park with the opening of the wildly popular Sunnyside Beach in 1922, it remained a popular destination for fun seekers right up to the latter part of the 1930s, when construction began on the Port George VI Island Airport.

———•———

THE BUILDING OF THE airport may have marked the end of an era for Hanlan's Point Amusement Park, but, interestingly, aviation has been intertwined with the story of the Island since the early twentieth century. On August 2, 1911, Canadian J.A.D. McCurdy flew his plane over the present-day Toronto shore at the completion of what was the first intercity air race in Canada, if not North America, and, according to the *Globe*, the longest cross-country flight in Canada up to that time. In 1909 McCurdy had become the first man ever to fly a controlled, heavier-than-air machine in Canada and the British Empire. His opponent in this race, Charles Foster Willard (whose story is detailed in the Beach section) was the first to fly over the Toronto shore.

Willard and McCurdy were already well known to each other on the flight circuit, and they were due to appear on August 3 for the opening of another air show at Donlands Farm, which was at that time located just outside the city limits. According to the *Globe*, the rivalry was intensified when McCurdy made a wager with Willard, who had the slower machine, that he could give him a head start and still beat him into Toronto. Accordingly, Willard left Burlington Bay, by all reports, at least ten minutes ahead of McCurdy. Willard chose to fly over the shore, while McCurdy chose the water route, flying over the lake, in the path of the steamers.

Reports by Frank Ellis, the *Globe*, and the *Toronto Daily Star* vary as to who reached Toronto first, but as they approached the city one thing is clear: atmospheric conditions, reported as thick haze and unfavourable wind currents, prevented both pilots from attempting a landing at Donlands Farm. In the circumstances, both men anxiously scanned the shore for a place to land. Flying over the Western Gap and skimming just above the surface of the water, McCurdy could make out the Island, just off the downtown shore, heavily girt with trees and rimmed by a broad band of sand. He made for it and circled it twice but, like Willard two years before at Scarborough Beach, he could not find a space clear enough for a safe landing. He finally settled on Fisherman's Island, which now lay on the far side of the Eastern Gap and was comparatively empty of people. Miss Hilda Smith, who according to the *Toronto Daily Star* lived on Fisherman's Island, was understandably shocked to see what she called "a lake bird" appear out of thin air and alight on the sands in front of her cottage.

Though accounts also vary as to whether Willard was the first to touch down, there is no dispute that McCurdy had the faster overall time. By the *Star*'s account, he was a full seven minutes ahead of Willard, who landed a short distance to the west at the Exhibition Grounds.

Some three years after J.A.D. McCurdy touched down on Fisherman's Island in 1911, the First World War broke out in Europe. Canada needed a place to train pilots. The Island provided an ideal location for the flying-boat base of the Curtiss Aviation School. The main facility was at Long Branch, just to the west of Etobicoke Creek, with J.A.D. McCurdy as manager of operations. According to Ellis, the Curtiss Aviation School, established in 1915 and popularly known as the Curtiss Flying School, was the first of its kind in Canada, with the Island housing the first ever seaplane base. The base was established at the northern tip of the western sandbar, near Hanlan's Point. An offshoot of the Curtiss Company of Hammondsport, New York, which had produced Charles Foster Willard's previously described *Golden Flyer*, the Toronto flying-boat division sported two

Flying boat, Toronto Island, c. 1912
CTA, F1244_it80

hangars and several two-seater Curtiss F-type flying boats, these having been shipped from Buffalo. T.C. MacCaulay, an early flying-boat pilot of some renown who had already many times flown over the lake in the vicinity of Toronto, was recruited to the train students. As Sally Gibson notes, many of the school's pilots had connections to the Island and went on to represent Canada during the dark days of the First World War. Among them was Grant A. Gooderham, who served Canada with distinction before returning to civilian life, as well as Fred Armstrong Jr. of Ward's Island, who became a squadron commander, and Jack Keens of Mohawk Avenue, who was shot down but survived.

Sally Gibson reports that the first venture into commercial passenger flight off the Island occurred just after the end of the First World War, when flying aces Billy Bishop and Billy Barker joined forces to create Bishop-Barker Airways. For a short time vacationing Torontonians could fly with Bishop-Barker from Toronto Bay to Muskoka, but in the early years of the twentieth century, most thought flying machines were too dangerous. The project was short-lived, yet the Island in the not-too-distant future would play a significant role in meeting Toronto's modest but growing need for the air transportation of goods and people.

During the Depression, the federal government was actively seeking infrastructure projects to stimulate the economy. It set its sights on the Island as a primary municipal flight centre for the city of Toronto. But first, people had to get there. In 1935 Prime Minister R.B. Bennett rolled out an impressive list of public works, including a million-dollar 2,000-foot-long tunnel to run from the foot of Bathurst Street under the Western Gap to the Island. The tunnel would facilitate the development and accessibility of the contemplated airport on Hanlan's Point. With lightening speed the city council jumped at the chance for development and jobs. Over the objections of Sam McBride, former and future mayor, city controller, and stalwart Islander, council approved the tunnel and the airport projects by a vote of fifteen to seven.

McBride believed that a tunnel would be the harbinger of total change for the Island. First of all, the very nature of the place, the fact that it was surrounded by water on all sides, would lose its significance, leaving it as little more than an adjunct to the mainland. Inevitably, with the building of a large airport to meet the needs of a rapidly expanding city, there would come mass transportation, pollution, noise, and all the other modern "conveniences," the very lack of which had contributed to the Island's evolution as a unique community. So McBride threw up every imaginable objection to the completion of the tunnel project, including a trip to Ottawa at his own expense.

In the end the tunnel, its construction already begun with unwonted speed, was nixed when the Liberal Party roundly defeated the Conservatives in the 1935 election. Shortly after McBride was elected mayor of Toronto for the second time, in 1936, city workers were dispatched over to the Island to fill in the hole at Hanlan's Point, where the tunnel was supposed to go. McBride died unexpectedly later that same year. In 1939 an Island ferry was named after him, in recognition of his faithful service to the Toronto Island community.

The debate over the need for expansion of flight services for Toronto, now growing at an exponential rate, did not go away. With the main opponent to an Island airport now gone, flying ace Billy Bishop was appointed titular head of the Advisory Airport Committee of the City of Toronto. Bishop already had a track record that supported air services on the Island, and it is therefore no surprise that on July 9, 1937, city council approved the Island airport project, which was initially planned to be the primary land

Along the Shore

and sea plane base for Toronto.

Almost immediately, the city embarked on an ambitious landfill project at Hanlan's Point to accommodate the airport. The old baseball stadium and part of Hanlan's Point Amusement Park were removed, and the Memorial Regatta Course was filled in. Fifty-four cottages were also uprooted, with many of the residences relocated to Sunfish Island. The overall land mass of this area was greatly increased due to extensive land reclamation to accommodate the cottages; shortly after this period it was renamed Algonquin Island. In 1939 the Port George VI Island Airport (later named the Toronto Island Airport) was opened. Though the facility was renamed the Billy Bishop Toronto City Airport in 2010, it is still referred to as the Island airport by most Islanders.

We will read in the next chapter that shortly after the airport's construction, it was used by the Norwegians during part of the Second World War as a training base for both fighter and bomber pilots. After the end of the Second World War, the Island airport played a significant part in the transportation needs of Torontonians, one that fitted in with the multiple uses of a still busy harbour that was also home to a growing residential community. During those years there were some commercial flights at the airport, including to the racetrack at Fort Erie, as well as many private flights to cottage country. In 1960 the Toronto Flying Club moved to the Island for a short period, causing a large increase in traffic volume. In March 1962 the *Globe and Mail* reported that Toronto Island Airport was Canada's busiest in terms of movement, though the

Lifelong Islander Tommy Swalwell, seated at the front left, chats it up with the nurses at the airport ferry terminal upon his return home during the Second World War

Courtesy Michael Swalwell

The Island

majority of those flights were for "local traffic, notably students." Throughout this busy period, passengers continued to cross the little stretch of water to the airport by way of ferry rather than a fixed link or bridge.

By the 1970s, pressure mounted for the Island to take on a greatly increased role in commercial passenger service. By the early 1980s, the Toronto Harbour Commission (now the Toronto Port Authority), the City of Toronto, and the federal government entered into a tripartite agreement that set out the rules of engagement for further airport expansion. Among other things, it set out cumulative noise levels and approved the type of commercial aircraft that could fly out of the downtown port (jets remain prohibited).

In tandem with the expansion of commercial flights at the airport in the 1980s was the explosion of condominium development along the downtown lakeshore, south of the Gardiner Expressway. This development necessitated that any plans for future airport expansion, which by its very nature raises legitimate issues of pollution, noise, traffic congestion, and safety, would now have to be balanced against the interests of not just a few hundred full-time residents of the Island but also thousands of mainlanders, not to mention the legions of summer tourists and yachting enthusiasts who plied the Toronto Bay and the Outer Harbour.

While Chicago announced plans to close its lakefront airport in 1994, Toronto was just getting started. Though the 1990s witnessed a period of decreased commercial activity at the airport, the prospect of further expansion of commercial flight services never died and was raised again in the early twenty-first century. It is not surprising that a fixed link to the airport, this time in the form of a bridge, became an issue in the municipal election of 2003. David Miller was elected mayor, and, in a dramatic turnaround similar to the era of Sam McBride, he convinced incoming city council to cancel a previously approved bridge project. The federal Liberal government, now for the second time, followed suit and withdrew its support for the fixed link.

In 2006 Porter Airlines began service at the airport, followed recently by Air Canada, with both carriers offering a boutique flight experience that focuses on quality of service. In the span of those six years, service from the airport has grown from 25,000 passengers to two million by the end of 2012, making it the ninth busiest airport in Canada.

Denied a bridge, the Toronto Port Authority is in the midst of constructing a pedestrian-only tunnel that will smooth out the flow of passengers to and from the airport. When the tunnel is completed, the Island will be connected to the mainland for the first time. Passengers will now be able to reach the Island more efficiently; common sense dictates that the stage will be set for further airport expansion at some point in the

Along the Shore

An aircraft makes its final descent to Billy Bishop Toronto City Airport, 2010 Keith Ellis

future. Geoffrey Wilson, president of the Toronto Port Authority, maintains that no such plans for expansion are on the table at present and that the airport is designed for efficiency and quality of experience, not for high volume: "We want it to be the best of its kind anywhere in the world . . . and that flows through to our environmental practices and our traffic management . . . so this airport will be very, very good, not very, very big."

Airport expansion has galvanized the communities on Ward's and Algonquin Islands and has led to the formation more than a decade ago of Community Air, which is also supported by some lakeside condominium dwellers. Community Air takes the position that people and planes on Toronto Bay simply do not go together and calls for the complete abolition of the airport. With air traffic having increased exponentially since 2006, along with attendant increases in airplane emissions and noise, future expansion of commercial airline services may well have reached the tipping point.

As for the future? It is virtually certain that the intricate dance on the bay between commercial and business interests and those who seek to live and play along the shore will continue, with all sides in the debate validly claiming a stake in the Island's history. It's getting that balance between these competing interests that's the challenge.

CHAPTER FIVE

An Island Village

In the early part of the twentieth century, after the cries of "play ball!" ended in the fall and the leading families made the ritual crossing back to their Rosedale mansions, a stillness descended on the Island, the same stillness that happens today when the concessions close at Centre and the children trade their sand pails for schoolbags. With the autumn frost, the frolickers vanished, and waves rolled in on deserted beaches, leaving the Island once again to a small handful of full-time residents. These Islanders — the fishermen and lighthouse keepers of days gone by — would in future decades slowly relinquish their nets and become the caretakers of a year-round Island village that has its roots in the early decades of the twentieth century — the boathouse keepers, the constables, the school superintendents and teachers, and even the bootleggers who were the backbone of the tiny but spirited community all year round.

By the 1930s, a full-time residential community had emerged at Hanlan's Point on the Island. Not numbering more than a few hundred souls, these dyed-in-the-wool Islanders were largely left to fend for themselves in winter on the frozen sandbar.

Without frequent transportation across the bay in winter, crossings to the mainland were particularly treacherous during the swing months of November and March.

During this time, Hanlan's Point residents travelled back and forth to the Island on the *Ned Hanlan*, a tug boat, which was also an efficient icebreaker. (Ice on the bay in those years, according to some accounts, could be as thick as three feet.) The *Ned Hanlan* ran between John Street and the Island in winter, transporting crews of workers to the Island Filtration Plant. Later, in the 1940s, as the pace of residential development picked up on the Island, lifesavers would place trees in the snow to alert fellow residents to open water. Another alternative to a hike across the bay was the old jalopy of the slightly off-base Bill Sutherland, proprietor of the Manitou Hotel. For a small fee you could hire Sutherland to careen you over to the other side, risking life and limb, regardless of the open water.

This photo of Gwendolyn MacEwen was taken by Sheldon Grimson at the Eastern Gap, as part of a series of poems and photographs, Fifteen Canadian Poets, *1970*

From the earliest period of European settlement, Toronto Bay was recognized as an unpredictable and dangerous place in winter, especially during periodic warm spells, when sections of the ice would become treacherously thin or even dislodge. As early as March 14, 1794, Mrs. Simcoe recorded her concern about the safety of the ice on the bay: "As I was riding across the bay I felt the horse sink under me, and supposing there was a hole in the ice, I threw myself off." Two years later, on Easter Day, March 27, 1796, she wrote, "The ice went out of the bay this morning driven by a strong east wind; in the evening the wind changed and it drove it back, and as it beat against the shore in a floating surface of very small pieces it made an uncommon and fine sound, which I listened to a great while from the terrace before the house."

Though the bay rarely freezes completely over today, the phenomena of rapid ice break-up in the harbour may still be observed, as in the days of Mrs. Simcoe. Novelist and poet Gwendolyn MacEwen lived on the Island for a brief period in the early 1960s with her then-husband and fellow poet Milton Acorn. In "Animal Syllables," she references her small Island house and writes, "When the ice-sheets groan and split on the lake they fracture the landscape for miles around. . . . Vast shorelines, tongues of continents like land-waves chasing the seas. Shorelines of souls, the beaches of consciousness strewn with a thousand little shells . . . Everything begins, everything is a continuum, everything organizes its death . . . How many languages can we know? We approach the end of utterance."

Iceboating, though in decline with the coming of the icebreaking tugs, was another popular sport that brought Islanders into direct contact with the bay and its hazards during winter. Not for the faint of heart, it was always uncomfortable and could be quite dangerous, given the cracks that would develop in the ice, often making pools of water or even gaps in a sudden warm spell. John Summers, in "The Coldest Sport in the World: Iceboating in Toronto Harbour, 1824–1941," points out that iceboats appear in Flemish and Dutch paintings as early as the sixteenth and seventeenth centuries. These paintings depict small sailing vessels fitted in winter with iron blades, like skates but held in position by a triangular wooden frame attached to the keel.

Like their Dutch predecessors, Toronto's iceboats were steered from the stern, though they differed slightly in form — the hull was a shallow, triangular wooden shell. Summers points out that by the turn of the twentieth century, iceboats in many other parts of North America had adopted a steering wheel and were steered from the front of the craft, as distinct from a tiller bar. Yet although these technological innovations could make for more speed, the Toronto boats in large part stayed faithful to the original Dutch form. Another unique feature of these boats was their lateen rigging, which meant that they were operated with a single sail unlike most other places in North America, which had adopted a two-sail Marconi rig. Their distinctive design remained a unique feature of the Toronto vessels right up until the days when iceboating all but disappeared from the bay at the beginning of the 1940s.

The earliest reference to iceboating in Toronto is in *Robertson's Landmarks of Toronto*, which notes that in 1824 a tradesman at York, one Isaac Columbus, was in the business of making the irons of an iceboat. Columbus must have been a living monument to versatility: he also made and fitted sets of false teeth, crafted firearms, designed delicate articles of ladies' jewellery, and forged stovepipes.

Every winter the waters of the harbour froze flat and smooth, making an ideal location for iceboating. By the 1850s Toronto Bay was described in local newspapers as the city's largest ice rink. The presence of skaters, cutters, curlers, horse-racing enthusiasts,

Iceboats are very prevalent in William Armstrong's
Landing Passengers on the Ice, *1852* TPL, JRR 517

and spectators, all out there on the blue, windswept ice, must have made a pretty sight, enhanced by the iceboats, with their black skates and crisp white sails.

From the very beginning these boats served the dual purposes of utility and recreation on the bay. Like skates and sleighs in the seventeenth century, these unique vessels provided a means of transport for freight and passengers and especially for Island residents, who would otherwise have been hemmed in by the ice, given that there was no winter ferry service at all until the early 1930s. They were also a valuable taxi service for others who needed to get to the Island, such as the workers employed in the water filtration plant at Gibraltar Point. Connie Stevenson writes in "Iceboating on Toronto Bay" that several of the ice taxis waited at the foot of John Street in the mornings and Blockhouse Bay in the afternoons to transport employees to and from the filtration plant.

It is difficult even now to imagine how fast those early vessels could move, harnessing the ferocious winds and gliding, almost drag-free, across the ice. While modern iceboats, with their advanced technology, can clock up to eighty-four miles per hour, their ancestors could achieve speeds of sixty miles per hour despite their simple structure. It is probably safe to say that iceboats were as fast as any means of transportation in Canada before the advent of the automobile.

Given the iceboat's capacity for speed, it comes as no surprise that from the early 1870s onward several Toronto iceboating clubs, including the Toronto Iceboat Association, engaged in races on the bay. While the simple construction and portable assembly of Toronto iceboats made the sport accessible to people on both sides of the bay, iceboat racing was largely the purview of Islanders and those who belonged to the various yacht clubs that were already well established. Sally Gibson notes that in 1871 these races were formalized with the addition of an iceboating cup donated by Mrs. Parkinson, who owned and managed Parkinson's hotel on Centre Island.

One notable race across Toronto Bay was a contest in 1911 between a motorcycle and the *Comet*, a large iceboat owned by the Wells brothers. The "Mile a Minute Race" is said to have clocked speeds of sixty miles per hour with the contest ending in a dead heat. Another twentieth-century race pitted Islander Eddie Durnan's *Jessica* (pronounced by Islanders as Jess-ee-ca) against the *Zoraya*, the crew of which included the late Lou Marsh, a well-known Toronto sportswriter. According to Stevenson, the *Jessica* was said to have achieved a speed of 120 miles per hour on the Ward's Island to York Street leg of the race with an east northeasterly gale blowing.

Lifelong Island resident Jimmy Jones Jr. remembers sailing in the *Jessica* with his father, Jimmy Jones Sr., some years later in the 1930s. "We'd huddle down in the hull on blankets and man — what a ride it was, it was unbelievable — and the speed — no cars went that fast in those days." Passengers on iceboats often hunkered down in the hull of the craft on mattresses, covered in blankets to avoid the extreme cold that came on as the boat picked up speed as well as to avoid the inevitable flurry of ice chips as the blades turned left and right in moving along the surface of the bay.

Island residents like Eddie Durnan became expert in the building of these vessels. Durnan, along with Walter Dean, a prominent Toronto boat builder, provided the Toronto market with a full array of iceboats when the sport was at its height, at the beginning of the twentieth century. However, as Summers writes, many of the boats seen on the

The "Mile a Minute Race," 1911 Judy L. Wells Darke, CanadianHeritage.ca, ID #23300n

The Island

bay were never produced in factories at all but were handcrafted by individual Island residents, who passed their skills on down through generations. The handmade nature of these boats, often involving the inclusion of disused materials from local yachts, may have shaped the distinctly "Torontonian" style of iceboat, which remained largely similar in form to its seventeenth-century counterpart.

Iceboating was dealt a hard blow by the Toronto Harbour Commission's Waterfront Plan of 1912, which brought about the filling of the bay and the Western Gap and, as Summers relates, the dredging out of a new and straighter channel to the south. Not surprisingly these changes irrevocably altered the lake currents and the water flow in the bay, making it more difficult for hard ice to form. One iceboating enthusiast was so vexed by the change in conditions that he filed an application to sue the federal government for ruining iceboating on the bay. His application was denied.

Icebreaking tugs that began providing winter ferry service to the west end of the Island around 1930 also contributed to the decline of ice boating on the bay. While safely transporting passengers to the mainland, these boats broke long pathways of open water through the ice. Moving and unloading other large vessels in the harbour during winter also caused the ice break-up. Within a few decades of the introduction of ice-breaking tugs, most of the unique Toronto iceboats, with names like *Jack Frost*, *Ice Witch*, *Snowflake*, *Snowbird*, and *Stormy Day*, were gone from the bay forever.

A few Islanders nonetheless kept iceboating alive in the years that followed, most notable among them being Tommy Swalwell, who rescued his father Bill Swalwell's iceboat, *Silver Heels*, from certain destruction when the Hanlan's Point and Centre Island communities were razed in the 1950s. Up to 1969 he and his son Michael could be seen riding over the lagoon and north shore of the Island. Iceboats may still be seen from time to time in the sheltered "spoon" of the Island, between the Hanlan's Point ferry dock and the Ward's Island ferry dock, where thick ice often forms during winter.

As for *Silver Heels* and another Toronto iceboat, the *Comet*, they are presently hidden away in a City of Toronto warehouse, as part of the city's Historical Collection, after the Pier Museum (formally the Upper Canada Marine Museum) fell victim to budget cuts in the early years of the present century. These boats bear witness to a once great Toronto tradition.

Some years ago traffic on the bay came to an unexpected halt in the dead of winter, and Islanders got a glimpse of a time they'd never known, or perhaps had almost forgotten. Transportation to Ward's Island was difficult that winter, with ferry service temporarily suspended while substantial repairs were made to the trusty *Ongiara*, which had plied

Along the Shore

the waters of the bay since the early 1960s. By coincidence, at the same time the *William Lyon Mackenzie*, Jones recalls that Toronto's harbour fireboat and the main icebreaker on the bay, was also out of the water, undergoing refurbishment on the mainland.

From his tiny cottage on Ward's Island, Jimmy Jones watched and waited while the ice advanced, as it would had advanced each winter in decades past, inward toward the deep water between the mainland and the Island shore. On one particularly still night, the temperature plunged far below zero and, without the presence of vessels to disturb the surface of the bay, an extensive pan of ice formed over the water. Jones awoke to see what looked like a sheet of glass spread out between his Island home and the towers that lined the shore of the mainland. In need of groceries and not wanting to take the shuttle bus to Hanlan's Point, where he would be ferried across the Western Gap to the mainland, Jones opted to take the more direct route and stepped out onto the ice. As he puts it, "I turned left and went straight to the city to get my groceries."

While this may seem dangerous, even foolhardy by our twenty-first-century standards, to this lifelong Islander it was a regular occurrence, harkening back to his days on the Island as a child in the 1930s. By the time Jimmy Jones got his provisions and stepped off the seawall at the foot of Parliament Street to head back home again, a game of pick-up hockey had begun at the Eastern Gap, with rival Islanders fighting it out for supremacy while keen onlookers encouraged them from the shore. The restoration of the

"I can still recall the smells of the old ropes and the wood varnish that emanated from the boat. Those days of iceboating with my father were the best of my childhood. The cold, the speed, and the wind became part of my routine as a child growing up on the Island."

— *Michael Swalwell* Courtesy Michael Swalwell

The Island

ferry service and the return of the icebreaker put an end to this scene, and the skaters retreated to the frozen inner lagoon of the Island. Within days the earlier life of the Island, so briefly revived by a strange cluster of coincidences, was once more only a memory, though this time one shared by the old and the young.

———— •◦• ————

REGARDLESS OF THE obvious perils faced by residents during the severe winters of the 1930s, the Island experienced modest growth during the Depression years. The Island offered many families struggling with the harsh economic realities of the Depression shelter and community. In the lean years, the Oldershaws lived in a tiny cottage on Hanlan's Point and raised their son Bert, three-time Olympic paddler, along with his eight other brothers and sisters. It was also during these years that Jimmy Jones, the Hanlan's Point Amusement Park Clown, moved his family from Parkdale to the Island, where rents were cheaper and the commute to work, at least during the summer months, a lot easier.

Hanlan's Point's main competitor during the 1930s was the wildly popular Sunnyside Amusement Park. Nevertheless, the park managed to hold its own, with the help of amusement park clown Jimmy Jones Sr., who amazed audiences with daring acrobatics. One stunt involved jumping from car to car while at full speed, on the ride known as "the Whip."

In 1935 Jones Sr. planned to ride across Lake Ontario on a jury-rigged bicycle that was attached to the wooden pontoons of a catamaran, owned by his boss Ed Rudd. The pedals of the bicycle were connected to the stern so as to turn the propeller, and the boat was steered by the handles of the bicycle. Apparently Ed Rudd was less than enthused with this idea, given that he planned to have a "female softball star" ride it across the lake in the not-too-distant future. When he got wind of what Jones intended to do, he told him that if he ever attempted to leave the bay with the vessel he'd have him arrested. Undaunted, Jones, along with one of his nephews, arrived at the lagoon where the vessel was moored, and in the wee hours of July 14 they carried it over to the west side of the Island, so as to avoid the watchful eye of the Harbour Police.

According to the *Mail and Empire* and the *Globe*, as noted on July 15, 1935, Jones ran into a series of difficulties along the way that included rough water and broken sunglasses. The capper was the left pontoon, which sprung a leak. According to Jones, he was left with no alternative but to hand pedal the bike for the rest of the journey, a seemingly superhuman feat. At any rate, about ten hours later Jones arrived, not in the United States as he intended but in Port Dalhousie, Ontario, thoroughly exhausted. How did he get there? Jimmy Jones Jr. explains, "He started to ride and he saw the smoke from the *Cayuga* and that's what he set his course on, the steam across the Lake."

———— •◦• ————

FOUR YEARS AFTER Jimmy Jones's trip across the lake, the urban landscape of Toronto and its sheltering Island changed forever. With Canada's declaration of war against Germany in 1939, wartime workers who needed accommodation flooded into the greater Toronto area. Near the end of the Second World War, the city was already filled beyond capacity, with vast numbers of returning servicemen and women all seeking lodging.

According to former Island resident Mrs. Vivienne Trudeau Doyle, it was during this time that the City of Toronto introduced a new rule that in her view forced summer Island residents to make a choice: either move to the Island permanently and relinquish their comfortable homes in the city, or give up their Island retreats, which ranged from the spacious homes on Centre, though now in need of repair, to little more than the makeshift tents on Ward's Island. This seems to be corroborated by a rather draconian federal order-in-council issued in December 1944 that declared Toronto and District an "Emergency Shelter Area" and restricted the rights of Torontonians to rent or lease property if they were already in occupation of "family quarters" in the city.

For the Trudeau family, the choice was easy: Vivienne Trudeau Doyle's father sold their substantial house on two acres in the city and hauled their worldly possessions over to the Island. Their home on Lakeshore Avenue overlooking the water, while substantial in size, initially lacked some city conveniences, yet all of this paled in comparison to the alternative: the prospect of losing their Island paradise, which became their full-time home. In later years, Vivienne and her younger sister Naomi (Noni) were the first women to become full-fledged members of the Queen City Yacht Club, on Algonquin Island. By the end of their first year at the QCYC, the sisters were third in club points and had won the Sportsman Trophy.

Neither of the Trudeau sisters ever shied away from a challenge, and this was particularly true of Noni, who by the age of twelve was winning paddling races at the Island Amateur Aquatic Association, though getting little recognition simply because she was a girl. In later years she set a Canadian swim record for the medley relay. At the age of sixty-four and almost legally blind, Naomi Trudeau Morris made her way down to the Balmy Beach Club in the Beach and signed up for masters paddling, competing in C2s and C4s (two- and four-person paddling events), as well as a variety of kayaking events. She finished her competitive career at the age of seventy-six.

In the 1940s Sergeant McLarty, the father of John McLarty, whom we met earlier, carried on a brisk business moving freight and people to and from the Island with his trusty one-lunger, a single-masted auxiliary sailboat, the *Noazark*. In previous decades, McLarty had been the face of law and order on the Island. Though having long since relinquished his position as Island constable, he was still known to Islanders simply as "Sergeant." During these earlier years as constable, he meted out a form of understated, even-handed justice. According to his son John McLarty, his approach was, "I know you didn't steal it, but make sure it's back in the morning." The trusty Sergeant was now transporting crates of cola, fuel oil, and produce across the bay to the local businesses on Manitou Road as well as coal to Island homes in the fall. In the spring, he ferried the inevitable flow of summer visitors and residents back to their Island homes.

Just before Canada's declaration of war on Germany on September 10, 1939, a seaplane bound for Rochester, New York, crashed into the *Noazark's* mast while en route to the Toronto Island Airport. It is said that while the airplane flipped into a ninety-degree arc and sank in the harbour, the *Noazark* kept right on chugging, all the way to the far Island shore, with Sergeant McLarty still on board.

German blitzkrieg operations in Europe led to the invasion of Norway in 1940, and during the early 1940s, expatriate Norwegians, both from German-occupied territory and naval operations stationed offshore, travelled to Toronto and used the Island airport as a training base for both fighter and bomber pilots. They and the ground crew personnel were billeted on the mainland, across from the Western Gap, in an area that came to be known as Little Norway. Actress Liv Ullmann is the daughter of one of the Norwegians who was stationed at Little Norway and lived in Toronto for a short time as a toddler.

While the Norwegians were well accepted in the Island community, resulting in a few Island marriages to local girls and at least one love child, their stay was not without controversy. The possibility of accidents in the harbour increased with the arrival of the Norwegians, with at least two pilots-in-training losing their lives in separate incidents. As reported in Sally Gibson's *More Than an Island*, the final straw came when a Northrop bomber crashed into the top deck of the Island ferry *Sam McBride*, carrying another two Norwegians to the bottom of the bay. Shortly after this incident, the Norwegian flight training school was moved north to a field in Muskoka, Ontario, for the duration of the war. Norway Park on the mainland, adjacent to the current ferry landing for the today's Island airport, commemorates this period.

In the years immediately after the Second World War, Toronto's housing crisis intensified to the point that Toronto mayor Robert Saunders placed an advertisement in

Along the Shore

Canadian newspapers of the day reading, "Acute Housing Shortage in Toronto, do not come." The city was left with little choice but to encourage housing growth on the Island, particularly for war veterans, many of whom took advantage of federal programs and grants. One area that saw particularly strong growth during this period was Algonquin Island, where many former residents of Hanlan's Point had already found a home after the building of the Port George VI Island Airport. After the war, many veterans erected their own bungalows on the interior of the island with their federal grant money.

By the late 1940s, the Island still retained a resort-town character, and in summer its main thoroughfares were packed with fun seekers and the holiday crowd from the city. But with the addition of the war veterans, the Island became, first and foremost, a vibrant small town of more than 3,000 eclectic residents. While some came seeking modest housing in a city gone mad, others came to escape life's inevitable tragedies — a marriage on the rocks, a business deal gone sour, a career scuttled by devotion to the bottle. Out of the disarray and ashes of their lives, they would form, of seemingly incompatible parts, something that approached, by all accounts, Utopia. The venerable old resort town of old had morphed into a quirky, loveable Island village — a self-declared duchy of sorts, lying just off the shore of starchy Toronto.

During these years Jimmy Jones Jr. spent lazy days with other Island children, exploring the still

The Royal Norwegian Air Force training facility, or "Little Norway," early 1940s

OA, C-109-18-11-35H

Edith Ward and milkman Percy Emslie, c. 1975 Ursula Heller, first published in Robert Sward's *The Toronto Islands*

inner lagoon. Of those days in the 1930s and 40s Jimmy Jones said, "It was a paradise — it was pretty free, pretty relaxed and pretty lovely. What we had here was totally unique in Toronto, or anywhere for that matter. There was a total mixture of people. You had good people here in the Depression, on relief, and then two doors down were the Gooderhams, or the Phelans, with a swimming pool, and who served you lobster sandwiches for lunch."

It is impossible to tell how such an interesting and diverse group of characters came to inhabit the Island during and after the Second World War. Maybe it was the Island itself that drew them there and the freedom that promised. Or maybe, after some strange twist of fate had brought them there, it was the Island itself that played a small part in their making. We will never know, but the Island boasted its fair share of characters, like the much-loved Percy Emslie, who until months before his death in 1982 delivered the milk and eggs right into residents' refrigerators, whether they happened to be home or not. As Jones recalls, "You knew he had been there by the cigar smoke as you opened your front door."

And then there was Doc Howard, who was a well-respected bacteriologist and the chemist at the Island Filtration Plant. Dr. Howard also had medical training, and he was the unofficial physician on the Island for many decades. He is credited with having saved many lives on the Island, never charging a cent for his services. In the winter months, all of the Island kids gathered at the local fire station to watch Freddy Langstaff, badly scarred from a barge fire in the bay, swallow the most disgusting substances, including waxed paper and old elastic bands. Bill Swalwell cleaned the underwater water filtration system and, in his antiquated bubble diving suit, removed more than one interesting conversation piece clogging the Island's intake pipe.

Added to this eclectic mix of personalities are the many artists who have also been drawn to the Island for generations. Among them was Irish engineer William Armstrong, who was one of the founders of the RCYC. Prior to 1880, he built a rustic cottage that he named Rendezvous on Hanlan's Point and painted many enduring scenes of Toronto Bay and the Island. Armstrong's work as a railway engineer allowed him to record many other scenes farther afield, which have left a valuable record of early Canada.

Here is William (Bill) Swalwell, all suited up for work on the Island Filtration Plant's intake pipe in the 1940s. According to Vivienne Trudeau Doyle, the suit had weighted feet and a "screw on globe top." The Ned Hanlan *and a scow would accompany Swalwell far out into the lake to a point above the intake pipe. Then Swalwell would descend into the inky blackness, while oxygen was pumped into his bubble helmet.*

Courtesy Michael Swalwell

The Moorings, located on Lakeshore Avenue, was the Murphy family cottage. The view is from Algonquin Island, overlooking the back of the cottage and the lagoon. Rowley Murphy, PC

Painter Rowley Murphy began his long association with the Island as a child, while summering at the Moorings, his family cottage at 118 Lakeshore. Murphy was a yachtsman and had a lifelong passion for ships. He also taught at the Ontario College of Art for over thirty years, and became one of Canada's leading marine artists. Murphy painted scenes of numerous harbours on the Great Lakes, from both historical and early twentieth century perspectives. He also rendered detailed and accurate images of the harbour and vessels on Toronto Bay. Like William Armstrong, the breadth of his subjects extended far beyond the bay; he also served in the navy and acted as an official war artist during the Second World War.

Another gifted marine artist was Alan Howard, who lived for many decades at 410 Lakeshore Avenue, near the Island Filtration Plant. Alan Howard was the son of Doc Howard, and, like his father, he played an important role in the life of the Island, acting as an effective advocate for the community, particularly in the 1950s. He was also the driving force behind the establishment of the now-closed Marine Museum of Upper Canada, serving as curator from 1961 to 1981. In more recent times, Christiane Pflug, who painted such affecting portraits of Toronto and the bay and left behind a poignant memory of herself, ended her life on Island shores in 1972.

Tom Hodgson (pronounced on the Island as "Hodson") was another Islander who left a lasting mark on the Canadian art scene. He was a founding member of the Painters Eleven, a group that pioneered abstract expressionism in English-speaking Canada. Born in the mid-1920s, he was raised on Centre Island and from around the age of twelve clearly showed an artist's gift. He started by drawing cartoons for the local newspaper, the *Centre Islander*, and then in due course joined the Painters Eleven. The group's work was seen as a bold departure from the conventional art scene of Toronto, where public perception in the 1950s still focused on the Group of Seven.

Initial recognition, slight to begin with, came through the efforts of another of the group's members, William Ronald, who also lived on the Island for a time. Ronald was doing design work for the Simpson Company and hung some of the group's work in the large display windows of the old Simpson building at Yonge and Queen, pairing the paintings with traditional and contemporary furnishings that were on offer. For the first time, Torontonians were able to visualize abstract art in the context of everyday life. Within a month the group added four new members, and that first glimpse at Simpson's led to the first formal showing of the Painters Eleven, held in Toronto at the Roberts Gallery in February 1954. By the time of Hodgson's death in 2006, his paintings were commanding prices in the $30,000 range.

Tom Hodgson grew up in a large house on Centre Island at 35 Iroquois Avenue, known throughout the Island as the "Hodgson House of Nonsense." The atmosphere was laissez-faire. Various parts were continually being rented out to a ragtag collection of Island characters who came and went at all hours of the day and night. The house was best known for the raucous parties held there by Hodgson's amiable and hard-drinking father, Dinny Hodgson, while the kids, including Tom and his younger sister Jane, all congregated at the Island Amateur Aquatic Association, later to become the Island Canoe Club. Virtually every child who grew up on the Island in the 1930s and 40s knew from an early age how to paddle a canoe. Young Tom Hodgson learned to do

that a little better than most. Later on, while he was gaining recognition as one of Canada's leading abstract painters, he was also gaining stardom as a national paddling champion, taking part in two Olympic Games, first at Helsinki in 1952 and then at Melbourne in 1956.

Many have suggested that there was in fact integration between Hodgson's seemingly contradictory worlds of art and sport. If that is so, it could most certainly be found on the Island. Hodgson's studio was attached to his house and built onto the bank of the lagoon on Centre Island. About the time the Centre Island community came crashing down in the 1950s, Hodgson moved to the mainland, where notorious parties were held at his studio. At one such affair, the centre piece of a midnight brunch was actually a nude model spread out on Hodgson's work table and laden with fruit, cold cuts, and assorted other delicacies.

Some of those familiar with Hodgson's style of painting in broad strokes suggest a physical commonality between his two worlds of painting and canoeing. Joan Murray, past curator of several Painters Eleven retrospectives, has said, "You see in his abstraction a reflection of the great sweep of

Tom Hodgson entitled this work It Became Green. *Iris Nowell, in* Painters Eleven: The Wild Ones of Canadian Art, 2010, *relates that Tom and a friend transported the large unfinished canvas over the frozen bay on the* Ned Hanlan *tug boat during the winter of 1955–1956. Once cityside, they travelled to New Jersey, where the canvas was finished that summer. The painting's development gave birth to the title — as Hodgson remarked, "It became green."* Oil on canvas

Collection of The Robert McLaughlin Gallery; Purchase, 1971

Along the Shore

his arm as a paddler." This could well be the case. There is good reason why a common popular name for "abstract expressionism" is "action painting."

Hodgson went on to teach at the Ontario College of Art, and he pursued work as a commercial artist. He continued both to paddle and to paint until he fell into the grip of disease and old age, passing away in 2006.

Although having lived away from the Island for decades, as late as 1995 he could still be seen paddling the silent interior lagoon and inner waterways of his youth. Shortly after he disappeared from Island shores forever, his beloved Island Canoe Club was res-urrected (now the Toronto Island Canoe Club), becoming once again an integral piece of Island life.

———— •◦• ————

IN THE POST-WAR YEARS, most of the leading families had vacated their large summer homes, and other families of modest means discovered their own Island paradise in these tired yet picturesque properties right on the beach. These were the days when a family would ride three abreast on bicycle to church at St. Andrew or St. Rita's and when the neighbours, when the plumbing gave way, would think nothing of lining up to use the shower down the street, or yours if it wasn't presently occupied. And then there was the exodus to the Island at the end of the workday. At the piers of Hanlan's and Ward's, weary men and women would toss off their ties and unpin their hair at the dock and walk barefoot in the long Island grass toward home, the cares of city life now a world away.

On Saturday night, the younger crowd headed down to Bill Sutherland's Manitou Hotel on Manitou Road, the "main drag" on Centre Island, once described as "a stage set from High Noon." Though the elaborate dance pavilion at Hanlan's Point had dis-appeared some time ago, there remained a number of lively dance halls at Centre Island — after the last ferry left for the mainland, Islanders danced on. There you could for fifty cents hear big name bands from the city or just socialize with friends into the wee hours of the morning. Others would take in a movie at the local theatre just off the main street or have dinner at Dick's Grill and afterwards a romantic stroll up to English's Boathouse, where you could hire a rowboat and paddle the lagoon with your sweetheart by the light of the moon. The Island's imperfections and eccentricities only added to its charm in these few short post-war years.

Just as the Island population was at its zenith in the mid-1950s, the winds of change blew over the shore, this time threatening the Island's destruction, all in the name of

Manitou Road, early 1950s
TPL, S 1-2043A

progress. As a prelude of things to come, the fall of 1954 brought Hurricane Hazel to Toronto, an intense and highly destructive storm for which the city was completely unprepared.

Hurricane Hazel collided head-on with the Toronto shore on October 15 and unleashed torrential rains that increased in intensity as the night progressed, sweeping boats, houses, and corpses out into the lake. When it was all over, more than eighty people were dead in Southern Ontario, the vast majority of whom were from Toronto and vicinity. The Lakeshore was the hardest-hit waterfront district, suffering major property damage and loss of life. Though the Island did suffer its share of flooded basements and other related water damage, it passed through the hurricane relatively unscathed.

A different story, however, unfolded out in the harbour, where long-time Islander Jimmy Jones Jr., who was operating a water taxi from John Durnan's boathouse. In the early evening of October 15, Jimmy Jones, oblivious to the seriousness of the situation, left the protected Island lagoon and headed into the bay for the city with one passenger, Jack Gale, a reporter for the *Toronto Star*. They were in the *Minnie D.*, a steady wooden round-bottomed vessel.

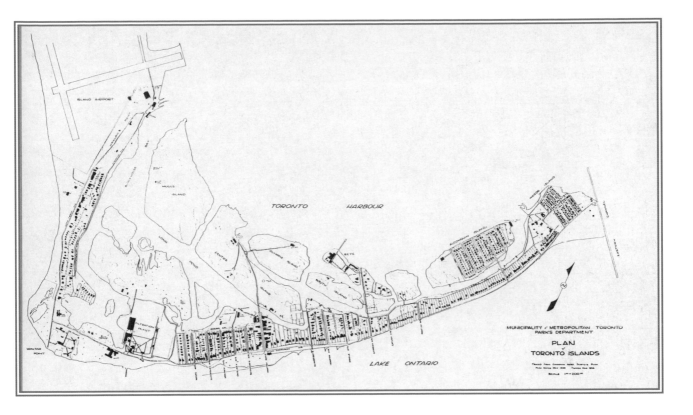

This 1955 map shows the Island at the height of residential development
CTA, F1047_ s1894_f4_b53093_f16

As Jones approached the open water, to his surprise he was faced with increasingly high easterly waves, waves that drove the boat into deep troughs where it shuddered, as if breaking apart. Jones let up on the throttle and gave the boat her way, and as Gale thrashed around on the bench seats, at times clinging on to the deckhead for dear life, they ploughed forward toward Toronto. When they reached the foot of York and Queen's Quay, street signs on cement poles were being tossed around in the roadway.

With ferry service from the mainland cancelled around 7 p.m., a group of increasingly numerous and worried Islanders started to gather, unsure of whether to run for cover or beg Jimmy to just take them home. Said Jones of the experience:

> They all just stood there, waiting to see what I would do, if I would take the chance and head back home. The *Minnie D.* could carry twenty-three passengers, and she was our most solid vessel, but I'd never seen anything like this before. At midnight I filled her to capacity, and with the rain coming down in sheets on Queen's Quay, I decided to make a run for it. I knew that going back

Hurricane Hazel left the worst of her wrath for the west end of the city. The normally placid Humber River became a rushing torrent that obliterated homes and carried many people to their deaths. Toronto Daily Star.
October 18, 1954, Paul Smith/GetStock.com

would be easier because the winds were out of the east, so I just pointed her towards Hanlan's and let the wind push me. . . . We boiled into Hanlan's and I thanked my lucky stars.

When I asked him if he would do it again, his answer was definitive: "I don't think so. I was twenty-four years old in 1954." Twenty years later, memories of the crossing had not faded. Jones found himself at an Island social gathering with John Fowlie, a passenger on the return trip, who, when asked if he had gone over to the Island during the hurricane, pointed directly at Jones and stated, "Yes I did. I came with that bastard over there."

Along the Shore

While Hazel was by no means the worst storm the Island had ever seen, the aftermath of the hurricane would be felt in the years to come. As Sally Gibson notes, Hazel became part of the official rationale for Metro's drive to convert the entire space to parkland in the years that followed.

CHAPTER SIX

Destruction and Loss

In the words of the *Toronto Star* on June 22, 1973, "No city that aspires to greatness can afford to trample its past on the way to the future." Some years later, in his autobiography *Life Begins at 65*, Hans Blumenfeld, an internationally recognized architect and planner, wrote of the Island: "Toronto, like most North American cities, had sacrificed the enjoyment of its waterfront to railroads and industries. However, God in his grace had given a second open waterfront to the citizens by locating a cluster of islands, covering about a square mile, at a distance of not less than a mile from the shore." The Island was the city's second chance, and it was about to go through a period of tremendous upheaval and change.

Since the late 1940s the matter of Island redevelopment had been at the forefront of Toronto city planning initiatives, and for the following number of years an assortment of proposals was put forward that envisioned wildly divergent schemes, with or without the inclusion of Island residents. Prior to the coming of Hurricane Hazel in 1954, none of these schemes had moved past the initial discussion stage, although Islanders remained somewhat on tenterhooks, given that their homes sat on city-owned land and were subject to long-term leases, the majority of which would expire within the coming years.

Without realizing it, Islanders were in the eye of a storm even before Hurricane Hazel arrived on the shores of Toronto Bay. With the passing of the Municipality of Metropolitan Toronto Act in 1953, the city and twelve outlying municipalities were federated into a regional government. Along with this change, residents had failed to grasp the significance of a decision by the City of Toronto earlier in 1954 that offered the Island to the newly formed Metro Council for redevelopment as a park and recreation centre. Metro accepted the offer in principle by March 1954, and the fate of the Island and its residents fell into the hands of the illustrious Metro Chairman Fred Gardiner, the same man who gave Toronto that architectural gem and mid-century monument to progress, the Gardiner Expressway, which still divides Torontonians from their waterfront.

Gardiner's self-appointed right-hand man, Parks Commissioner Tommy Thompson, was pursuing his mission to develop parkland in the newly formed Metropolitan Toronto with religious zeal, and he had the Island locked firmly in his sites. Thompson, while still held in high regard today by many Torontonians for giving the city a vast array of parkland, was the face of the enemy on the Island. In the end, he would not and could not envisage a park that had, at the same time, people in it.

During this period, Hans Blumenfeld, the assistant director of Metro planning, prepared a report that recommended blending residents and parkland — a strategy that would have saved many of the historic properties and residences. According to Blumenfeld, he showed the report to Thompson in advance of its release, and Thompson initially agreed that the houses were "more of an asset than a liability." However, Thompson

Poster produced by Rick/Simon at Coach House Press for the Save Island Homes Campaign

later changed his position to align with the views of Gardiner, who was already pressing for the eradication of the community. Thompson came to see the community as a roadblock to change, an impediment to the tunnel that would bring picnickers and their automobiles within a stone's throw of the beach, a Frisbee park in place of the old Massey residence, chrysanthemums instead of the old Pierson Hotel.

With the first blows of the wrecking ball and with barely a voice of protest raised city-side, the age of innocence for Toronto's Island paradise was over and, buoyed up by tyrannical reform, Toronto moved headlong into the future with callous disregard for our past. As one former Island resident put it, "What they would do is get the people out fast as soon as their leases were up, back the bulldozer up and bash it right down. Then everything would be slammed into a big pit they'd dug in advance and set on fire. You have no idea what they destroyed when they pulled the Island apart."

It started slowly at first, a house missing here and there, with the residents increasingly leaving voluntarily and seeking compensation for their houses before their leases were up. By the late 1950s the Island looked similar in character to a bombed-out English neighbourhood during the Blitz. With masses of razed frozen earth, the remaining children stood around in snowsuits, watching the chewed up remains of the neighbour's house being piled into a shallow grave. Then there was the O'Shea family who, with the help of Island friends, packed up their possessions into a skiff, took a final journey across the bay, and then moved like refugees single file up Bay Street to a city they did not remember. Their photographs, balanced precariously between the rudder and the goldfish bowl, spilled out into the bay and were never recovered, though the memories remain.

Destruction of an Island home CTA, F1047_s872_it24, (image originally held in Toronto Island Archives)

Along the Shore

Due to the years of uncertainty that followed, many Island homes fell into disrepair and ranged in description from "charming and quaint" to "squalid," depending on one's perspective on the community and whether it should be saved. The destruction meted out to the Island in the 1950s and 1960s was not just directed at the wartime housing and post-war bungalows, some of which were hastily built in the middle years of the twentieth century. A large number of properties with significant heritage features were also lost during this period, including the summer homes and mansions of Toronto's leading families, Ward's Hotel, the Pierson Hotel, English's Boathouse, and many other businesses that had been long established along Manitou Road on Centre Island.

The St.-Andrew-by-the-Lake Anglican Church miraculously escaped the wrecking ball and survives to the present day, remaining not only a fully operating church but a vibrant focal point for the life of the community. In a sense, the story of the little parish is intertwined with the story of the Island itself.

Robertson's Landmarks of Toronto describes services held at the church in the late nineteenth century: "The first thing noticeable was the unconventional style of dress characterizing many persons there. . . . This variety of dress, taken with the plainly furnished chapel, the open windows, through which the breezes came laden with vigour and health, the sound of the surf on the shore and the gay laughter of little children playing on the sand made the room pleasant, cool, airy and bright."

This description dates from some fifteen years after the celebration of the first services at St. Andrew, which took place on July 27, 1884. At that time the church was located on the south shore of Centre Island, at the corner of what would in later years become Cherokee and Lakeshore Avenues. The church owed its inception to an Island summer resident, Bishop Arthur Sweatman (later Archbishop of Toronto and then Primate of Canada). It was built to meet the needs of a growing summer community on the Island that by then included the prominent Gooderham and Massey families, who were leading members of the congregation at St. Andrew.

The tiny church was affiliated to the Parish of St. James, though bearing no other resemblance to the Cathedral Church of St. James on the mainland. In 1950, after the Island's full-time population increased at the end of the Second World War, St. Andrew was declared a separate parish of the Diocese of York. Designed by architect Arthur Denison, who summered on the Island at that time, St. Andrew was built in the stick-style of construction then prevalent on the Island but elaborated into a charming semi-Gothic variation. It was also conveniently located next door to the summer residence of Bishop Sweatman, which was also designed by Denison and was aptly named Happy-Go-Lucky. Although modest and in keeping with its Island surroundings, the interior of Saint Andrew was then and still is now by no means commonplace. The original walls and vaulted ceiling remain clad in tongue-and-groove fir. Several windows in the chancel were made in 1885 by the renowned McCausland studio in Toronto, while another memorial window by N.T. Lyon pays tribute to the remarkable contribution that Islanders made during the First World War.

During the dark years of the late 1950s, when the communities of Hanlan's Point and Centre Island were destroyed to make way for an island park, St. Andrew was sold to the city but leased back to the archdiocese for an indefinite period. In 1959–60, the church was moved to its present location on Centre Island, closer to Ward's Island, along with its Roman Catholic counterpart, St. Rita's. By 1974 the congregation had dwindled to about fifteen families, and in 1979 the City of Toronto condemned St. Andrew, just four years after the parish had celebrated its centennial. With a six-foot-high wire fence put up

Here is English's Boathouse, which stood on the south side of the lagoon at the top end of Manitou Road until the late 1950s. Just imagine how wonderful it would be to get off the ferry at Centre Island, walk south toward the lake, and see it there still. Related to the Englishes were the Durnans, whose boathouse stood at Hanlan's Point, though they maintained a dock for water taxis on the west side of English's Boathouse as well. CTA, F1244_it0165a

around it and the few remaining parishioners facing eviction, it seemed that the church was destined to be reduced to rubble, like so many other historic Island properties.

However, the forces of desecration that passed themselves off as "progress" were not to have the last word. In the first place, they had not reckoned with the determination of the Islanders themselves. Using wire cutters retrieved from one of the nearby homes, parishioners John Fowlie and Liz Amer cut through a section of the fence shortly after the church was condemned. The congregation went in, and the Sunday services continued despite the eviction notice. The community continued to use its church through the years of uncertainty that followed.

Eventually, in 1984, St. Andrew was saved by an agreement between the city and the Anglican Archdiocese of Toronto. Reverend Michael Marshall, the present incumbent

Relics of the past are still quite prevalent today on the Island. Though his dwelling is long gone, Freddy Poole's house number is still firmly attached to the old sea wall on Lakeshore Drive.

Jane Fairburn

of St. Andrew, explains that the remaining Islanders never lost sight of the fact that St. Andrew was "part of their heritage and legacy. They recognized the need to maintain their use of it, so it didn't become a pawn in the struggle between the forces who would destroy the Island community and those who would save it."

Sadly, St. Rita's was indeed demolished, while its remaining parishioners attended separate worship services at St. Andrew. Items salvaged from St. Rita's, such as its wooden oak pews and the stations of the cross that now adorn St. Andrew's dark-panelled walls, all add to the richness of a setting that has developed there for more than a century. St. Andrew now represents more than just itself. Perhaps unwittingly, this little church has become a symbol for a good and simple way of living and a repository for the relics of past Island life.

———— • ————

ON A SUNNY FEBRUARY MORNING, Jimmy Jones Jr. and I ride our creaky Island bicycles down the old Manitou Road on Centre Island, the one-time "main street" for Islanders and the very heart of the community. The buildings have long disappeared and it is

Along the Shore

Dug out, Ward's Island beach,
2012 April Hickox Katzman Kamen
Gallery, AprilHickox.com

eerily quiet now, the sides of the old boulevard neatly bordered with flower beds that in summer form a complex display of geraniums and baby's breath that stretches down to the water as far as the eye can see.

Beyond our frivolity and Jones's gregarious nature, there is an underlying sadness here — a sense of loss for what was — as he gives me a tour of landmarks long gone:

> Down there on the left, that was the Manitou Hotel . . . at the corner was the Casino, nothing to do with gambling, but they danced in there all night. Lionel P. Conacher awarded our Toronto Island Hockey Club the cup for outstanding achievement there one night around 1940. . . . And up there, that's where we lived on the second floor. Mom and Dad ran the restaurant, Jimmy's Coffee Shop. There was a fire one night and the staircases were already up in flames. I squeezed through the second floor window on a rope to get the fire department . . . they saved my whole family.

Ted English, the great-great nephew of Ned Hanlan, moved away from the Island in the 1950s, when it all came apart, and although a long-time resident of California, he still returns occasionally to his old Island home: "The first time I came back, I looked down toward the boathouse and saw the flowers all lined up in rows . . . it was a terrible feeling. Gone were the enticing pleasures of Manitou Road."

Only the old-timers know that just under the flowers of Centre Island, a few inches under the earth, lies a graveyard of artifacts and memory. At any given moment, you could excavate that self-made land of enchantment, right here, under the earth. Yet all that remains visible now are the gnarled tree-lined entrance ways, the broken steps leading nowhere, and Freddy Poole's house number, 170 Lakeshore Avenue, cemented in time to the original seawall. These are the sad relics of another age in the life of an Island community that against all odds would endure to another day.

DURNAN'S SONG
by Michael Jones

The other day I went walking
to a place I haven't been to
for a while
I found myself at Durnan's Boathouse
a flood of memories
and a smile
the day itself was kind of foggy
a light rain was blowing in
across the bay
the kind of day for remembering
conjuring up some old spirits
that got away
and as I stood there listening
I thought I heard an old voice say

Tell Billy Ward and Jimmy Jones
that I'm okay
don't rue the day
I passed away
and left them standing all alone
along the shoreline
of the bay

Along the Shore

CHAPTER SEVEN
Renewal

The communities of Ward's and Algonquin in the 1960s and 1970s were as diverse a group of people as you would find anywhere on the earth at that time. War veterans and old-timers — some displaced from other areas of the Island and whose roots extended back to the pioneer days of the 1830s, including Bill Durnan and the curmudgeonly but lovable Bill Ward — were living next to the Vietnam draft dodgers, hippies, and Bohemian types of the "new age," all refugees imported from a city still too conservative to accept them. Then there were the thinkers, the writers, and the poets, some who lived there seasonally, others full-time, including the soon-to-be-famous Canadian journalist and broadcaster Peter Gzowski, journalist Robert Fulford, and for a brief period novelist and poet Gwendolyn MacEwen, not to mention the other poets and writers who frequented the Island or had visited there, including Victor Coleman, Alan Ginsberg, and William Burroughs.

By 1970 Manitou Road was long gone, and the vast majority of the residences west of Algonquin and Ward's Island were no more, yet change was afoot in the city

of Toronto that would eventually assist
the remaining Islanders' cause. Author
and journalist Robert Fulford suggests
that Toronto began to develop civic
consciousness back in the early 1960s,
with the building of New City Hall. Along with that civic consciousness came new city
councillors in 1969 — many of whom had ties to the Island, among them John Sewell
and William Kilbourn as well as future Toronto mayor David Crombie — who carried
forward an exciting new vision for the city, one that included a heavy measure of respect
for communities and grassroots urban development.

Crombie and another newcomer to the city, urbanologist Jane Jacobs, who had
authored *The Death and Life of Great American Cities*, were already embroiled in another
battle to prevent the building of the Spadina Expressway, which threatened to do to the
Annex what had already been meted out to the Island. With the dawning of a new age

Here is the Butscher family in 1980. Speedskater Tom Butscher, the man on the left, who still lives on the Island today with his wife, Luisa, until recently was the oldest man ever to have rowed across the Atlantic. Ursula Heller

in the life of Toronto came the thought that maybe, just maybe, you could fight city hall and win. So the remaining Islanders did what they had always done through the life of the Island, through the snow and the ice, without provisions and in the driving rain: they stuck together on their island and organized a military-style campaign the likes of which Toronto had never seen.

By the summer of 1969, the writing was on the wall for the removal of the rest of the Islanders, who had been given a final extension of their leases until August 31, 1970. But rather than surrendering their leases early or standing by helplessly as moving day rapidly approached, the remaining Islanders dared to organize an army of protesters with the singular goal of preserving their community. They called themselves the Island Residents Association (IRA for short; the association of the acronym IRA with the Irish Republican

The Island

Army was lost on no one). While the name was ultimately changed to the Toronto Island Residents Association (TIRA), the message was still the same: Islanders were up for a fight and they would not be moved.

In the years that followed, the City of Toronto, with the support of reform-minded councillors, became increasingly supportive of the Islanders' right to remain, granting further lease extensions. In the end, however, Metro politicians would not be moved. The anti-Island faction had exposed the fact that a small group of Islanders were actually using their homes as secondary properties and sometimes as money-making propositions, subletting them to tenants on a seasonal basis. This practice did political damage to the Islanders' cause, though it was uncharacteristic of the financial situation of most Islanders, many of whom did not have high incomes and who, by and large, occupied their homes on a full-time basis. In the end, Metro simply lacked the largesse to allow the remaining several hundred souls to stay in their homes on nineteen acres in a 600-acre park that was otherwise lifeless and in the middle of a frozen bay at least eight months of the year. Tommy Thompson's ugly little vendetta against the Island community had turned personal. He wanted them out. This was war.

Any military campaign has its skirmishes before the decisive battle, and so it was with the fight for the Island. Many Island residents, while lacking deep pockets, had connections, and the conflict proceeded on many fronts, not only the political realm but also the courts. Islanders mounted a series of legal challenges that involved their authority to remain on the Island, culminating in a decision by the Supreme Court of Canada that upheld the validity of the eviction notices in 1977.

Sally Gibson writes that further legal wrangling and a series of reprieves followed this ruling, which brought Islanders all the way to July 24, 1980, when Mr. Justice John O'Driscoll of the Supreme Court of Ontario ruled that the writs of possession, the legal documents which gave Metro the authority to physically remove Islanders from their homes, were valid. Metro smelled blood. The decision was definitive, and all bets were off as to whether Islanders would be able to secure leave to appeal this ruling

Islanders had known for some time that, in the absence of legal roadblocks, Metro would move quickly toward eviction — it was only a matter of time before the sheriff came knocking. Metro's enthusiasm for eviction was only matched, and perhaps surpassed, by the Islanders' conviction to stay, and this included a plan to counter any attempt at eviction in the event that all court challenges were unsuccessful. In one such strategy session, little Matthew Ferguson, who at that time was no more than seven years of age, asked in a squeaky voice, "When the sheriff comes, will he be wearing a hat and have those big guns?"

Along the Shore

Kay Walker rallies the troops Ursula Heller
in Robert Sward's, *The Toronto Islands*

Meanwhile Island residents, including the aforementioned collection of Second World War veterans,
Island pioneers, artists, poets, and anarchists, joined
forces to protect their little duchy. Members of the
Home Guard donned yellow hard hats and remained at the ready, scanning the harbour
for invading ships that would bring the sheriff, and along with him the writs of possession. They also established the Toronto Island Radio Network on the Citizen's Band (CB)
radio with broadcaster Kay Walker, who maintained, as reported in Robert Sward's *The
Toronto Islands*, "I'm as radical as a pussycat, but don't step on my tail. I'm here to stay. If I
have to go to jail, I might as well go for something reasonable like fighting for my house."
Having lived through the London Blitz, Walker cajoled the troops by reading the local
news of the day interspersed with calls to action, while remaining at all times poised for
the inevitable, when the sheriff would come calling and all Islanders, near and far, would
be called to their battle stations.

Among Island leaders was TIRA co-chairperson and future city councillor Liz Amer, whose experiences later inspired her to write a book on community action entitled *Yes We Can! How to Organize Citizen Action*. Amer's grandmother and aunt had been part of the original Ward's Island tent community in the early twentieth century. From the age of eight, Amer spent her summers on the Island with her grandparents. By the time she was fifteen, she was living there year round. Speaking of her deep connection to the Island, she stated in *The Toronto Islands*, "Sometimes I feel as if I own this community. I don't but it's as if it belongs to me and I certainly feel as if I belong to it. It is the opposite of alienation." In the days to come, Amer would lead the charge as the spokesperson for the residents at the bridge, along with fellow TIRA co-chair Ron Mazza.

The day of infamy finally came to the Island on July 28, 1980, a day so central to the psychology and lore of the community that it is referred to as "The Day of the Bridge." The story goes that Islanders received a tip about the sheriff's intention to begin the process of removal. The tip set off the war service siren mounted atop the Ward's Island clubhouse, and it screamed out over the bay, alerting Islanders city-side of the imminent invasion. At that moment, the action plan, rehearsed over and over, kicked into high gear, and city-side Islanders sprinted down Bay Street and jumped into a waiting flotilla of private boats and water taxis that carried them home.

By three thirty in the afternoon, every single rain-sodden Islander had converged at the foot of the Algonquin Bridge with the children in the front, along with throngs of reporters, their canvas tents stretching out to the very edges of the lagoon, to await the oncoming offensive. There they all stood in silence while Acting Sherriff Bremner and Deputy Sherriff Kashuba, accompanied by an ambulance and a city bus, began their slow campaign eastward from Hanlan's Point to the bridge. Liz Amer remembers how Acting Sherriff Bremner's hands shook as he got out of his cruiser and approached the crowd — he had a job to do, and he was intent on delivering the notices to quit and getting the hell off the Island. Amer, on the other hand, clung to the only card she had left — the moral authority to remain.

And so it was that a twenty-five-year-long conflict was compressed into a few moments on the Algonquin Bridge in the rain. "It was a moment and all the other moments fed into it," said Amer, who, with the strength of the assembled crowd behind her, grabbed Sherriff Bremner's hand and said:

> How do you do? I am Elizabeth Amer, co-chair of the Toronto Island Residents' Association. We are 700 people. Two hundred of us are children. We are in a desperate situation. We are being thrown out of our homes without compensation.

We've got no place to go. All we're asking you to do is give us twenty-four hours while we continue to work with the political people and the legal people. We'd like you to go back, take the boxes of notices, and take no further action until the political and legal matters are resolved, which we think is imminent.

Acting Sheriff Bremner approaches the crowd on July 28, 1980 Ursula Heller

In the end, sheriffs Bremner and Kashuba backed off, granted Amer's request for twenty-four further hours, and got back into their cars without serving a single notice. Metro may have won the legal battle, but Islanders, from that moment, had won the war.

Within six months of the Day of the Bridge, the Report of the Commission of Inquiry into the Toronto Islands, entitled *Pressure Island*, was delivered, recommending that the community be allowed to stay for twenty-five years, until July 31, 2005. Premier Bill Davis then undertook to overrule Metro, introducing legislation that stayed the writs of possession. The Ontario NDP government solidified the Islanders' right to remain with

Liz Amer (centre) meets acting Sheriff Bremner as TIRA *co-chair Ron Mazza (right) and executive member Sarah Miller (left) look on* Douglas Ganton

the Toronto Islands Residential Community Stewardship Act. With the passing of the act, the province acquired the Island land in exchange for giving the Lakeshore Psychiatric Hospital property to the city.

The Act created the Toronto Island Land Trust Corporation to administer the land and buildings on the Island as well as to provide stewardship to the Island community. Under the scheme, Islanders were to make a one-time payment to the trust for a ninety-nine-year lease on the land and own their own houses. Restrictions are placed on resale of the homes so that profit cannot be made on the land or the house. In an effort to ensure that Island homes are not used to generate income, those holding title to Island properties must use their home as a principal residence. It is further specified that Island residences cannot be used as part-time or "summer homes" or as rental properties.

With the creation of the land trust, an epic struggle of some forty years came to an end. Toronto had entered a new era, and the destruction and loss meted out to Toronto and its Island were over. Perhaps the iconic Jane Jacobs, who attended the Dominion Day Rally in 1980, days before the confrontation at the bridge, best summed up the soul of the Island when she said, "You don't need to invoke practical reasons as to why this community shouldn't be destroyed. It shouldn't be destroyed because it's lovable. It's unique. It's a lovely thing. It's wicked to destroy lovable, unique and lovely things."

In the coming decades, more and more Torontonians would rediscover that loveliness, too, a loveliness that comes from the unique pairing of the village against the backdrop of the metropolis, which is so rarely seen in any other city. This tiny little community had endured, and, although forever changed, it would not be piled up on the shrine of memory and loss, as had so many other pieces of Toronto's past.

More than fifty years have gone by since the homes on Hanlan's Point and Centre Island were bulldozed under the earth. The areas that the Hanlans, the Durnans, the Hodgsons, and the Englishes once called home now provide a vast open space for thou-

sands of visitors, both city residents and tourists alike, primarily during the summer months. While picnic sites are located throughout the Island, the majority of the attractions and activities are concentrated around Centre Island, now home to the Centreville Amusement Park and Far Enough Farm.

At the time of writing, recent budget cuts at the City of Toronto have called the existence of the farm into question, but with the prospect of a larger amusement park replacing the small hobby farm, Islanders and non-Islanders alike have rallied and plans are afoot to save it. Boat and bike rentals and restaurants may also be found there. Centre Island has also served as a venue for many large-scale political, social, and athletic events over the years.

Though the past century has seen plenty of changes to haberdashery and even ferry design, the general concept — escape, entertainment and fun in the great outdoors — has remained the same CT/MS, 1996,18,69,144

The surprisingly clean beaches on the south and western shores of the Island, including the sheltered bay at Ward's beach and the "clothing optional" beach at Hanlan's Point, continue to attract large numbers of swimmers and sunbathers during the summer months. The boating and yachting clubs also play an important role in maintaining the vitality of the Island in summer. The Island was home to the Mariposa Folk Festival in the 1970s, with Neil Young, Joni Mitchell, Gordon Lightfoot, and Bob Dylan making surprise guest appearances there in 1972. With ever-increasing attendance numbers, and with several exuberant fans swimming across the lagoon to crash the event on at least one occasion, the festival was moved to Molson Park in Barrie in the 1980s. Today the Island continues to be a place for people to enjoy the great outdoors, whether it be in large groups for a family picnic or political event or alone in a quiet corner, contemplating the metropolis under the shade of a giant willow.

These days, the remaining Islanders are still undergoing the long and difficult process of renewal. As with any such process, there are bumps along the road as competing visions of the Island and its future collide. Politics still abound on the Island, and although the battle with Metro is long behind them, the land trust, which amounts to an additional layer of government, has polarized Islanders on issues as diverse as property use, site planning, taxes, and the environment. Infighting has become at times intense, leading a dizzying number of committees to administer Island affairs. Rather than sticking together to fight the enemy, Islanders are now sometimes divided.

Readers will recall that since the late 1930s, the northwest tip of the Island at Hanlan's Point has also been home to an airport, the very existence of which has remained a matter of considerable debate and controversy over the decades. With the introduction of Porter Airlines in 2006, the Billy Bishop Toronto City Airport has experienced an intense period of growth, and there is little doubt that its existence and any further plans for expansion will continue to be debated by Islanders and Torontonians alike, as people increasingly find their way back to the water's edge.

———•———

NO ONE UNDERSTOOD the competing interests that affect Island life and politics better than lifelong resident Bill Durnan. Until his death in 2003 at the age of eighty-seven, he survived the decades of debate, conflict, and open warfare over "what to do about the Island" while faithfully keeping in touch with "his girls" on the mainland. These "girls," a group of octogenarians and aging widows who had left the Island decades earlier when the destruction began, were spread out over greater Toronto and environs beyond. And

Moonlight Sail, on the Bay, Toronto.

"The waves recur, the light, the seasons; memories flash and turn and guide the ships of wisdom in."
— *Gwendolyn MacEwen, "Animal Syllables"* CT/MS, 1996.18.69.117

though distance separated them, it was no impediment to the bonds of friendship that continued and began decades earlier on the Island they so loved.

What is remarkable is that so many Islanders stayed so close to their waterfront, to the west and east, after the community was almost extinguished. Bert Oldershaw, three-time Olympian and stalwart member of both the Island Amateur Aquatic Association and later the Island Canoe Club, moved west along the lakefront after Centre Island was demolished and founded the Mississauga Canoe Club in 1957. He would be evicted twice from the lakefront during his lifetime, remaining the last holdout on his area of Burlington Beach in the 1990s, before his cottage was destroyed to make way for park-land. In his final years, he spent countless hours collecting odd shells and curious objects that he later converted into folk art — all gathered from the shore of a lake he first dis-covered as a child on Toronto Island.

IN THE WANING LIGHT of midwinter, warm lights twinkle on the cottages at Ward's Island, fairy-like, covered in snow. Across the bay, the gleaming city beckons, and it is with reluctance that I climb aboard the *Ongiara* for the return trip, having now completed my exploration of these Island shores. As the city looms ever closer, we bump up against the docks of the ferry terminal and exit the vessel. Within moments my fellow passengers are expertly threading themselves up Bay Street and are subsumed into the texture of the city, yet I hesitate, unsure of my direction. In my mind's eye, I am still out in the bay, moving with the waves, carrying the Island with me still, a small village sunk deep within the heart of the metropolis. Maybe, in a small way, we are all Islanders here.

The Lakeshore

PART IV

Lake Shore Boulevard East, under the feet of the
Leviathan (view is to the west), 2005 John Wallace

CHAPTER ONE

The Nature of the Place

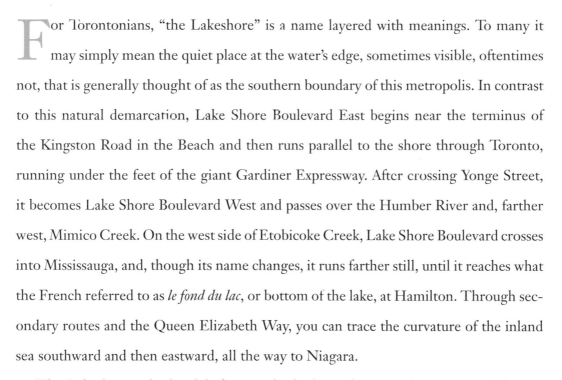

For Torontonians, "the Lakeshore" is a name layered with meanings. To many it may simply mean the quiet place at the water's edge, sometimes visible, oftentimes not, that is generally thought of as the southern boundary of this metropolis. In contrast to this natural demarcation, Lake Shore Boulevard East begins near the terminus of the Kingston Road in the Beach and then runs parallel to the shore through Toronto, running under the feet of the giant Gardiner Expressway. After crossing Yonge Street, it becomes Lake Shore Boulevard West and passes over the Humber River and, farther west, Mimico Creek. On the west side of Etobicoke Creek, Lake Shore Boulevard crosses into Mississauga, and, though its name changes, it runs farther still, until it reaches what the French referred to as *le fond du lac*, or bottom of the lake, at Hamilton. Through secondary routes and the Queen Elizabeth Way, you can trace the curvature of the inland sea southward and then eastward, all the way to Niagara.

The Lakeshore is both a lakefront and a highway, but it is also a string of former villages and towns that stretch along the highway for almost six miles beyond the Humber

Lake Shore Boulevard runs parallel to the lake under "the Gardiner" at the southern periphery of Toronto's downtown core John Wallace

River, from the forgotten district of Humber Bay and on to Mimico, New Toronto, and finally Long Branch, on the east side of Etobicoke Creek.

Long before Europeans ever touched these shores, the precursor to Lake Shore Boulevard was a sandy aboriginal trail that traversed the many ponds and marshes along the waterfront. While moving inland in some sections, the trail connected the eighteenth-century Seneca village of Ganatsekwyagon on the Rouge River to its sister village of Teiaiagon, located in the west near the mouth of the Humber River.

Massive infilling of the lake, which took place in the late nineteenth and early twentieth centuries, pushed the water far to the south of this original pathway west, so much so that the downtown portion of the original trail now lies buried under asphalt, in some sections close to half a mile north of the present shore.

So it is on this "new" lakeshore trail, Lake Shore Boulevard, that we begin our journey westward, into a realm that is set apart from the city by a series of rivers yet linked to it by a shore and a highway that are rich with relics, many of which are intertwined with the history of the Lakeshore district itself. Near the foot of Bathurst Street but blocked off from our sight stand the nineteenth-century barracks and fortifications of the British

View of the west side of Fort York, painted by Owen Staples, 1816–1912 TPL, JRR 671

garrison that we know as Fort York. A military base was established near here, on the east side of the long-buried Garrison Creek, in 1793. Slightly to the west of this, the French built Fort Rouillé, a defensive trading post that was established by 1751; its foundations now lie buried near the bottom of Dufferin Street on the grounds of the Canadian National Exhibition.

A little farther along the shore, we pass Marilyn Bell Park. This is where a sixteen-year-old Toronto schoolgirl from the Lakeshore Swimming Club is honoured for becoming the first person to swim across Lake Ontario, though she came ashore about a mile west of here. Farther along are the Toronto Argonaut Rowing Club and the Boulevard Club, which began life as the Parkdale Canoe Club. These places bear witness to a time in the nineteenth and early twentieth century when many Torontonians enjoyed leisure time at the water's edge, at the numerous boathouses and rowing, canoe, and yacht clubs that lined the shore. Farther west is the Palais Royale, Toronto's historic lakefront dance hall. Next we come upon the Gus Ryder Swimming Pool and the Sunnyside Bathing Pavilion, collectively the remnants of what many would say was Toronto's greatest lakeside amusement park.

Near the westerly edge of former Sunnyside, in Sir Casimir Gzowski Park, stands a

The Lakeshore

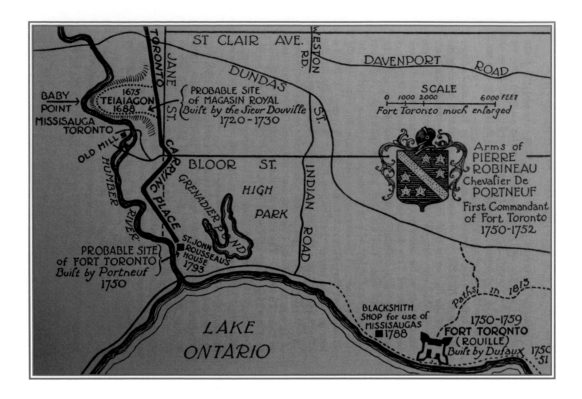

This map of early Toronto shows the probable location of Jean-Baptiste Rousseaux's home and the three successive French posts established at or near the Humber River. The map appears in Percy J. Robinson's Toronto During the French Régime University of Toronto Press (2nd ed.), 1965

miniature French château, the Joy Oil Gas Station, which was originally located on the north side of the highway. The gas station, one of a number of similar stations introduced to the Toronto region in the late 1930s, was strategically placed on the east side of the Humber to service westbound traffic. It presented a last chance to fill up alongside the main thoroughfare before leaving the city, the limits of which then stretched to the Humber River.

A slight bump in the road and a hurried glance to the right give us the only indications that we have sped past thousands of years of human history. We have just crossed over the Humber, the source of the largest watershed in the city — a Canadian Heritage River, a transportation and communications hub for thousands of centuries, and the birthplace of modern Toronto.

Here is the place, near the river mouth, where successive groups of Aboriginal peoples established encampments and villages, among them the ancestral Huron-Wendat, the Seneca, and the Mississaugas. Here is the point of entry to the Toronto Carrying Place Trail, the gateway to the interior of Canada, used not only by first peoples but also, in later

Along the Shore

years, by coureurs de bois, explorers seeking fame and fortune, and missionaries seeking souls. And here is the place, on the east bank of the river, where Indian Department interpreter and trader Jean-Baptiste Rousseaux established his trading post in the wilderness years before the arrival of Lieutenant Governor John Graves Simcoe. But it is on the west bank of the river that our present story begins. We have now arrived in the Lakeshore.

———— ◆ ————

THE GREATER LAKESHORE AREA begins in the arch of Humber Bay, from which the district of Humber Bay takes its name. When moving west along Lake Shore Boulevard from the district of Humber Bay, the shoreline inclines to the southwest, and farther on in Mimico for a short period, due south. For our purposes, we will refer at all times to Lake Shore Boulevard as running east-west and the waterfront as directionally south of the highway in the Lakeshore. Humber Bay's southern boundary extends from the Humber River westward along the shore to both sides of Mimico Creek. In the latter part of the nineteenth century, it was one of Toronto's primary recreational areas; in the twentieth century, it developed into an eclectic collection of holiday motels, inns, and private beaches along the shore. The district, described by many as a former "village," though never officially achieving that status, once radiated northward from the lake as a series of market gardens, commercial areas, and residences, all the way to present-day Berry Road, north of what was then the Queen Elizabeth Way highway.

Humber Bay has seen many changes over its history. For one thing, intensive lake-filling in the twentieth century pushed the shoreline farther and farther to the south of the original Lake Shore Road, which hugged the line of the water. Humber Bay Park, located at the mouth of Mimico Creek and opened in 1984, extends east and west along the lakefront, with Toronto's Waterfront Trail threading through the newly extended shoreline. Behind the trail are the condominiums, which stand shoulder to shoulder at the former shore and near-shore waters of the lake.

Indeed, when I began writing this book, over ten years ago, Humber Bay looked very different. At that time, this area was still referred to as the Motel Strip, and until very recently, a number of small, respectable motels and inns with open views to the lake were still hanging on here, many with architecture straight out of *Happy Days*. Notable among them were the well-loved Casa Mendoza and the Shore Breeze Motel, last operated by Ron Butwell, whose family traces its roots in Humber Bay back to the 1850s. This so-called strip earned itself a bad reputation in the 1970s and 1980s, owing to some nasty goings-on that are now the stuff of legend. Some time ago, the Casa Mendoza was

The Hillcrest Motel fell to the wrecking ball before the Shore Breeze and the Casa Mendoza. With its sleek lines and art deco feel, it often acted as a movie set. Jane Fairburn

bulldozed to the ground, and the Shore Breeze disappeared behind hoardings to make way for sky-high residential towers of concrete and glass.

As we move westward, beyond the quiet marshes of Mimico Creek, it is not long before the built landscape alters dramatically. Gone are the sky-high condominiums of Humber Bay. As we travel along Lake Shore Boulevard West, beyond the unremarkable low-rise apartment buildings of the 1950s, we see remnants of another era begin to emerge on the south side of the highway, near the water's edge: the estates and homes — some time-worn and decrepit, others restored to their former glory — of Toronto's wealthy industrialists, businessmen, and tycoons of the late nineteenth and early twentieth century.

To the north of the highway, away from the water, are the modest streets and homes of the former town of Mimico, which today extends northward from the lake beyond the railway corridor to just south of the Gardiner Expressway. Incorporated as a village in 1911 and a town in 1917, Mimico was one of Toronto's first suburbs, though without any of the derogatory or detrimental aspects of that term. Mimico was never a vacuous dormitory suburb, nor did it mirror the snobbish enclaves described in Phyllis Brett Young's novel *The Torontonians*. If anything, it was comparable with the garden suburbs of a bygone era, a time of widespread hope that everyday life could retain a pastoral echo of Arcadia. This led to a unique residential pattern in Mimico, with a commercial and residential sector along the waterfront (now referred to as Mimico-by-the-Lake) and a large number of folks living north of the lake in modest single-family homes with small gardens, supported by a commercial presence on Royal York Road, north of the highway.

Farther to the west, beginning at Dwight Avenue, is the former industrial satellite town of New Toronto. Bounded to the south by Lake Ontario and to the north by the Canadian National Railway's mainline, the community extends west to Twenty-Third Street, south of Lake Shore Boulevard, and to the north of the highway, at the midpoint between Twenty-Second and Twenty-Fourth Streets.

In New Toronto, and equally so in Mimico and Long Branch, which lies farther to the west, we have come to a place that still knows the meaning of households, lawnmowers, and the girl next door. Gentrification has not quite managed to shove aside the good old folks, those next-door neighbours, now in their sixties, seventies, and eighties, who spent their working lives mainly to the north of the highway, in factories of the industrial age that are almost all now defunct, boarded up, or redeveloped for new uses. These are the factories that turned out the copperware, tires, munitions, and bricks that helped fuel the war effort and the rapid growth of modern Toronto and Canada throughout the first half of the twentieth century.

Farther to the west — beyond the border of Twenty-Third Street, south of Lake Shore Boulevard West, and north of the highway, at the midpoint between Twenty-Second and Twenty-Fourth Streets — lies Long Branch. Etobicoke Creek serves as the dividing line between Long Branch and Mississauga, though it is little known that Long Branch (and Toronto, for that matter) extends over to the west side of the creek, south of Lake Shore Boulevard, following the original pathway of what was once referred to as the Etobicoke River.

Beginning as part of a large land grant to Loyalist Colonel Samuel Smith, Long Branch eventually developed, in the late nineteenth and early twentieth centuries, into a resort area and was incorporated as a village in 1930. As the district made the transition to a suburban community later in the twentieth century, many of its residents found work in the factories that sprang up north of the highway, both in Long Branch and Mimico and in the booming town of New Toronto. Still others, including large numbers of housewives and single women, crossed Etobicoke Creek in the 1940s and went to work at Small Arms Ltd. in southwest Mississauga, churning out massive quantities of firearms and ammunition for the war effort.

George E. Elliott's eclectic variety store in New Toronto offered something for everyone

CT/MS, Montgomery's Inn, 031_030 Box1

DESPITE THE AMALGAMATION of the whole area — Humber Bay, Mimico, New Toronto, and Long Branch — into the Borough of Etobicoke in 1967, and then into the city of Toronto in 1998, each area continues to retain a distinct identity. With the exception of Humber Bay, these communities have, for the most part, not yet been gentrified, prettified, or primped. Rather, the district as a whole is somewhat like the Beach of yesteryear, in the days before the multi-wheeled designer strollers took command and before the Woolworth's and the family hardware store were driven out by banks, trust companies, fast food outlets, fashion boutiques, and temples to the low-fat cappuccino.

Rather than aspiring to such exotica, the Lakeshore opts for eccentricity. Where full-service stores along the highway once offered staples and modern conveniences to the burgeoning local working and middle classes, there is now an eclectic medley of merchandisers, from an antique store crammed with fascinating memorabilia of the Second World War to a horticultural seed store with a dressmaker's dummy in the window to a second-hand bookstore with paperbacks piled to the ceiling but pride of

Dr. E.B. Sisley's painting Creek at the Hospital Grounds. *The creek ran north of the now demolished Lakehouse on the historic Mimico Asylum grounds.* Courtesy John and Muriel Easton

place given to a matched pair of plaster dinosaur footprints, provenance undefined.

Step back from these strange, endearing shop windows and you see the wide, multi-laned, divided streetscape that seems to go on forever. As on the Kingston Road along the Scarborough shore, the lake is nowhere to be seen. Yet the streetcar that runs parallel to the lake and began its journey at Neville Park Avenue in the Beach earlier this morning is squeaking along the track, making its way to the turnaround a little farther west at the Long Branch loop, near Etobicoke Creek.

IT IS FROM THE corner of Seventh Street and Lake Shore Boulevard in New Toronto that we begin our journey south to find the water, through the quiet neighbourhood that stretches down to the shore. As for the people out on their front porches and hanging out their laundry in their backyards, some of them are elderly and many of them seem friendly. You're back in the 1950s.

In the 1930s and 1940s, members of Gus Ryder's Lakeshore Swimming Club trained

The Lakeshore

out in the lake at the foot of Seventh Street, long before they had the luxury of an indoor pool. In the early days, his Lakeshore swimmers also swam farther to the west in Etobicoke Creek and could often be spotted moving southward in the water at dusk, steadily and rhythmically, arm over arm.

Many miles to the east of the Humber River, the Rouge River meanders out into Lake Ontario at the Scarborough shore through a deeply cut valley. Closer to the centre of the city, the Don River, though now channelized in its lower reaches, flows into the lake at the westerly edge of what was once Ashbridge's Bay, and so it draws a kind of demarcation line between the Beach on the east of it and the Island on the west.

Yet no other lakefront district in Toronto has been so clearly defined by its river systems than the Lakeshore. Maps and accounts of the area from the late eighteenth and early nineteenth centuries reveal that it was bisected by a series of arterial waterways that led down to the lake from Etobicoke and Mimico Creeks and the Humber River to a number of smaller rivulets, creeks, and streams. Intense development, primarily in the twentieth century, has erased the evidence of many of these smaller watercourses, particularly in New Toronto, though recent efforts have begun to undo some of that damage.

The Etobicoke, though now channelized, still flows out to Lake Ontario at Marie Curtis Park. Farther to the east, Mimico Creek ambles down through its quiet marsh to the shore. Following the curve of the lake eastward, the Pedestrian and Cycling Bridge spans the Humber River, with the downtown angling out into the water, toward the Island. Directly in front of you is a seemingly endless expanse of blue.

This photo of Goodyear workers is believed to have been taken in 1917, the year the plant opened in New Toronto Courtesy Wendy Gamble

AS IN THE BEACH, on the Island, and along the Scarborough shore, the roots of the Lakeshore district are in the lake that forms its southern boundary. After a lengthy and important Aboriginal presence that extended over the millennia, the first Europeans came to the Toronto area in the seventeenth century. Settlement along the present-day Toronto shore began in the late eighteenth century, and soon after that, traders, fishermen, boat builders, and entrepreneurial millers took advantage of the natural harbours and resources at the mouths of the Humber River and Mimico and Etobicoke Creeks. In time, pioneers moved across the lakeshore and contributed to and prospered from this early commercial and industrial development that began on the waterways.

In later decades, seasonal resort communities came to Humber Bay, Long Branch, and Mimico. Permanent residential development followed a little later, in the last decades of the nineteenth century and the early decades of the twentieth century. Unlike the other waterfront districts covered in this book, however, the communities that took root here were supported by a strong railway and industrial presence that developed first and foremost in New Toronto but also in the other adjoining areas along and north of the highway.

In the high-technology, post-industrial Toronto, some may be inclined to look askance at what we take to be a bland, banal, and even slightly rundown neighbourhood — one that, until recently, presented as its principal landmark to the east nothing more than a motel strip straight out of the 1950s and has neither the wit nor the imagination to do better than name itself after the road that runs through it. No matter. Such observations miss everything of significance about the Lakeshore.

This neighbourhood is like a well-thumbed book, an early edition that has been through many hands. The jacket has shelf wear: a slight tear on one edge, a crease along another. The paper inside is faintly discoloured, made of old stuff, not acid free. The type has faded a little but the tale it tells is remarkable, with its own share of memorable happenings, some of them of national significance. This is a story of first peoples, traders, pioneers, and settlers, of factory hands, sailors, and swimmers, of floods and hurricanes, of wartimes and heroics, and of urban and industrial development. This is the story of how a waterfront, an ancient trail turned highway, and the people who settled here evolved together to create the Lakeshore that we know today.

The Lakeshore

CHAPTER TWO

Beginnings

The Scarborough section of this book describes the final retreat of the ice sheet from the Toronto region some 12,500 years ago and looks at how, after this event, a giant meltwater basin formed, known as Lake Iroquois. During this early period, the area that would become the Lakeshore district was entirely submerged, with the shore-cliff of this ancient glacial lake located very near to present-day Dundas Street.

This lake rapidly drained, and the smaller Lake Admiralty was left in its wake, with its shore far to the south of today's Lake Ontario. Water draining down to this basin carved river and creek valleys that empty into the lake along the present-day Toronto shore, including at the Humber River and Etobicoke Creek. In the Lower Humber River Valley, from Étienne Brûlé Park to the river mouth, deposits laid down during the advance and retreat of the last glacial period, known as the Wisconsin Glacial Episode, were deeply eroded by this process. In fact, some of the same deposits present in the lower Humber are also prominently displayed in the Scarborough Bluffs, including the Scarborough, Meadowcliffe, and Seminary formations.

Today, the 450-million-year-old Upper Ordovician Georgian Bay Formation is exposed on the deeply carved ravine walls of the lower Humber. This Ordovician marine shale, commonly known in Toronto as Dundas shale, is also a noted feature of Etobicoke Creek and was at one time very prominent along the Toronto shore, including the Lakeshore. In the early nineteenth century, Thomas Douglas, the Fifth Earl of Selkirk and future Lord Selkirk, visited one of the first patentees and settlers of the Lakeshore, Colonel Samuel Smith, who held a large tract of land fronting the lake and Etobicoke Creek. As quoted by Etobicoke historian Robert Given in *Etobicoke Remembered*, in May of 1804, Douglas remarked, "[Smith] is inclosing [*sic*] a garden — proposes to fence with stone of which he has some fine beds on the shore — thin Strata of Sandstone some almost fit for flags or slating, & some look like tolerable limestone — the stone is almost on the level of the water — & the beds run in below a clay bank apparently diluvian."

We read in the Scarborough section that increasing lake levels over the millennia have backed up Toronto's tributary rivers and streams that lead down to the waterfront. The gradual flooding of the mouths of these watercourses, a process that still continues today, has created substantial wetland complexes as well as meandering rivers and streams in wide valleys. These river marshes, combined with the periodic flooding that took place adjacent to the river meanders and oxbows, created rich soil for cultivation

conditions that supported a wide variety of plant and animal life for first peoples who congregated there, establishing encampments and settlements near the shore. After European settlement, industrialization began at the mouths of these same rivers and creeks, though these endeavours were not without their own share of difficulties, such as natural periods of flooding exacerbated by the rapid deforestation of the river valleys.

Though greatly diminished is size, these wetlands persist, even when they flow underneath major transportation corridors. Beneath the Queensway and up to Dundas Street is the Lower Humber River Wetland Complex, which has been recently affirmed, in the "Review of Provincially Significant Wetlands Within the City of Toronto," as provincially significant. According to this report, prepared by the City of Toronto, the area is composed of fifteen wetlands and has an overall area of just over sixty-three acres of swamp and marsh. Floating and submerged aquatic vegetation may be seen in coastal bays of the marsh and in a pond in an old oxbow, near present-day Baby Point. The marsh complex is a noted stopover point for songbirds and contains a habitat that supports over fifty fish species, along with many bird and animal species, including the provincially rare Red-headed Woodpecker and the Blanding's Turtle. The marshes, including the surrounding uplands, have also been designated a Life Science Area of Natural and Scientific Interest (ANSI)

Humber River Marshes, c. 2008

Jane Fairburn

by the Ontario Ministry of Natural Resources and an Environmentally Significant Area (ESA) by the Toronto and Region Conservation Authority.

———•———

JUST A FEW INCHES under the soil, in the creek beds, valleys, and few remaining areas of the original remnant Toronto shore, lies evidence of a much earlier human presence, one that extended from east to west all the way along the waterfront of modern-day Toronto. In 2006 Toronto Region and Conservation Authority archaeologist Catherine Crinnion conducted an archaeological survey on the beachfront south of Lake Shore Boulevard in Mimico. This particular area of the beach has been tentatively identified as part of the original shoreline, though urban expansion and landfill and a high level of activity surround the site. Remarkably, three stone items, deemed to be "probable" artifacts, were removed from the site. The items were all considered to pre-date European contact.

Though a limited archaeological record exists for the Lakeshore, long-time residents of the district did, from time to time, collect interesting objects from the soil. George Chowns was born in his family home on what is now Stephens Drive, north of the Queensway, to market gardeners in 1927. According to Chowns, his mother, Jessie Todd, was born in a log cabin on what is now the Queensway in 1884. In planting and

Along the Shore

harvesting seasons, he often helped his uncles, who ran market gardens on Salisbury Avenue (now Park Lawn Road), north of the Queensway, in Humber Bay. When they harrowed the ground, interesting things were always popping up. He said, "As a kid I had a whole collection of arrowheads. You could find them practically anywhere when you where plowing." He has since given his finds to a museum.

This archaeological presence is no surprise, since the rich marshlands of the Lakeshore waterways were of great importance to successive groups of indigenous peoples who moved through and occupied the shore and nearshore areas of the district.

The Humber River was of great strategic significance because it lay at the juncture of two important aboriginal pathways. The Lakeshore Trail deviated north at the Humber to ford the river near Bloor Street, in the vicinity of the present-day Old Mill Bridge, and then continued south to the waterfront, moving westward through the Lakeshore district all the way down to Niagara. To the north of the Old Mill Bridge, on a high promontory overlooking the river, was the commencement of another trail, the western branch of the Toronto Carrying Place, a shortcut that led Aboriginal people northward to Lake Simcoe, the Upper Great Lakes, and the interior regions of Canada.

In the 1800s, artifacts, perhaps related to the ancestral Huron-Wendat, were found on the west side of the lower Humber Valley, below Bloor Street, in the vicinity of Humber Marshes Park. These included stone axes, clay tobacco pipes, ceramic vessels, and bone tools, which provide us with clues to the nature of their lifestyle and occupation of the lower Humber River Valley. To date, no intact habitation site has been found.

By the late sixteenth century, the ancestral Huron-Wendat had moved north to where we know today as Huronia. In the mid-1660s, the Seneca, a branch of the Iroquois Confederacy normally resident in what is now New York State, established a number of villages along the north shore of Lake Ontario, including two villages with about 500 to 800 people each in what is now Toronto.

Projectile points from the Niagara Peninsula that are similar to the kind of points that have been found across Toronto PC

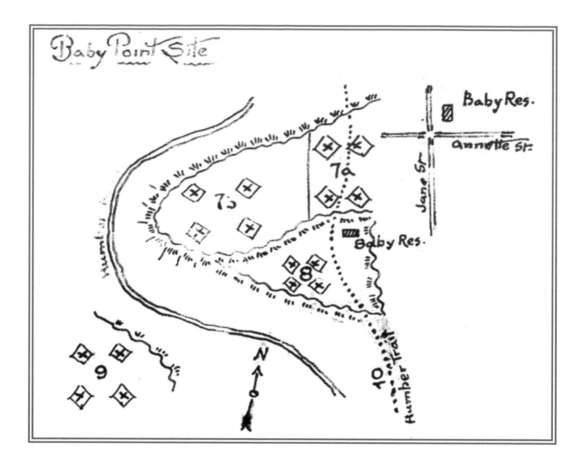

Archeological map of Teiaiagon drawn by
A.J. Clark in the early twentieth century

Canadian Museum of Civilization, A.J. Clark Collection,

Archaeology fieldnotes, Box 1, File 2 AJC

On a high promontory on the east bank of the Humber River in the area of what is now Baby Point, west of Jane Street and south of St. Clair Avenue, lay Teiaiagon, a sister village to Ganatsekwyagon, located near the mouth of the Rouge River (described in the Scarborough section of this book). Teiaiagon was connected to Ganatsekwyagon by the Lakeshore Trail and was situated about a mile and a half up from the mouth of the Humber, just above the ford in the river, north of today's Bloor Street and the Old Mill Bridge. Interestingly, archaeologist Ronald F. Williamson points out that Teiaiagon is an Iroquois word meaning "cross the river." The Humber was no longer navigable in the vicinity of this village, and it was at this point that the Carrying Place Trail began.

The village was about the same distance that Ganatsekwyagon was from the mouth of the Rouge. Here, in the rich valley lands and the marsh, the Seneca practised agriculture, hunted game, and fished abundant salmon from the river. Archaeologist Mima

Kapches writes that the Baby Point area, when viewed from the air, reveals "a classic and impressive Iroquoian site. Situated on a high plateau of land and bordered on its north, south, and west sides by the meandering Humber River, it was easily defensible, a characteristic that the Iroquois usually sought for their sites."

As we have seen, one of the probable reasons for the establishment of these villages was to command control of the complex fur trade network that had intensified after the appearance of the Europeans in the region in the seventeenth century. The most efficient way to control access to the interior, along routes such as the Carrying Place Trail (or Passage de Toronto, as it was called by the French), was to establish a village at the base of the trail.

As for the first European to travel along the Carrying Place, that honour has often been given to Étienne Brûlé, emissary of the early French explorer Champlain. The theory is that Brûlé followed the Carrying Place Trail south to Humber Bay on his way to the territory south of the Susquehanna Valley in 1615. While compelling, this theory has recently been refuted by scholars. There is strong evidence that once Brûlé reached the south shore of the Great Lakes, he followed a route to the south of Lake Erie, making the Carrying Place Trail simply too far out of his way to be a convenient route. Many have also argued that the Passage de Toronto would have been seen as too dangerous at that time because it was frequented by the Iroquois normally domiciled south of Lake Ontario, who were enemies of the French during that period.

Historian Percy J. Robinson maintains that Sulpician priests François d'Urfé and Abbé Fénelon would have preached at Teiaiagon, after a mission was established at Ganatsekwyagon in 1669. However, it is through Father Louis Hennepin, a member of the Récollet mission in Fort Frontenac (now Kingston), that we are given one of the first European accounts of the village. In November 1678, Hennepin was en route to Niagara in a brigantine when foul weather forced the ship's captain to put in at the mouth of the Humber River. In his words:

> The Winds and the Cold of Autumn were then very violent. . . . On the 26th, we were in great danger . . . but at length the Wind coming to the North-East, we sail'd on and arriv'd safely at the further end of Lake Ontario, call'd by the Iroquoese, Skannadario. We came pretty near to one of their Villages call'd Tejajagon, lying about Seventy Leagues from Fort Frontenac. . . . We barter'd some Indian corn with the Iroquoese, who could not sufficiently admire us, and came frequently to see us on board our Brigantine, which for our greater security, we had brought to an anchor into a River.

Likewise, the explorer René-Robert Cavelier de La Salle camped at Teiaiagon in the summer of 1680 and possibly twice the following year. The Passage de Toronto was a key route to Michilimackinac, the French fort located on the Island of Mackinac on the south shore of the Straits of Mackinac, which connects Lake Huron and Lake Michigan. This fort, located in present-day Michigan, was the key staging ground for La Salle's explorations of the interior reaches of North America. Robinson also points out a very early reference to a group of La Salle's men having visited Teiaiagon in the 1670s, engaging in a "drunken debauch . . . a rather melancholy beginning for Toronto the good!"

Though no professional archaeological investigation of the Teiaiagon site has taken place until very recently, many artifacts have nonetheless been discovered, with many finds dating back to the nineteenth century. An unsigned document held at the Ontario Archives entitled "Indians of the Humber Valley," probably written in the late nineteenth century, notes three aboriginal sites on the Humber, all relatively close to the river mouth. The first site, overlooking the Humber on a high bluff facing Lambton Mills, was "the old Indian camping ground," and "tons of bones have been excavated from the crest of this elevation, among these bones several very valuable relics . . . some of which are splendid specimens of bone implements most beautifully carved and decorated."

The second site, in the vicinity of the rapids near Teiaiagon, was deemed to be a workshop that "at the present day is strewn over with flint chippings, broken arrow heads & pieces of decorated pottery." An old burial ground was said to be located farther south, in a grove of pine trees at the mouth of the river.

Williamson notes that hundreds of graves were documented when the Baby Point area was first developed. Archaeologists and relic hunters also recorded remnants of a stockade

Comb found at the site of Teiaiagon, carved and etched with aboriginal religious symbols Courtesy John Howarth, Archaeological Services Inc.

(a fence forming a defensive barrier) and campfires in the late nineteenth century, though details of this excavation have since been lost.

Discoveries continue. As late as 2005, two shallow graves were unearthed at Baby Point in service trenches during the installation of natural gas lines. Archaeologists found two late-seventeenth-century Seneca women, both in their twenties, buried with a number of artifacts, which, according to Williamson, were meant to "accompany them to the next world. . . . The first woman had three brass finger rings . . . and a finely made moose-antler hair comb, carved to depict two human figures wearing European style clothes flanking an aboriginal figure. With the other woman was a brass pot containing an ash bowl that in turn contained squash, acorn, and grape remains; . . . an iron axe; and another carved and engraved moose-antler comb, which had carved representations of a panther (with a rattlesnake tail), possibly representing Mishipizheu (Mi-shi-pi-zhiw), the chief manitou of the underwater realm."

By the late seventeenth century, the Seneca had abandoned their villages on the north shore of the lake, including Teiaiagon and Ganatsekwyagon, and returned to the region of what is now New York State. By 1700, the Anishinabeg had moved down from their traditional territory on the north shore of Lake Superior and Lake Huron. A branch of the Anishinabeg who settled along the north shore of Lake Ontario were known to the Europeans as Mississaugas. The territory of the Mississaugas in the Toronto region stretched from Long Point on Lake Erie to the Rouge River at the southeastern edge of what is now Toronto and extended back inland to the height of land.

Though they were concentrated at the mouth of the Credit River on a seasonal basis, their semi-nomadic lifestyle allowed for a significant Humber Bay presence, which has been often overlooked. Kathleen MacFarlane Lizars, in *The Valley of the Humber, 1615–1913*, specifically references the presence of the Mississaugas at the Humber River, referring to them as the Humber River Indians. Indeed, the same archaeologists who documented the remains of the occupation on Baby Point in the nineteenth century also noted remnants of a settlement on the *west* side of the Humber River, in the former Township of Etobicoke. This site may have been occupied by the Mississaugas. Esther Heyes, in *Etobicoke: From Furrow to Burrow*, also points to the "Mississaugas on the Humber" and their Chief Tequakareigh, who negotiated peace with the British shortly after the latter defeated the French at Fort Niagara and gained control of Lake Ontario.

As late as 1825, some Mississaugas along with their leader, Chief Kahkewaquonaby (Sacred Feathers), who was also known as the Reverend Peter Jones and was a convert to the Methodist Christian faith, attended an important council fire, or meeting, at the mouth of the Humber with the British including, among others, Reverend John Strachan. After the meeting and the distribution of annual presents, the Reverend Peter Jones and his followers decided to radically alter their traditional lifestyle and move permanently to lands adjacent to the Credit River.

With the surrender of lands in 1805 that confirmed the Toronto Purchase of 1787 and the Mississauga Purchase of 1805, the Mississaugas conveyed a vast portion of their territory along the north shore of the lake to the British, though they reserved the sole right of fishery in some creeks and in the Etobicoke and Credit Rivers. The Mississaugas also initially retained a mile on each side of the Credit River, together with the "flats or low grounds" on several creeks and the Etobicoke.

As time went on, the Mississaugas relinquished their sole right of fishery in even these waterways. Kathleen Lizars maintains that they continued to frequent the Humber River Marshes into the last years of the nineteenth century, where they collected material for baskets that were later sold in Lambton.

Though the Mississaugas have long left the banks of the Lakeshore's river and creeks, the name Etobicoke, derived from the Mississaugas, lives on. The lands west of the Humber River, in which they hunted and fished, were called the "A-doo-pe-

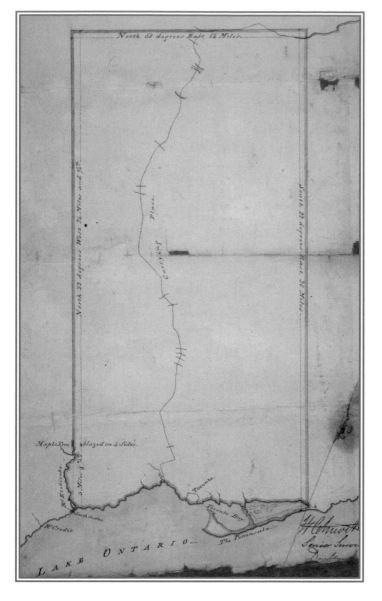

A vast portion of present-day Toronto is included in the Toronto Purchase map, *1805* William Chewett, 1805, LAC, RG 10, Vol 1841, IT 039

Along the Shore

kog," according to the Reverend Peter Jones in his *History of the Ojebway Indians; etc*. This name, phonetically close to "Etobicoke," is translated, according to Peter Jones, as "place of the black alder." Remarkably, the "A-doo-pe-kog" name, despite early attempts to call the area "Toby Cook," survived, though in an anglicized form. Etobicoke Creek, the most westerly waterway in the Lakeshore, takes its name from the region through which it flows. Likewise, the Humber River was earlier called the Cobechenock, meaning "leave their canoes and go back," according to surveyor Augustus Jones's 1796 list of "Names of the Rivers, and Creeks, as they are called by the Mississaugas." This watercourse was also referred to as the Rivière Toronto by the French and St. John's Creek by the English, but the name was changed to the Humber, undoubtedly after the name of a river that runs through the north of England, at about the time of official settlement, in 1793.

The Humber River took on a variety of names that marked various historical periods of transition in Toronto. Mimico Creek and the surrounding area, however, managed to retain a version of the original Mississauga name that marked this territory, Omimeca. Historical geographer Wayne Reeves translates the name as the "Resting Place of the Wild Pigeons," for Mimico was home to the vast nesting grounds of the now extinct passenger pigeon. For nearly 100 years after the founding of York, the skies would darken around the mouth of the creek as the pigeons gathered during the fall and spring migrations. These birds, which had never developed a fear of humans, were shot down and slaughtered in tens of thousands; they were pickled in barrels of salt and made into a ready source of protein for settlers of the Lakeshore and beyond. By the latter years of the nineteenth century, the skies were silent.

———————— ◆ ————————

A YEAR AFTER THE original Toronto Purchase in 1787, Alexander Aitken (also spelled Aitkin) arrived in Toronto to draw up a survey of the lands apparently ceded by the Mississaugas to the British. The Mississaugas strenuously objected to Aitken crossing the Humber River, maintaining that the territory west of the Humber was never ceded to the Crown. In a letter sent from Kingston on September 15, 1788, Aitken detailed his experience, stating that with the assistance of an interpreter, he eventually was allowed to cross the Humber but was prevented from going any farther than the Etobicoke River, for "the creek they said was a Boundary that could not be altered or moved." Aitken nonetheless followed a straight line northward from the mouth of the creek to a maple tree "blazed on four sides"; however, the lower portion of the creek was later recognized as the boundary of the purchase, in keeping with the wishes of the Mississaugas.

The significance of the waterways to Aboriginal people in the Lakeshore also made them important natural boundaries. Yet we shall also see that the creeks and river were no less important to the handful of Europeans who lived along the Toronto shore prior to the commencement of official settlement, with the arrival of the Simcoes in 1793.

CHAPTER THREE
Settlement

When Lieutenant Governor Simcoe and Mrs. Simcoe stepped ashore at Toronto on July 30, 1793, the period of official British settlement began, though the actual European presence in Toronto extends back much farther in time. Father Hennepin and others from Fort Frontenac, though by no means the first Europeans in Toronto, took shelter in the lower Humber River near Teiaiagon, about 115 years before the Simcoes' arrival. Their presence was followed in the early to mid-1700s with a succession of French trading posts at or near the Carrying Place Trail. These were established in an attempt to stem the flow of goods to the English, who were accessing the rich beaver peltry north of the lake. In 1720 the Magasin Royal was established on the east side of the Humber, near the former site of Teiaiagon. Next came the short-lived Fort Toronto, near the mouth of the river in 1750, and within a year the establishment of Fort Rouillé three miles to the east, on the grounds of the present-day Canadian National Exhibition. In 1759, with news of the English pillaging Fort Niagara, the French abandoned and burned Fort Rouillé before making a hasty retreat to Montréal. With the

Jean-Baptiste Rousseaux's account ledger AO, F 493-1, MS 7924

Treaty of Paris in 1763, the Seven Years' War between Britain, France, and other nations officially ended. Though the British gained control of the Great Lakes region, a period of some thirty years would elapse before the Simcoes' arrival in Toronto Bay.

During these intervening years, the earliest seeds of full-time occupation in the greater Toronto area were planted by a small number of United Empire Loyalists and French traders living near the river mouths to the east and west of the bay. These early residents included the William Peak (or Peek) family, who established themselves in the vicinity east of the Don River sometime after 1782. Decades later, Peak describes in a land petition how he came to leave the Don, eventually becoming the first settler in the Township of Pickering.

Farther west, on the banks of the Humber, was a fascinating cross-cultural and multi-lingual couple: French trader, interpreter, and merchant Jean-Baptiste Rousseaux and

Along the Shore

his wife, Margaret Cline (also variously spelled as Clyne or Klein), a Caucasian woman who had been raised by the family of the great Mohawk warrior Joseph Brant.

Fort Rouillé, as drawn by Hans Jensen in 1936 Hans Jensen, 1936, TPL, 987-6-5

Rousseaux had previously acted as an interpreter in the American War of Independence. Sometime after 1779, he established himself at the mouth of the Humber River and lived there seasonally, very near or at the location of the second French trading post, Fort Toronto. In his speech in 1951 to the Ontario Historical Society, T. Roy Woodhouse indicated that Rousseaux probably brought Cline to the Humber for the first time in 1792 and shortly thereafter settled there on a full-time basis, before the arrival of the Simcoes. The Rousseauxs lived at their home on the Humber until 1795. Margaret Cline gave birth to their fourth child, Reine, six days before Jean-Baptiste piloted the Simcoes into Toronto Bay. Reine is said to be the first European child born in Toronto.

The Lakeshore

Pages of account books drawn up between Rousseaux and his business partner, Thomas Barry, indicate that Rousseaux did a stiff trade not only with first peoples but also with early members of York society and settlers along the shore. The ledgers include many names that are consistent with people described in this book, as well as other early settlers in the Lakeshore whom we shall meet in this section.

By the time of Jean-Baptiste's residence in Toronto, his family was already generationally acquainted with the Lower Great Lakes region. According to Woodhouse, Rousseaux's grandfather married a French woman at Fort Détroit (now Detroit) and also acted as a trader and aboriginal interpreter. Rousseaux's father, Jean Bonaventure, had carried on an active trade at the Humber from at least 1770 and probably earlier. Sometime in the early eighteenth century, the family became associated with the name St. Jean — or St. John, to the English — and Woodhouse points out that at least one map of the Toronto region drawn prior to 1770 does show the Humber as St. John.

As for Margaret Cline, she is said to have been born in the Mohawk Valley in what is now New York State in 1759, the year that Fort Rouillé burned. According to oral tradition, her parents and most of her family members were killed in a violent confrontation with Mohawk warriors. Upon the death of her parents, Cline and one of her young sisters were said to have been taken into this society and later adopted by Chief Joseph Brant. (A letter certifying her marriage to Rousseaux, executed in 1795, states Cline to be "formerly a prisoner among the Mohawk Indian Reserve.") The Mohawks, along with other members of the Iroquois Confederacy, were given land on the Grand River, in what would become Southwestern Ontario, for their loyalty to the English during the American War of Independence. Raised by the Mohawks, Cline spoke their language, and though European by descent, she was culturally aboriginal.

Jean-Baptiste Rousseaux eventually petitioned Simcoe for more land along the Humber River. Unsuccessful in his request, he moved to the vicinity of what is now Ancaster, Ontario, in 1795, where he became, among other things, a mill owner, eventually acquiring extensive lands of about 1,200 acres. During the War of 1812, he acted as captain in the Indian Department; he died of a pleurisy attack during service at Niagara-on-the-Lake.

It is fitting in a city as diverse as Toronto that among our first full-time residents are Jean-Baptiste Rousseaux and Margaret Cline, who bridged the worlds of the French, English, and aboriginal cultures all present in Toronto in the late eighteenth century. Many historians have called them "transitional figures," and while this is certainly true, I like to think of them first and foremost as Torontonians, in the best sense of that word.

MRS. SIMCOE WAS ONE of the first newcomers to recognize and record the natural beauty of the shoreline areas featured in this book, and the Lakeshore is no exception. Of her first recorded journey west to the remains of the old French fort, she writes enthusiastically, "It rained very hard, and I was as completely wet as if I had walked through a river, for being in a shower in the woods is quite different from being exposed to it in open country; every tree acted as a shower bath, as the path was just wide enough to admit of one person. We passed some creeks and unhewn trees thrown across, a matter of some difficulty to those unaccustomed to them. I should think it might be done with less danger of falling with moccasins on the feet."

On September 4, 1793, she writes of her experience visiting the wild Humber River Valley and the house of Jean-Baptiste Rousseaux, which stood on the east side of the waterway, just below the commencement of the Carrying Place Trail: "I rode to St. John's Creek (the Humber River). There is a ridge of land extending near a mile beyond St. John's House, 300 feet high and not more than three feet wide; the bank toward the river is of smooth turf. There is a great deal of hemlock spruce on this river; the banks are dry and very pleasant."

That same year, a large tract of forested lands on the west side of the Humber was reserved for use at the government-owned King's Mill, also erected on the west side of the river in 1793. This structure was Toronto's first industrial building. A steady supply of lumber for milling operations could be drawn from these lands, with the size of the reserve expanding over time. According to Carl Benn in *The King's Mill on the Humber 1793–1803*, the building was a double sawmill constructed of wood and measuring about ninety feet by fifty feet. Benn relates that the mill supplied York's earliest needs for the construction of government buildings and likely supplied lumber for a number of early buildings in or near the vicinity of York, including blockhouses at Gibraltar Point and the garrison, two brick Parliament Houses, and one government-owned inn, the King's Head, at the mouth of the Credit River. Benn also notes that it is not clear what role, if any, the mill played in furnishing lumber products for private settlement and that production at the mill was probably significantly below its capacity.

We do know from Benn, and other sources, that it is "almost certain" that the original King's Mill supplied lumber for an early nearby boat-building initiative on the east side of the Humber River. Master boat builder John Dennis (sometimes mistakenly referred to as Denison) built the government yacht *Toronto* — launched in 1799 and wrecked on the southern shore of the Island in 1811 — at this facility near the mouth of the Humber. As noted by Benn, Dennis was given permission to cut his own planks at the King's Mill.

C.H.J. Snider, in an *Evening Telegram* "Schooner Days" column of April 18, 1953, described the *Toronto* as having more extensive and comfortable accommodations than other government vessels at that time, including six staterooms and "ample deck space." Indeed, the *Upper Canada Gazette* of September 14, 1799, stated that the *Toronto* "will, in the course of a few days, be ready to make her first trip. She is one of the handsomest vessels, of her size, that ever swam upon the Ontario; and if we are permitted to judge from her appearance, and to do her justice, we must say, she bids fair to be one of the swiftest sailing vessels. . . . Her master builder was a Mr. Denison, an American, on whom she reflects much honor."

Other vessels built at the Humber dockyard, possibly by Dennis, included a scow, a bateau, and "at least three gunboats," the latest of them constructed in 1796. John Dennis's son, Joseph, would follow in his father's footsteps and build the early steamship the *Canada* at the mouth of the Rouge in 1826, possibly with his father's assistance. Many early settlers also built boats at the mouths of the Mimico and Etobicoke waterways and participated in active local trade, much like their fellow pioneers along the Scarborough shore and in the Beach.

———— • ————

WITH A GARRISON to establish and, later, a town to develop, Simcoe brought back into service the Queen's Rangers. It was a military unit that had its roots in the former American colonies during the Seven Years' War. The unit had distinguished itself during the American War of Independence and was commanded for most of the war by none other than John Graves Simcoe. The Rangers assisted with the initial land surveys and built roads from present-day Hamilton to Toronto, among them Yonge Street and much of Dundas Street, as well as the bridges, the government buildings, and the garrison for defence. Edith Firth's *The Town of York 1793–1815* contains a letter from Peter Russell, administrator of Upper Canada, to Robert Prescott, lieutenant governor of Lower Canada, that was written from Niagara in August 1796 and mentions these men in connection with the early development of York: "At present York is in a matter isolated, being cut off by the want of Roads from an easy land Communication with the rest of the Province. . . . Our Dependence rested wholly upon the Queen's Rangers for assistance to raise these necessary Buildings, make bridges, cut Roads of Communication &ca." The Queen's Rangers were disbanded in 1802.

Along the Shore

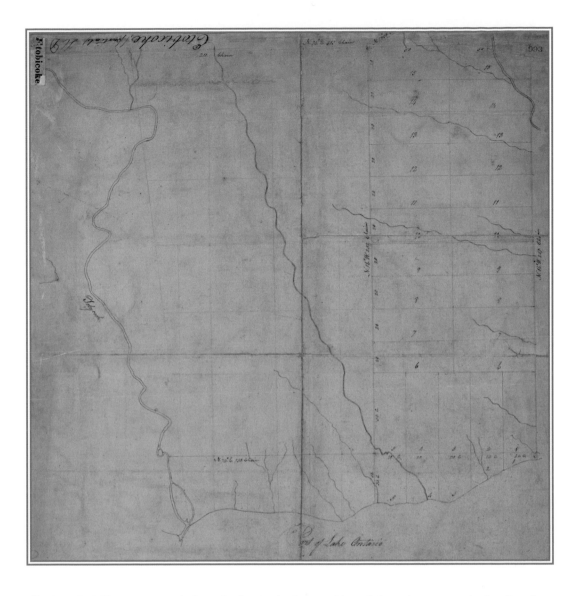

Abraham Iredell's 1795 survey laid out the first lots in the township and shows the many creeks that flowed south, down to the shore AO, Etobicoke, 1795, RG 1-470-0-0-304, Ministry of Natural Resources township survey plans

During the late eighteenth and early nineteenth centuries, the government of the day considered the lakefront at Etobicoke, from the Humber River to what is now Etobicoke Creek, to be what we would call a buffer zone in the event of an attack on York. With this in mind, Abraham Iredell was commissioned to make a survey for settlement, with the lands to be taken up by semi-retired officers and militiamen, from today's Royal York Road to Kipling Avenue and from the lake north to Bloor Street.

The Lakeshore

Samuel Smith home, c. 1953

CT/MS, Montgomery's Inn, 011_047 Box1

After the survey was completed, some officers and sergeants of the Queen's Rangers obtained land patents in the Lakeshore for their services, with many of these parcels fronting the lake. This distribution would substantially delay development near the lakefront in the years to come. As was the case in other areas of the lakefront, some of the choice lots near the front of the township were held for land speculation and not improved by the original patentees.

In a land patent dated June 12, 1798, a significant portion of what is now New Toronto was granted as "Lot 1 with the broken front," along with other lands, to "Serjeant [*sic*] Patrick Mealey of the Queen's Rangers." Robert Given reports that the sergeant was the first person to receive a land patent in the Township of Tobacook, or Etobicoke. In the years that followed, some of these discharged and half-pay officers and soldiers, including Mealey and William Hooten, whose lots fronted the lake, did improve their property. Many, however, also had interests elsewhere; they owned businesses in York and maintained substantial land holdings in other areas of Etobicoke that were far removed from the shore.

One Queen's Ranger who had fought alongside Simcoe in the American Revolutionary War was Samuel Smith, who became lieutenant colonel of the Queen's Rangers in York and was twice briefly the administrator of Upper Canada. Smith eventually received a very substantial amount of property that extended down to the broken front, or water's edge, including most of today's Long Branch all the way to the westernmost reaches

Along the Shore

of New Toronto, at the historic Mimico Asylum grounds. These lands are commonly referred to as the Smith tract. Along with other parcels in the Township of Etobicoke and the County of York, *The Domesday Book* records that Smith received patents in the amount of 2,100 acres in total.

Smith erected a dwelling and, eventually, outbuildings on his property, near the east side of the Etobicoke River. He also built a mill on the same waterway before 1820. Colonel Smith, along with other Queen's Rangers, was rich in status and land but simply did not have the resources to maintain and develop his domain. Reformer Robert Gourlay, a political adversary of Smith's, wrote the following description of Smith's Etobicoke home, several years after it had been built, from memory, in his 1822 *Statistical Account of Upper Canada*:

> For many miles not a house had appeared, when I came to that of Colonel Smith, lonely and desolate. It once had been genteel and comfortable; but now was going to decay. A vista had been opened up through the woods towards Lake Ontario; but the riotous and dangling undergrowth seemed threatening to retake possession from the Colonel all that had once been cleared. . . . How could a solitary half-pay officer help himself, settled down upon a block of land, whose very extent barred out the assistance and convenience of neighbours?

Another challenge to development was transporting materials, since the Lakeshore Trail, which served first peoples so well for millennia was inadequate for the horses, stagecoaches, and ox carts of the new order, partly, at least, because of a lack of manpower to maintain it. Crossing the Humber was made somewhat easier with the addition of a bridge that was, according to Wayne Reeves, "erected some twenty-five feet above the marsh in 1809."

Smith died in 1826, and the family retained a substantial portion of their lands until well into the nineteenth century. The remaining property near the front was sold to James Eastwood in the 1870s. Residency, however, may not have been continuous. The sketch attached to H. Noble's 1861 census report, part of the "Census Rolls for District Number One of the Township of Etobicoke," does show the Smith lands in Ward 1, fronting the lake, as "vacant," though there are reports of other families living in the house before the 1860s.

One stretch of the Smith homestead later became the most westerly part of the historic Mimico Asylum grounds (in 1964 named the Lakeshore Psychiatric Hospital), and another portion, farther to the west, became Long Branch Park. In 1952 Colonel Smith's home, one of the oldest at York and a place of obvious historical significance, was demolished so a shopping development and then a school could be built in its place.

The Samuel Smith name survives, though, in the archaeological record (portions of two Dundas shale foundations and thousands of artifacts were discovered on the school grounds in 1984) and in Colonel Samuel Smith Park, which was developed after the closing of the Lakeshore Psychiatric Hospital in 1979.

While settlement may have been slow to take hold in some of these waterfront areas, a major transformation was nevertheless unfolding on the waterways that flowed down to the lake. Industry was taking hold, not only near the busy downtown harbour but also at the outlying creeks and river mouths, a development that would in turn hasten the pace of change in Lakeshore. The first settlers along the shore and in the regions north of the lake needed industry in order to finish, store, and transport their crops to outlying markets. While the King's Mill burned down in 1803, a series of sawmills, gristmills, and woollen mills soon lined the rivers and creeks of the Toronto region.

Among the first founding families of the Lakeshore was the Gambles, who became prominent in the ruling elite of Upper Canada. Loyalist John Gamble had been an assistant surgeon with the Queen's Rangers during the American War of Independence. He followed Simcoe to Upper Canada in 1796, where he became a surgeon to Simcoe's reconstituted rangers. Two of Gamble's sons — John William being the elder and plain William the younger — may be considered among the founding fathers of Lakeshore and Etobicoke. Settling near the lakefront, both brothers were merchant millers who helped develop the economic infrastructure — roads, mills, and bridges — that allowed for the growth of villages and settlements.

In the early 1820s, John William and his wife, Mary (née Macaulay), established themselves on the east side of Mimico Creek, near the outlet to the lake, on lands first patented by his father. John William constructed a sawmill on the west side of Mimico Creek in 1823. He also erected a pier at the mouth of Mimico Creek, where the freshly cut timber was loaded onto ships. As Harvey Currell writes in *The Mimico Story*, workmen "threw up huts of rough-hewn planks," which were the humble beginnings of the town of Mimico.

John William was not only a businessman but also active in the affairs of church and state. Entering the Legislative Assembly of Upper Canada in 1838, he was instrumental in establishing the Anglican Parish of Christ Church, which, according to Sidney Fisher in *The Merchant Millers of the Humber Valley*, was built on lands he secured that were formerly held as part of the King's Mill Reserve. A later iteration of Christ Church stood, until recently, north of the lake on Royal York Road in Mimico. Sadly, the church succumbed to two successive fires in 2006; only the cemetery, dating back to 1832, now remains.

The original Christ Church was erected in 1832 and stood north of the lake on what is now Royal York Road. Sadly, the third iteration of Christ Church was destroyed by fire in 2006. CT/MS, Montgomery's Inn, 012_045 Box1

Gamble is said to have read services in his own home prior to the building of the church, possibly at the urging of one of his workmen, millwright Herod Noble. The report of Enumerator H. Noble, appended to the abovementioned "Census Rolls for District Number One of the Township of Etobicoke," describes Christ Church as follows: "There is A Church of England, worth About Seven Hundred Dollars, with Pew Accomadation [*sic*] for One Hundred & twelve Persons . . . with an average congregation of from Eighty five to One Hundred persons, Service once every Sunday, with a Sunday School Eight Months in the year."

In the mid-1830s, John William Gamble's brother, William, assumed operations on the King's Mill site at the lower Humber. Under Gamble's direction, the site, which already included a sawmill, nail factory, inn, stables, and store, developed into a little hub of industry and commerce. Renaming the area Milton Mill, Gamble added a distillery to the complex and erected a gristmill that was destroyed by fire, then rebuilt. The romantic ruin of the latter mill remained a notable feature on the west bank of the Humber in Etobicoke until 2001, when, sadly, the building's stones were incorporated into the Old Mill Hotel & Spa. Gamble also later acquired a woollen mill near the Humber and Dundas Street.

In the 1840s, William Gamble began commercial development at the mouth of the Humber. Despite mounting financial pressures and flooding that damaged mill operations, he, along with others, founded the Humber Harbour & Road Co. They erected a wharf and warehouse on the west side of the river at the outlet to the lake and, according to Wayne Reeves, "a considerable export trade emerged" by about 1850.

Gamble's Mill ruins, 1907 CTA, F1244_it1239

Though little information exists about the details of the business conducted there, it was undoubtedly the centre of much commercial activity, with produce from the mills and surrounding hinterlands being loaded onto schooners that came to port regularly. A similar operation, the Scarborough and Pickering Wharf Company, began about the same time at the mouth of the Rouge.

But these economic engines began to fail with the railway age in the mid-1850s, which allowed goods to be easily and efficiently transported overland. As H. Noble's 1861 census report reveals, "There is a Pier Wharfe and Storehouse at the Mouth of the River Humber coast [*sic*] of 11,000 thousand [*sic*] five hundred Dollars, and being A good business, previous to the Railroad, coming Into operation, that having ruined the business wharfe & Storehouse, there have [*sic*] not been anything Notice [*sic*] done Since."

Along the Shore

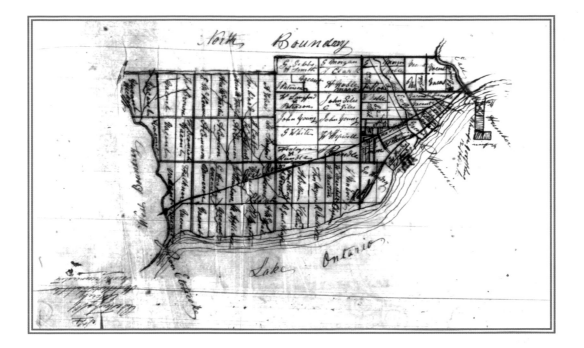

The sketch attached to H. Noble's 1861 census report for District Number One provides us with a treasure trove of information about the Lakeshore during the mid-nineteenth century. Note Gamble's wharfe and storehouse that appears at the mouth of the Humber River. AO, Census Rolls for District Number One, Township of Ontario, reel C-1087 (original records held at LAC)

In the latter half of the nineteenth century, conventional water-powered milling also proved to be an industry that was increasingly fraught with difficulty. Regular flooding in Toronto's river valleys, known then as "freshets," was exacerbated by the deforestation and industrialization that came with settlement. The Humber and Etobicoke waterways in particular would experience disastrous flooding well into the twentieth century, with the onslaught brought on by Hurricane Hazel in 1954. As a precursor of things to come, the flood of 1878 is said to have washed out almost all of the remaining water-powered mill operations on the Humber River. This was true for parts of the Don River as well. As if flooding was not enough, water-powered mills were also facing stiff competition from more reliable and efficient steam-powered mills.

John William Gamble moved north up the Humber River Valley to the township of Vaughan around 1840 and died in 1873. His death was followed by William's eight years later. William had suffered declining financial fortunes later in life, and many of the family's enterprises had suffered from the consequences of the industrial change. They had been born into a squirearchy. By the time they died, that world was gone.

The Lakeshore

BY THE MID-1820S, the Mississauga band was in crisis. They had surrendered the vast majority of their fishing rights as well as their hunting territory, which included the A-doo-pe-kog. In the span of one generation, their population base decreased by half and alcohol abuse was rampant among many members.

Their permanent relocation to the Credit, a traditional seasonal gathering place and the next major river west of the Humber, offered some hope that the Mississaugas would endure, but adaptation to the white man's world was the price they would pay for their ultimate survival. The aforementioned Reverend Peter Jones — also known as Kahkewaquonaby and Sacred Feathers — led this process of transformation and accommodation. Like Jean-Baptiste Rousseaux, Peter Jones may also be viewed as a transitional figure.

Jones was born in a wigwam on Burlington Heights to Tuhbenahneequay, or Sarah Henry, who was the daughter of Wahbanosay, a Mississauga chief. Peter Jones's father was Augustus Jones, who had surveyed the Humber River, Dundas and Yonge Streets, and many townships along the shore, including York and Scarborough, in the late eighteenth century. According to Donald Smith, in his book *Sacred Feathers*, Peter Jones was raised in the traditional lifestyle by his mother until the age of about fourteen. Later, he was brought into European society by his father and received a formal education among whites.

This unique pairing of both cultures allowed Jones to advocate for his people, record their history, and adjust to the European presence. Jones's work on behalf

Portrait of Kahkewaquonaby, Reverend Peter Jones

Peter Jones Collection, with permission from the Victoria

University Library (Toronto), Matilda Jones, 1832

of his people led to an audience with Queen Victoria in 1838. Upon Jones's death in 1856, Egerton Ryerson stated that he had "enjoyed the esteem of, and had access to, every class of Canadian society."

In 1847, over 200 band members moved from the banks of the Credit to the southwest corner of the Six Nations Territory on the Grand River, where they continue to live today as the Mississaugas of the New Credit Nation.

———— • ————

BY THE TIME THE Mississaugas had moved to the banks of the Credit, log cabins were well established on cleared fields — sure signs that settlement had taken hold in earnest. Early settlers included Peter Van Every, of Dutch and United Empire Loyalist stock, who, according to Harvey Currell, came to Etobicoke shortly after fighting in the War of 1812. His farm, on lands originally patented by Patrick Mealey, reached northward from the lake to just south of the railway tracks on the west side of Royal York Road. Currell indicates that Van Every married Agnes Barry, whose father, Thomas, a merchant, was in partnership with Jean-Baptiste Rousseaux.

As in Scarborough, pioneers did a substantial local trade, slipping into the small rivers and creeks along the shore to load cordwood, potash, apples, and other pioneer produce and making their return trip with other goods that sustained the homesteads. C.H.J. Snider reminds us in his "Schooner Days" column of September 5, 1931: "Lake Ontario bristled with ports. The lights are maintained at Oakville and Bronte, but the trade is gone . . . at the turn of the Toronto-Hamilton highway — Port Credit, Duck's Bay, the Etobicoke, Hooten's point, and the Dutchman's Bar, Mimico Creek, and the Humber — all those once had their Lake commerce and now have nothing."

One family who conducted such a trade in the Lakeshore was the Goldrings. In *English Immigrant Voices: Labourers' Letters from Upper Canada*, a William Goldring is said to have emigrated from South Bersted, England, along with his wife, Sarah (née Pratt), and children in 1832. Being coastal people, it would have been natural for the Goldrings to settle near the waterfront, and they probably did so in the Township of Etobicoke as early as the 1830s. Indeed, the *Directory of Toronto and Home District* for Etobicoke and the census returns for Etobicoke of 1851–52 indicate the presence of a Goldring in the southwest corner of the Township of Etobicoke, at or near the mouth of Etobicoke Creek.

Quoted in Cameron et al. is an early letter back to England from two of the sons, William and James, in which they describe themselves as living "about 8 miles above York, Upper Canada," with one acre of garden that "runs down to Lake Ontario."

The Maple Leaf *was a schooner of 100 tons, according to C.H.J. Snider, "rebuilt from a scow after . . . [the] Esplanade fire, 1885. Long sailed by the Goldring family."* Charles I. Gibbons, CT/MS, 1972.27.1

C.H.J. Snider recorded the memories of one of the sons of William Goldring, lake captain Richard Goldring, in a series of columns running in 1943. In the "Building of the Betsey," Snider recounts the family's experiences living at the mouths of Mimico and Etobicoke Creeks in the 1860s. William Goldring is described, like many early pioneers along the shore, as a jack of all trades: "a shoemaker, fisherman, sailor, carpenter, wharfinger, (and) ship-owner, as required."

As Snider recounts, in 1862 the family moved from Mimico Creek to the Etobicoke, where William Goldring had a fisherman's licence and fisherman's rights in the river mouth, which apparently entitled him to a "fishlot." Licensees of this period may have exercised certain property rights at the mouths of the rivers and creeks, though conflicting land and riparian rights remained a controversial issue throughout the nineteenth century. Indeed, the stonehooker the *Defiance* was built at the mouth of the Etobicoke in 1845, said to be named in "defiance" of farmer's claims to riparian rights at the river mouths along the shore.

The Goldring schooners were not the only vessels to have been built at the mouth of the Etobicoke. According to C.H.J. Snider, Boss Harris of Port Credit built the Defiance *there in 1845.* Defiance at Queen's Wharf, Jan 6th 1898, first arrival, C.H.J. Snider, CT/MS, 1972.6

The Goldring family is reported to have built a few small vessels at the mouth of Etobicoke Creek, behind the sandbar that extended westward at the opening to the lake. A natural harbour was created behind this little peninsula near the mouth of the creek that lasted until well into the twentieth century. Goldring maintained that one vessel, the *Betsey*, was built from the remnants of a schooner wrecked at what was referred to as Van Every's Point, in the vicinity of the former water treatment plant in New Toronto. In later years, Richard Goldring is reported to have first crossed the lake to Wilson, New York, in the *Betsey* and also to have ferried crude oil in the little vessel up 16 Mile Creek to a refinery established in the 1850s in Oakville.

Later, Richard Goldring, in collaboration with his father and other family members, owned and sailed a substantial fleet of schooners and stonehookers from the downtown harbour. The Toronto region needed stone to build foundations and roads. Accordingly,

This snapshot of the mouth of the Humber River in 1892 shows John Duck's Wimbledon House on the west side
W. Topham, 1892, CT/MS, 1970.220.19A

from April to November each year, stonehookers would pry, blast, and scrape away the Dundas shale that lined Toronto's shore and nearshore waters from east to west, thereby dramatically altering the water's natural edge.

On the "high shaly banks" of Van Every's Point (also referred to by Snider as Hooten's/Houten's Point and Two Tree Point), there reportedly lived the mysterious "old Dutchman," who was said to have lived in the vicinity of the former water treatment plant in New Toronto. There, Snider relates, a working model of a steam vessel was built: "The boat was almost sixty feet long, put together with pins, the ribs so close they formed a solid wall. She had paddles like duck's feet, and as soon as the inventor was satisfied with the engine to turn them over she was going to be launched." The strange vessel is said to have burned one night, "with the Dutchman's house a charred ruin, and he himself a frozen corpse in a newly heaped snowdrift." The details of this vessel, its owner's identity, and its mysterious demise remain, at least for the present, a mystery.

Remnants from a lost age: an abandoned old boat and miniature windmill/lighthouse formed part of the clutter behind the Casa Mendoza after its closure in 2012 Jane Fairburn

THE GOLDRINGS' EARLY livelihood in the Lakeshore was tied to a diverse number of waterfront-related trades and pursuits, and by the 1870s, possibly earlier, a similarly diverse group of entrepreneurs, shipbuilders, and tradesmen had established themselves on the west bank of the Humber River, where they built three hotels. John Duck's Wimbledon House was opened in 1872, a full eight years before Ned Hanlan opened his stick-style hotel on the Island. By 1878, Wimbledon House featured a pleasure ground and menagerie, possibly the first of its kind in the Lakeshore. Octavius Hicks, owner of the Royal Oak Hotel, was also a well-known boat builder. According to volume 2 of Adam and Mulvany's *History of Toronto and County of York, Ontario; etc.* (1885), Hicks took orders for yachts and pleasure boats and was "the inventor and patentee of the roller sliding-seats for racing boats, similar to those used by Mr. Hanlan." (Islander Ned Hanlan notably rowed using a sliding seat, and this feature, along with his natural rowing prowess, led him to several back-to-back world championships.)

Another "boat builder, carpenter, and fisherman" was Roy Nurse, who also operated a hotel and pleasure ground in the immediate vicinity. Adam and Mulvany note that he did "quite a business in fishing in the spring of which he markets in the city." Sometime prior to 1885, hoteliers Nurse, Hicks, and Duck, along with Toronto brewer Eugene O'Keefe, began the Humber Steam Ferry Company and operated the steamer *Annie Craig*, which made four round trips a day between Toronto and Humber Bay.

The tradition of the hotelier–boat builder continued on the west side of the Humber until well into the twentieth century. One of the last establishments demolished near the waterfront at Humber Bay was the Casa Mendoza, known in earlier days as the Dutch Sisters. The Dutch Sisters property originally stretched down to the water, and it was from the shipyard behind the original restaurant and, later, inn that proprietor Hans Sachau, a German naval architect, built his ships. Vessels of note include the eighty-eight-foot-long, sixty-ton schooner the *Alvee*, which was constructed from 1939 to 1940, and the 112-foot wooden Fairmiles that were built there during the Second World War.

On New Years Eve 2011, piano player Tomanel Raposo sung his heart out for the last time at the Casa Mendoza while the crowd lingered to the wee hours of the morning, reluctant to leave until the very last song had been sung. By daybreak, the last establishment on the Lakeshore's motel strip had closed its doors forever. Let's now take a look back at an earlier time in the life of the district, when the shoreline was dotted with such motels, restaurants, and lakeside mansions, and with day trippers seeking frivolity and relaxation in the summer sun.

CHAPTER FOUR

Resort Era

By the 1870s, Humber Bay sported a series of hotels and pleasure gardens that offered Torontonians a place of refuge from the heat and drudgery of the city during the hottest months of the year. By 1879, both Victoria Park and Kew Gardens were up and running in the east end of the city, while Ned Hanlan followed suit with his hotel on the Island in 1880 and, later, an amusement park. Not to be outdone, plans were well under way in the west end of the Lakeshore district for Long Branch Park in October 1883, when the Eastwoods sold over fifty acres of the Samuel Smith tract for development. The land stretched down from the Lake Shore Road to the water. A year later, a plan for Sea Breeze Park was registered, allowing for 219 cottage lots and a park that fronted on the lake. By 1887, at least twenty lots had been sold, and a hotel, built in the Japanese pagoda style and with similarities in design to Ned Hanlan's Island hotel of the same era, was erected.

Investors and brothers Thomas J. Wilkie, who was one of the pioneers of the YMCA movement in Ontario, and John N. Wilkie spearheaded the project. Thomas's first wife

TORONTO'S FAVORITE SUMMER RESORT

was Charlotte (née Cornell), whose ancestors were early settlers along the Scarborough shore, and though she was deceased by this time, her brother, William Edward Cornell, was one of the primary investors in the hotel and park. With frequent ferry service from the docks at the foot of Bay Street to the Long Branch Pier, the park became a popular escape for the middle class. In *Villages of Etobicoke*, it is reported that, in the summer of 1888 alone, more than 50,000 patrons embarked from downtown steamers, and headed for Long Branch Wharf. A brochure promoting Long Branch Park, entitled "A Souvenir of Long Branch," targets a more "discerning" crowd of pleasure seekers, thereby distinguishing the area from the humbler, more raucous resorts at Humber Bay. The brochure speaks of the need to prevent the "incursion on the part of the rougher element" and provides rules and restrictions for the "respectable pleasure seeking community."

Mrs. J.A. Smythe, in "Long Branch Park Historical Sketch," confirms the exclusivity of the Long Branch crowd. She recalled, "There were two brick pillars at either side of the street, near where St. Agnes Church now stands. Atop these pillars were two very beautiful lamps sitting very majestically, blinking and winking at all those who came near its portals. At one time there stood an attendant or gate-keeper inquiring into the why

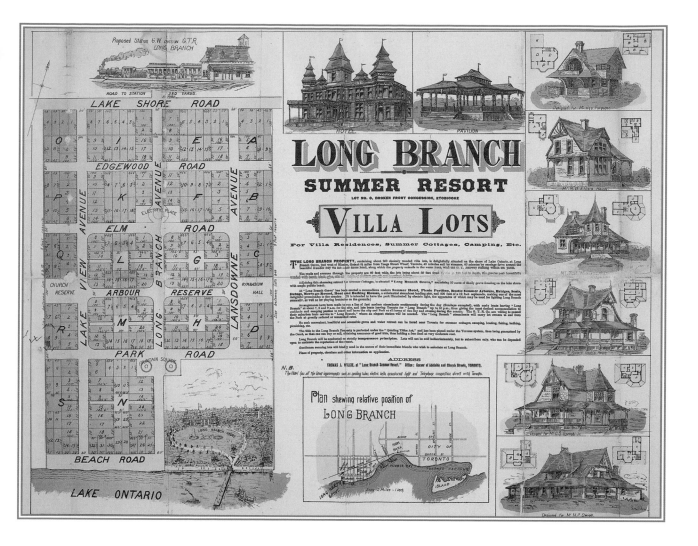

A few of the homes standing in Long Branch today are similar in design to the dwellings featured in this promotional broadsheet for Long Branch. The Long Branch Hotel is featured at the top middle. TPL, Mpbds 1887

and the therefore [*sic*] of your presence there." Regardless of the strict moral overtones of the early literature, the park did offer several amusements, including a carousel, a pavilion for dancing, and an early version of a water toboggan ride that disgorged its passengers directly into the lake.

A substantial cottage community also developed at Long Branch that lasted well into the twentieth century. Some of these original cottages, now renovated and used as full-time residences, may still be spotted near the lake and remain as tangible reminders of Long Branch's rich waterfront past.

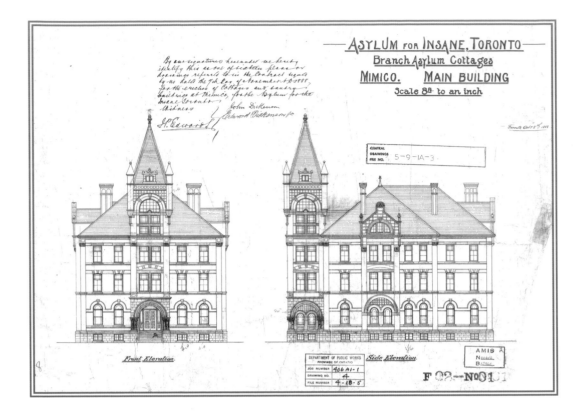

Architect's elevation drawings for the Main (Administration) Building at Mimico Branch Asylum (later renamed Lakeshore Psychiatric Hospital), late 1880s AO, Asylum for Insane, Toronto: Branch Asylum Cottages, Mimico — Main Building, RG 15-13-2

A little farther to the west, on the grounds that are now Colonel Samuel Smith Park, another type of refuge was erected in the late 1800s. The Mimico Branch Asylum received its first patients from its parent institution, the Asylum for the Insane in Toronto (now the Centre for Addiction and Mental Health), in 1890. The Mimico institution was predicated on the most modern principles for treating "chronically insane" populations. It was believed that patients should be treated in a setting where they could take full advantage of the outdoors and participate in the work of a self-supporting institution. In keeping with the "colony system," an approach that had already been adopted in the United States, patients were housed in a series of small, two-storey "cottages."

According to I.K. Bond, in a "History of Lakeshore Psychiatric Hospital," patients from the Toronto asylum largely built the Mimico facility. The original quadrangle of buildings, now house Humber College's Robert A. Gordon Learning Centre, and are surrounded by Colonel Samuel Smith Park, south of Lakeshore Boulevard in New Toronto.

Lakeshore hospital farm workers harvesting potatoes, c. 1930 Courtesy CAMH Archives

Mimico asylum residents reportedly made a number of structural improvements to the property over the years and built the large circular recreation ground behind the main quadrangle, where cricket and soccer games often took place. Sometime early in the history of the facility, a wharf was also constructed at the waterfront, along with a decorative pavilion that provided shade near the lake.

In the early years, particularly under the supervision of Superintendant N.H. Beemer, the grounds were enjoyed by patients and summer visitors alike. Bond notes, "On a summer evening cricket and soccer games took place on extensive and beautiful grounds . . . Boating was enjoyed from the hospital marina while local gentry took tea while enjoying the cricket matches. After dusk magic lanterns hung in the trees to the accompaniment of music concerts as all staff had to be proficient in either music or sport. In those days the hospital and community were entirely a British culture."

A review of the annual reports filed by Superintendant Beemer, found in the *Ontario Sessional Papers*, reveals that the Mimico facility used the waterfront for a variety of purposes, including, in the early years, as a water supply and for recreation. The 1897 report indicates that the patients enjoyed "boating in the summer" and the 1900 report that

Lakehouse, c. 1940 Anonymous,
Courtesy John and Muriel Easton

"daily outings by the lake-side are very much enjoyed." According to the 1907 report, the old wharf, "which time had nearly destroyed," was reconstructed of cement. Sadly, the use of the waterfront by patients had declined by the mid-1920s, while the institution, though it went through a number of name changes, continued. Reports about the conditions at the facility vary during its long history, including, in the 1960s and 1970s, accounts of substantial hardship suffered by some of the patients at the hands of a few of the employees.

John Easton, whose father, Norman, was a psychiatrist at the Lakeshore Psychiatric Facility, was raised in a house on the grounds of the institution in the 1940s. His family lived in the Lakehouse, which, according to Easton, was the original powerhouse for the institution. (It was demolished in the 1990s.) John described his experience there as a child in the 1940s: "We played all along that shore and launched our kayaks out into the Lake as kids. There was a great big crumbly concrete dock out there from the house — we could dive off it . . . They marched the prisoners of war from the Mimico Reformatory down to the dock, [and they] dived right in off the end. When they started heading for Buffalo, they'd fire bullets over their head and get 'em to come back."

Along the Shore

Before the war years and throughout the decades that led up to the closure of the Lakeshore Psychiatric Hospital in 1979, many patients at the facility were prisoners of another sort — they were Ontario's unwanted. Some women labelled chronically insane gave birth in the institution, while others, afflicted with senility and no longer able to cope on their own, were held there for years and sometimes decades. Many people spent their entire lives there, and though confined, they were viewed by many as an integral part of the wider Lakeshore community.

The graves of well over 1,000 patients, including some of the children born to them, remain on what is left of the agricultural farm north of the highway, on the corner of Evans and Horner Avenues. The Lakeshore Asylum Project, a local community group headed by former hospital employee Ed Janiszewski, tends these graves in an ongoing act of respect and remembrance.

———— • ————

WELL BEFORE THE establishment of the Mimico Branch Asylum and Long Branch Park, the first of the Lakeshore's grand homes was erected at the water's edge. In his Mimico Beach Estates blog, Lakeshore historian Michael Harrison provides an extensive review of the mansions and high-end residences that were built by many of Toronto's wealthiest industrialists, manufacturers, architects, lawyers, professionals, and businessmen along the shore at Mimico. He recounts that the first three summer homes were established by two Toronto merchants, W.H. Sparrow and William Hewitt, along with William Irving in 1875. John Kay, who is described by Harvey Currell as Toronto's first commuter, came a few years later.

Fetherstonhaugh's palatial guest house was known as the Tower. Pianist and silent film accompanist Horace Lapp lived in the Tower in the 1950s.

CT/MS, Montgomery's Inn, 012_025 Box1

George Paginton's The Bay in Winter, *c. 1955, shows the apartment blocks that began to appear on the lakefront in the 1950s. Fetherstonhaugh's Tower may be just made out in the distance.* Courtesy Tony Paginton

Between 1890 and 1930, many other lakeside mansions were built, including F.B. Fetherstonhaugh's Lynne Lodge — a residence described in *A History of Ontario* as "one of the most beautiful homes in the city." (Mike Filey in *The Way We Were: Toronto Sketches 8* also identifies the prominent lawyer as one of the pioneers of the electric car. According to Filey, his Toronto-built electric vehicle was in use for almost fifteen years and was displayed on more than one occasion at what is now known as the Canadian National Exhibition.) Fetherstonhaugh also commissioned a three-storey "guest castle" near the shore that boasted medieval battlements. The boathouse and gardener's cottage are the only substantial surviving remnants of this once-unique property.

Just as original was Miles Park, the creation of Arthur William Miles, a leading undertaker. His claim to fame was not so much that he introduced the motor-driven hearse to Ontario as that he turned part of his estate into a zoological garden with a menagerie that included an elephant, two camels, monkeys, donkeys, and other assorted fauna and built a pavilion, a pier, and a breakwater as well, all of these being for public use and entertainment. Wayne Reeves makes note of a "unique race," sponsored by one of the local churches in 1930, between a camel and "the fat women of Etobicoke." No victor was recorded; perhaps fortunately, the camel broke for the road.

The second Lakeshore residence of the well-known distiller Lawrence McGuinness is still a noted feature on Lake Shore Boulevard. It was erected in 1927 and is now the Polish Consulate. He is said to have built the English Tudor home with the profits of bootlegging, and he established a distillery and bottling plant in Mimico in 1938.

Another estate, Ormscliffe, was developed around 1906 by a steel manufacturer as his family's summer retreat, although he courteously allowed public access across the grounds to the lake on Sundays, a practice continued by the next owner, the prominent Italian-Canadian James Franceschini, when he bought the property in 1925 and developed it into Myrtle Villa. Franceschini added many features to the estate, including additional residential accommodations and stables and training facilities for his prize-winning horses.

Franceschini, who arrived in Canada in the first years of the twentieth century as a penniless boy of fifteen, went on to own an important construction company that had helped to complete the Toronto-to-Hamilton highway (the Lake Shore Road) in the 1910s. In 1940, although one of his companies was building minesweepers for the Canadian government, he was arrested and interned on suspicion of working for Fascist Italy against the Allies. He spent 1940–41 in prison, after which he was fully exonerated by a judicial inquiry. Wayne Reeves indicates that after the war, Franceschini rented the adjoining estate, earlier acquired from T.P. Loblaw (of grocery store fame), for use as veterans' housing.

Toronto's elite began to gradually migrate north to extravagant lakeside retreats in the earlier decades of the twentieth century. As taxes made many of these gracious mansions more difficult to maintain for successive generations, the properties were often subdivided, with low-rise apartment buildings appearing on some of the lots south of Lake Shore Boulevard in front of the lake. A judicial inquiry held in 1961 found that many of the apartment buildings erected during the 1950s were built in flagrant contempt of town bylaws in a period when "the builders, real estate men, and the speculators took over." Many of these apartments are now badly in need of improvement.

In 1950 the Myrtle Villa property was sold for redevelopment. The mansion and some of the original buildings, along with an outdoor sculpture and water fountain, now exist as part of a low-rise apartment complex known as Amadeo Garden Court Complex. In the mid-1960s and early 1970s, Oscar Peterson lived with his second wife in two apartments on the property overlooking the lake. For years Peterson frequented the mom-and-pop shops along the Lakeshore and according to his widow, Kelly Peterson, loved spending time near the water. Though he eventually moved to Mississauga, he could, in his later years, be spotted from time to time at the bottom of Marie Curtis Park. Oscar Peterson was in good company; according to longtime New Toronto resident Tony Paginton, pianist and silent film accompanist Horace Lapp also moved into the same building after vacating the Fetherstonhaugh "Tower." The trombone player Butch Watanabe, a good friend of Peterson's, also lived in New Toronto during this period.

At the time of writing there is a movement afoot to designate the historic elements of the Ormsby/Franceschini estate, as the community enters into a period of gentrification, with some developers eager to construct soaring lakeside condominium towers all along the edge of the lake. Residents await the outcome of the current planning process.

———————•———————

IN THE LATE NINETEENTH CENTURY, a middle class with time and money to spare emerged, and so did a leisure industry that was concentrated along the lakefront. The other crucial factor was transportation, and nothing made a seasonal community, hotel, or pleasure garden take off like the availability of mass transit. According to historian Robert Stamp, the Toronto and Mimico Electric Railway and Light Company provided radial service along the Lake Shore Road, first to the Humber River in 1892. William Mackenzie's Toronto Railway Company took over this service in July 1893, extending service to Mimico Creek the same month. By September of that year, you could ride the radial to present-day Kipling Avenue; by 1895, service had reached Etobicoke Creek, with the line successfully completed to Port Credit in 1905.

The unique features of the radial system have been addressed in the Scarborough section of this book; suffice it to say that with the advent of relatively inexpensive, reliable, and frequent service and tracks laid alongside the previously laid roads, more people than ever flooded into Toronto's outlying waterfront areas in the summer months, including the Lakeshore. The TRC promoted these destinations to its riders and established railway parks in other areas of the waterfront. An advertisement in the *Globe* from July 16, 1898, notes, "The Street Railway Company is devoting a great deal of attention to amusement-seekers. At Monro Park in the east and Long-Branch [*sic*] in the west are parks to which citizens are carried rapidly and with comfort. . . . The band of the Queen's Own will play

Along the Shore

to-night at Monro Park, and there will be a programme of amusements in the afternoon. There are cheap excursions to Long Branch every Tuesday and Friday."

Another popular area, noted by the TRC in "Toronto as Seen from the Streetcars," was Mimico Creek: "A short distance west is another little river, too small for boating, but just the thing for bathing; it has a fine sandy bottom and is deep enough for a swim without fear of drowning."

Travel on the radial, however, was not without its challenges. In the summer months, the radials to the east and west of Toronto were often filled to capacity and that, along with the usual delays that are experienced by Torontonians even today, could try people's patience. Mary Fitzpatrick (née Gamble), at the time of speaking to me in her 100th year, was raised both at Humber Bay and New Toronto. Near her family's home on Salisbury Avenue was Mimico Bridge, which was also the territory of an old goat. Says Fitzpatrick, "That old goat considered the track going over Mimico Creek to be his own personal territory. He would stand his ground as the car approached, and the conductor, or whoever else was on the car, would have to get out and chase him off the track."

The Lakeshore

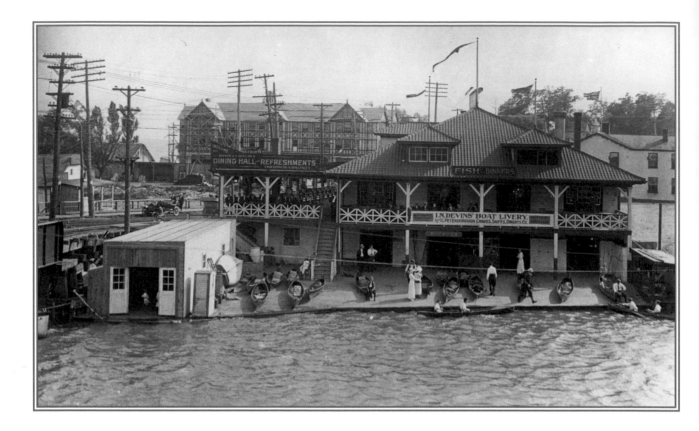

I.N. Devin's Boat Livery did a stiff business at the Humber in 1910, offering boat rentals, refreshments, and fish dinners CTA, F1244_it 2523

BY 1917, ONTARIO'S FIRST highway designed for motor traffic was completed with the paving of the Lake Shore Road between Toronto and Hamilton. This feature would bolster the influx of day trippers and fun seekers into the Humber in the years and decades to come. The area still offered a number of boat livery services, including the Isaac Devin's Boathouse near the mouth of the river, later known as the Riverview Boat Livery. Later came the Toby Jeck's Boathouse, which, according to George Chowns, lasted well into the 1930s. Like many young children growing up in Humber Bay, Chowns yearned to get into the canoes that were on offer at the mouth of the River. As he remembers, in the 1930s:

> In order to get a free boat, we'd collect all the abandoned canoes in the Humber, almost right up to Bloor Street. Then we'd bring them back to Mr. Wellwood at Toby Jeck's Boathouse. Most of the time the folks who rented the canoes would ditch them in the gut of the marsh, and walk up the banks of the Humber River.

We'd spend hours down there looking for canoes in Boyd's marsh, Scott Jack's marsh, Riley's marsh and the Dead marsh (the one they filled in for a park). When they filled in the Dead marsh, they must have lost a million and a half turtles. My brother and I once carried one home — it must have weighed about fifty or sixty pounds.

For those looking for racier thrills, the Humber Bay district offered gambling houses and bars, even through the Prohibition era, when bootleggers did brisk business there. Harry and Blanche Hall's *Memories of a Place Called Humber Bay* relates that one boat, the *Helinda*, regularly loaded her wares on the west side of the Humber, about a mile up from the river mouth (near today's Toronto Humber Yacht Club), and then made for the United States.

By the 1920s, many others ventured over the Humber on the paved Lake Shore Road, where tourist camps and cabins were being erected on the west side of the river by the 1920s. As Etobicoke historian Denise Harris notes, camping in Humber Bay began when some Americans received permission to camp in tents on the property of the Hicks establishment, near the Royal Oak Hotel. Soon, Hicks Humber Bay Tourist Camp was begun beside their boat-livery business. Other Lakeshore residents followed suit and began offering similar accommodations, including groups of individual cabins, on narrow properties that stretched down to the shore and offered private beaches.

As Mary Gamble recalls, the Butwells also had a "tent camp" and later opened the Shore Breeze Motel. According to Denise Harris, it was the first "modern" motel, and, soon after, a number of other low-slung, drive-up motels were built, including the Hillcrest, the Seahorse, the Rainbow, and the Beach.

———— • ————

ANOTHER AREA LINKED TO the history of Long Branch, though in present-day Mississauga, is the property on the west side of Etobicoke Creek, between Lake Shore Road and the lake, that is now known as the Lakeview lands. These lands housed the former Lakeview Generating Station, which was demolished in 2007.

In the late nineteenth century, this area was open farmland, some of which was originally patented to Samuel Smith. In 1891 the Ontario Rifle Association and the federal government established the Long Branch Rifle Ranges there. The ranges remained at Lakeview until 1957 and played an important role in training cadets, militia, and personnel of the Department of National Defence, though the area was also popular with local residents from both sides of Etobicoke Creek.

Fewer than twenty-five years after the establishment of the Rifle Ranges, Canada entered the First World War, and in 1915 these same lands housed the country's first flight-training facility, the Curtiss Aviation School, which also maintained a seaplane base on the Island. We owe the beginnings of military flight training in this country largely to J.A.D. McCurdy, who flew his *Silver Dart* out over the frozen shores of Baddeck Bay in February 1909, becoming the first person in Canada, and in the British Empire, to fly a controlled heavier-than-air machine. McCurdy, also discussed in the Beach and Island sections, participated in the first cross-country intercity air race in Canada, landing on Fisherman's Island in 1911.

According to Liwen Chen's "Canada's First Aerodrome: Long Branch Curtiss Aviation School," it was McCurdy who suggested that Canada's developing air service should be bolstered by home manufacturing. Accordingly, the Toronto branch of the Curtiss Aeroplane Company was established, with the company also offering flight instruction. (The definitive biography of J.A.D. McCurdy, *The Silver Dart* by H. Gordon Green, interestingly notes the aviation instruction facility as the McCurdy Aviation School.)

In any case, aviation historian Frank Ellis indicates that McCurdy was named manager of both operations, and Canada's first aerodrome and runway were constructed on the Lakeview grounds. The Curtiss operation lasted for only two seasons; according to Chen, it was then taken over by the Royal Flying Corps, which used it as a flight-training camp from the beginning of the 1917 season.

———◆———

AS IN THE BEACH, the introduction of street railways in the Lakeshore made it possible for middle-class people to live in the Lakeshore and work in the city. In the first decades of the twentieth century, many seasonal residents did just that. Pockets of subdivisions began in earnest in the Lakeshore by about 1910, and the charming little cottages in Long Branch and in other areas of the Lakeshore were eventually winterized, while others were torn down to make room for larger, more substantial year-round housing.

Despite the steady move toward suburbanization, the cottage community at Long Branch hung on until the 1930s. As a young child, Canadian landscape painter Doris McCarthy summered in Long Branch while living in the Beach. Toronto lawyer Carl Keyfetz, who also cottaged at Long Branch as a boy, recalls that the area, like the Beach, had a small community of Jewish summer residents, including the Bennett family, who were involved in real-estate development. The oldest son, Archie, later became president of the Canadian Jewish Congress. His son, Avie Bennett, went on to acquire McClelland

Sunnyside Amusement Park offered a world
of delights on the edge of the lake, c. 1920s

and Stewart in 1986, the large Canadian publishing house formerly owned by Jack McClelland.

The Lakeshore, like the Beach, also experienced some unfortunate anti-Semitic signage in local waterfront establishments. According to Keyfetz, in 1939 signs in Long Branch Park read, "No Jews or dogs allowed." During the years that Crowe's Beach operated in Humber Bay, a similar sign appeared reading, "Gentiles Only."

As the cottage community at Long Branch began to wane, many full-time residents from the Lakeshore increasingly sought entertainment on the east side of the Humber River. Sunnyside, which opened in 1922, was possibly Toronto's greatest amusement park. Toronto historian Mike Filey points out in *I Remember Sunnyside* that provision for a waterfront park on the east side of the Humber River was made in the Toronto Harbour Commission's Waterfront Plan of 1912. The ambitious plan mandated the dredging of

Toronto Harbour to accommodate larger ocean-going vessels along with a massive land-reclamation project that included Humber Bay, allowing for the development of parkland and recreational facilities on the western waterfront. Construction on a massive breakwater to protect this development began in 1913. Dubbed the "Poor Man's Riviera," the publicly owned and controlled Sunnyside Bathing Pavilion and Amusement Park, with the Harbour Commission as "landlord," drew, in its heyday, crowds in the tens of thousands weekly.

The Bathing Pavilion was designed by Chapman and Oxley, the same architects who built the humble but iconic Leuty Lifeguard Station in the Beach and, later, the Princes' Gates at the Canadian National Exhibition. The impressive facility, which still stands today, provided changing areas, showers, and, on the top floor, a full-length upper terrace that offered a broad and expansive view of the lake. On July 29, 1925, the massive Sunnyside pool, which had a capacity of up to 2,000 swimmers and was affectionately known as the "Tank," opened just to the east of the pavilion and was frequented by those patrons of the park who found the frigid waters of the lake a little too bracing. The Toronto Transportation Commission offered free rides to the Tank for children on many of its routes, including the Lakeshore west of the Humber.

At the east end of the park was another building designed by Chapman and Oxley, along with a third party, Bishop. Initially the structure was given over to two entirely different pursuits: boat-building and carpentry. Boat builder Walter Dean initially occupied the basement and part of the first floor, while the rest of the structure was used as a dance hall. Dean later left the premises, though the much-loved Palais Royale dance hall remained. Known for its "swing style" jazz, this structure still stands to the east of the Sunnyside Bathing Pavilion, and is a wonderful reminder of the many dance halls and pavilions that once dotted the Toronto shore from east to west.

By comparison, the original amusement park was quite modest. It boasted seven rides and nine games, which were quickly replaced with ever faster and more up-to-date thrill-seeking rides, such as the roller coaster known as the Flyer, which was rebuilt in 1933 and could reportedly achieve a speed of sixty miles per hour. In 1924 the Derby Racer was installed, mimicking a steeplechase.

Toronto's other waterfront amusement parks, namely Hanlan's Point and Scarboro' Beach, though waning in popularity, hung on after Sunnyside's opening in 1922. Both of these parks had a history of hosting numerous popular attractions and stunt events. The new kid on the block, Sunnyside, followed suit with parachute jumping and flagpole sitting events, a high-wire act, and at least one person who was buried alive.

Along the Shore

At night, the park was transformed by sound and a profusion of light. Patrons could take in an evening softball game at the Sunnyside stadium, purported to be the first such park in Toronto to install lights. Musical concerts were staged in the Sunnyside bandstand, along with sing-alongs. Open air dancing was in the offing at the Seabreeze dance pavilion, situated to the east of the Sunnyside Tank.

In *I Remember Sunnyside*, former mayor of Toronto David Crombie, who was raised on the east side of the Humber, in Swansea, recalls this of the park itself: "Across the short field and a narrow Lake Shore Road we would run to get to our first goal — the boardwalk! . . . A kind of yellow-brick road that stretched as far as the eye could see. . . . And there it was! The water, the break wall, the colours, the people, the smells, the happy noise — the sheer energy of it all. A world of rides, Honey Dew, music and chips with vinegar and salt."

By the late 1940s the writing was on the wall for Sunnyside. The last concessions were torn down in 1956, and the people's park on the lake gave way to the automobile age, the commute to cottage country, and the Gardiner Expressway.

———— •✦• ————

THOUGH THE RIDES have been carted away and the concession stands have long since closed at Sunnyside, relics from those days may still be found in the waters off Sunnyside Beach. The *Julia B. Merrill* and several Island wooden-hulled ferries met their end here, lit up as spectacles for the gathered crowds. Notorious among these burned vessels is the *Lyman M. Davis*, ignited in 1934. She is believed to have been one of the last, if not the last, indigenous working commercial sailing vessel left on the Great Lakes.

As Douglas Hunter notes in "An Undefiled Heritage," the *Lyman M. Davis* was built in Muskegan, Michigan, in 1873. In her later years she had sailed out of Napanee and Kingston, hauling coal from Oswego, New York, to Canadian ports on the lower lakes until the early 1930s. Still a strong and reliable servant, the proprietors of Toronto's Sunnyside Amusement Park bought her in 1933 for a fiery spectacle. Some city residents fought to save her, in large measure because she was the last, or very near the last, of her kind.

C.H.J. Snider, who we know from his "Schooner Days" columns, led the movement. The Beach's Great Lakes schoonerman Captain John Williams also joined in the fight and was quoted in the *Evening Telegram* of February 1, 1934, as saying, "Burning that old schooner would be an act of savagery. . . . It would be on par with tying cans to the tail of some faithful old dog that had outlived its usefulness, and kicking him out on the street just to see how fast he would run."

The Lakeshore

Sailing Ship 'LYMAN M. DAVIS'
Lying at Sunnyside Beach, Toronto

The Lyman M. Davis, *Sunnyside Beach*

"Shall you destroy the last old schooner
Put from your sight that work well done,
Of thousands of sailors, builders, captains,
Who laid foundation of years to come?

She is built of the stuff of which they were made.
Strong and reliable, swift and true,
She is fit to represent them now
To let posterity give them their due."

— G. Harrington Wilson, "Passing Hails,"
"Schooner Days," March 3, 1934

CTA, S330_F39_sheetIV_id001

Today it is difficult to comprehend an action so callous, but by the standards of the 1930s, in the midst of the Great Depression, these ships of a bygone era were seen as losers. They could not compete financially with the steamers that were able to move much heavier loads in much less time. Lorne Joyce, a former fisherman from Port Credit who is now in his eighties, told me that many schooners in the vicinity of Toronto were simply abandoned by their owners and, having no value as scrap metal, were filled with stones and sunk. Further, the early 1930s was a grim time. During the Great Depression, people simply wanted to go to a place like Sunnyside and forget their troubles, to be part of any distraction that might free them for a moment from the anxiety of their everyday lives.

Along the Shore

This spectacular photo of the Lyman M. Davis, *taken by David Sheard of Save Ontario Shipwrecks, shows the ship as it appears today, off the shore of Sunnyside Beach* David Sheard

Efforts to save the ship were in vain. According to the *Evening Telegram*, just before midnight on June 29, 1934, the *Lyman M. Davis* was towed from the Sunnyside anchorage to about 300 yards beyond the seawall. There she was blown up and burned to the glee of thousands of onlookers. She was then towed out to deep water, where a further blasting sent her tortured remains to the bottom of the lake. The bones of the *Lyman M. Davis* are out there still, just beyond Sunnyside Beach.

CHAPTER FIVE

Lakeshore Towns and Villages

Though the *Lyman M. Davis* met her end in 1934, Sunnyside continued for over twenty more years. By the time of its demolition in 1956, Toronto had witnessed a period of enormous growth. While the Lakeshore was by no means immune to the changes brought on by this expansion, the district remained, to a degree, set apart from the city on the other side of the Humber.

Some areas of the Lakeshore trace their roots to the coming of the railways through Toronto in the mid-1850s. A branch of the Great Western Railway was the first line across Etobicoke Township. A station was opened almost a mile north of the Lake Shore Road at Mimico in 1855. Goods could now be transported year round into what had been until then a remote area. Easier access, coupled with a plentiful source of fresh water and relatively cheap, undeveloped land that was close to the Port of Toronto and the downtown markets, brought about the possibility of industry and jobs.

With a view to the further industrialization that was certain to take hold in the Lakeshore area, prominent religious leaders, including Anglicans and Christian Socialists, banded together in the 1850s to establish an early model village for workers at Mimico. While a few homes were erected, the scheme failed, not for lack of merits but simply because the concept was ahead of its time; the lack of jobs in the area and a reliable source of flexible, inexpensive transportation, coupled with an economic downturn, meant that mass migration into the district would be left for another day.

The seeds of suburban development began some decades later, with the appearance in the *Globe* of an advertisement sponsored by the Mimico Real Estate and Security Company for a subdivision of 550 acres of land in what is now New Toronto. The plan envisioned a group of industries just west of the developing hamlet of Mimico, north of the Lake Shore Road, with a large number of lots that would provide housing for factory workers. As the *Globe* reported in October 1890, "There is an embryo town growing up which with its past development and its future prospects promises in time to equal, if not surpass, old Toronto as a commercial centre."

An added feature for would-be residents was an electric railway service, which was to be built between the city and New Toronto. The Mimico Real Estate and Security Company's optimistic projections for the growth of their planned community outpaced reality, however. Though the Toronto and Mimico Electric Railway and Light Company reached the Humber River in 1892, historian Robert Stamp reports that it languished there until William Mackenzie took over operations in July of 1893. The radial line was pushed to Mimico Creek and then to present-day Kipling Avenue by September 29 of that year. By July 1, 1895, you could ride the radial all the way to Etobicoke Creek. With the coming of the radial, a frequent, reliable, and comparatively cheap form of mass transportation was offered to working and middle-class people for the first time. Though the seeds of development were planted, the Mimico Real Estate and Security Company declared bankruptcy in 1896.

In the present-day area of New Toronto, a small industrial base had nonetheless developed by the turn of the twentieth century, and a small number of workers' homes had been constructed. With the coming of the Grand Trunk Railway's westerly marshalling yards in the area north of the Lakeshore in 1906, the rest was history. Richard Harris, in *Unplanned Suburbs*, notes, "Here, as elsewhere, radial lines and freight yards shaped the industrial geography of the urban area." A ready workforce moved to the area in droves.

To promote industry and growth, Wayne Reeves indicates that New Toronto's village council offered "an adequate and constant supply of pure water for all purposes." From 1915 onward, the New Toronto Filtration Plant, later renamed the Lakeshore Pumping Station, stood at the foot of Sixth and Seventh Streets. Eventually the plant began to serve not only New Toronto but Mimico and Long Branch as well.

Paternalism and concern for the well-being of workers were part of the business model Goodyear opened their doors in New Toronto in 1917, and a concept that was evident for decades to come in many of the other industrial plants that followed. In return, the workers were incredibly loyal to their employers, with many spending their whole working lives in one factory shop. A headline from an article in the *Star Weekly* from September 1917 says it all: "Toronto's Newest Factory One of the Finest in Canada. Workmen Well Cared For, Given Ideal Surroundings."

Indeed, local industry never threatened the Lakeshore with "dark satanic mills" like those of nineteenth-century industrial England. Rather, the industries became the corporate partners of the district, contributing greatly to the services, sports, and sense of citizenship that knitted them all together. According to Ross Bonar, son of local fisherman William Bonar, who was raised near the mouth of Mimico Creek in the 1940s, "That's how you got a job in those days, if you could play sports, you were in — the local factories sponsored the teams. . . . There was a real rivalry and local industry was always scouting the better players."

J.O. Browne's Plan of the Town of Mimico *shows a plan of subdivision that failed to materialize in the 1850s* AO, B 66-06

GOODYEAR'S MOVE TO New Toronto in 1917 roughly doubled the number of available jobs in the Lakeshore, and workers in need of housing flooded into the area. In 1918 the New Toronto Housing Commission was formed, and, taking advantage of a federal housing program offered in 1919, they built a number of cottage-style homes for

Along the Shore

workers, the majority of which were semi-detached, borrowing aspects from the industrial and garden suburbs of England and Europe. A smattering of these original homes remain in New Toronto, with some examples on Eighth Street.

Shortly after the arrival of Goodyear, Anaconda Brass, the Donnell and Mudge Tannery, and Continental Can all followed, with Campbell Soup arriving in the 1930s. The new subdivisions that grew up north and south of the highway kept pace with this industrial development by housing the workers and also those who simply wished to escape the city.

By 1913, New Toronto attained status as a village separate from the Township of Etobicoke, and by 1923, it was a full-fledged town. Statistics collected by Harris reveal that by 1928, a full seventy-eight per cent of workers employed at Goodyear were living in either New Toronto or Mimico. In 1941 an overwhelming number of New Toronto residents worked in New Toronto, with eighty-five per cent of residents living within a three-mile radius of their place of work. By 1963 New Toronto had earned the reputation of being Canada's most productive square mile.

Goodyear plant, New Toronto, c. 1950s

Though industry was nearby (north of the highway), it did not prevent local workers from taking advantage of the natural world of the lake that lay virtually at their feet. At the age of ninety, Ross Gamble fondly remembered growing up in New Toronto after moving from the village of Humber Bay in about 1927. The lake lay just beyond his front door, at the bottom of Third Street:

> I slept on the porch and if I left my window open, I could feel the spray of the water on my face as I slept. When the winter came, we'd skate out onto the ice. Those were the days when the Lake would sometimes freeze right over. . . . We'd skate across to the Island. You had to learn to follow the heavy ice. Lots

The Lakeshore

of times our feet would go through where it was too thin. . . . Mother was so mad. . . . In summer we'd take the streetcar all the way through the city to the Bluffs for a picnic. My Aunt Dolly had a cottage out there right next to the cliffs.

It was a long ride . . . across the Lake Shore to the other side.

Whereas the subdivisions at New Toronto were intended for the working class, those at Mimico were intended for the middle-class buyers who sought to escape the squalor and smoke of Toronto's inner core. To the west of the Franceschini estate, Cecil White, who controlled White & Co. Real Estate, commenced one such early development — Crescent Point — in 1910. White was active in real-estate development not only along the Scarborough shore but also in Etobicoke. An article in the *Toronto Daily Star* in May 1928 indicates that White had sometime later purchased a large parcel of land with frontage on the Humber River, which would likely be added to the Riverside Golf and Country Club, of which White held "the controlling interest."

White, whom we met in the Scarborough section as the self-styled "pioneer" of Scarborough lakeside development, promoted the Lakeshore property in a similar fashion to those in the eastern lakefront district. As with the Sandown Park promotional brochure, a promotional article that appeared in the *Toronto World* on July 31, 1910, leveraged the natural surroundings, the lake, and the healthful environment. The proximity of the Mimico Beach Estates was also mentioned, which guaranteed "an excellent neighbourhood and the best class of people."

Though overtures were made to the upper-middle class as potential buyers, White's article on Crescent Point in the *Toronto Daily Star* of August 5, 1910, emphasizes low taxes, the proximity of industry, and the availability of transit as primary selling features. Regardless of his intention, with the exception of the waterfront estates on the lakefront, Mimico developed for the most part as a middle-class residential community and was considered to be one the prettiest outlying neighbourhoods in the vicinity of Toronto.

The character of planned development in Mimico featured, in varying degrees, elements derived from the garden suburb movement that had begun in late nineteenth century England as a reaction to the loss of aesthetic creativity to mechanization. It rejected the soul-destroying regimented nature of the recent industrial revolution. The new emphasis in Mimico, and in various suburban developments across North America, was on greenery, neighbourhood, and self-contained communities, in contrast to the stark, grim uniformity that had encircled the towns and villages of industrialized areas in England. The principles of the movement held that each dwelling was to have "ample room, ample air and a place in the yard for a garden" and an advantageous mix of industry,

Labels on image: Humber River · High Park · Sunnyside · Parkdale · Exhibition Park · Toronto Harbor · The Island · LAKE SHORE ROAD · CRESCENT POINT · EASTBOURNE · SYMONS STREET · DARTMOUTH CRESCENT · CHURCH STREET

commerce, residential accommodation, and verdant spaces.

Cecil White's Crescent Point estate, as it appeared in the Toronto Daily Star, *August 5, 1910* GetStock.com

As in the Scarborough shore, suburban development in the Lakeshore did not proceed uniformly, particularly in the years prior to the Second World War. The district of Humber Bay remained a sort of semi-rural borderland into the 1930s, with cabins and tenting facilities along the shore. Market gardens, though more prevalent north of the Queensway, were also in evidence, growing apples, pears, strawberries, and raspberries. Farmers delivered their produce to local Lakeshore residents and to markets in downtown Toronto by horse and wagon.

Fisherman William (Bill) Bonar, like the Goldrings who had preceded him in the nineteenth century, lived on the banks of Mimico Creek with his wife, Letitia (Letty), and their five children. The Bonar property was the playground of many Lakeshore children, who swam in the deep bend in Mimico Creek near his home. Said former Humber Bay and New Toronto resident Mary Gamble, "Right after Bonar's house was a sharp turn in the creek, and that was where the deepest part was. The boys used to go up there and swing from a willow tree into the water. The girls were not allowed there because they went bare, but we could watch from where ever we were walking!"

From 1916, Bonar set out nightly in his one-lunger boat to cast his gillnets four or five miles offshore. According to Mary Gamble, her brother Frank would sometimes go

The Bonar home, Mimico Creek

Courtesy Ross Bonar

out with him early in the morning and bring back the nets full of fish. Said Gamble, "When I think of Mr. Bonar, I think of the word stalwart. . . . He lived in the smallest little house I have ever been in. His wife had beautiful red hair and I just can see her standing in the doorway. . . . A lot of kids grew up there on the banks of Mimico Creek and they were very important to us."

A gentleman's agreement between the Joyce commercial fishermen of Port Credit and Mr. Bonar allowed him the sole right to fish the waters off Mimico Creek. According to Bonar's son Ross, another favourite spot that his father cast his nets was directly south of the Palace Pier, a popular dance hall opened on the west side of the Humber River in 1941. After hauling in his whitefish, frosties, and the occasional salmon, Bonar stood on Mimico Bridge and sold his catch, greeting his customers with a hardy "I say boy!" right up until the 1950s.

Along the Shore

WHILE MIMICO ACQUIRED town status by 1917, development proceeded at a much slower pace to the west, in Long Branch. The subdivisions of Lakeshore Gardens, Lake Shore Gardens Annex, the Pines, and Pine Beach all appear on the *Toronto Daily Star's* 1912 "Graphic Presentation of Toronto's Real Estate Activity," yet few of these had been fully developed by the time Long Branch attained village status in 1930 (as late as the 1940s, lots on Thirty-sixth and Thirty-seventh Streets were offered for sale to returning war veterans for ten dollars.)

Instead, this area evolved in the 1930s, to an extent, like the Scarborough shore, becoming what was referred to by S.D. Clark as a "backland utopia" for some, who settled on empty lots of subdivisions and built their homes in stages as finances allowed, sometimes forgoing direct access to water mains or indoor plumbing in the early years. Strong bonds of friendship were forged out of hardship during the years of the Great Depression. As former resident Don Smith said of those years: "I remember the love and kindness each person in Long Branch viewed each other. We didn't have much but it was shared by all."

During these years, a community of homes also developed in the "flats" along the banks of the Etobicoke Creek. According to John Ernest (Erney) Collict, one business in particular, Oates for Boats, sold groceries and rented out their little vessels to the local clientele for twenty-five cents. Many Long Branch children paddled down to the "lagoon" where the creek took a sharp turn to the west, creating a little marsh at the outlet to the lake, which had in the nineteenth century been occupied by the Goldrings and where "Boss Harris" built his schooner the *Defiance* in the 1845.

The Long Branch of those years, up to and including the 1950s, had its share of characters, among them the prim and proper church lady married to the bookie who ran the variety store along the highway and the indomitable chief at Long Branch, an old Irish copper, who worked the beat on his bicycle. His daughter Daphne Scale (née Smyth) told me, "The red light on top of the pole at the

Fisherman Bill Bonar (with a pet squirrel on his right shoulder)
Courtesy Ross Bonar

The Lakeshore

highway signalled trouble in the Long Branch area and the Chief, ending a shift, would return to the station no matter what time of day or night it was." When the town went bankrupt for a short period, the Chief kept right on working — for free.

As one long-time Lakeshore resident related, there was also the gentleman who, whenever given a day pass from the psychiatric hospital, would set off, smartly dressed, and call upon one of the local real estate offices. He always made the same request. He would consider it most kind if he could be shown any suitable residential property that might happen to have come up for purchase in the Lakeshore. With an obliging smile the realtor would politely refer him to one of the newer, unsuspecting members of the office, who would graciously escort the gentleman around for a couple of hours. At the end of the day, the resident would request to be returned to the hospital.

———— ◆ ————

THOSE WHO LIVE in the dormitory suburbs of today may well spend most of the day-light hours far away from their homes and communities, either working or shopping or driving back and forth between widely dispersed locations. By contrast, most of the Lakeshore residents would simply go from home to their work in the factories north of the highway, come back home for lunch at noon, and then go back to work in the afternoon. Right up until the end of the Second World War, market gardeners tended their vegetable plots in Humber Bay while a significant number of office workers and professionals, especially in Mimico, would pack their briefcases and commute to downtown on the radial, and later the streetcar, that ran just a few blocks away from their doors.

Despite local differences, these towns were linked, first by the shore on the south and then by the common highway and the factories on the north. Although someone living near Etobicoke Creek might retain an allegiance to Long Branch, he might likely work in New Toronto. Admittedly Long Branch itself had its own share of industry along the highway, but on a smaller scale than New Toronto. The memory of shared experiences, a collective memory drawn together over the course of time by residents past and present, could well be what makes this area more than the sum of its parts, giving it heart and soul, even today.

———————— • ————————

COMMUNITY SPIRIT IS often forged out of hardship, and this was certainly true of Long Branch, New Toronto, Mimico, and Humber Bay during the Second World War. The breadth of the contribution that each made to the war effort is astonishing, given that these communities were so small compared to Toronto at that time. Given their unique position on Lake Ontario, it is fitting that each of Mimico, New Toronto, and Long Branch sent a naval ship into service, respectively the HMCS *Mimico*, HMCS *New Toronto*, and HMCS *Long Branch*.

Among the Lakeshore heroes of the Second World War was Flight Lieutenant David Hornell, who is said to have been born on Toronto Island. Raised in Mimico, he was posthumously awarded the Victoria Cross for action over the North Atlantic in 1944. Attacked by a German U-boat, he nonetheless managed to sink the enemy submarine before crash-landing his blazing plane on the water. Mortally wounded and with only one dinghy for the eight men in his crew, Hornell, along with the others, took turns in the frigid water. He died soon after his rescue from the North Atlantic. One of the ferries to the Billy Bishop Toronto City Airport is named for Hornell.

Decades after the cessation of hostilities in 1945, the industries of the Lakeshore were filled with our brave servicemen and women of the Second World War. Ernie Scale is just one of many who landed at Juno Beach, survived the horrors of the Falaise Gap for our freedom, and then, at the end of the war, returned home to Canada and found a job on the factory floor of Continental Can. In 2004 he was given the Knight of the Legion of Honour Medal by the government of France for service during the Second World War.

The Lakeshore

An overwhelmingly female workforce is pictured outside the Small Arms plant, c. 1943 Courtesy Hilda Insley

The factories on the highway also played a unique role during the war, turning out the tires and machining the copper for the war effort. Many married women of the Lakeshore, housewives at home in pre-war days, now joined the war effort themselves, taking up employment to make firearms, among them the Sten submachine gun and the Lee Enfield rifle at Small Arms Limited, a munitions factory that was ready for operation in 1941 and located on the present-day Lakeview lands, on the west side of the Etobicoke Creek in Mississauga.

Lifelong Port Credit resident Hilda Insley (née Briscoe) remembers well her days at Small Arms, where she inspected the Lee Enfield and the Sten. Said Briscoe:

> We had to make sure the guns fired properly. . . . I would put the artificial bullets down in the magazine and then make sure that then when I pulled the bolt back, when I shot that bullet, that it didn't just drop beside the gun. It had to fire out properly. . . . I left Small Arms early one day . . . and got married in the Christie Street Hospital with a padre. My husband was sent out from there and went overseas, so naturally you wanted to make sure you were making a good gun.

The Lakeshore even had a prisoner of war camp. It was known as Internment Camp "M" and was located on the grounds of what is now known as the Mimico Correctional

Centre. Long-time Lakeshore residents remember the Home Guard marching the prisoners every Wednesday down to Lake Ontario for a swim. Robert Given writes in "New Toronto" that many of the prisoners were merchant marines and U-boat crewmen and were dressed in blue with "a red patch on the back of their coat." Despite the protests from local council, some of the prisoners were put to work at the Donnell and Mudge Tannery, located in New Toronto at the corner of Birmingham and Eighth Streets, where many war-related materials were being produced.

The Second World War hit especially close to home when practice bombs were dropped in various locales in Lake Ontario, including south of Long Branch, about a half a mile to three-quarters of a mile offshore. Many of the fishermen active in the Toronto area during this period observed these flights and knew the approximate locations where the bombs were dropped. One such family was the Joyces of Port Credit, who trace their roots in the fishing trade back to 1834 on Burlington Beach. After the war, Lorne Joyce scuba dived into the deep water and collected these bombs off Long Branch and other areas of the Great Lakes and salvaged the lead. Said Joyce:

> After the war the fishery was not as good as it had been . . . for about three years after the Second World War, that's about all what we did. Most of the bombs would have exploded and there would just be the bottom section, or the nose section of it; it would still have the same eight pounds of lead in each one. . . . We taught ourselves how to get the bombs back up by walking on the bottom. At Long Branch it was hard out there . . . generally speaking we didn't do much above over sixty to sixty-five feet of water — the effect on your body you know — you'd have limitations. We tended to say not too much about this . . . Other people would have been going after them, and wouldn't know properly how to get them . . . so we kind of held that to ourselves.

Lorne Joyce with a practice bomb, 2011
Wayne LeFort

ALMOST A DECADE before the Second World War, in 1930, Gus Ryder moved to the Lakeshore and opened a customs brokerage business in New Toronto. Later that summer he revealed his true passion when he started the Lakeshore Swimming Club. Gus Ryder came by his uncanny ability to teach swimming and lifesaving honestly. Ron McAllister's *Swim to Glory* indicates that some years before moving to the Lakeshore, Ryder, himself an excellent athlete, pulled a skater from the icy water of Grenadier Pond in High Park. From that time on, Ryder vowed to learn and master the art of lifesaving and become an accomplished swimmer.

Although Ryder never had children of his own, in a sense he had thousands of them, teaching swimming to countless Lakeshore children of all ages and abilities. In the summer months he ran an instructional swimming program under the sponsorship of the Red Cross for local kids at the Sunnyside Tank, now known as the Sunnyside–Gus Ryder Outdoor Pool. Lakeshore kids travelled back and forth to the pool using the free streetcar service for children that was provided by the Toronto Transportation Commission on many of its routes, including the Lakeshore.

Until 1952 the Lakeshore Swimming Club was without its own indoor pool. Before this, its athletes swam out in the lake in the summer months — in the early years from the bottom of Seventh Street and near the mouth of the Etobicoke Creek, and later near the mouth of the Credit River. Ryder's rise to pre-eminence as a swimming coach coincided with Toronto's rising profile as the premier place in North America for marathon swimming. That story began when Toronto teenager George Young rode down to California on a battered motorcycle and was the surprise winner of the first marathon swim across California's Catalina Strait in 1926. The trophy, donated by Arthur Wrigley Jr., named Young the Champion of the World for his twenty-mile crossing. For years after that, highly competitive marathon swimming events were held in Lake Ontario, in front of the Canadian National Exhibition, with a cast of local and international athletes.

As Bill Leveridge writes in *Fair Sport: A History of Sports at the Canadian National Exhibition Since 1879*, the Wrigley trophy that Young won for crossing the strait moved to Toronto the following year. On August 31, 1927, the first "Big Swim" for the Championship of the World was held at the Canadian National Exhibition with Ernst Vierkoetter, "the Black Shark of Germany," taking first place in the twenty-one mile course. During this first marathon swim, Gus Ryder saved two men who were floundering in the frigid water along the breakwater. To ward off the cold, both swimmers had covered their bodies in graphite grease, which was now threatening to suffocate them.

The Wrigley swims lasted until 1937, with many of Gus Ryder's athletes from the Lakeshore Swimming Club participating in its later years. Ryder's first swimming star was long-time Seventh Street resident and community volunteer Lucille (Lou) Gamble (née Wylie), the sister-in-law of Mary Fitzpatrick (née Gamble), whom we met earlier in this section. Though she achieved much success throughout her competitive swimming career, her prized possession was the Mayor Jackson Trophy, which she earned by winning the mile race at the New Toronto waterfront three times in a row. From Coach Ryder, Gamble not only learned to swim but also, according to her daughter Wendy Gamble, "the watchwords of her life: personal commitment, community service, and dedication to her sport."

Ryder devoted as much time to teaching disabled children to swim as to coaching his star athletes. And he made sure that all of his swimmers participated in teaching these children, too. Many, including Lou Gamble, volunteered alongside Ryder for decades and took up his work after his death, making community service their life's work, both in the Lakeshore and farther afield. Another of Ryder's swimming stars, Marilyn Bell, had this to say of her coach, "Everything that I've done in my lifetime in terms of trying to be understanding of people who are less fortunate, be it physically less fortunate or whatever, it all came from Gus Ryder and the Lakeshore Swimming Club. He set the bar high for himself but he also set it high for us . . . I really felt like he gave so much of himself to make me whatever I could be."

Another Lakeshore swimmer who had a tremendous impact on community life was local hero Cliff Lumsdon, who won his first World Marathon Swimming Championship at the Exhibition in 1949, a feat that earned him the Lou Marsh Trophy for best Canadian athlete of that year. He would be awarded five individual world championships at the Exhibition in all and would cross the Juan de Fuca Strait, between British Columbia and Washington State, in 1956.

Called "one of the epic swims of the century" by the *Toronto Daily Star*, Lumsdon's effort in the 1955 World Championship at the Exhibition is perhaps his most legendary performance. In lieu of an earlier planned lake crossing, the swim involved a thirty-two-mile triangular-shaped course, in front of the Exhibition grounds. At the outset of the race, which began about one a.m. on September 9, the water temperature was reported to be close to fifty degrees Fahrenheit, a dangerously low swimming temperature.

By daylight, all but three in the field of internationally known marathoners were out of the lake. Before the halfway point, the only swimmer left in the punishing water was Lumsdon. By mile fifteen he was suffering from terrible groin cramps and was dragging his legs behind him, but as thousands of Torontonians began to gather on the lakeshore, he somehow was able to summon the courage to plow forward, with Coach Gus Ryder at his side in the guide boat. At the finish, Lumsdon, semi-conscious, was unable to pull himself up onto the barge. As Lumsdon was removed from the platform on a stretcher, Gus Ryder collapsed, no doubt due to the strain of watching one of his star athletes endure such a test. Fortunately, one hot cup of coffee later, Ryder recovered.

A lifetime resident of the Lakeshore, Lumsdon was made a member of the Order of Canada in 1982, seven years after Coach Gus Ryder had received the same honour. Before his early death in 1991, he accompanied his daughter Kim Lumsdon, also a top marathon swimmer, during her initial crossing of Lake Ontario in 1976.

The first crossing of our great inland sea came more than two decades earlier, when, in 1954, the Lakeshore Swimming Club's Marilyn Bell (now Bell Di Lascio), a spritely, otherwise average Toronto teenager, took on Lake Ontario and won. In the ensuing decades, many other successful and impressive swimmers have followed Bell across the lake. Among them is Cindy Nicholas, who remains, almost forty years after her record-

setting crossing in 1974, the fastest woman to have swum the lake. The tenacious and talented Vicki Keith crossed Lake Ontario five times, and her many achievements include a double crossing in 1987. In 2012 Annaleise Carr stole Torontonians' hearts when, at age fourteen, she became the youngest person to have ever made the crossing.

Despite these other remarkable achievements, Bell's epic David-and-Goliath struggle with the lake remains as an enduring story of faith, perseverance, and courage. Stories of her swim have been repeated in the kitchens and living rooms of many Torontonians for decades, and in the 1950s and 1960s, a whole generation of mothers wanted their daughters to grow up just like Marilyn Bell. In 2010 the Toronto Port Authority's new ferry to the Billy Bishop Toronto City Airport was named for her.

Prior to her history-making swim across the lake, Bell had an otherwise normal and uneventful upbringing in the west end of Toronto. Her parents were raised in the Humber Bay area and, according to Bell, courted in a canoe rented at the mouth of the Humber River. In the early days of their relationship, they spent a lot of time along the lakefront, and during the Canadian National Exhibition they would paddle out into the lake and watch the marathon swims. In an interview I did with Marilyn Bell Di Lascio in November 2011, she told me, "I got my first introduction to long distance swimming through the stories Daddy would tell me about the different swimmers that he and Mom watched at the Exhibition. I knew all about George Young and his story before ever I swam Lake Ontario."

Years later, Bell's parents bought her a season ticket to the Oakwood Swimming Club in Toronto to keep her busy during the summer, and a short time after that, she was invited to join the Dolphinettes Swimming Club. Much anticipated in those early years was the swimming competition and other water events held at the Exhibition on Children's Day. Said Bell Di Lascio, "We used to live, just live for those two weeks in the summer when the Ex was open. We knew that we were going to be swimming in front of crowds of people, cheering and clapping for us."

In 1949 twelve-year-old Marilyn Bell swam her first mile race with twenty- and thirty-year-olds in the open lake at the Exhibition. Though she didn't win the race, she caught the eye of Lakeshore Swimming Club coach Gus Ryder, whose swimmers were also competing. After finishing the swim, Ryder introduced himself to Bell and her father and encouraged her, noting that, according to Bell Di Lascio, "I had shown such courage and that I had a lot of heart." Bell began swimming with the Lakeshore Club shortly after that.

Over the next few years Bell had a number of competitive showings in the long-distance swims at the Exhibition. In 1954, at the age of sixteen, Ryder and Bell came to an agreement that if she could swim in the Credit River non-stop for ten hours, Ryder would enter her in the Atlantic City Marathon around Absecon Island. Bell successfully completed her ten hours in the Credit, and Ryder duly entered her in the race. Perhaps less well known is the fact that Bell won the ladies' event at Atlantic City.

In the summer of 1954, the Canadian National Exhibition offered an enormous purse of $10,000 to the thirty-six-year-old American long-distance swimming star Florence Chadwick if she could become the first to swim across a thirty-mile stretch of Lake Ontario. Her solo swim of the yet-uncrossed lake was to begin on the beach at Youngstown, New York, and end at the Canadian National Exhibition grounds as the grand finale of the Exhibition season.

Bell maintains that it was during the Atlantic City swim that Gus Ryder realized the Lakeshore Swimming Club needed to provide a contender. Interest became excitement when Bell and Gus Ryder challenged Chadwick to a race across the lake. Bell was not after the money. She was offered no financial reward. She simply felt that Canadians "shouldn't let an American hog a Canadian show."

At sixteen, little Marilyn Bell stood only five foot one. She weighed only 119 pounds. Commentators of the time thought her prospects laughable: such a wisp of a girl could hardly survive more than a few hours in the frigid lake, let alone challenge a strongly built champion who, in 1953, had become the fastest person, man or woman, to ever cross the English Channel from England to France.

Bell Di Lascio told me that she wasn't at all confident of her chances of crossing the lake. "My determined goal, although I never spoke about it until afterwards, was to swim as far as Florence did, even if I just went one stroke or two strokes past where she finished or where she got out, because I really didn't think anybody could do it. My goal was to swim further than she swam."

Though sponsored by the *Toronto Daily Star*, Bell was an unofficial participant in the Exhibition's lake swim. What has often been forgotten is that she shared that status with another challenger also sponsored by the same newspaper — Port Credit–born Winnifred (Winnie) Roach-Leuszler, who was a gifted Canadian athlete and swimmer.

Among her achievements, Roach-Leuszler was the first Canadian across the English Channel, in 1951.

As the swim's only official entrant, it was up to Chadwick alone to determine when the race would begin, and when the word finally came on the evening of September 8, 1954, Bell's father and coach Ryder couldn't be immediately located. In the circumstances, it wasn't possible for her guide boat to be taken to the coast guard station in Youngstown, New York, where the race was to begin. In order not to miss Chadwick's start, Bell was raced overland to the coast guard station by one of the reporters covering the story.

This photo was captured at Coach Gus Ryder's home on September 4, 1954. It shows a hopeful Marilyn Bell days before the start of her historic swim across the lake. YUL/CTSC, Toronto Telegram fonds, ASC07788

Under intense media scrutiny, Florence Chadwick lowered herself into the water at Youngstown and swam off into the night with her coach and guide boat. A minute later Marilyn Bell entered the same depths alone and headed north up the Niagara River, without the assistance of an adult, a boat, or even a compass. For the next twenty-one hours, Bell would be involved in a herculean struggle with Lake Ontario that would give rise to one of the most triumphant and inspiring passages of Toronto's history. "Gus had said to me, when you start, dive in and try to get yourself out into the centre of the river and just swim out of the mouth of the river and we'll find you. It was pitch black and raining, eleven o'clock at night. . . . I was petrified, I was really petrified. I remember stopping and looking around and the only lights I could see were lights to my left, up ahead. I could see Florence's boat because it was all rigged with lights." Miraculously, Ryder did find her. Roach-Leuszler, who started the race in similar circumstances to Bell, wasn't as lucky. Picked up later by a fisherman, the twenty-eight-year-old mother of three began again some hours later, though she was later pulled from the water thoroughly exhausted.

As Bell told me, "We weren't set up for any kind of communication on the Lake. We had an escort boat and whatever charts the yachtsman and fisherman used. Gus had a chalkboard to give me instruction and to keep my attention but of course, swimming through the night, you couldn't see it . . . Gus had a very large high-powered flashlight and he was shining it just ahead of where I was swimming." Bell swam to that light all through the night, but, unfortunately for her, the flashlight had the unwelcome effect of attracting the night-feeding, snake-like eels, which she repeatedly ripped off her body and flung into the night.

Also problematic were the great swells in the lake, higher than anything she had ever experienced before: "I distinctly remember sailing on the crest of the wave and pulling in air." Chadwick, violently ill from the waves, was pulled from the water dejected at dawn; Bell remained in the water, and though in great discomfort, she was buoyed up in those early morning hours by the vision of the sun breaking over the surface of the lake, a powerful experience that has stayed with her to this day:

> Fortunately for me I breathe on the right, so I was breathing to the east and I could see traces of light, streaks of light at first, in the sky. I remember being disconcerted by that, it was just very strange and then gradually I could see more light, more light, and that's when I realized, "Oh, my God, the night is almost over, I've swum all night!" I watched the colours, the yellows, the pinks and then the sun, oh my goodness, the sun! I've never forgotten that sunrise. It was

Marilyn takes a break the following day to have some sustenance, delivered to her in a paper cup. Her guideboat, the Mipepa, *is loaded down almost to the gunwales with Coach Gus Ryder, her friend Joan Cooke, and Toronto Star reporter George Bryant. Jack Russell is at the tiller.* YUL/CTSC, *Toronto Telegram* fonds, ASC07789

glorious. When I saw that red sun pop up on the horizon, it was just *springing* out of the water. To this day it still reminds me of what I think Easter Sunday morning should be like, it was like a resurrection! I had swum all through this blackness and then I was in the light and I've never ever forgotten the joy that I felt at that particular time, it was just so beautiful.

Later that day, the city of Toronto would learn that though the lake had felled the great American champion, a sixteen-year-old teenager, their sixteen-year-old teenager, was determinedly crawling arm over arm to shore. Toronto — still so tight-lipped and starchy as to seem incapable of expressing much emotion — went nuts. In the tradition of sculler Ned Hanlan and marathon-swimmer George Young, Marilyn Bell was drawing the focus of Toronto's attention to the waterfront. Eager spectators clutched their radios on the roof of the Royal York Hotel, vying for a first sight of Bell through their

The Lakeshore

binoculars. The event also sparked a newspaper rivalry between the Toronto *Telegram* and the *Daily Star*; throughout the day, reporters sped offshore in water taxis to obtain updates and photos of Bell as she inched ever closer to Toronto. By late afternoon, offices were empty and thousands of people were gathering at the Exhibition grounds and along the lakeshore in expectation of her arrival.

From about mid-morning on Bell was, in her words, "in difficulty . . . stopping and starting." It was sometime after that that Bell's friend Joan Cooke, the future wife of Cliff Lumsdon, stripped down to the bare essentials and joined her in the water, encouraging Bell to plow forward. Bell rallied, but by about mid-afternoon, she told Ryder definitively that she could go no further. Says Bell Di Lascio:

> I remember telling Gus, "I'm paralyzed, I can't move my legs and I feel like I don't have a stomach," because the muscles were beginning to spasm. He said, "Okay, if you're absolutely sure that you want to get out then swim to the boat and I'll take you out." Well, with that, I started swimming to the boat and I didn't know this but I was kicking ferociously and that was when he realized that I wasn't done so he had the boatmen pull away. I recall swimming and swimming and I wasn't getting closer to the boat. Then I realized he was moving away. I yelled at him, "What are you doing, you're moving the boat! You said to swim to the boat!" and then he said, "And you told me your legs were paralyzed!" He did what a good coach would do but I was furious with him. . . . Later on he said that was when he knew I wasn't

Photographer Ted Dinsmore snapped this award-winning shot of Marilyn Bell at the Sunnyside breakwater after he was ferried into position by his water taxi driver, fellow Islander Jimmy Jones Sr. The shot changed the course of his career — shortly thereafter he began working full-time as a staff photographer for the Toronto Star.

Courtesy the Dinsmore family

Along the Shore

going to give up and he took so much criticism for that, so much criticism. . . . You know it's not pretty. Marathon swimming is not pretty.

Fuelled by those moments of anger and frustration and beyond the point of exhaustion, Bell put her face back in the water. Buffeted by strong winds from the east, she was driven almost parallel to the shore and away from the Exhibition grounds. She would swim many miles more than the agreed distance as she inched ever closer to the Toronto shore. As darkness fell, Bell took her last tormented strokes toward Toronto. A motley flotilla bearing businessmen in suits, mothers with babies, and harbour officials had gathered around her and onlookers had crowded the breakwater just off the beach to share in these final moments of her journey, willing her to shore.

Marilyn Bell was drifting in and out of consciousness and does not remember the frantic crowds, the joyous cacophony, and the exploding rocket flares as she approached the shore a mile west of the Exhibition grounds on September 9, 1954. But when she touched the breakwater with her left hand, she claimed Lake Ontario for our own.

CHAPTER SIX

Destruction and Loss

A month after Marilyn Bell came to shore just west of the Exhibition grounds, every Torontonian's eyes were again turned to the lake, but this time to face a catastrophic force that slammed into the lakefront on the afternoon of October 15, 1954. Hurricane Hazel cut a wide swath of destruction along the greater Toronto shore area and up its river valleys, including its far eastern reaches.

Just east of the Rouge River, my own mother's life "flashed before her eyes" as she and her lifelong friend Jane Lenartz (née Roberts) were bowled off their feet into what was a normally placid Petticoat Creek. The girls were swept out into the lake and at the mercy of the howling wind, driving rain, and waves that crashed headlong into the shore. In the end it was the trunk of an old felled willow tree that saved them; Jane grabbed onto the tree and then onto my mother, and as they inched their way through its branches toward shore, the tree steadfastly refused to be dislodged from the beach. Though the vicious storm affected all of the Toronto region, and southern Ontario, it saved the worst of its wrath for the Humber River, Etobicoke Creek, and the Lakeshore.

Rescuers wade into the swollen Humber River in October 1954 YUL/CTSC, *Toronto Telegram* fonds, ASC05565

We have earlier touched on the "freshets" that periodically wreaked havoc on the Humber River Valley in the nineteenth century, wiping out bridges, gristmills, and sawmills. The deforestation that occurred on the tablelands into the twentieth century, coupled with the development that took place in the river valley, only increased the intensity of these floods — a circumstance that was repeated along the banks of Metropolitan Toronto's other waterways, including the Don and the Rouge. By the 1950s, with a substantial number of people now actually living in the valley flood plains of Toronto and vicinity, Hazel's devastation was a nightmare waiting to happen.

North of the Lakeshore, part of the Lawrence Avenue Bridge was swept away by the rushing torrent, and the river's next target was the community of homes a little farther south, at the lower end of Raymore Drive. As the river burst its banks, the angry water severed the footbridge to the north; houses were lifted off their foundations and launched into the deluge. When it was all over, more than thirty people were killed from this community alone. Farther south, near Dundas Street, the Humber swept five Etobicoke volunteer firemen into its churning clutches, claiming their lives. As the storm boiled downstream to Lake Shore Road's Humber Bridge, it carried with it battered homes, cars, pianos, and corpses.

George Chowns was one of many CN Railway employees who stood on the rail-

way bridge near the mouth of the river that night. The roar of the water was so loud that "you could have shot a cannon off the bridge and not heard it," while "the streetcar lines on the Lakeshore bridge hung like ribbons." For what seemed like an eternity, Chowns and others stood on top of the railway bridge and threw coal and stone down on the surface to stabilize it, while it pitched and trembled under their feet. Thanks in large part to their efforts, the railway bridge held. According to Chowns, the storm demolished the western approach to the Lakeshore bridge, and so the rail line served as a vital link between the city and the lands west of the Humber in the days to come. Farther to the west, the hurricane tore through the Island Road community on the previously mentioned flats at the mouth of Etobicoke Creek in Long Branch.

Some full-time residents of the flats clung to the roofs and rafters of their houses as forty-foot homes from the Pleasant Valley Trailer Camp, located just north of the highway on the west side of the creek, surged past them to the outlet of the lake. Few old-timers in Long Branch have forgotten the story of the Thorpe family, who, clinging to their rooftop, passed their four-month-old baby, Nancy, to Deputy Fire Chief Albert Houston. The rest of the family sadly perished after being swept out into the lake.

The day after the storm, along with the police and firefighters, Lakeshore residents, including Chowns, went from house to house in search of survivors. On Forty-Third

Street they found an old couple miraculously still standing in water on their kitchen table. Afraid even to move, the terrified couple had clung to each other all night in the freezing water, praying for the help that finally came.

After the storm came the necessary rebuilding of the area, spearheaded by Long Branch's well-loved reeve, Marie Curtis. Priorities included channelizing Etobicoke Creek and condemning more than 100 homes and cottages in the Island Road community, including a number of residences that were located along the sandy bank in front of the waterway. Lakeshore residents, like many others living in Metropolitan Toronto, would no longer be able to inhabit the flood plains of their waterways, where the deadly torrent of water had been unleashed. By 1957, a new government agency, the Metropolitan Toronto and Region Conservation Authority, would manage the region's green spaces, rivers, biodiversity, and shorelines.

Along with its physical devastation, Hazel and its aftermath signalled an era of decline in the lands west of the Humber. In 1958 Long Branch resident Wayne Carscadden was walking home when he saw a giant plume of smoke rising from the park near the Long Branch Hotel. By the time he got to the fire, the old wooden hotel was lit up "like a pile of orange crates," and in half an hour it was gone. All that remained were some of the original oak and ash trees, many 100 to 150 feet high, now scorched on one side from the intensity of the flame.

By this time, Mimico Creek, once the summer playground of Humber Bay residents and pleasure seekers from across Toronto, was badly degenerated. Fisherman Bill Bonar had already closed up shop, and the Joyces of Port Credit followed suit around the same time, reckoning the lake had been all fished out. During this period, some of the last remaining portions of the smaller creeks throughout the Lakeshore

Islander Ted Dinsmore also captured this image of Mrs. Thorpe Sr. coming to terms with the loss of her son and daughter-in-law on the day after the storm

YUL/CTSC, Toronto Telegram fonds, ASC0557O

Gus Ryder's Lakeshore swimmers, c. 1955. Second from left is one of Ryder's early champions, Lucille Gamble.
Courtesy Wendy Gamble

disappeared underground, trading their natural, time-worn pathways for concrete sewers that flowed out to the lake.

The building of the Queen Elizabeth Way in the 1930s (later renamed the Gardiner Expressway inside the current city limits), increasingly drew people away from the shops and services along the highway. According to some residents, the mass urbanization of the post-war years and the building of Sherway Gardens in the 1960s only contributed to this problem, with fewer and fewer of the well-established mom-and-pop stores on the highway making a go of it.

Just as the Lakeshore shopping area fell into decline, so did the motel strip in Humber Bay. The borderland once occupied by market gardeners, holiday campers, and boy scouts was now increasing the haunt of the nefarious crowd from "the city," including sex workers, drug addicts, and criminals. By 1948, some of the humble dwellings and small businesses north of the Lake Shore Road had been replaced by a massive bakery operation, the forerunner to Mr. Christie Cookies, which is now slated for closure. The Ontario Food Terminal, the primary produce distribution centre for Ontario, was established in the same vicinity in 1954.

By the 1960s the wrecking ball had demolished or dramatically altered most of the gracious homes and estates in Mimico. During a period of political corruption in the 1950s, many of these mansions were replaced with low-rise housing developments along the lake, complete with parking lots that reached down to the water's edge.

The sense of separateness from the city that had always defined the area was dealt a hard blow when in 1967, Mimico, New Toronto, and Long Branch were amalgamated with the Township of Etobicoke, forming the Borough of Etobicoke. By 1998, Etobicoke had graduated to city status and was part of the merger that formed the new City of Toronto. Globalization and post-industrialism, factors far beyond local control, dealt the final blow. The industrial plants, in former days the lifeblood of the Lakeshore, began to close in the 1970s. Goodyear closed its doors in 1987, and in 1992 the Daniels group began constructing a large residential apartment complex on the former industrial site. With Goodyear's closure came the pervasive view that "the Lakeshore will always be held down by its past."

CHAPTER SEVEN

Renewal

It is a testament to the strength of the Lakeshore community that as Toronto moved to a post-industrial economy, the district did not disintegrate into a classic rust belt area, as happened to similarly situated cities and towns across North America. By the time of the Goodyear closure, only a small percentage of the overall community was still working locally. Instead, residents were moving on and joining the commute to the downtown core, only six miles away.

Meanwhile, residents with homes on the lake have started to see real estate values climb as high as the condominium towers being erected along the shore in Humber Bay. The Campbell Soup plant is still on Birmingham Street in New Toronto, but if you want to buy a house by the water, you'll need a million dollars just to get started.

Change is coming to the Lakeshore yet again, and residents are strengthening their ties to Lake Ontario — a constant presence that is central to the shared history of the community. The quadrangle of nineteenth-century buildings on the historic Mimico Asylum grounds is now restored and surrounded by Colonel Samuel Smith Park, which extends down to the lake. The Lakeshore Yacht Club resides at the bottom of the park.

The mouth of Mimico Creek has been rejuvenated, and marshlands have been reintroduced, attracting wildlife back into the once verdant corridor. A new section of the Waterfront Trail and Greenway ambles through the freshly minted Mimico Waterfront Park, extending from Norris Crescent all the way to Humber Bay Park.

In the spirit of Humber Bay's former glory days as a recreational hub, the park contains a fully accessible fishing pier and is home to numerous boating and yachting organizations. The four- and two-storey lighthouses that stood from 1895 at the entrance to the Eastern Gap were acquired by the Mimico Cruising Club and the Etobicoke Yacht Club and are now refurbished and proudly standing in Mimico Harbour.

The rejuvenation of the Lakeshore's waterfront has not been the only change that has come to the district. In recent years, development pressures have been brought to bear in the Lakeshore, much like they have in the Beach community much farther to the east. With pressure mounting from some quarters to build higher and higher condominiums along the lake, the experience of Mimico stands as an example. Mimico-by-the-Lake is currently undergoing a revision process that will result in the formulation of a city-mandated secondary plan that will guide future development in the area. It is hoped that through this process, heritage buildings and unique streetscapes will be preserved while the sense of community and connections to the lake are further strengthened. As past president of the Mimico Residents Association Bob Poldon maintains, plans for future growth will need to take into account the mixed economic nature of the community and that "Mimico is a village in a large city — people are passionate to ensure our village continues."

Despite all this change, the essence of the Lakeshore, its history and its stories, lives on in the old-timers who have survived the transition to the present day. Rather than "held down by its past," perhaps it is better said that the Lakeshore is held together by its past.

———— • ————

IT HAS BEEN SAID that a layer of Dundas shale still lines the lake bed at the foot of Seventh Street, the same shale that was scraped away by stonehookers more than a century ago to build the roads and foundations of old Toronto. In the early days, the first of Gus Ryder's champions would ease themselves down onto the flat, hard surface of the shale, and race to a rock — what the stonehookers referred to as a hardhead — though it has long been buried by lakefill. 5,280 feet out and 5,280 feet back, swimming, turning, being the best they could be. The future of the Lakeshore was built by hard work and industry, by pioneers and fishermen, sailors and swimmers. The events of yesteryear have passed, but Humber Bay, Mimico, New Toronto, and Long Branch remain, forever changed, with new chapters yet to be written.

Epilogue

IN SEARCH OF THE SHORE

FROM THE CORNER of Jane and Bloor Streets in the city of Toronto, you cannot see the lake or hear the water lapping rhythmically against the shore. On any steamy afternoon in late summer, weary mothers in heels are hauling vegetables and kids home for the day, while drivers inch their way west into Etobicoke, bumper to bumper, with few or none giving a thought to the lake.

Yet you can walk north a few blocks on Jane, escape the madness, and clamber down into a deep gully of oak and maple. The city retreats like a distant memory. The coolness of the ravine gives way to the sound of rushing water as the Humber River forms a subterranean pathway to the inland sea. Like a diviner, you continue on your journey to find the water, moving with the river southward.

The city closes in. You pass under the great arch of the Humber Bridge and the mouth of the river spreads open into Lake Ontario, where it dies and is born again in the dark, cold expanse.

— • —

AFTER A VIVID and personal experience with Lake Ontario some fifteen years ago, I began a journey — indeed, the writing of this book — with a simple question: Where am I? The question, so obviously rooted in the innermost nature of place, led me to a detailed examination of the landscape and geography, history and people of the Toronto shore, through the lens of four waterfront communities and districts that retain a connection to Lake Ontario and the natural world: the Scarborough shore, the Beach, the Island, and the Lakeshore. Though each of these areas retains its own unique identity, collectively they are part of the larger, integrated story of Toronto's waterfront history and heritage — a heritage that for decades has gone largely unrecognized.

We have read that in 1934, during the heyday of Sunnyside Amusement Park, tickets were sold to view the torching of one of the last of the Great Lake schooners, the *Lyman M. Davis*. Thousands of thrilled onlookers cheered as the great ship succumbed to the flames and its charred skeleton sank below the surface of the lake forever. Its tortured remains lie out there still, beyond the Palais Royale and the beach.

After the Storm Mike Maclaverty,

TheAccidentalPhotographer.ca

Toronto's waterfront heritage suffered its first body blow with the burning of that old, venerable ship. Some twenty years later, Hurricane Hazel collided head-on with the Toronto shore and cut a swath of destruction through Toronto's river valleys, leaving eighty-one people dead, the vast majority of whom were from the Greater Toronto Area. The demolition of Sunnyside Amusement Park began the next year, and in 1956 the Gardiner Expressway was rammed through the old park grounds, near the shore. It was as though a collective amnesia preceded and followed these events, a forgetting that left many of us unsure of our connection to the water.

Yet a cultural identity is a birthright. It is an inherited group of characteristics that may be forgotten for a time but can never be completely erased. And the water, a fundamental part of our identity as Torontonians, slips back into our consciousness at unexpected moments, as when we suddenly glimpse the lake through the buildings of the downtown core or from above while weaving through traffic on the Gardiner Expressway.

We have heard the lament time and again that Toronto is bereft of a shared mythology

— a common creation story that gives this city a deep sense of identity and purpose. Yet at least part of that story may be found in the rich seam of our own past that is rooted at the water's edge, a past that is alive in the depths of the ravines that lead down to the shore and the waterfront communities and districts outlined in this book. As Amy Lavender Harris notes in *Imagining Toronto*, even the origin of Toronto's name, "trees standing in water," leads us down an ancient pathway through the wilderness and along a river valley that gradually descends toward the inland sea.

One of our greatest challenges in this century will be to envision Toronto again as a waterfront community. To do this, we will have to learn to respect our past — to value and protect both our established and developing waterfront communities and districts and to cherish the history and the stories that are central to our own unique waterfront culture. Marilyn Bell's triumph, William Ward's tragedy, R.C. Harris's endurance, the Goldring family's ingenuity, Spencer and Rosa Clark's vision and creativity, all these stories and others like them resonate and transcend the diverse cultures and creeds of our forward-thinking, post-modern city. Collectively, they are our stories.

As Norman Jewison said to me, "It was the lake that pulled us together." For people who come from the past and the present and from every corner of the world, there can be no better way for all of us to appreciate each other as neighbours, and for our children to come to know one another as friends, than to walk and to wander, to rest and to play, to splash and to picnic side by side along the lakeshore of our own hometown.

Torontonians are busy people. We need only to find our way back to the water — to descend into a ravine, to gaze out from the Bluffs, to meander the Boardwalk, or board a ferry for the Island — to experience the history that lives along the shore.

Epilogue

ACKNOWLEDGEMENTS

I OWE A DEBT of gratitude to Roger Boulton, who edited the first draft of *Along the Shore* and who has been an unfailing source of encouragement, assistance, and support throughout this lengthy process.

Any work of local history is ultimately a collaborative effort. It's the alchemy of historical fact, blended with the anecdotes and remembrances of people, places, and events, that has breathed life into this project. I'd like to thank the scores of Torontonians who shared their photographs, artwork, and stories about living along the shore. Your life experiences, and the friendships that have been forged, will remain with me for a lifetime.

Along the Shore is based on a period of research that spans more than a decade. The foundations of that research have been strengthened through the contributions of historians, archaeologists, academics, archivists, librarians, city and other government officials, private institutions, authors, artists, and photographers who have generously given of their time, expertise, and talent. I would also like to thank Wayne LeFort, the principal photographer on the project, and Keith Ellis for their dedication and technical expertise throughout.

I would specifically like to thank those who provided comment on the text, including Wayne Reeves, Chief Curator, Museum Services, Toronto; Martin Cooper and Robert MacDonald of Archaeological Services Inc.; Nancy Gaffney, Dena Lewis, Margie Kenedy and the staff of the Toronto and Region Conservation Authority; historian Donald Smith; author Kevin Bazzana; John Carley of Friends of the Spit; Michelle Holmes and Vicki MacDonald at Rouge Park; local historians Michael Harrison and Jane Beecroft O.M.C.; Professors Victor Konrad and Ian Brookes; Ken Bingham; Graham Segger; Liz Amer; and James Bow. Thanks also to Donald Bastian, who believed in this project from the very beginning — your professional assistance was invaluable.

I would like to also recognize Colin McFarquhar and Laurie Leclair of Leclair Historical Research, and Jeremy Hopkin for their tremendous ongoing assistance with targeted research tasks. I've also benefitted from the assistance of numerous archival institutions, libraries, and others, including Alan Walker and the staff at the Toronto Public Library; Alex Avdichuk and Lisa Buchanan at Museum Services, Toronto; Marlaine Koehler of the Waterfront Regeneration Trust; John Court at the CAMH Archives; Jeff Hubbell at the Toronto Port Authority; the staff at the City of Toronto

Archives, Archives of Ontario, Library and Archives Canada, Marine Museum of the Great Lakes, Roman Catholic Archdiocese of Toronto, Archives of the Sisters of St. Joseph (Toronto), Montgomery's Inn, and the Clara Thomas Archives and Special Collections, York University. Thanks also to Fortunato Aglialoro, Dena Doroszenko, Dana Poulton, Scarlett Janusas, Jay Bascom, Andrea Carnevale, Matthew Wilkinson, Michael Levine, Richard Hicken, Barbara Breuner, Tona Dodge, Rachel Keane, Richard Harris, Gillian Watts, Moyra Rodger, Lana Deluca, Gary Travis, and Cindy Vail — all your contributions have enriched this book.

I have also benefitted from the assistance of those who have dedicated themselves to the preservation of memory and the protection of the natural world in the waterfront communities in which they live, or have lived, including Albert and Emily Fulton and Peter Holt of the Toronto Island Archives, Wendy Gamble of the New Toronto Historical Society, Gene Domagala and Kevin McConnell in the Beach, Richard Schofield of the Scarborough Historical Society, Denise Harris of the Etobicoke Historical Society, Tom Mohr and John Sabean of the Pickering Historical Society, Madeleine McDowell, Jaan Pill (Preserved Stories), Paul Chomik, Natalie Lisowiec, and Bert Crandall.

Thanks to my husband, children, and dear family and friends who stood by me and celebrated the little benchmarks along the way to building this book — to each of you I am truly grateful.

And finally I'd like to thank my editor Jennifer Knoch, designer Tania Craan, production manager Carolyn McNeillie, typesetter Kendra Martin, publisher Jack David, and the whole team at ECW Press for taking on this project and shepherding it through to its successful conclusion — it has been a wonderful, illuminating journey.

Jane Fairburn
Doire Naomh,
Scarborough Bluffs, 2013

WORKS CITED

The following works are mentioned in the text. An appendix of interviews conducted during the course of research for *Along the Shore*, including interviews referred to by the author in the text, is available online at JaneFairburn.com.

INTRODUCTION

Raweno:kwas, William Woodworth. "Foreword." In *The Archaeological Master Plan of the Central Waterfront — City of Toronto, Ontario*. Prepared for Heritage Preservation Services, Archaeological Services, Toronto, 2003.

Williamson, Ronald F., ed. *The Archaeological Master Plan of the Central Waterfront — City of Toronto, Ontario*. Prepared for Heritage Preservation Services, Archaeological Services, Toronto, 2003.

PART ONE: THE SCARBOROUGH SHORE

Adam, Graeme Mercer, and Charles Pelham Mulvany. *History of Toronto and County of York, Containing an Outline of the History of the Dominion of Canada; A History of the City of Toronto and the County of York, with the Townships, Towns, Villages, Churches, School; General and Local Statistics; Biographical Sketches, Etc., Etc.*, vols. 1 and 2. Toronto: C. Blackett Robinson, 1885.

Allen, Don. "The Willows Park." *Scarborough Historical Notes and Comments* 22 (2011).

Archives of the Sisters of St. Joseph, Toronto. Annals of the Sisters of St. Joseph. 1919.

Bascom, Jay, ed. "Ship of the Month No. 49 Alexandria." *Scanner* 7, no. 8 (1975).

Belisle, Donica. "A Labour Force for the Consumer Century: Commodification in Canada's Largest Department Stores, 1890 to 1940." *Labour/Le Travail* (Fall 2006).

Benn, Carl. "The History of Toronto: An 11,000-year Journey." City of Toronto Museums and Heritage Services, 2006. www.toronto.ca/culture/history/credits.htm.

Bonis, Robert, ed. *A History of Scarborough*. Scarborough: Scarborough Public Library, 1968.

Booth, Karen Marshall, ed. *The People Cry — "Send Us Priests": The First Seventy-five Years of St. Augustine's Seminary of Toronto, 1913–1988*. Toronto: Metro Press, 1988.

Bouchette, Joseph. *The British Dominions in North America; Or, A Topographical and Statistical Description of the Provinces of Lower and Upper Canada, New Brunswick, Nova Scotia, the Islands of Newfoundland, Prince Edward, and Cape Breton*. London: Longman, Rees, Orme, Brown, Green, and Longman, 1832. Reprinted, Charleston, SC: Nabu Press, 2010.

Boyle, David, ed. *The Township of Scarboro 1796–1896*. Toronto: William Briggs, 1896.

Brown, Ron. *Toronto's Lost Villages*. Toronto: Polar Bear Press, 1997.

Brown, William. *America: A Four Years' Residence in the United States and Canada*. Leeds: William Brown, 1849. www.archive.org/details/americaafouryea00browgoog.

Canniff, William. "An Historical Sketch of the County of York." *Illustrated Historical Atlas of the County of York*. Toronto: Miles and Co., 1878.

Carr, Margaret. "Extracts from the Letters of Ruth McCowan and John Heron, 1916–1919." *Scarborough Historical Notes and Comments* 13, no. 1 (S/F 1989).

Cavanagh, Jack. "Parks in Scarborough Remembered: Leisure, Amusements, Picnics and Dancing." *Scarborough Historical Notes and Comments* 11, no. 2 (November 1987).

Census records for 1861, Ward 2, as reported by Census Enumerators, "Scarborough in 1861," *Scarborough Historical Notes and Comments* 1, no. 1 (November 1976).

Central Mortgage and Housing Corporation. *67 Homes for Canadians*. (Catalogue). Ottawa, 1947.

Charron, Mathieu. *Neighbourhood Characteristics and the Distribution of Police-reported Crime in the City of Toronto*. Ottawa: Statistics Canada, Canadian Centre for Justice Statistics, 2009. statcan.gc.ca/pub/85-561-m/85-561-m2009018-eng.htm.

Clark, S.D. *The Suburban Society*. Toronto: University of Toronto Press, 1966.

Coleman, A.P., H.L. Kerr, F.B. Taylor. "Map of Toronto and Vicinity." *Annual Report of the Bureau of Mines*. 22, ARM22G (1913).

Dollier de Casson, François. *A History of Montreal 1640–1672*. New York: Dutton & Co., 1928.

Einstein, Albert. March 21, 1955, as quoted in *The Oxford Dictionary of Quotations*, 5th ed. Oxford University Press, 1999.

Evening Telegram, "Six Years in Building; an Asset to Kingston Road." July 20, 1920.

Eyles, Nicholas. "Ravines, Lagoons, Cliffs and Spits: The Ups and Downs of Lake Ontario." In *HTO: Toronto's Water from Lake Iroquois to Lost Rivers to Low-flow Toilets*. Toronto: Coach House Books, 2008.

———. *Toronto Rocks: The Geological Legacy of the Toronto Region*, 2nd ed. Toronto: Fitzhenry & Whiteside, 2004.

Globe and Mail. "Cecil White." July 8, 1946.

Gray, William. A *History of the Toronto Hunt 1843–1993*. Scarborough: Toronto Hunt Club, 1993.

Guillet, Edwin C. *Pioneer Life in the County of York*. Toronto: Edwin C. Guillet, 1946.

Hall, Basil. *Travels in North America in the Years 1827 and 1828*, vol. 1. Philadelphia: Carey, Lea & Carey, 1829.

Harris, Richard. *Unplanned Suburbs: Toronto's American Tragedy 1900 to 1950*. Baltimore: The Johns Hopkins University Press, 1996.

Havard, Gilles. *The Great Peace of Montreal of 1701: French-Native Diplomacy in the Seventeenth Century.* Montreal: McGill-Queen's University Press, 2001. English translation of the Montreal Treaty, 1701; see Appendix III, pp. 210–215.

Higginson, T.B. "Alexander Glendinning — 'The Scarborough Settler.'" *Scarborough Historical Notes and Comments* 2, no. 4 (November 1978).

Hinde, George Jennings. "The Glacial and Interglacial Strata of Scarboro' Heights and Other Localities Near Toronto, Ontario." *Canadian Journal of Science* (new series) 15, (1878): 388–413.

Jones, Augustus. "Names of the Rivers, and Creeks, as they are Called by the Mississaugas . . ." Archives of Ontario, RG 1-2-1, vol. 32, Correspondence relating to surveys, reel MS 7433, pp. 103–105. (Many of these names are reproduced in Donald B. Smith, *Sacred Feathers.* Toronto: University of Toronto Press, 1987, pp. 255–257.)

Latta, Martha. *The Guild Log Cabin*, AkGt-51. Report to the Minister of Citizenship, Culture, and Recreation, September 1998.

Lidgold, Carole. *The History of the Guild Inn.* Scarborough: Brookridge Publishing House, 2000.

Little, Jean. "The Neilsons of Scarborough." *Scarborough Historical Notes and Comments* 5, no. 2 & 3 (May/September 1981).

MacDonald, Robert I. "Toronto's Natural History." In *Toronto: An Illustrated History of Its First 12,000 Years.* Toronto: James Lorimer & Company, 2008.

Makovsky, Paul, ed. *The Stuff Dreams Are Made Of: The Art and Design of Frederick and Louise Coates.* (Catalogue). Toronto: Governing Council, University of Toronto, University of Toronto Library, 1997.

Mayer, Pihl, Poulton and Associates. *The Archaeological Master Plan Study of the Northeast Scarborough Study Area: An Interim Report — Survey Methods and Results.* Submitted to the City of Scarborough, November 1988.

Mays, John Bentley. *Emerald City: Toronto Visited.* Toronto: Penguin, 1994.

McCarthy, Doris. *A Fool in Paradise: An Artist's Early Years.* Toronto: Macfarlane Walter & Ross, 1990.

McCowan, D.B. "A Lakefront Estate Residential Development, 1890–1940, An Introduction." *Scarborough Historical Notes and Comments* 13, no. 2 (S/F 1989).

———. "The McCowans of Scarborough." *Scarborough Historical Notes and Comments* 7, no. 4, supplement (November 1983).

———. *Neigh the Front: Exploring Scarboro Heights.* Toronto: The Scarboro Heights Record and The James McCowan Memorial Social History Society, 2001.

McCowan, James. Letter to William Begg. In *Neigh the Front: Exploring Scarboro Heights,* Toronto: The Scarboro Heights Record and The James McCowan Memorial Social History Society, 2001.

McLachlan, W.W. "Royal Canadian Air Force Personnel on Radar in Canada During World War II." www.rquirk.com/cdnradar/cor/chapter20.pdf.

The Metropolitan Toronto and Region Conservation Authority. *Integrated Shoreline Management Plan: Tommy Thompson Park to Frenchman's Bay.* December 1996. www.trca.on.ca/trca-user-uploads/ IntegratedShorelineManagementPlan.pdf.

Middleton, W.E. Knowles. *Radar Development in Canada: The Radio Branch of the National Research Council of Canada 1939–1946.* Waterloo: Wilfrid Laurier University Press, 1981.

Moodie, Susanna. *Roughing It in the Bush.* London: Richard Bentley, 1852. www.digital.library.upenn .edu/women/moodie/roughing/roughing.html.

Mosser, Christine, ed. *York, Upper Canada Minutes of Town Meetings and Lists of Inhabitants 1793–1823.* Toronto: Metropolitan Toronto Library Board, 1984.

Myrvold, Barbara. *The People of Scarborough: A History.* Toronto: Public Library Board, 1997.

Patent Plan, Scarborough Township, 1811, Archives of Ontario, RG 1-100, Patent Plans, Scarborough Township, Map No. A25, Container C-52, barcode D752020.

Reeves, Wayne C. *Regional Heritage Features on the Metropolitan Toronto Waterfront: A Report to the Metropolitan Toronto Planning Department.* Toronto: Metropolitan Toronto Planning Department, 1992.

Reeves, Wayne, and Christina Palassio, ed. *HTO: Toronto's Water from Lake Iroquois to Lost Rivers to Low-flow Toilets.* Toronto: Coach House Books, 2008.

Robertson, J. Ross, ed. *The Diary of Mrs. Simcoe.* Toronto: William Briggs, 1911.

———. *Robertson's Landmarks of Toronto: A Collection of Historical Sketches of the Old Town of York from 1792 Until 1833 and from 1834 to 1914,* vols. 1–6. Toronto: J. Ross Robertson, 1894–1914.

Robinson, Percy J. *Toronto During the French Régime, 1615–1793,* 2nd ed. Toronto: University of Toronto Press, 1965.

Ryan, Grace, ed. *The Log Cabin at the Guild, Scarborough: Historical and Archaeological Research.* Toronto: Municipality of Metropolitan Toronto, 1996.

Scarborough Settler's Lament. youtube.com/watch?v=HIjFgsDAZWM.

Scheler, Auguste. *Dictionnaire d'étymologie française d'après les résultats de la science moderne.* Bruxelles: M.W. Weissenbruch, 1873.

Schofield, Richard, Meredyth Schofield, and Karen Whynot. *Scarborough: Then and Now (1796–1996),* 3rd printing, revised. Heritage Scarborough, 1997.

Schroeder, Bruce. "Evidence for Early Human Presence in Scarborough." *Scarborough Historical Notes and Comments* 8, no. 1 (W/S 1989).

Seton, Ernest Thompson. "Seton's Ashbridge's." In *Ashbridge's Bay: An Anthology of Writings by Those Who Knew and Loved Ashbridge's Bay*. Toronto: Toronto Ornithological Club, 1998.

Snider, C.H.J. Schooner Days columns, *The Evening Telegram*
    "The Last of the Stonehookers." Marine Museum of the Great Lakes, Schooner Days Index, no. 117.
    "One Try for the Treasure: Rainbow's End in Highland Creek Marsh." August 15, 1942.
    "Perhaps This Solves Highlands' Secret." November 29, 1941.
    "In Search of Frenchman's Bay." September 23, 1944.
    "Turning Back Clock — Builder's List Does It." July 13, 1935.

Spilsbury, John. *Fact and Folklore*. Cobourg, ON: Haynes Printing Company, 1973.

Stamp, Robert M. *Riding the Radials: Toronto's Suburban Electric Streetcar Lines*. Erin, ON: Boston Mills Press, 1989.

Toronto & Canadian Building Company brochure (promoting Sandown Park), c. 1913. London and Toronto.

Toronto Daily Star
    "Edgely Park Right on the Car Line." May 17, 1912.
    "'I Just Took a Line,' Says Hero Modestly." August 4, 1915.
    "James F. Harris." October 17, 1955.
    "Opening Sale: Kalmar Heights, October 21st to 26th." October 22, 1912.
    "Park Hill, Scarboro, Lakeside Homes for Particular People." September 22, 1911.
    "Ready to Start on Scarboro $50,000,000 Community." April 9, 1955.
    "Rouge Hills: A Wonderful Place to Live." June 30, 1926.
    "Suburban Bungalows 'Kingston Road.'" October 23, 1913.
    "Tear Down House Ere It Falls Over Bluff: 18 Others in Danger." February 21, 1951.

Toronto Purchase of 1787. *Indenture Made at the Carrying Place, head of the Bay of Quinté the twenty-third day of September, in the year of Our Lord one thousand seven hundred and eighty seven*, vol. 1. Saskatoon: Fifth House Publishers, 1992.

Toronto Purchase Settlement. Ref. #2-3420, "Canada and the Mississaugas of the New Credit First Nation Celebrate Historic Claim Settlement," dated October 29, 2010. See Aboriginal Affairs and Northern Development Canada at www.aadnc-aandc.gc.ca.

Treaty 13 of 1805. *Indenture made at the River Credit on Lake Ontario on the first day of August in the Year of Our Lord one thousand eight hundred and five between William Claus, Esquire, Deputy Superintendent General and Deputy Inspector General of Indians and of their Affairs . . . and the Principal Chiefs, Warriors and people of the Mississague Nation of Indians*, no. 13 in Canada, *Indian Treaties and Surrenders*, vol. 1. Saskatoon: Fifth House Publishers, 1992.

Vartanian, Hrag. "Chine Drive: An Arts and Crafts suburb and its context." *The Stuff Dreams Are Made*

Of: The Art and Design of Frederick and Louise Coates. Toronto: University of Toronto Library, 1996.

Waterfront Toronto. Waterfront Toronto: Archaeological Conservation and Management Strategy. Prepared by Archaeological Services Inc., Toronto, October 2008. www.waterfrontoronto.ca/about_us/history_and_heritage/archaeological_conservation_and_management_strategy.

Williams Treaties of 1923. Library and Archives Canada, RG10, vol. 1853, ITs 483-488, microfilm reel T-9941.

Williamson, Ronald F., and Robert I. MacDonald. "A Resource Like No Other: Understanding the 11,000-Year-Old Relationship Between People and Water." In *HTO: Toronto's Water from Lake Iroquois to Lost Rivers to Low-flow Toilets.* Toronto: Coach House Books, 2008.

Young, Peter. *Let's Dance: A Celebration of Ontario's Dance Halls and Summer Dance Pavilions.* Toronto: Natural Heritage/Natural History Inc., 2002.

PART TWO: THE BEACH

Adam, Graeme Mercer, and Charles Pelham Mulvany. *History of Toronto and County of York, Containing an Outline of the History of the Dominion of Canada; A History of the City of Toronto and the County of York, with the Townships, Towns, Villages, Churches, School; General and Local Statistics; Biographical Sketches, Etc., Etc.,* vols. 1 and 2. Toronto: C. Blackett Robinson, 1885.

Baird, George. "Waterworks: A Commentary." *Artviews* (S/S 1988).

Bazzana, Kevin. *Wondrous Strange: The Life and Art of Glenn Gould.* Toronto: McClelland & Stewart, 2003.

Beaches Living Guide. "Lost Villages of Norway and Ben Lamond." *Beaches Living.* December 6, 2011. www.beachesliving.ca/pages/index.php?act=landmark&id=9.

Bonnycastle, R.H. *No. 1 Plan of the Town and Harbour of York Upper Canada, 1833.* Library and Archives Canada, NMC 16818.

Bouchette, Joseph. *Joseph Bouchette's Plan of Toronto Harbour with the Rocks, Shoals, & Soundings, 1792.* Toronto Public Library, T [1792]/4Msm.

———. *Plan of York Harbour,* 1815. Toronto Public Library T1815/fold.

Boyer, Barbaranne. *The Boardwalk Album: Memories of the Beach.* Erin, ON: Boston Mills Press, 1988 (reprinted 2000).

Campbell, Mary, and Barbara Myrvold. *The Beach in Pictures, 1793–1932.* Toronto: Toronto Public Library, 1988.

———. *Historical Walking Tour of Kew Beach,* revised edition. Toronto: Toronto Public Library Board, 1995.

Careless, J.M.S. *Toronto to 1918: An Illustrated History.* Toronto: Lorimer and National Museum of Man, National Museums of Canada, 1984.

Carroll, Jock. *Glenn Gould: Some Portraits of the Artist as a Young Man*. Toronto: Stoddart, 1995.

Cauz, Louis. *The Woodbine 1875–1993*. Canada: Old Woodbine Memorabilia, 1997.

Cities: Glenn Gould's Toronto. Director John McGreevy, TV film, 1979. See "Glenn Gould's Toronto — The Complete Film,"parts 1-6 on YouTube.

Commins, Cathy, and Olga Marie Commins. "A History of Balmy Beach." *Ward 9 News*, April 8, 1980.

Death Registration of Dr. William Daniel Young. Archives of Ontario, RG 80-8, 1918, vol. 1, #1078, reel MS 935/238.

Domagala, Gene. "A History Tour of the Beach." *Travel and Transitions*. www.travelandtransitions.com/ inspiring-you/interesting-and-inspiring-people/beach-mission-mercy-gene-domagala/3/.

Doroszenko, Dena, and Martha Latta. "'Down by the Bay': The Ashbridge Estate in Toronto, ON." Prepared for the Council for Northeast Archaeology Annual Meeting, St. Mary's City, Maryland, Oct. 22–24, 1999.

E.R.A. Architects Inc. "Balmy Beach Heritage Conservation District Study: Balmy Avenue." Toronto, June 6, 2006. www.toronto.ca/heritage-preservation/hcd_balmy_beach.htm.

Ellis, Frank. *Canada's Flying Heritage*. Toronto: University of Toronto Press, 1954.

Evening Telegram. "Record Crowds at Beaches." August 16, 1920.

Fairfield, George, ed. *Ashbridge's Bay: An Anthology of Writings by Those Who Knew and Loved Ashbridge's Bay*. Toronto: Toronto Ornithological Club, 1998.

Fulford, Robert. *Accidental City: The Transformation of Toronto*. Toronto: Macfarlane Walter & Ross, 1995.

———. "Memories of the Beach: The Evolution of a Village in Our Biggest City." *Canadian Geographic*, December 1989/January 1990.

Globe
  "Balmy Beach." August 3, 1901.
  "Cross Country Flight." August 14, 1909.
  "To Fly Over the Lake." August 24, 1909.
  "New French Aviator." August 9, 1909.
  "Willard Flies." September 10, 1909.

Gould, Glenn. Autobiographical Notes (unpublished), 1982. The Glenn Gould Archive, Library and Archives Canada, Ottawa (MUS 109), Writings, 22, 25: p. 3.

———. Letter to Mr. Albert Emid Jr., April 20, 1961. The Glenn Gould Archive, Library and Archives Canada, Ottawa (MUS 109), Correspondence (Outgoing): 31, 14, 30.

Howard, Marjorie. The History of the Beaches District. Unpublished. 1938.

Hume, Christopher. "Toronto's Accidental Treasure." *Toronto Star*, April 13, 2008.

Jewison, Norman. *This Terrible Business Has Been Good to Me*. Toronto: Key Porter, 2004.

Lang, Dawson. "Biographical sketches of Hillyard and Norman Lang." Lang family photographs and papers. Toronto Port Authority, 1988.

Lang family fonds. Special fishery license issued to George Lang, 1894. Lang family photographs and papers, 1894–1988. Toronto Port Authority, SC 40/1.

Mannell, Steven. "A Civic Vision for Water Supply: The Toronto Water Works Extension Project." In *HTO: Toronto's Water from Lake Iroquois to Lost Rivers to Low-flow Toilets*. Toronto: Coach House Books, 2008.

Masemann (Ward), Vandra, Donna Halliday (Robb), and Paula Warder. *Malvern Collegiate Institute Centennial Book*. Toronto: Britannia, 2003.

McGrath, Paul. "The Lost Village of Norway." *Toronto Tree* (September 2005). www.ontarioroots.com/content/04/04_02/article_004.html.

McGreevy, John, ed. *Glenn Gould: Variations*. Toronto: Doubleday, 1983.

Monthly Reports of the Department of Public Health, October 1918, City of Toronto Archives, Fonds 200, Series 365, file 21, Box 225022, folio 2.

Ondaatje, Michael. *In the Skin of a Lion*. Toronto: McClelland & Stewart, 1987.

Peak, William. Letter to Sir Francis Bond Head, April 12, 1837. Archives of Ontario, Upper Canada Land Petitions, reel #C-2732.

"Plane Lands on Beach." *Beach Metro Community News* 23, no. 13 (October 11, 1994).

Reeve, Ted. *More Beach Reminuisances*. Beaches Library Local History Collection.

Reeves, Wayne C. *Regional Heritage Features on the Metropolitan Toronto Waterfront: A Report to the Metropolitan Toronto Planning Department*. Toronto: Metropolitan Toronto Planning Department, 1992.

———. "Building Storeys — Architect Unveiled: T.C. Pomphrey and the R.C. Harris Water Treatment Plant." Spacing.ca. February 10, 2010.

Robertson, J. Ross. *Robertson's Landmarks of Toronto: A Collection of Historical Sketches of the Old Town of York from 1792 Until 1833 and from 1834 to 1914*, vols. 1–6. Toronto: J. Ross Robertson, 1894–1914.

Saloranta, Kevin, ed. "The Church of St. John the Baptist Norway," 2002. St. John the Baptist Norway, 470 Woodbine Avenue, Toronto.

Scadding, Henry, D.D. *Toronto of Old*, 2nd ed. Toronto: Willing & Williamson, 1878.

Smith, Frank. "Hunting Days." In *Ashbridge's Bay: An Anthology of Writings by Those Who Knew and Loved Ashbridge's Bay*. Toronto: Toronto Ornithological Club, 1998.

Smyth, Sir David William. *A Short Topographical Description of His Majesty's Province of Upper Canada in North America: To Which Is Annexed a Provincial Gazetteer*. London: W. Faden, 1799.

Snider, C.H.J. Schooner Days column, *The Evening Telegram*.
 "Brothers Under Horns." February 4, 1933.
 "Roving with The Rover — 3: One 24th of May." Beaches Library Local History Collection.
 "Roving with The Rover — 4: Little Wood Box." Beaches Library Local History Collection.

Stott, Greg. "Canada Journal: The Beaches, Toronto, Ontario: Streets of Attitude." *Equinox* (September/October 1991).

Taylor, Robert. "Saw-whet Owls." In *Ashbridge's Bay: An Anthology of Writings by Those Who Knew and Loved Ashbridge's Bay*. Toronto: Toronto Ornithological Club, 1998.

Temple, Joseph. Waterfront Dreams. Unpublished. Beaches Library Local History Collection, September 2009.

Toronto Daily Star
 "On the Site of Scarboro Beach Amusement Park and Athletic Grounds There Are Now — Over 50 Homes Ready for Sale." Advertisement. September 23, 1926.
 "Crowd of 2,000 Saw Memorial Unveiled." August 3, 1920.

Toronto Harbour Commissioners. *Toronto Waterfront Development, 1912–1920*. Toronto, [1913]. Fonds 2, series 60, item 1968, box 225027.

Toronto Patriot. "Norway Steam Sawmill, City of Toronto." June 2, 1835.

Toronto Star
 Millar, Cal. "Plane Lands on City Beach." September 29, 1994.
 Smith, Greg. "A World Away." April 13, 2008.

Toronto Urban Design Guidelines: Queen Street East, Coxwell Avenue to Nursewood Road. Toronto City Planning, 2012. www.toronto.ca/legdocs/mmis/2012/te/bgrd/backgroundfile-51604.pdf.

Toronto World. "The Ashbridge Bay District." November 3, 1894.

"Toronto's First Synagogues." Beach Hebrew Institute, 2006.

Townsend, Robert B. *Tales from the Great Lakes*. Toronto: Dundurn, 1995.

———. *When Canvas Was King, Captain John Williams: Master Mariner*. Carrying Place: Odyssey Publishing, 2001.

PART THREE: THE ISLAND
Amer, Liz. *Yes We Can! How to Organize Citizen Action*. Ottawa: Synergistics Consulting, 1980.

Baldwin, Dr. William Warren. Letter to Pheobe Baldwin, April 2, 1812. Archives of Ontario, F 17, William Baldwin family fonds, reel MS 88/1.

———. Letter to William Firth, April 22, 1812. Archives of Ontario, F 17, William Baldwin family fonds, reel MS 88/1.

Berton, Pierre. "The Greatest Oarsman of All Time." *Reader's Digest*, April 1984. Condensed from *My Country: The Remarkable Past*. Toronto: McClelland & Stewart, 1976.

Blumenfeld, Hans. *Life Begins After 65*. Montreal: Harvest House, 1987.

Bonnycastle, R.H. *No. 1 Plan of the Town and Harbour of York Upper Canada, 1833*. Library and Archives Canada, NMC 16818.

Ellis, Frank. *Canada's Flying Heritage*. Toronto: University of Toronto Press, 1954.

Fleming, Elizabeth J., ed. *The Song of Hiawatha by Henry Wadsworth Longfellow: Edited, with an Introduction, Biographical and Explanatory Notes, and a Pronouncing Vocabulary of Proper Names*. London: Macmillan & Co., 1905.

Gibson, Sally. *More Than an Island*. Toronto: Irwin Publishing, 1984.

———. "Visiting John Paul's Ghost." *Canadian Heritage* 13, no. 4 (1987): 6-7.

Globe
> "Captain W. Ward Dead: 184 Lives to His Credit." January 25, 1912.
> "Crosses Lake on Bicycle in Ten Hours." July 15, 1935.
> "Deplorable Accident: Five Sisters Drowned in the Bay." May 12, 1862.
> "The Late Captain Ward." January 26, 1912.
> "The Melancholy Accident on Sunday." May 1862.
> "A Triumph for Aviators: Raced from Hamilton." August 3, 1911.

Globe and Mail
> Chandler, Al. "Island Made in Hurricane." December 18, 1954.
> "Traffic Volume Makes Toronto Air Capital." March 1, 1962.

Hood, Sarah. "J.P. Radelmüller Arrives in Canada." Suite101.com. January 3, 2009.

Jacobs, Jane. *The Death and Life of Great American Cities*. New York: Random House, 1961.

Jones, Michael. "Durnan's Song." 2004.

Jones, Peter. *History of the Ojebway Indians; With Especial Reference to Their Conversion to Christianity*. London: Houlston and Wright, Paternoster Row, 1861.

MacEwen, Gwendolyn. "Animal Syllables." *The Fire Eaters*. Ottawa: Oberon Press, 1982.

———. "Dark Pines Under Water." *The Shadow Maker*. Toronto: Macmillan, 1972.

Mail and Empire. "Water-bike Rider Wins Tilt with Lake Ontario." July 15, 1935.

Marriage record of Chief George King to Susannah Russell, October 7, 1863. Archives of Ontario, RG

Works Cited

80-27-2, County Marriage Registers, vol. 1, Brant County, p. 126, reel MS 248/5.

Nowell, Iris. *Painters Eleven: The Wild Ones of Canadian Art.* Vancouver: Douglas & McIntyre, 2010.

O'Brien, Brendan. *Speedy Justice: The Tragic Last Voyage of His Majesty's Vessel Speedy.* Toronto: University of Toronto Press for the Osgoode Society, 1992.

Order-in-Council, LAC, RG 2, series A-1-a, vol. 1873, P.C. 9439, December 19, 1944.

Radelmüller, J.P. Letter, January 1, 1808. Civil Secretary's Correspondance, Upper Canada, Upper Canada Sundries, January — June 1808, RG 5, A 1, volume 7.

Richardson, Hugh. "York Harbour" (R. Stanton, printer), 1833, photocopy, Toronto Port Authority Archives.

Richmond, John. *A Tearful Tour of Toronto's Riviera of Yesteryear.* Toronto: Macmillan, 1961.

Robertson, J. Ross, ed. *The Diary of Mrs. Simcoe.* Toronto: William Briggs, 1911.

———. *Robertson's Landmarks of Toronto: A Collection of Historical Sketches of the Old Town of York from 1792 Until 1833 and from 1834 to 1914*, vols. 1–6. Toronto: J. Ross Robertson, 1894–1914.

Scadding, Henry, D.D. *Toronto of Old*, 2nd ed. Toronto: Willing & Williamson, 1878.

Scott, David. Letter, March 10, 1909. Albert Fulton subject files. (Now housed at the City of Toronto Archives, Fonds 1047.)

Simcoe, Elizabeth. Letter to Miss Hunt, August 23, 1793. Archives of Ontario, F 1174-3, file 2, J. Ross Robertson family fonds, J. Ross Robertson's Simcoe papers, reel MS 8757.

Smith, Donald. *Sacred Feathers.* Toronto: University of Toronto Press, 1987.

"Snatched 142 from Death: Work of One Life Saver." January 24, 1912. Toronto Public Library, Toronto Public Library Biographical Scrapbooks, vol. 2.

Star Weekly. "65 Years a Dweller on Toronto Island." February 3, 1912.

Stevenson, Connie. "Iceboating on Toronto Bay." Excerpted from *News from the Archives*, March 1977. Toronto Island Archives, Albert Fulton subject files. (Now housed at the City of Toronto Archives, Fonds 1047.)

Summers, John. "The Coldest Sport in the World: Iceboating in Toronto Harbour, 1824–1941." *Material History Review* 35 (Spring 1992): 35–46.

Swadron, Barry. *Pressure Island: The Report of the Commission of Inquiry into the Toronto Islands.* Toronto: Government of Ontario, 1983.

Sward, Robert. *The Toronto Islands: An Illustrated History.* Toronto: Dreadnaught, 1983.

Tobico, James. Affidavit, February 7, 1888, New Credit Reserve. Ontario Archives, R.G. 10, vol. 2238, folder 45, 742, C-12780.

Toronto Daily Star
"The Aviation Meet Opens in Toronto Today." August 3, 1911.
"McCurdy and Willard Flew 35 Miles, Hamilton to Toronto, Successfully." August 3, 1911.

Toronto Harbour Commissioners. *Toronto Waterfront Development, 1912-1920*. Toronto, [1913]. Fonds 2, series 60, item 1968, box 225027.

Williamson, Ronald F., ed. *Toronto: A Short Illustrated History of Its First 12,000 Years*. Toronto: Lorimer, 2008.

The York Gazette. "Died." January 14, 1815.

Young, Peter. *Let's Dance: A Celebration of Ontario's Dance Halls and Summer Dance Pavilions*. Toronto: Natural Heritage/Natural History, 2002.

PART FOUR: THE LAKESHORE
Account books drawn up between Rousseaux and Thomas Barry. Archives of Ontario, Series F 493-1, File 1 (Jean Baptiste Rousseau family genealogical material).

Adam, Graeme Mercer, and Charles Pelham Mulvany. *History of Toronto and County of York, Containing an Outline of the History of the Dominion of Canada; A History of the City of Toronto and the County of York, with the Townships, Towns, Villages, Churches, Schools; General and Local Statistics; Biographical Sketches, Etc., Etc.*, vols. 1 and 2. Toronto: C. Blackett Robinson, 1885.

Addison, Robert. Letter certifying marriage of Margaret Cline and Jean-Baptiste Rousseaux, October 15, 1795, F493, Jean Baptiste Rousseau family fonds, reel MS 7294.

Aitkin, Alexander. Letter to the Honourable John Collins Esq., Deputy Surveyor-General, 1788. In *Toronto During the French Régime, 1615–1793*, 2nd. ed. Toronto: University of Toronto Press, 1965.

Benn, Carl. *The King's Mill on the Humber 1793–1803: Toronto's First Industrial Building*. Etobicoke: Etobicoke Historical Society, 1979.

———. *Historic Fort York: 1793–1993*. Toronto: Natural Heritage/Natural History Inc., 1993.

Bingham and Webber. *A Souvenir of Long Branch*. Promotional brochure, c. 1888.

Bond, I.K. "History of Lakeshore Psychiatric Hospital." Unpublished, July 1976. CAMH Archives, Lakeshore Psychiatric Hospital fonds, 2–18.

Cameron, Wendy, Sheila Haines, and Mary McDougall Maude. *English Immigrant Voices: Labourers' Letters from Upper Canada in the 1830s*. Montreal and Kingston: McGill-Queen's University Press, 2000.

Census Rolls for District Number One of the Township of Etobicoke, 1861, Archives of Ontario, reel C-1087.

Census Rolls for Etobicoke Township, 1851, Archives of Ontario, reel C11761.

Chen, Liwen. "Canada's First Acrodrome: Long Branch Curtiss Aviation School." Local History Files, Heritage Mississauga, 2010.

Works Cited

The City of Toronto and the Home District Commercial Directory (1837). Archives of Ontario, B70, series D-5, reel 2.

Crinnion, C. Archaeological Assessment (Stage 1-3) of TRCA Property in the City of Toronto: Amos Waites Park Project, 2006. On file at the Ministry of Tourism, Culture and Sport.

Currell, Harvey. *The Mimico Story*. Town of Mimico & Library Board, 1967.

Directory of Toronto and Home District for Etobicoke (1837). Archives of Ontario, B70, series D-5, reel 2.

Domesday Book. Archives of Ontario, Archives of Ontario, RG 1-63, no. 3.

Ellis, Frank. *Canada's Flying Heritage*. Toronto: University of Toronto Press, 1954.

Etobicoke Historical Board/Local Architectural Conservation Advisory Committee. *Villages of Etobicoke*. Weston: Argyle Printing Company, 1985.

Evening Telegram
> "Would be 'Act of Savagery' to Burn the Lyman M. Davis." February 1, 1934.
> "Fire Struck Thrill Seekers Watch End of Old Schooner." June 30, 1934.

Filey, Mike. *I Remember Sunnyside*. Toronto: Brownstone Press, 1981.

———. *"The Way We Were": Toronto Sketches 8*. Toronto: Dundurn, 2004.

Firth, Edith G. *The Town of York 1793–1815: A Collection of Documents of Early Toronto*. Toronto: University of Toronto Press for the Champlain Society, 1962.

Fisher, Sidney Thomson. *The Merchant-Millers of the Humber Valley*. Toronto: NC Press, 1985.

Fraser, Alexander. *A History of Ontario: Its Resources and Development*, vol. 1 (2 vols.). Toronto: The Canada History Company, 1907.

Given, Robert A. *Etobicoke Remembered*. Toronto: Pro Familia Publishing, 2007.

———. "New Toronto." Etobicoke Historical Society website. www.etobicokehistorical.com/Stories/New_Toronto/new_toronto.html.

Globe
> "Street Railway Amusements." July 16, 1898.
> "Toronto's Growing Suburb: 'New Toronto' As It Is and What It Will Be." October 25, 1890.

Gourlay, Robert. *Statistical Account of Upper Canada, Compiled with a View to a Grand System of Emigration*, vol. 2 (2 vols.). London: Simpkin & Marshall, 1822.

Green, Henry Gordon. *The Silver Dart: The Authentic Story of the Hon. J.A.D. McCurdy, Canada's First Pilot*. Fredericton, NB: Brunswick Press, 1959.

Hall, Blanche, and Harry Hall. *Memories of a Place Called Humber Bay*. 1991. (Privately published.)

Harris, Denise. "The Village of Humber Bay Walking Tour" (unpublished). Revised version, September 16, 2011.

Harris, Richard. *Unplanned Suburbs: Toronto's American Tragedy 1900 to 1950*. Baltimore: The Johns Hopkins University Press, 1996.

Harrison, Michael. "Mimico Building Scandal, Judicial Inquiry 1961." *History of the Town of Mimico* (blog). December 15, 2011. mimicohistory.blogspot.ca.

———. MimicoEstates.Blogspot.com.
"Lynne Lodge — Fetherstonhaugh Estate." February 23, 2011.
"McGuinness Estate II — 2603 Lake Shore Blvd. West." April 23, 2010.
"Mimico Building Scandal, Judicial Inquiry 1961." December 15, 2011.
"Ormscliffe/Myrtle Villa Estate." April 22, 2010.

Hennepin, Father Louis. As quoted in *Toronto During the French Régime, 1615–1793*, 2nd ed. Toronto: University of Toronto Press, 1965.

Heyes, Esther. *Etobicoke: From Furrow to Borough*, 2nd printing. Borough of Etobicoke Civic Centre, 1974.

Hunter, Doug. "An Undefiled Heritage." *GAM on Yachting*. February 1983.

"Indians of the Humber Valley." c. late 1800s, Archives of Ontario, F 775, Miscellaneous Collection MU 2096, #69.

Jones, Augustus. "Names of the Rivers, and Creeks, as they are Called by the Mississaugas . . ." Archives of Ontario, RG 1-2-1, vol. 32, Correspondence relating to surveys, reel MS 7433, pp. 103-105. (Many of these names are reproduced in Donald B. Smith, *Sacred Feathers*, Toronto: University of Toronto Press, 1987, pp. 255–257.)

Jones, Peter. *History of the Ojebway Indians; With Especial Reference to Their Conversion to Christianity*. London: Houlston and Wright, Paternoster Row, 1861.

Kapches, Mima. "An Archaeological View of Toronto: Life in the Past Lanes." *Rotunda* (Spring 1987): 19–24.

Leveridge, Bill. *Fair Sport: A History of Sports at the Canadian National Exhibition Since 1879*. Toronto: Canadian National Exhibition and MS Printers, 1978.

Lizars, Kathleen MacFarlane. *The Valley of the Humber 1615–1913*. Toronto: William Briggs, 1913.

McAllister, Ron. *Swim to Glory*. Toronto: McClelland & Stewart, 1954.

Mealcy, Patrick. Patent, Township of Tobacook or Etobicoake. Archives of Ontario, June 12, 1798. RG 53-1, vol. D., folio 265, reel MS.

Mulvany, Charles Pelham. *History of Toronto and County of York, Containing an Outline of the History of the Dominion of Canada*, vols. 1 and 2. Toronto: C. Blackett Robinson, 1885.

North-South Environmental Inc. "Review of Provincially Significant Wetlands Within the City of Toronto." Toronto, 2009. www.toronto.ca/planning/environment/pdf/wetland_report_aug09_small.pdf.

Pendleton, Glenna Mack, and the Etobicoke Historical Board. "Long Branch Park Historical Sketch."*Historical Planning: Cottages in Long Branch Park*, c. 1981. Long Branch Library Historical Collection.

Reeves, Wayne C. *Regional Heritage Features on the Metropolitan Toronto Waterfront: A Report to the Metropolitan Toronto Planning Department*. Toronto: Metropolitan Toronto Planning Department, 1992.

"Reports of Dr. N.H. Beemer, Medical Superintendent of Mimico Asylum/Medical Superintendent of the Hospital for the Insane/Superintendent of the Ontario Hospital, Mimico." Archives of Ontario, Ontario Sessional Papers, reels B 97/54 (1896) - B 97/178 (1923).

Robertson, J. Ross, ed. *The Diary of Mrs. Simcoe*. Toronto: William Briggs, 1911.

Robinson, Percy J. *Toronto During the French Régime, 1615–1793*, 2nd ed. Toronto: University of Toronto Press, 1965.

Ryerson, Egerton. As quoted in *Dictionary of Canadian Biography Online*. University of Toronto and Université Laval, 1990. www.biographi.ca/index-e.html. Quotation dated c. 1856.

Smith, Donald. *Sacred Feathers*. Toronto: University of Toronto Press, 1987.

Snider, C.H.J. Schooner Days column, *The Evening Telegram*
    "Building of the Betsey." December 24, 1943.
    "Junior League of the Gay Nineties." December 4, 1943.
    "The Maple Leaf Man." December 18, 1943.
    "They Missed the Toronto Yacht." April 18, 1953.
    "More Stonehookers." December 3, 1933.
    "Of Wellington Square." September 5, 1931.

Stamp, Robert M. *Riding the Radials: Toronto's Suburban Electric Streetcar Lines*. Erin, ON: Boston Mills Press, 1989.

Star Weekly. "Toronto's Newest Factory One of the Finest in Canada. Workmen Well Cared For, Given Ideal Surroundings." September 29, 1917.

Toronto Purchase of 1787. *Indenture Made at the Carrying Place, head of the Bay of Quinté the twenty-third day of September, in the year of Our Lord one thousand seven hundred and eighty seven*, vol. 1. Saskatoon: Fifth House Publishers, 1992.

Toronto as Seen from the Streetcars: A Passenger Souvenir for Visitors and Residents of Toronto. Toronto: Toronto Railway Company, 1894.

Toronto Daily Star
    "Crescent Point: The Lakeside Suburb." August 5, 1910.

"Graphic Presentation of Toronto's Real Estate Activity." May 1, 1912.

"Marathon Not Brutal." September 10, 1955.

"Sidney G. Holley Is the Vendor . . ." May 2, 1928.

Toronto Harbour Commissioners. *Toronto Waterfront Development, 1912–1920.* Toronto, [1913]. Fonds 2, series 60, item 1968, box 225027.

Toronto Purchase Settlement. Ref. # 2-3420, "Canada and the Mississaugas of the New Credit First Nation Celebrate Historic Claim Settlement," dated October 29, 2010. See Aboriginal Affairs and Northern Development Canada at www.aadnc-aandc.gc.ca.

Toronto World. "Crescent Point." July 31, 1910.

Treaty 13 of 1805. *Indenture made at the River Credit on Lake Ontario on the first day of August in the Year of Our Lord one thousand eight hundred and five between William Claus, Esquire, Deputy Superintendent General and Deputy Inspector General of Indians and of their Affairs . . . and the Principal Chiefs, Warriors and people of the Mississagua Nation of Indians*, no. 13 in Canada, *Indian Treaties and Surrenders*, vol. 1. Saskatoon: Fifth House Publishers, 1992.

Treaty 13a of 1805 (otherwise known as the Mississauga Purchase). *Indenture made at the River Credit on Lake Ontario on the second day of August in the Year of Our Lord one thousand eight hundred and five between William Claus, Esquire, Deputy Superintendent General and Deputy Inspector General of Indians and of their Affairs . . . and the Principal Chiefs, Warriors and People of the Mississagua Nation of Indians*, no. 13a in Canada, *Indian Treaties and Surrenders*, vol. 1. Saskatoon: Fifth House Publishers, 1992.

Upper Canada Gazette. "The Oracle." York, Saturday, September 14, 1799.

Williamson, Ronald F. *Toronto: A Short Illustrated History of Its First 12,000 Years.* Toronto: Lorimer, 2008.

Woodhouse, Roy T. "The Romance and Tragedy of Jean Baptiste Rousseau." An address given at the annual meeting of the Ontario Historical Society at McMaster University, June 28–30, 1951. Archives of Ontario, Series F 493-5 (Jean Baptiste Rousseau family genealogical material).

Young, Phyllis Brett. *The Torontonians*, 2nd ed. Montreal: McGill-Queen's University Press, 2007.

EPILOGUE

Harris, Amy Lavender. *Imagining Toronto.* Toronto: Mansfield Press, 2010.

Index

Along the Shore

Along the Shore

Queen City Yacht Club, 246, 269
Queen Elizabeth Way, 305, 392
Queen's Rangers, 40, 332, 334–35, 336
Queen Street East, 116, 148, 195–96, 199–200, 201
Quick, William, 55
Quinn, John, 239
Quinn's Hotel, 238–39

Radelmüller, J.P., 211, 226–28
radial railways (interurban electric railways), 73–75
    Beach, 159–60
    Lakeshore, 356–57, 367
    Scarborough, 19, 73–74, 81, 88
Ranelagh Park, 71–72. See also Guild of All Arts
Raposo, Tomanel, 346
Rawano:kwas (William Woodworth), 7
R.C. Harris Water Treatment Plant, 9, 178–82
Rebellion of 1837, 55
Reeve, Ted, 156, 159, 165, 171
Reeves, Wayne, 52, 90, 141, 182, 325, 335, 338, 355, 367
Research Enterprises Limited (REL), 96
Resolute, 236
Reuben Dowd, 236, 237
R.B. Rice and Sons, 81
Richards, Phil, 85, **100**, 101
Richardson, Hugh, 216–17
Riverside Golf and Country Club, 370
Riverview Boat Livery, 358
Roach-Leuszler, Winnifred, 383, 384
Robertson, John Ross, 248–49
Robinson, Percy J., 36, 321, 322
Rogers, Stan, 51
Ronald, William, 275
Rosebank, 66–67
Rouge Hills (subdivision), 89–90
Rouge Hills Golf and Country Club, 89, 90
Rouge Park, 29–30
Rouge River, 44, 52, 53-54, 90, 314, 338, 389
    Aboriginal name, 39
    marshes, 21, 29–30
    name origin, 36
Rousseaux, Jean-Baptiste, 15, **308**, 309, 328–30, 331
Rousseaux, Jean Bonaventure, 330
Rousseaux, Reine, 329
rowing and paddling
    Beach, 139, 164
    Island, 241–44, 269, 275–76
    Lakeshore, 307, 358–59
Royal Canadian Yacht Club, 245–46
Royal Norwegian Air Force, 249, 257, 270, **271**
Royal Oak Hotel, 345
Rudd, Ed, 268
Russell, Jack, **385**

Ruth, Babe, 253
Ryan, Grace, 48–49
Ryder, Gus, 313–14, 378–80, 382, 383, 384, **385**, 386–87
Ryerson, Egerton, 341

Sachau, Hans, 346
Sacred Feathers. See Jones, Peter (Kahkewaquonaby)
sailing ships, vessels
    Beach, 145–48
    Island, 234, 237
    Lakeshore, **342**, 343, 346, 364–65
    Scarborough, 52, 54, 56, 62
Sam McBride, 270
Sandown Park, 81, 89
Saunders, Robert, 270–71
Scadding, Henry, 127, 218
Scadding, John, 136
Scale, Daphne (née Smyth), 373–74
Scale, Ernie, 375
Scantlon family, 148
Scarboro' Beach Amusement Park, 112–14, 167–68, 170
Scarboro Foreign Mission Society, 72
Scarboro Golf and Country Club, 67–68
Scarborough, 23, 86
    as township, 17–18, 64, 75, 81
    as village, 20, 63
Scarborough and Pickering Wharf Company, 60–62, 338
Scarborough Bluffs, 16–18, 69
    cliffs, 21, 75, 106
    dangers, 2–3, 56–58, 97
    erosion, 30, 31–32, 77, 106, 126, 215–17, 226
    Flats, **28**, 29, 48, 92
    Front, 40, 43, 44, 45, 49–50, 58, 59
    gullies, 56, 105, 106
Scarborough Hall (hospital), 95
Scarborough Heights Park, 20, 74–75
Scarborough shore, 9, 15, 20–21
    beaches, 75, 105–6
    name origin, 21–22
Schofield, Richard, 63, 70
Schroeder, Bruce, 33
Scott, David, 252–53
Seabreeze dance pavilion, 363
Sea Breeze Park, 347. See also Long Branch Park
Seaway Market, 195
Second World War
    Island, 257, 269, 270–71
    Lakeshore, 355, 375–77
    Scarborough, 95–96
Selkirk, Earl of (Thomas Douglas), 317
Seneca, 34–37, 218, 306, 308, 319–23
Seton, Ernest Thompson, **41**, 68
Sewell, John, 292

Along the Shore

Toronto lawyer Jane Fairburn has for many years lived at or near the north shore of Lake Ontario. Born in Toronto, Jane graduated from the University of Toronto with an honours B.A. in Political Science. Thereafter she studied law and was called to the Bar in 1990. Jane currently lives in the Scarborough Bluffs with her husband and three children.